No Man's Land

JAMAICAN GUESTWORKERS IN AMERICA
AND THE GLOBAL HISTORY OF
DEPORTABLE LABOR

Cindy Hahamovitch

PRINCETON UNIVERSITY PRESS

PRINCETON AND OXFORD

Copyright © 2011 by Princeton University Press

Published by Princeton University Press, 41 William Street, Princeton, New Jersey 08540
In the United Kingdom: Princeton University Press, 6 Oxford Street, Woodstock,
Oxfordshire OX20 1TW

press.princeton.edu

Library of Congress Cataloging-in-Publication Data

Hahamovitch, Cindy.
    No man's land : Jamaican guestworkers in America and the global history of deportable
labor / Cindy Hahamovitch.
        p. cm.
    Includes bibliographical references and index.
    ISBN 978-0-691-10268-9 (hardcover : alk. paper)   1. Foreign workers—United States.
2. Jamaica—Emigration and immigration.   3. Foreign workers.   4. Deportation.   I. Title.

    HD8081.A5H34 2011
    331.6'27292073—dc22   2011012260

British Library Cataloging-in-Publication Data is available

This book has been composed in Stempel Garamond
Printed on acid-free paper. ∞

Printed in the United States of America

10 9 8 7 6 5 4 3 2 1

No ebery ting wha got sugar a sweet.

    —*Jamaican proverb*[1]

Contents

Acknowledgments

When you've been working on a book as long as I've been working on this one, you rack up as many debts as a sharecropper, though these are debts I'd be happy to pay. I would like to thank the numerous and talented graduate students who have worked on this project over the years: Ellen Adams, Evan Bennett, Jarrett Brown, Fred Carroll, Michael Simoncelli, and John Weber. I'd like to thank the staff members here at William & Mary and at Yale University who provided support: Gail Conner, Betty Flanigan, Kay "the Principal" Mansfield, and Roz Stearns. Special thanks go to the librarians who answered all my crazy questions, especially Marian Smith, Don Welsh, Hope Yellich, Allen Zoellner, and William & Mary's incredibly efficient Inter-Library Loan staff. Lindsey Allen, Jarrett Brown, and Patti Brown helped me find my way around Jamaica. Jarrett's mother, Rose, and brother, Dayan, put me up in their lovely house in Effort, Jamaica. Sheryl Reid shared her research and her home in Port More, Jamaica. Prize-winning filmmaker Stephanie Black shared the interviews that she conducted when working on her brilliant film, *H2 Worker*.

Thanks to Taylor & Francis for letting me reproduce sections of my articles, "Creating Perfect Immigrants: Guestworkers of the World in Historical Perspective," *Labor History* 44, 1 (January 2003): 69–94; and "The Worst Job in the World": Reform, Revolution, and the Secret Rebellion in Florida's Cane Fields," *Journal of Peasant Studies* 4, 35 (October 2008): 770–800. Thanks to Cornell University Press for permission to reuse sections of "In America Life Is Given Away: Jamaican Farmworkers and the Making of Agricultural Immigration Policy," from *The Countryside in the Age of the Modern State: Political Histories of Rural America*, edited by Catherine McNicol Stock and Robert D. Johnston (2001). Copyright © 2001 by Cornell University. Used by permission of the publisher, Cornell University Press.

The Agrarian Studies Program at Yale University, the Lyon G. Tyler Department of History, William & Mary's Tyler Grant Program, the U.S.-Irish Fulbright Commission, and the Wendy and Emory Reves Center all provided much needed financial support and time. Phil Daileader, Judith Ewell, Jim McCord, and James P. Whittenburg, all chairs of the Lyon G. Tyler Department of History at William & Mary during this project, helped me get where I needed to go. Lindsey Allen, Eric Arnesen, Joan Bak, Evan Bennett, Anne Effland, Judith Ewell, Leon Fink, Jessica Hahamovitch, Rick Halpern, Rhys Isaac, Will Jones, Jeanette Keith, Steve Knaus, Laurie Koloski, Kathy Levitan, Alex Lichtenstein, Jennifer Luff,

Nancy MacLean, Leisa Meyer, Gary Mormino, Jason Parker, Richard Price, Kendra Smith, Rohan D'Souza, John Weber, and Robert T. Vinson commented on sections of the manuscript, shared invaluable sources, or answered questions (sometimes the same question twice). Linda Gordon, Mae Ngai, and Karin Wulf read the manuscript from cover to cover and offered invaluable suggestions. Thanks also to Karen Verde, who copyedited the manuscript, and to Sarah Wolf and all the staff at Princeton University Press for a job well done. Walter Comrie, and attorneys Sarah Cleveland, Bruce Goldstein, David Gorman, Steve Routh, Greg Schell, Joe Segor, and Edward Tuddenham shared records with me. A special thanks to the members of the Agrarian Studies Breakfast Club, the Richmond Labor History Group, the William & Mary History Department Brown Bag Series, and the Newberry Library Labor History Group for encouragement and advice. To my colleagues at William & Mary, thanks for making work a joy. To my parents, who babysat so often they might as well have adopted, I couldn't have done it without you. To my son, Renny (a.k.a. Shaggy), who was raised by wolves, thanks for always remembering to ask how it was going. And to Annie, yes, I can play with you now.

Most of all, I want to thank my brilliant husband, Scott Reynolds Nelson, who has walked on eggs for ten years while still managing to offer advice, editorial suggestions, support, love, and lots of latte. Every hoot owl is for you.

Abbreviations

BITU	Bustamente Industrial Trade Union
CIA	Central Intelligence Agency
CIO	Congress of Industrial Organizations
FSA	Farm Security Administration
GAO	Government Accountability Office
G&W	Gulf & Western
INS	Immigration and Naturalization Service
NAWU	National Agricultural Workers Union (formerly NFLU)
NFLU	National Farm Labor Union (formerly STFU)
OEO	Office of Economic Opportunity
PNP	People's National Party
SAWs	Special Agricultural Workers
SFMLS	South Florida Migrant Legal Services
STFU	Southern Tenant Farmers Union
UCAPAWA	United Cannery Agricultural Packinghouse and Allied Workers Union
UFW	United Farm Workers of America
USES	United States Employment Service
WFA	War Food Administration
WICLO	West Indian Central Labour Organization

No Man's Land

Introduction

THE AMERICANS WERE COMING. In the spring of 1943, Jamaican radio stations buzzed with the news. American officials were coming to recruit Jamaican men for war work in the United States. When word reached the tiny mountain hamlet of Mulgrave—3,000 feet above sea level and twenty-five miles inland from Montego Bay—eighteen-year-old Leaford Williams and his family were thrilled and nervous. "Everywhere we went during the days and weeks that followed," Leaford recalled, "small groups gathered under the eaves of someone's house or on the front porch of the local shops sharing news about the recruiting program 'for going to foreign.'" The prospect of work in the United States was big news in Mulgrave, which was so small that there was "no crime and no policeman." So little happened in Mulgrave, in fact, that law enforcement consisted of a "Pan Head" who gave out tickets for cursing. There was no crime, but also few prospects for advancement. Boys grew up to be "rum drinkers and farm hands," Leaford recalled. Hoping to be neither, he and his older brother Enoch walked twenty-fives miles to be first in line at the recruitment station at Balaclava.[1]

Leaford didn't want to end up a farmhand in Jamaica, but he would happily do farmwork in the United States if that's what it would take to get ahead. Securing tickets from their local member of Parliament, the brothers made their way back to Mulgrave and from there another twenty-five miles north and downward to the coast, where a Montego Bay schoolhouse had been commandeered by the Jamaican government as a screening facility. The floor had been marked off into sections, and a doctor stood in each one. Along with thousands of others, Leaford and Enoch would have entered the room naked, and passed from station to station until they had completed all the tests.[2] Declared fit and eligible to work in the United States, the brothers returned home. "God be praised," their "Dada" shouted when they walked back into Mulgrave, "God is in His Holy Temple."

A few weeks later, they set off for the United States, carrying the cedar "grips" Enoch had made. Each contained an extra pair of pants, a shirt, and two sets of underwear sewn by their mother and sister. They walked five miles to Elderslie, where they boarded a truck sent to take them back to Montego Bay. Dozens of other young recruits traveled with them, singing and waving to people along the way. They bounced over potholes, rolled blindly around hairpin turns, and strayed perilously close to sheer drops as they traveled down from Jamaica's Cockpit Country to the coast. By the time they arrived safely in Montego Bay's railway yard, Leaford felt like a war hero. Singing "We all are jolly good fellows," they boarded cow cars bound for Kingston's harbor.

When the doors of the cars opened in Jamaica's capitol the following morning, Leaford was struck by the sight of more "white people at one location" than he had ever seen before. The Americans rushed them up the gangplank of a waiting battleship, saying, "Hurry up, hurry up—come on, get your asses [up] here quickly." Once on board, most of the Jamaicans stood on deck, watching the Blue Mountains recede into shadow. Leaford lay on his bunk, reflecting on the slaves who had made the same journey before him and "[o]ur good fortune . . . that we were not bound in chains the way they were."

Leaford and Enoch Williams were not slaves. They had jumped at the chance to do fieldwork in the United States, walked many miles to secure recruitment tickets, waited in line for their physical examinations, and boarded a truck and train with great hopes and expectations. They had visas admitting them to the United States and work contracts that promised them conditions far superior to the treatment American farmworkers received. They were paid for their work, and they could quit and leave if they wanted to go home. But although they were not slaves, neither were they free. Leaford, his brother, and the millions of other Caribbean and Mexican men who followed them to the United States in the sixty-five years since World War II were recruited by the government to enter the country and work for American employers, but they were not free to settle down, look for better work, go west (or east!), or do any of the other things that immigrants have done (and still do) to make good in the United States. They came to the United States under contracts that promised them wages and benefits far beyond what domestic farmworkers received, but they could not invoke it without risk of deportation. If they broke their contract by trying to stay in the United States, their status changed automatically from "non-immigrant temporary worker" to "illegal alien." Leaford and Enoch were neither slaves nor free men; they were guestworkers, a quintessentially modern form of international migrant.

Guestworkers have been called different names in different parts of the world: H2 Workers and Braceros in the United States, European Voluntary Labourers in England, expatriate workers in the Persian Gulf, servants in Singapore, or simply "our Filipina" in Montreal.[3] But the names all represent a relatively new form of labor migrant, one designed to balance employers' desire for contingent, less expensive, and presumably pliable foreign labor and native populations' antipathy toward those same workers.[4] Unlike immigrants who stay, settle, and in some countries naturalize, vote, and qualify for social services, guestworkers exist in a no man's land between nations; they provide labor to their host societies but often fall outside the protections of those societies' labor laws. Ineligible for social benefits in their host country, they are often poorly protected by their home governments, despite the value of the remittances they send home. Guestworkers exist somewhere on the spectrum between slavery and freedom. Just where is this book's central question.

The term "guestworker"—a translation of the German *gastarbeiter*—hadn't been coined when Leaford and his brother arrived in the United States in 1943. The word would be a product of the massive programs that would bring some 30 million contract workers to central Europe beginning a few years later.[5] Nevertheless, state-sanctioned temporary worker programs, which came to be known as guestworker programs, had long been in existence. The first such programs were created in Prussia and South Africa in the 1880s. The next appeared in Australia at the turn of the century, and in the American Southwest and Europe during World War I. Like their later counterparts, these early programs all aimed to give employers access to foreign workers whom nativists sought to ban. With the exception of South Africa's long-running program, which supplied labor to gold and diamond mines, all of these programs ended during the Great Depression, a period in which foreign workers were more likely to be expelled than imported.

After a few years, war mobilization created new demand for temporary foreign workers in the United States, Germany, and Japan, setting off a second wave of state-mobilized migration. In this second phase in the history of guestworker programs far greater numbers of workers moved about. While 30 million guestworkers journeyed from Europe's periphery to its center in the decades after World War II, some five million Mexican and Caribbean guestworkers cycled in and out of the United States. The first wartime guestworkers in the United States were Mexican men, who came by train, and Bahamian men and women who flew in on planes starting in 1942. The Immigration and Naturalization Service (INS) soon banned women from the program when a few Bahamians had abortions after being threatened with deportation for becoming pregnant. The ban would last for decades, forcing women to stay at home and male guestworkers to choose between living with their families and providing for them. In 1943, just a couple of months after the arrival of the first Bahamian recruits, the British Colonial Office agreed to let the United States recruit tens of thousands of Jamaican men as well. Jamaicans soon dwarfed the number of Bahamians on contract and would remain the vast majority of Caribbean guestworkers in the United States. A trickle of Barbadians joined in a year after the Jamaicans, followed by recruits from other British West Indian colonies. Together the separately negotiated Mexican, Bahamian, and British West Indian wartime programs were known as the Emergency Labor Importation Program. In the last year of the war, it brought 106,000 guestworkers to the United States. Canadians came too but no one bothered to count them; they were not bound by contracts; and officials didn't seem to worry about whether they left. In the imagination of U.S. officials, guestworkers were men of color whose movements had to be carefully monitored.

The war began the second phase in the history of guestworker programs but it didn't end it. After the war, new European guestworkers began rebuilding Europe's flattened cities and factories. The U.S. guestworker programs continued and grew, though U.S. officials reauthorized the importation of foreign labor for agriculture only. A small fraction of the nation's growers used hired labor—perhaps 2 percent—but that tiny minority of growers had employed guestworkers during the war and they wanted to keep doing so. Farm employers had also organized themselves into a powerful lobby. Its efforts kept U.S. guestworker programs alive despite ample evidence that, in the postwar period, the domestic supply of migrant farmworkers was growing, not shrinking. Although the U.S. guestworker programs lived on, the federal government largely withdrew from its wartime role as protector of guestworkers' wages and conditions.

Indeed, the role of the state is most remarkable in this second phase, and it is here that this book's comparative approach proves particularly useful. The U.S. government was intensely involved in the wartime guestworker programs. U.S. officials negotiated contracts; recruited, transported, housed, and fed the guestworkers; contracted them to employers; and dealt with their problems and complaints. Yet the U.S. government rapidly withdrew from its supervisory role after the war's end. Indeed, rather than protect workers or at least arbitrate grower-farmworker relations, U.S. officials increasingly served growers' interests. They authorized growers' requests for labor without question, detained workers who protested their treatment, pursued those who jumped their contracts, and suspended raids during harvests. In contrast, state actors in Europe became progressively more involved in protecting guestworkers from exploitation as time went on. As a result, guestworkers' experiences on either side of the Atlantic diverged dramatically. In Europe, temporary workers—who ended up being not so temporary—gradually gained many of the benefits and rights that unionized European workers enjoyed. Guestworkers in the United States rapidly joined the ranks of the nation's most impoverished and exploited workers. The key to that difference, I suggest, was that only European states had the power to deport workers who displeased European employers, and they used it judiciously. In the United States, employers quickly gained and still retain the power to deport the workers they imported.

Phase two in the history of guestworker programs shrieked to a halt in the 1960s and early 1970s as the European and U.S. economies sank into recession. The more European guestworkers won the right to settle and move around, the more antagonism they engendered. In the United States, an anti-guestworker campaign bubbled up from below as farmworkers in California organized a powerful and popular movement, which insisted that American farmworkers' rights depended on guestworkers' departure. This movement brought about the demise of the Mexican guestworker program—which was known as the Bracero Program for *brazo*, the Spanish word for arm. The last Braceros left the United States in 1964. The oil shocks of the early 1970s brought an end to the European guestworker programs.

The economic slump may have spelled the end of most postwar guest-worker programs in the United States and Europe, but it did not put a stop to temporary labor schemes in other parts of the world or in the United States. Indeed, the oil crisis of 1973 launched the third phase in the history of guest-worker schemes: the movement of temporary labor migrants from oil-poor countries in Asia to the booming oil economies of the Middle East and Pacific Rim. This third phase in the history of guestworker programs resulted in majority foreign work forces in four Middle Eastern countries and the growing dependence of sending states on the remittances workers sent home.[6] It also brought some innovations. Guestworker programs still supplied workers for dirty, dangerous, and difficult work, but they now also recruited highly skilled workers and professionals, such as engineers, nurses, and computer analysts. Migration programs also became increasingly feminized as "the Maid Trade" overtook the traditional trade in miners, agricultural laborers, and construction workers. With remittances in the billions, sending governments exhibited far greater enthusiasm for the idea of exporting their people as contract workers, and many actively marketed their citizens abroad.[7] But the greater the role sending nations played in charting the paths labor migrants took, the less influence they exerted on the conditions under which their nationals lived and worked. Guestworkers, whose global numbers are now enormous, are more easily exploited than ever before.

The Mexican Bracero Program fits neatly into this three-phase rubric. It began in 1942 and continued until 1964, bringing half a million workers to the United States annually at its peak. However, the Caribbean program, which is the subject of this book, fits less neatly into this scheme. Always much smaller than its Mexican counterpart, the Caribbean Program (really *programs* initially) continued to operate long after the Bracero Program went down in a hail of controversy, although most Americans were oblivious to its existence. In 1952 Caribbean guestworkers were dubbed "H2 workers," after the sub-section of the immigration law which reauthorized their presence, and in 1986 they were divided into H2-As (agricultural workers) and H2-Bs (non-agricultural workers). But, otherwise, this employer-dominated migration scheme continued with only minor changes. After 1986 it was feminized (by the inclusion of maids, waitresses, and other women workers) and gentrified (by the addition of high-tech and other highly educated people). It also got bigger—until the economic slump of recent years, the program was importing some 100,000 farmworkers a year and even more nonagricultural workers. And, after 1986, it became a mostly Mexican program, though Jamaicans continue to come to the United States as apple pickers, and H2 workers come from as far away as Thailand. Despite these modifications, the H2 Program has spanned the last two of these three phases, and it continues to this day, making it the oldest guestworker program in U.S. history and the second oldest in world history, after South Africa's.

I began to consider the history of guestworkers in the United States in the 1990s, when working on my first book, *The Fruits of Their Labor: Atlantic Coast Farmworkers and the Making of Migrant Poverty, 1870–1945*.[8] There I argued that farmworkers still suffer from low wages and even worse living conditions, not because farmworker poverty is inevitable but because the federal government intervened time and again on the growers' behalf, undermining farmworkers' bargaining power and relieving growers' need to recruit labor by improving wages and conditions. During World War I, for example, the federal government encouraged Work-or-Fight campaigns that threatened to imprison or deploy black men and women who abandoned farmwork for better-paying war jobs. During World War II, when African American, Mexican American, and Filipino American farmworkers took advantage of relative labor scarcity by organizing and striking to raise their wages, Congress passed a law that confined domestic farmworkers to their home counties even as it authorized the importation of tens of thousands of guestworkers from Mexico and the Caribbean on fixed, no-strike contracts that bound them to particular employers and forced them to cycle in and out of the country. One book led to the other, just as a labor system based on forced immobility (sharecropping, convict labor, the Work-or-Fight regime) rapidly gave way to a new one based on forced mobility.[9]

Although guestworkers came from all over the British West Indies and the Bahamas, this book focuses on Jamaicans because they made up the vast majority of *Caribbean* guestworkers in the United States and, for two decades after the demise of the Bracero Program, they represented the vast majority of all U.S.-bound guestworkers. Only since 1986 have Mexicans once again become the guestworkers of choice. For over forty years, the H2 Program was primarily a Jamaican program. The book devotes a great deal of ink to Florida's sugar industry because, from 1943 until the 1990s, it was the largest employer of H2 workers, with 5,000 to 20,000 guestworkers cutting sugar cane for five- to six-month seasons every year.

This book may seem like much ado about a small number of workers concentrated primarily in one industry, but the H2 Program's significance has long been completely disproportionate to its size. Besides being the longest running guestworker program in U.S. history, and the object of years of litigation and investigation, the H2 Program has been symbolically important as a legal alternative to unauthorized or "illegal" immigration. Since the Second World War, whenever concern about the number of "illegal aliens" in the United States reached a fever pitch, guestworkers gained legitimacy. In fact, within a few years of the war's end, the INS began dealing with the unauthorized Mexican immigrants it apprehended by transforming them into Braceros, a process that the agency unfortunately called "Drying Out the Wetbacks."[10] Since the termination of the Bracero Program, whenever the U.S. public has fixated on "illegal immigration," the H2 Program has grown in importance as a purportedly managed alternative to a seemingly unmanageable issue. The same is true today. In recent debates about immigration reform, both parties have considered proposals that would legalize millions of unauthorized immigrants by transforming them into legal but temporary guestworkers. As we shall see, however, the story of Leaford Williams and the thousands of other H2 workers who exited boats and airplanes to work in American fields and orchards is not a story of carefully managed migration. The history of the H2 Program is a tale of exploitation, protest, litigation, and mass deportation.

The H2 Program is not just important to U.S. history. The program looms even larger in Jamaica, where veterans of the program are ubiquitous. On my first trip to the island, the taxi driver who drove me from the airport to my hotel was a former guestworker. The security guard at the pharmacy in the suburb of Port More where I stopped for supplies was still traveling to the United States every fall to pick apples. The Jamaican graduate student who became my research assistant—then one of just three Jamaicans at the College of William & Mary—turned out to be the son of an H2 worker. He led me to his tiny home village of Effort, where many of his relatives and neighbors were guestworkers. His brother had tried unsuccessfully to become one. On another occasion, when I stopped in the slightly larger town of Brandon Hill to ask directions during a torrential downpour, the man at the side of the road who got in the car to direct me was a former U.S. cane cutter. He pointed the way to a "Dead House," where a body was laid up inside, and a small group of men, including two former guestworkers, were playing dominoes on the porch. Two more H2 workers—one still "traveling"—soon joined them. You can't shake a palm frond in the Jamaican countryside without hitting a former guestworker or the family members his remittances helped support.

Asked about their experiences as farmworkers in the United States, almost all the Jamaican men I interviewed or spoke to informally responded with the same words: "it was rough." The work—especially cane cutting in Florida—was physically punishing and dangerous. "It is rough work," said Carlton Nelson, who worked in the United States off and on from 1963 to 1986, using the money to pay school fees for his children and nephew. "The food is rough. The work is rough. It is rough always." The work was physically punishing, but it was also "rough" in the sense that it rarely produced the sort of wages the men expected. To make enough to come home with significant savings or goods, men had to work at a dangerously fast pace, a pace that increased dramatically as the sugar industry boomed in the 1960s. Veteran guestworkers insist that they were underpaid for the work they did and defrauded of wages they were promised. Yet for rural men who were desperately poor and who had little hope of changing that fact at home, the program seemed worth the risk, if not for themselves then for their children. Few would turn down an opportunity to "reach over" to the United States, if they could get one. "Some won't cut because it is so rough," said Nelson. "But I will. If you work, you get money."[11] Even men who were badly injured or who alleged wage fraud were often eager to try again. Wynston White complained bitterly about timecard fraud, but asked if he would go to Florida again, he answered, "I wouldn't mind to leave right now."[12]

Jamaican men came to the United States as guestworkers and ran to their cane rows in the morning because, to rural Jamaicans, the prospect of paid work was irresistible. In Jamaica in 1980, the average worker earned $1,406 (US) a year; the average rural Jamaican far less. In contrast, during the five- to six-month period Jamaican H2 workers spent in the United States during the winter of 1980/81, the average worker grossed $4,000. Even after deductions totaling $2,327, men still earned nearly twice as much in a few months in the United States as they could have earned in a year in Jamaica.[13] Few H2 workers made enough to buy land or build a house, even after years of five- to six-month journeys to the United States. But rural Jamaicans' ability to pay for groceries, their utility bills, and, most importantly, their children's school fees has long depended on temporary farmwork in the United States. The average H2 worker supported a family of six.[14] The H2 Program allowed men to be providers, even as it separated them from their families. Highly skilled and educated Jamaicans often left the island for jobs as nurses, doctors, and teachers in the United States, Canada, and England. But for less educated rural people, the "farmworker programme," as Jamaicans call it, has long been the best—and often the only—way to earn the cash that made the difference between a decent life and desperation.

Guestworkers' desperation goes a long way toward explaining why employers fought long and hard to retain them. Time, space, and longing produced an unbeatable work ethic. But there was more to growers' fondness for the H2 Program than that. There are two other explanations. The first is the kind of workers employers could get through the H2 Program. The Jamaican government has long defended the guestworker system as a foreign aid program that cost the United States nothing. But the H2 Program and its West Coast counterpart did more than send U.S. dollars to poorer countries. Perversely, sending countries sent foreign aid *to* the United States in the form of young men in their peak years of physical fitness. Traveling without their families, men could be housed and transported more efficiently than domestic workers who came with families in tow. Guestworkers didn't demand space for people who didn't work; they didn't require schools or Head Start Programs; they didn't attract as much attention from misty-eyed reformers; they didn't get pregnant and give birth to citizen children. Their wives and girlfriends had their children back in Jamaica, Barbados, St. Kitts, and Mexico, and there they stayed. Local midwives or hospitals delivered them. Local schools taught them. When guestworkers' children became young adults, they too might follow their fathers to Florida, New York, or Virginia, but until then, they remained offshore. And when guestworkers were too old to travel, they wouldn't be called back. By hiring a young, male labor force, agricultural employers banished the most persistent and media-worthy problems that had plagued the nation's fields since the late nineteenth century—child labor and illiteracy, abysmal maternal health care, and aged former farmworkers. They did so not by solving those problems but by out-sourcing them to the United States' poorest neighbors. These neighbors gave the United States men in their prime, and took them back when they were old or sick. The United States took the fittest, letting other nations worry about their survival.

Second, guestworkers proved to be especially desirable sort of workers, not just because of their youth and work ethic, but because of their deportabil-ity. Much to growers' chagrin, guestworkers weren't always willing to put up with conditions that domestic workers would reject; they frequently resented the conditions they were offered. And, in fact, Jamaican and other Caribbean guestworkers were often far more militant in defense of their interests than their domestic counterparts, who were more likely to protest by quitting and quietly walking away. Guestworkers, who couldn't change employers with-out transforming themselves into illegal immigrants, were far more likely to strike. Their militancy was rendered impotent, however, by the fact that their American employers had the power to repatriate them. It wasn't complacency but deportability that made guestworkers particularly vulnerable to exploita-tion. This deportability also weakened domestic farmworkers, who were vul-nerable to replacement by vulnerable guestworkers.

To study the H2 Program, I made four trips to Jamaica to search for records and to interview former guestworkers. I traveled into Jamaica's mountainous interior, where mudslides are common and potholes can swallow a compact car. Most of my interviews took place in two mountainous Clarendon Parish hamlets: Effort, which is so lush and tiny that none of the houses are vis-ible from the road; and Brandon Hill, a slightly larger, one-store village on a mountaintop ridge. I chose the first because it was the home of my research assistant; I chose the second because Sheryl Reid, a fellow student of the "farmworker programme," had generously provided me with a list of former guestworkers who lived there. Both towns could stand in for the communities of rural smallholders that dot the Jamaican countryside, though only the sec-ond appeared on my road map. Even in Frankfield, the bustling market town about a half hour from Brandon Hill, two women standing in front of a corner shop could point out half a dozen former guestworkers among the men mill-ing about. When it came to locating research subjects, my method was about as complicated as having people point.

Finding guestworkers to interview was easy. Finding government docu-ments in Jamaica's National Archives was another story. The key Jamaican agency involved in "the U.S. Farmworker Programme" was the Jamaican Ministry of Labour, but its records were neither at the National Archives nor at the Ministry itself. According to the Ministry official I interviewed— whose name I will omit to protect his job—the Ministry periodically burned its records instead of turning them over to the Archives. Given the fact that J.A.G. Smith, Jamaica's Minister of Labour in the 1980s, went to prison in 1990 for embezzling from the Canadian farmworker program, one can only presume that the Ministry's bonfires were meant to shield the workings of the agency from inquiring minds like mine. Fortunately, Florida's cane companies had copies of government records such as the minutes of the Regional Labour Board, the intra-Caribbean agency that annually negotiated guestworkers' contracts with employer representatives. Those copies were made available to guestworkers' attorneys as part of the discovery process in a long series of lawsuits, and those attorneys shared their records with me. It's sad to say that I now have more records of the Ministry of Labour in my attic than Jamaica has in its National Archives.

Besides the cache of records I have built up as a result of visits to attorneys' offices, I have cut a swath through governmental records in the U.S. National Archives, and the British Colonial Office papers in the Public Records Office in Kew Garden, England. Unfortunately, U.S. and British sources are only bountiful through the World War II era. At that time, the U.S. officials who ran the labor camps that housed guestworkers wrote weekly reports and the secretary of state for the Colonies investigated charges of abuse, fearing that mistreatment of black British subjects in the United States would tarnish the Allies' international reputation. As England began to disentangle itself from its colonies in the 1950s, and as the United States withdrew from daily supervision of the guestworker programs, government records began to peter out. Fortunately, one of the Jamaican liaison officers who accompanied guestworkers to the United States, a white Jamaican named Walter Comrie, kept copies in triplicate of every report he wrote and every bit of correspondence he sent in his twenty-plus years on the job in Florida. He gave one set of copies to me. He also kept a sort of diary and, after retiring, wrote an unpublished memoir of his experiences. The H2 Program has also been the subject of countless investigations by journalists and governmental bodies ranging from the Government Accountability Office to the House Subcommittee on Education and Labor. Together, they produced reams of reports, correspondence, and hearing minutes.

Finding former guestworkers in Jamaica and archival records in the United States and England was easy. Finding U.S. employers who would speak frankly with me was more difficult. For the H2 Program's first forty years, beginning in 1943, the vast majority of guestworkers labored in Florida's sugarcane industry, a business dominated by five large companies. U.S. Sugar—the oldest and the biggest of the five—responded to my inquiries by sending me a little white pamphlet with gold lettering on the cover that touted the miracle of sugar production in the Everglades. No answer to my request for an interview nor access to corporate records was forthcoming. George Wedgeworth, the CEO of the Sugarcane Growers Cooperative, did agree to meet me, but his attorney and public relations director remained in the room. It was not my most productive interview. Wedgeworth promised to send me a long list of names of Jamaicans who would sing the praises of the Co-op and the H2 Program in general, but the list never arrived.

Fortunately, growers' views are well represented in a wide array of sources from federal hearings to correspondence with government officials to letters to the editor and depositions. The small number of employers who used guestworkers formed a powerful lobby during World War II and succeeded in making their views well known. And because public interest lawyers who began suing the sugar companies on behalf of cane cutters in 1968 have shared reams of corporate records they secured through the discovery process, I was able to read some revealing internal company documents as well.

Not surprisingly, many of these sources privilege moments of conflict between guestworkers and their employers. Far more ink has been spilled over workers who struck or protested than over those who worked quietly and contentedly. Yet the records reveal that guestworkers who resented their treatment and guestworkers who desperately wanted to return to the United States were not separate people. Employers could deport hundreds of workers en masse for disrupting a harvest by striking and within a day have hundreds more workers waiting at the Kingston airport to replace them. Workers might be sent home, blacklisted for protesting their condition, and return under an assumed name as soon as they could arrange it. Guestworkers were neither slaves nor free; they were both. In the wide world of international migration, dissatisfaction and desire are two sides of the same coin.

For all the protests, investigations, and litigation that have surrounded the H2 Program over the past sixty years, its essential purposes and functions have remained the same. It has offered some of the nation's biggest commercial farmers an alternative to domestic workers who can organize for change without fear of deportation. It has offered the state a perceived alternative to undocumented immigrants whose presence has generated periodic panic. And, as in other parts of the world where guestworkers are in use, the H2 Program has arrested the development of wages and conditions for some of the nation's most neglected workers. To quote Jamaica's former prime minister, Michael Manley, "better must come."[15]

CHAPTER ONE

Guestworkers of the World, Unite!

You Have Nothing to Lose but Your Passport, Your Visa,
Your Immigration Status

LEAFORD AND ENOCH WILLIAMS and the thousands of other Caribbean and Mexican workers who entered the United States on government contracts during World War II weren't the first guestworkers in the world. The first phase in the global history of guestworker programs began in the late nineteenth century and lasted until the Great Depression of the 1930s. Before that time, there were no guestworker programs because there were no immigration restrictions. Immigration restrictions led to guestworker programs as states sought to guarantee employers access to the immigrant workers that restrictionists were trying to deny them.

For much of modern history, to the extent that immigration laws existed, they tended to bar emigrants from leaving, not new immigrants from coming.[1] All that began to change at the end of the nineteenth century. As capitalism cut the final fetters that had bound Europeans to particular lands and lords and as Europeans blasted open the doors to China's massive labor force, 60–70 million Europeans and seven million Chinese workers emigrated in search of gold, land, and work.[2] And the more people moved—sped by railroads, steam travel, and global markets—the more they fed the fires of nationalism. Nationalism fostered state formation as nation-states responded to popular anti-immigrant sentiment by increasingly asserting the right to regulate migrants' movements across national borders. Through passports, birth certificates, and visas, nation-states determined who was a legitimate member of the nation-state and who was not. The rise of welfare states only heightened this scrutiny. The more states promised their citizenry in terms of services—workers' compensation, old-age and mothers' pensions, public education—the more state officials struggled to identify who was and who was not entitled to such services. By the early twentieth century, industrialized nation-states around the world had enacted legislation requiring immigrants to register, to be literate, to pay head taxes, or to stay out altogether. Unregulated border crossings were criminalized.[3]

Restrictionists were particularly opposed to the immigrants who indentured themselves to employers or recruiters to make the journey from home to work. As the slave trade declined in the early nineteenth century, indentured servitude experienced a huge revival around the world, particularly in the British Empire, as planters struggled to find cheap, pliable, and ostensibly voluntary alternatives to slaves. Similarly, in the United States after the Civil War, American planters in the U.S. South schemed about importing Chinese workers, whom they called "coolies," to supplant newly freed slaves. Planters abandoned their schemes when they found the Chinese neither cheap nor pliable. Yet U.S. workers and former abolitionists denounced Chinese migrant workers for their apparent willingness to accept substandard wages and conditions. Although Chinese immigrants were stereotyped as slavish "coolies," Irish and later eastern and southern European labor migrants entered into very similar financial arrangements in which they owed employers or recruiters for their passage. Bound by debt or contracts, nineteenth-century labor migrants to the United States and many other nations often had little choice but to accept the difficult, dangerous, and low-paid work to which they were assigned, even in the midst of strikes and other labor struggles.[4]

Not surprisingly then, the assumption—which was sometimes correct—that immigrant workers undercut native-born workers' wages and organizing efforts led to a growing chorus of critics, which considered the various forms of transnational debt migration to be slavery, poorly disguised. The first immigration restrictions were therefore efforts to prohibit the movement of any immigrants who crossed an ocean by indebting themselves or by signing a labor contract with a prospective employer. Chinese migrants engendered the most violent reactions and the first immigration restrictions, but European immigrants were also the targets of restriction campaigns, though the press often painted them sympathetically as victims of "white slavery."[5] Congress, which had encouraged transnational contract labor schemes during the Civil War, reversed itself in the years that followed. In 1882, lawmakers banned all Chinese laborers from entering the United States. Three years later, the Foran Act extended the contract labor ban to immigrants of all nationalities. The best way to protect domestic workers from unfair competition, lawmakers seemed to suggest, was to ensure that immigrant workers entered the United States freely or not at all.

The ban against Chinese laborers in Victoria (Australia) and the United States (in 1881 and 1882, respectively) set off a global rush to block the Chinese. Colonies and nations from New South Wales to Venezuela followed suit, constructing what Aristide Zohlberg calls "A Great Wall Against China."[6]

Chinese exclusion was just the beginning, however. The years that followed saw a flurry of even broader restrictive legislation in the United States and around the world. Between 1887 and 1918, the Netherlands,

Sweden, Argentina, and Chile, among others, all asserted their "sovereign right" to exclude immigrants for any reason, whether or not they had the means or inclination to actually do so. In 1893, France required that immigrants register as they crossed land borders. Other governments singled out particular immigrant groups. In 1897, Natal restricted Indian immigration by means of a dictation test in a European language and by imposing a head tax of £25. Venezuela banned all non-Europeans, while in 1914 Colombia simply restricted the immigration of "dangerous aliens." Haiti, Costa Rica, and Panama all denied admission to Syrians among others.[7] The United States imposed a head tax, then a bar against anarchists and other radicals, then a literacy test during World War I, and finally a quota system rigged to vastly reduce the number of immigrants from eastern and southern Europe, and to block Asians of all nationalities.

This global trend toward exclusion was the context for the world's first guestworker programs. Temporary immigration schemes—guestworker programs—were state-brokered compromises designed to placate employers' demands for labor and nativists' demands for restriction. Not surprisingly, the first guestworker programs appeared in new nation-states—Prussia, Australia, and South Africa—where nationalist sentiment was particularly fevered and where restrictionist policies threatened rapid economic development. There guestworker programs offered clear-cut distinctions between citizens and noncitizens, natives and aliens, insiders and outsiders, Germans and non-Germans, whites and nonwhites.

This first phase in the history of guestworker programs is worth exploring in some detail because it reveals the essential features of the guestworker programs to come. The earliest program was in Prussia, where in the 1880s the countryside was undergoing rapid commercialization, mechanization, and concentration (instigated at least in part by a crisis caused by competition from American-grown grain). Because large grain and beet planters needed few year-round farm hands but many short-term seasonal laborers, these changes simultaneously displaced rural people and generated complaints of labor shortages. The problem was not, in fact, a lack of potential workers—the Reich's population increased by 25 percent between 1873 and 1895—the problem was attracting and keeping short-term seasonal laborers at a time when year-round jobs in factories and coal mines beckoned.[8]

To secure a short-term labor force without raising wages for farmworkers, Prussian farm owners in the 1880s did what many other nineteenth-century employers around the world were doing: they recruited workers from abroad—in this case, tens of thousands of Poles from Russia and Austria (Poland itself had been disassembled by its neighbors in the late eighteenth century). Many thousands of ethnic Poles already lived and worked in Prussian provinces as a result of earlier annexations of Polish territory, but landowners imported tens of thousands more, driving the rapid development of mining and the commercialization of agriculture.[9]

Though the new arrivals were relatively few compared to the numbers of Poles already in Prussia and to the Prussian population as a whole, the presence of new Slavic immigrants fed a rising tide of German nationalism. By the mid-1880s, the hue and cry over the so-called Polanization of Prussia reached a fever pitch, forcing Bismark to choose between placating nativists, on the one hand, and placating landed capitalists, on the other. He went with the nativists, deporting some 40,000 unnaturalized Poles in 1885 and supporting harsh measures to block further immigration.[10]

These measures outraged the owners of large estates in eastern Prussia, whose appeals became all the more strident as labor-intensive beet cultivation spread in the East, exacerbating their seasonal labor problems. Recognizing the power of anti-Polish forces, growers petitioned not for an open border but for the right to import agricultural labor on a *temporary* basis. Promising that their recruitment efforts would be subject to government controls, landowners won a compromise five years later. In 1890, the government reopened the eastern provinces of Prussia to Polish migrants, but with conditions.[11] Prussia discouraged migrants from settling by allowing entry only to single men and by requiring those men to leave every winter. Migrants were issued identification cards, color-coded to indicate their nation of origin, and were banned from speaking German or conducting meetings in Polish. The policy's object, according to Ulrich Herbert, was to "repeatedly impress upon both the Polish farmworkers *and* the local German population that such workers were merely aliens whose presence was tolerated and that their permanent settlement in Prussia was out of the question."[12]

The state became involved, in other words, not so much because of employers' demands for foreign workers—they had already had them—but because of rising public opposition to foreign workers' presence. Draconian immigration restrictions were staved off by the promise that, with state power, immigrants could be deployed temporarily and thus kept from integrating into German society. By segregating foreign workers from the general population, Prussia's system pitted foreigners against domestic workers and intimidated Poles who might have formed or joined labor organizations. When foreign workers did organize, employers could threaten them with deportation, with the force of the state undergirding the threat.

A similar process transformed contract laborers into guestworkers in turn-of-the-century Australia, where late nineteenth-century sugar planters had been recruiting Pacific Islanders as indentured servants. Many cane cutters were kidnapped and forced into indentures, a process known as blackbirding. The use of Pacific Islanders, who were called Kanakas, generated little comment from white Australians until the worldwide depression of the 1890s forced unemployed white workers to seek jobs in the cane fields. White Australians' anger at having to compete for work with nonwhites fed the popular campaign to make the continent's newly unified British colonies into a single, independent, "White Australia." Almost immediately on its formation in 1901, Australia's new Commonwealth Parliament expelled the Kanakas and passed an Immigration Restriction Act that required immigrants to pass a "dictation test" in a European language. Two years later, the 1903 Commonwealth Naturalization Act limited the right of naturalization to European immigrants. Only then did Australia's parliament allow sugar planters to re-import Kanakas, and then only on temporary visas. Australia had transformed indentured servants into guestworkers.[13]

Recognizing that guestworker schemes went back at least as far as the late nineteenth century—even if the word gastarbeiter did not—forces us to consider how guestworker programs differ from other systems by which labor moved around in the late nineteenth century. What separated the Poles and Kanakas from the indentured servants and "white slaves" who lived and worked at the same time? What, for that matter, separates late twentieth-century guestworkers from nineteenth-century indentured servants? Are Jamaican guestworkers today simply modern coolies?

The South African example should disabuse us of that notion. As in the case of the 1890 Prussian compromise that mediated between Germans who wanted to hire Poles and those who wanted to banish them, South Africa's labor supply system was designed to simultaneously placate whites who wanted to isolate themselves from nonwhites and satisfy white employers who sought a larger and more controllable labor force. In devising a guestworker system—an "oscillating" system of labor supply, as South African scholars put it—South African mining companies categorically rejected indentured servitude in favor of a modern form of migration.[14]

After the annexation of Natal in 1842, Britain's colonial government responded to the rising number of Africans in the territory by removing about half of them to "locations," a sort of British colonial precursor to the American "reservation." Producers of wine and wool complained that they could not get sufficient labor as a result, and complaints of labor scarcity grew louder still after the proliferation of sugarcane plantations in 1860 and the discovery of diamonds in the Cape Colony and gold in the Transvaal (in 1870 and 1871, respectively). It wasn't that Africans weren't available locally, but mine managers complained that local blacks resisted signing long contracts, preferring instead to remain free to return at will to subsistence farming or hunting.[15]

Employers responded in different ways. Planters turned to indentured labor from India, importing six thousand people on five-year contracts between 1860 and 1866. In doing so, however, they incurred the wrath of white settlers who didn't want to rub elbows with Indians any more than they did with Africans. To make matters worse from white settlers' perspective, the planters were clearly encouraging Indians to stay when their indenture bonds were up.[16]

Mine managers sought alternatives. In 1872, the Kimberley diamond mine complex resurrected old slave pass laws to restrict miners' movements. In 1881, Kimberley began importing miners on contracts from Portuguese East Africa (now Mozambique) in a bald effort to depress local wages by pitting local workers against foreigners in a competition for work and wages. In 1885, the mines combined the two strategies, instituting a policy of "closed compounds," which involved locking miners in for the duration of their contracts, and paying them every six months instead of weekly. Unlike the South Asian indentured servants, who had been encouraged to settle in Natal, however, foreign miners were shuttled out of the mining region when their contracts ended to guarantee against permanent settlement.[17] This was indentured servitude with a difference: laborers had to leave when their contract was up. This oscillating labor supply system soon spread to other mines and regions, allowing South Africa's mining companies to expand rapidly while keeping miners' real wages flat for fifty years.[18]

As in Prussia and Australia, employers created South Africa's temporary labor scheme with the sanction and active support of state authorities. But in newly unified South Africa, the state took its very identity from its foreign labor supply system. The Native Labour Regulation Act, enacted by the Union of South Africa in 1910, required all male, black African workers, foreign and domestic, to carry passes. Three years later, the 1913 Land Act created overcrowded "reserves," much like the old "locations," which could be mined for cheap labor. A decade after that, the Natives Act amended the pass laws to keep blacks out of urban areas, except when they had to be there "to minister to the needs of the white man." This apartheid system mirrored Prussia's efforts to import *and* segregate Poles, but with an insidious twist: while Prussia's foreign worker program helped distinguish "foreigners" from "Germans," South Africa's plan helped reduce black South Africans to the status of foreigners in their own land.[19] These three labor migration systems—Prussia's, Australia's, and South Africa's—were the granddaddies of modern guestworker programs, though the word "guest" seems particularly inappropriate in all three cases. It would rarely be more appropriate later.

Guestworker programs did not proliferate immediately. In the United States, the 1885 Foran Act specifically forbade the importation of contract workers. Employers got around the law, but they did so without state sanction. Canada too generally refused to allow the admission of industrial workers on temporary permits. France was generally open to immigrants, so there was no need to seek immigrants on a temporary basis.[20]

It was the outbreak of World War I that accelerated the spread of guest-worker programs. The war generated precisely the sort of contradictory impulses that had midwifed the earlier programs. It inspired belligerents to throw open their arms to immigrants in the name of maximizing war production, while at the same time it heightened xenophobia and exacerbated fears of supposedly subversive foreigners. These contradictory sentiments—the desire to admit immigrant workers and the urge to expel them—encouraged even the most liberal states to get into the business of recruiting *and* policing immigrants, using the very sort of methods pioneered by Prussia, South Africa, and Australia.[21]

The French state stepped in to recruit colonial labor from North Africa, Indochina, and Madagascar as well as Chinese men for docks and military construction sites. French farmers joined forces to import Iberian and Italian workers, and the French government actively assisted industrialists in securing southern Europeans for mines and factories. Government officials soon discovered, however, that sponsoring labor supply schemes was more complicated than they had expected. While French workers seemed to accept the necessity of immigration during the war, they responded virulently and even violently to the presence of nonwhite workers, who were regularly paid half as much as French workers for the same jobs. Socialists called for "equal pay for equal work" and tried to organize foreign workers, but more conservative trade unions insisted that French workers be given priority for all jobs and that nonwhite workers be directed only to the most onerous, unattractive work. Agricultural employers and mine owners complained that European immigrants, who enjoyed greater freedom of movement than the nonwhite workers, tended to break their six-month contracts and migrate to cities in search of better paying and less difficult work.[22]

French officials responded by collaborating with employers and trade unions to direct nonwhite foreigners to jobs and lodging deemed "unsuitable for Frenchmen" and to guard them closely to keep them from looking for better work. With European migrants, in contrast, the French Foreign Labor Service employed a carrot and stick approach, awarding bonuses to workers who completed their contracts and threatening "troublemakers" with expulsion. Like the South Africans and Prussians, the French devised a pass system, issuing identification cards, which, Gary Cross notes, "designated the geographical limits within which [immigrant workers] could travel and whether they were farm or industrial workers." Copies of the cards were sent to local police departments, which were instructed to "threaten to expel workers who broke their contracts."[23]

Though immigrants had no legal right to remain in France once their contracts expired, only nonwhite workers were summarily repatriated after the armistice. In contrast, European immigrants were allowed and, indeed, encouraged to remain to help clear rubble and aid in the country's reconstruction. Interestingly, their increasing numbers led in the 1920s to calls for measures that would speed their assimilation (not their expulsion). Likewise, French officials encouraged Polish farmworkers to settle down in company housing instead of jumping their contracts in search of better work by allowing them to bring their family members to join them. In other words, European workers were offered what John Torpey calls the "embrace" of the French state; nonwhite workers got nothing but a cold shoulder and a long boat ride home.[24]

The war instigated a similar change of direction in U.S. immigration policy because the outbreak of war cut off European migration to the United States, just as American industry expanded in the interests of war mobilization. Mass migration of white and black southerners to cities North and South made up some of the difference but the loss of a million and a half rural people merely shifted the sense of crisis to the countryside. U.S. officials responded to complaints of labor scarcity in a variety of ways. The Labor Department tried to organize a labor distribution system that would relocate workers from pockets of surplus to areas of scarcity, simultaneously recruiting Boy Scouts, high school students, and a Woman's Land Army to make up the shortfall. The U.S. Department of Agriculture took a different tack, encouraging southern legislatures to pass "work-or-fight" ordinances that would compel black workers to return to white people's fields and kitchens. Men who didn't were put at the top of the draft rolls. Women, who couldn't be drafted, were simply arrested (and sometimes released into the custody of their former employers to work off their fines). But when neither proposition satisfied the owners of large farms, the Department of Labor's Immigration Service—the precursor to the INS—encouraged the migration of agricultural workers from Mexico, Canada, Puerto Rico, and the Bahamas on temporary labor contracts.[25] This was the first American guestworker program, though it was far less formal than its World War II counterpart.

The wartime importation of temporary contract labor would seem to have violated both the 1885 Foran Act and the new 1917 Immigration Act, which required immigrants to pay a head tax and be literate in their own language. But the 1917 act included a loophole for employers seeking foreign labor on a temporary basis. The act's "ninth proviso" authorized the Commission-General of Immigration together with the Secretary of Labor to "control and regulate the admission and return *of otherwise inadmissible aliens* applying for temporary admission."[26] Just after the United States entered the war, moreover, the Secretary of Labor waived the head tax and literacy test for agricultural labor. Later, he included railroad, mining, and construction labor in his exception. The ninth proviso gave southwestern farmers continued access to Mexicans; Maine potato growers a greater number of French Canadians; New Bedford, Massachussetts growers access to "Bravas" from Cape Verde Island; and Floridian truck farmers more Bahamians. None of these labor sources were new, but they would have been lost to growers had immigration restrictions been applied to farm workers.[27]

These World War I importation schemes not only reversed the thirty-year-old congressional ban on importing contract labor, they *required* that aliens entering for temporary farmwork sign contracts for the duration of their stay. Employers had to apply to the Immigration Service or U.S. Employment Service for labor, after which the required number of workers would be admitted and photographed. To ensure that the Mexican workers remained only temporarily, the Labor Department demanded that employers withhold a portion of their pay and sent it to Mexico by money order. Any worker who failed to claim his funds at the end of his contract forfeited them. Growers had to sign performance bonds in which they promised to personally deport their employees at the expiration of their contracts or the end of the war.[28]

Though the lifting of the U.S. contract labor ban lasted only for the duration, migration often continued unofficially after the war. In fact, the number of Mexicans entering the United States increased as Mexicans fled the turmoil of the Revolution south of the border. The World War I guestworker programs dissolved into unmanaged, informal migration, which was relatively uncontroversial as long as jobs were plentiful and migrants stuck to agriculture.

If they hadn't already been stopped by plummeting farm prices in the 1920s, these early guestworker programs came to a screeching halt when the stock market crashed in 1929 (except in South Africa, where the doubling of gold prices and the discovery of new seams led to a large-scale expansion of the migrant labor program). In settler countries worldwide, returning migrants outnumbered new immigrants during the Great Depression, a process that some governments, including the United States, helped along by expelling hundreds of thousands of foreign workers they had actively sought earlier. Germany, which had transformed its migrant workers into forced laborers during the Great War, closed its German-Polish frontier to migrant workers during the Depression.[29] U.S. and state officials in the American southwest forcefully deported many thousands of Mexicans and Mexican Americans and terrified even more into leaving on their own. In the Dominican Republic, the army massacred twenty- to thirty thousand Haitian cane cutters and sent hundreds of thousands of others fleeing over the border that divides the island into two nations. Thus the Great Depression ended the first phase in the history of temporary labor recruitment.

In the long run, however, these reversals turned out to be temporary interruptions in the overall trend toward state-sponsored temporary labor migration. Once the demands of war mobilization began to raise wages, guestworker programs would begin again, and Leaford and Enoch Williams would be at the head of the line.

CHAPTER TWO

Everything But a Gun to Their Heads

The Politics of Labor Scarcity and the Birth of World War II Guestworker Programs

THE SECOND PHASE in the history of guestworker programs began as the mobilization for world war led once again to rising wages and thus to the rekindling of interest in temporary foreign workers. Outlasting the war by more than thirty years, this phase involved far more nations and migrants, and far greater state involvement in labor supply schemes. During the Great Depression—or "the Great Slump" as the British called it—nation-states expelled foreign workers in the name of taking care of their own; during World War II, they invited them back, beginning a new and much larger trend toward admitting foreign workers on a temporary basis. In 1936, just four years after Germany closed its eastern border for a second time, the German government began negotiating with Polish authorities to revive the controlled importation of farmworkers. In another three years, Germany had signed similar agreements with five other European nations from Holland to Bulgaria. South Africa, which had by this time been importing migrant workers for almost fifty years, doubled its workforce in the mining industry and expanded the migrant labor program to funnel workers to farms as well. Japan fueled its military buildup by recruiting workers from its "co-prosperity sphere," facilitating this labor migration by issuing Japanese passports in the countries it colonized.[1]

Yet war has a strange way of mobilizing and immobilizing labor at the same time. Just a few years after reopening their borders to foreign workers, Germany and Japan transformed their foreign labor schemes into forced labor systems. By August 1944, there were 5.7 million civilian conscripts working in Germany and its occupied territories alone, including every second agricultural worker and every third worker in mining, construction, and metals.[2]

U.S. growers also demanded renewed access to foreign workers. An "unholy holler from the farm bloc" followed the outbreak of war in Europe as American farmers predicted that a draft and war economy would mean a disastrous labor shortage.[3] Indeed, rural Americans were abandoning the countryside like never before. They were answering draft calls, traveling to remote areas to construct vast military bases, and searching for better paying war jobs. By the war's end, 15 million Americans—one-third of the prewar workforce—would have taken advantage of the war economy to switch to better jobs, and four million of them would have left their home states to do so. The rural South would see the biggest exodus, as about 10 percent of its population headed north or west and another 10 percent abandoned the countryside for the city.[4]

Yet even the movement of millions doesn't necessarily mean a labor crisis in the countryside. The "great migration" of rural people to the cities and of southerners to the North and West surely reduced the rural labor supply, but it had been so glutted by the slump in agricultural prices in the 1920s and then by the Great Depression in the 1930s that it took a long time for the war to make a dent in the surplus of desperately poor and often homeless people. Rural poverty, unemployment, and underemployment were deeply entrenched, especially in the U.S. South.

Yet growers certainly feared labor scarcity. Exacerbating their sense of insecurity was the fact that many could recall the pressures of World War I, when they or their parents were called on to win the war by increasing their production with less labor. The circumstances were not identical, however. The early twentieth century had been a "Golden Age of Agriculture," during which prices and wages rose. The outbreak of World War I had sent wages spiraling even further and farmworkers racing for better paying jobs and the front lines. World War II came on the heels of nearly twenty years of agricultural depression and the biggest labor glut in American history.[5]

In some regions, growers did lose their labor to the military, manufacturing plants, and base construction during the war, but in many parts of the country—particularly in the South where prewar wages were lowest—the press of destitute workers for farm jobs was so large that the war only relieved it a little. What occurred in the South during World War II was less a dearth of labor than a seismic shift in the balance of power between growers and farm laborers. Farm laborers hadn't vanished, but their reduced numbers gave them the courage to demand more for their services. And farmworkers'—especially black farmworkers'—ability to make demands infuriated employers, who refused to admit that the ground beneath them had shifted.

As farmworkers used the exigencies of war to demand a new deal, growers looked for alternative sources of labor. "I want 6 Bahama [sic] Laborers and need them now," wrote Mrs. William J. Krome on January 29, 1943, in a telegram to the Secretary of Agriculture; "Bahamians are far better help than riffraff now walking our roads and shooting craps in our fields." Another grower, one of many who wrote to Washington that

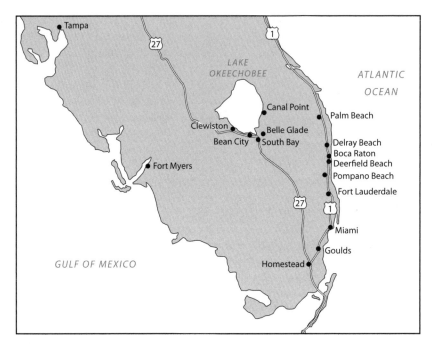

Map of South Florida

year, warned that the War Manpower Commission's "refusal to allow us to import Bahaman labor" was sabotaging Florida's war effort: "Your action," he wrote, "will show whether you are working for the allies or the axis."[6]

In the East, many growers demanded a new immigration policy that would give them access to Bahamian workers. South Florida vegetable and sugarcane growers, who paid some of the lowest wages in the nation, hollered the loudest for foreign labor. Organized into a formidable lobby under the tireless leadership of a tomato farmer and self-appointed diplomat named Luther L. Chandler, they wrote letters, sent telegrams, called their congressmen, marched into officials' offices, and testified at hearings. Chandler and his neighbors weren't the only growers demanding Bahamians. Al French, the labor manager at Seabrook Farms, New Jersey, was lobbying hard, as were shade tobacco growers in Connecticut. But no one was more persistent and more effective than Chandler, who organized South Florida growers to demand renewed access to the Bahamians who had built Miami, dived for sponges off Key West, harvested and processed crops along the east coast of Florida, and cooked, cleaned, and minded white children since the turn of the century. Bahamians had come to Florida by the thousands and then, impeded by immigration restrictions, most stopped coming. With a war on, South Florida growers wanted them back.

Chandler envisioned a return to Bahamian labor, but under new terms. Instead of a return to the days when Bahamian men and women came and went at will, Chandler envisioned migrant Bahamians who could be immobilized and deported at growers' will, and he realized his dream not by convincing federal officials that growers' labor needs were real but by badgering politicians, public officials, and even one disgraced former monarch into doing his bidding. His heart set on a sort of Florida variant on apartheid, Chandler's efforts resulted in the creation of the nation's longest-running guestworker program.

Down and Out

Like California, Florida was a destination for the down-and-out during the Great Depression. As forty- to sixty thousand destitute people hurried to Florida every winter during the Great Depression, wages deteriorated, despite the vegetable industry's boom. By all accounts farmworkers' wages fell dramatically over the decade. As one veteran farmworker who had worked in thirty-three states put it, "Florida is the sorriest wages in the United States."[7]

South Florida was so oversupplied with labor during the 1930s, in fact, that the black men and women who lived in Belle Glade's ramshackle flophouses and outhouse-like sheds had to compete for work every morning at a street corner "roundup." Though bean growers offered only 15 to 25 cents a hamper (down from 40 cents in the 1920s), workers raced to growers' trucks, cramming themselves upright into the flatbeds and hanging onto the sideboards. Drivers' helpers beat the men and women who clung to the hood and sides of the trucks until they let go, and the trucks could drive off into the fields.[8]

Ironically, the New Deal made things worse, not better. Farmworkers were excluded from all the labor and relief measures passed during the legislative whirlwind of the New Deal's first hundred days. Farmworkers were not specifically excluded from Section 7(a) of the 1933 National Industrial Recovery Act, which granted workers the right of collective bargaining, but Franklin Roosevelt's presidential decree excluded them three weeks later. In 1933, Congress established a Federal Transient Program within the Federal Emergency Relief Administration (FERA), and set aside millions of dollars for the relief of "transients," but FERA excluded migrant farmworkers from its definition of transients, arguing that federal aid to farmworkers would subsidize industries that benefited from cheap, casual labor. FERA required that states employ the "utmost vigilance" to insure that federal relief funds went to "bona fide transients," *not* to farmworkers. Equally important, the Agricultural Adjustment Act sought to revive agricultural prices by paying growers to grow less. By requir-

FIGURE 2.1 Migrant family from Tennessee at their shelter in Winter Haven, Florida, 1937 (Arthur Rothstein, State Archives of Florida).

ing growers to share their allotment payment with their sharecroppers, the law inadvertently encouraged growers to evict their sharecroppers and hire them back as casual labor during peak planting, chopping, and harvest seasons. By any measure, farmworkers got a raw deal.[9]

Many arrivals were homeless country people who had either lost their farms to the bank or the boll weevil. Some were tenants who lost their leases to federal crop reduction programs. A few, no doubt, were unemployed factory workers. Poor people—black and white—came to Florida, not only because homelessness was more tolerable under a palm tree, but because the draining of the Everglades had recently exposed rich farmland that could produce hundreds of thousands of acres of vegetables in the winter when there was little work elsewhere. There the prices of perishable "truck crops" remained high. Small farmers who gambled on Florida agriculture often lost out to freezes and floods, but big, diversified farms prospered, making truck farming—the production of perishable fruits and vegetables for direct sale—the state's leading agricultural industry. Acreage in green beans increased sevenfold during the depths of the Great Depression, and the value of that harvest alone rose from $59 to $86 an acre.[10]

FIGURE 2.2 Farmworker housing in Belle Glade, Florida, 1941. Housing like this was still in use in the 1970s (Marion Post Wolcott, Library of Congress).

Florida farmers may not have paid much but they paid cash, something sharecroppers rarely got to see, let alone earn. Mary Jenkins and her brother, Freddy Young, fled a cotton farm in Dublin, Georgia, hoping for new lives in Florida. Both swore never to marry "a girl or boy that wanted to farm." Trying to escape rural life, they ended up at work on Butts Farm, one of the nation's biggest commercial farms. Freddy had gone south first in 1935. Returning with his own car and cash in his pocket, he talked Mary into going back with him. To her Butts Farm was nothing but beans, a thousand stooped laborers, and a long row of pickers' shacks. Standing by Freddy's car in the dawn light, she thought the farm was the worst place she "had ever seen."[11] Yet so many people came to Florida seeking work that the Florida state police established a border patrol along the main highways into the state to turn back "undesirables" who might flood relief rolls.[12]

A decade later, the tables had turned. Workers hadn't vanished, and the flophouses and sheds they lived in hadn't changed because of World War II, but those who remained farmworkers were suddenly in a position to influence the price of their labor, simply by shunning the poorest paying growers. As the war drew away surplus labor, anxious growers were reduced to employing barkers to advertise the day's offerings to increasingly choosey farmworkers. "First picking! Bountifuls! Good stand! Fifty cents." "Tendergreens, second picking, good yield! Sixty cents!" men cried from the truck beds. Growers secretly paid a few farmworkers to clamber enthusiastically onto their trucks to sway the waiting crowd. What a difference a war makes.[13]

Employers' complaints of labor scarcity reveal that workers were present but increasingly demanding. "50% of the crops are wasting in the fields," L. L. Stuckey, chairman of the Florida Farm Bureau's Vegetable

Committee wrote in a letter to the U.S. Secretary of Agriculture in 1942: "1,000 farm laborers idle in the communities and a majority of those working effectively employing delaying tactics."[14] Farm employers found themselves forced to negotiate with workers, and they didn't like it one bit. "*Negroes have got to be bossed*," insisted Mrs. William Krome, of Glades County, Florida, the wife of the engineer who had surveyed Henry Morrison Flagler's daring oversea railroad connecting Miami and Key West. "[Y]ou can't boss them when they make that kind of money and when they can get another job anywhere they want it." "I haven't fired a Negro in I don't know when," she complained; "they quit first."[15] L. L. Stuckey agreed. Tens of thousands of acres of vegetables and sugar needed for the war effort would be lost, he argued, if foreign workers weren't imported in time for the harvest.[16] What the country needed was "fewer negroes in uniforms," added Mrs. J. W. Wallace from up in Florence, South Carolina: "[R]eturn them to their homes on the plantation."[17] After twenty years of agricultural depression, and three hundred years of white supremacy, the notion that black farmworkers could quit, sit idle, or delay was unthinkable. And if African American workers wouldn't accept what they were willing to offer without question, growers thought they knew other black workers who would. Bahamians were just off the mainland, eager for work.

Worse Than the Chain Gang

Growers didn't all strike on the same solution by coincidence. In South Florida, their leader was L. L. Chandler, an irrepressible agricultural entrepreneur with a talent for talk. Born in 1896 in Fort Drum, Florida—once a Seminole War army post—Chandler was the son of a central Florida cattleman father and a missionary mother. Her mission was saving souls; his was cultivating South Florida's agricultural economy. In 1906, when L. L. and Miami were both a decade old, he and his family moved to nearby Homestead. The arrival of Flagler's East Coast Railway two years earlier made the settlement an ideal place to produce crops that northerners couldn't get in winter, especially the tomatoes coveted by new city dwellers from Italy. Chandler enlisted in the Navy in World War I, but returned "just as fast as [he] could" to plant tomatoes. He bought land one railroad stop away from Homestead in a place called Goulds, where he planted crops and built a general store and a packinghouse.[18]

By 1941, Chandler was forty-five years old, successful, a co-founder of Holsom's Bread (the South's largest bakery), and a leader of his community. He was president of Dade County's chapter of the American Farm Bureau Federation, the nation's largest and most powerful growers' lobby, and had served for the previous six years on the Florida Citrus Commission. He was a Rotarian, an Elk, a Mason, and a Shriner. Soon, he would be a diplomat of sorts.

In his role as Farm Bureau president and community booster, Chandler began the drive for Bahamian labor five months before the attack on Pearl Harbor. Dade and Broward County growers supported him enthusiastically, as did the U.S. Sugar Corporation in Palm Beach County. Florida's largest and best-connected agricultural company, U.S. Sugar—or "Big Sugar" as workers called it—had been having labor troubles since 1931 when its founders Charles S. Mott (of General Motors) and his partner Clarence Bitting bought up 100,000 acres from a failed sugar company and began producing sugar on a massive scale. Finding year-round employers and mill workers was never a problem, especially during the Depression, but retaining harvest labor was. Cutting sugarcane with a razor-sharp machete is dirty, difficult, and dangerous work, and the surroundings didn't help. U.S. Sugar was located on recently reclaimed Everglades, which meant cane cutters lived and worked in the midst of miles of cane and canals, home to alligators, snakes, very large spiders, and biting insects of infinite variety. The flophouses and bean fields of Belle Glade seemed like the Riviera in comparison.[19]

Since its start in 1931, U.S. Sugar had taken a carrot-and-stick approach to its labor problems. First it built model housing for harvest hands, ten-by-twenty-foot wooden cottages with screened windows (though no plumbing or electricity). White mill workers got more substantial houses with gardens out front, but the humble cottages in U.S. Sugar's "negro villages" were such a remarkable improvement over Florida's norm that Eleanor Roosevelt came for the ribbon cutting.[20] Black workers continued to leave for Belle Glade's bean fields.

When the carrot failed, U.S. Sugar's managers turned immediately to the stick. They recruited African Americans farther afield in Georgia, Alabama, and Louisiana, promising them free transportation, Bar-B-Qs, and good pay. But when workers arrived, they discovered that their wages were half what they expected, transportation and equipment costs were deducted from that, and what little was left came in scrip. When they tried to leave, they encountered camp managers brandishing pistols and blackjacks, and sheriff's deputies patrolling the roads for runaways. Those caught were beaten. Not long after Mrs. Roosevelt had flown home after the opening of U.S. Sugar's neat little labor village, Florida's governor received a letter from one of Big Sugar's cane cutters who complained, "They works us from dark to dark," and paid less than the dollar a ton recruiters had promised. It was "worse than the chain gang," one sympathetic white resident of nearby West Palm Beach explained in a letter of protest to the governor. Local black people avoided working there

FIGURE 2.3 A U.S. Sugar Corporation village for African American families (c. 1941) (Marion Post Wolcott, Library of Congress).

because payday meant "an empty envelope or one with a few cents in it."[21] One father wrote to the U.S. Attorney in Memphis to report that his son had been killed trying to escape from the company. A local resident named C. A. Coldman claimed that local law enforcement officials were in league with U.S. Sugar, and insisted that a Palm Beach County sheriff who had found the body of a sugarcane cutter along the banks of a canal had set fire to the corpse instead of investigating the man's death.[22] Summarizing workers' statements to investigating FBI agents, Jerrill Shofner writes, "Nearly all workers testified that they had been offered from three to six dollars a day and free transportation to Florida. After arriving they were told that wages were $1.80 per day and that they were being charged for transportation, the equipment necessary for cutting cane, and an identification badge. They were also informed in graphic terms that they could not leave until they had worked off their debts." "Men stated that" after deductions, they received "only a few cents at each of several successive pay days." "The three supervisors wore guns and carried black-jacks," which they frequently threatened to use. The workers were told that "if they tried to leave on the sugar trains, all of which the company owned, they would be shot. If they tried to escape by public roads they

FIGURE 2.4 African American cane cutters in Leon County, Florida. (Photo courtesy of State Archives of Florida.)

would be arrested as vagrants and returned to camp with an additional fine to work off . . . Numerous men testified that they had been beaten or had seen others beaten with blackjacks."[23] By 1941, Eleanor Roosevelt, President Roosevelt, Florida Governor Doyle Carlton, and the FBI had all received complaints from men who were being held against their will by U.S. Sugar.

As a result of these complaints, the FBI launched an investigation into U.S. Sugar's labor policies, producing deposition after deposition that documented the use of overbearing force at U.S. Sugar.[24] The investigation signaled a major change of policy for the federal government, which for decades had refused to prosecute employers for violating the Thirteenth Amendment to the U.S. Constitution, the Civil War era amendment which prohibited forced labor. Federal officials had long insisted that forced labor was not slavery unless it was justified by debt. Although debt was a factor at U.S. Sugar, federal inaction in cases involving the use or threat of force encouraged growers to make the blackjack and the shotgun their principal labor management tools. Now, in 1942, in the midst of a war for freedom and democracy, the Justice Department had changed its position and indicted U.S. Sugar's labor camp managers for kidnapping, imprisoning, and shooting at African American workers. The case, which went to trial in April 1943, was quashed on a technicality, but it was embarrassing to U.S. Sugar nonetheless. Bahamians seemed a much better solution to U.S. Sugar's labor troubles than meddling First Ladies and G-men.[25]

The federal government didn't immediately embrace Chandler's proposal to replace African American workers with black workers from abroad. The Farm Security Administration first tried to help U.S. Sugar meet its labor needs with domestic labor. It built migratory labor camps near the sugar fields and used the offices of the U.S. Employment Service to secure labor from farther afield, but U.S. Sugar's reputation for brutality stymied recruiters. "I will endeavor to give you a picture of the recruitment activities in Alabama," an FSA official reported to the Washington office, after talking to 350 men in a seven-hour period. "Whenever [Florida] was mentioned to these colored men," he reported, "they shut up like a clam and shook their heads, and others say that FL is the place you get shackled or locked up and they don't want to go down there to work." Only two out of the 350 were willing to go to U.S. Sugar.[26]

U.S. Sugar's managers weren't much interested in the federal labor supply system either, especially when federal camp managers refused to evict residents who went on strike. Camp residents had "stopped all work and were loafing," U.S. Sugar officials complained. They were not mollified when FSA camp managers replied that camp residents had simply gone to work for other farmers or that it was "not within [their] power to require individuals to work at any specified point."[27]

Impatient with the federal employment service system, growers concentrated on lobbying for Bahamians. Al French, previously of Seabrook Farms, but now the manager of the West Palm Beach U.S. Employment Service office, "was very anxious to complete arrangements for placing [Bahamian] workers with the Sugar Corporation," wrote a Mr. Levine in a Bureau of Employment Security Report. Asked if local sources of labor supply had been tapped to meet the company's needs, French explained that "no attempt had been made to recruit Florida labor for cane cutting, first, because no definite orders were on hand [employers not even having bothered to put in an application for domestic recruits], and second because Negro labor in Florida will not work for the Sugar Corporation." "Mr. French could not explain this situation," Levine noted, "except that certain 'rumors' about poor treatment at the hands of Sugar Corporation foremen had always circulated among the Negro population." These rumors "were unfounded," French insisted, though he noted without irony that, "it was true that Negroes were occasionally beaten for attempting to leave the job when they owed debts at the company's commissary, and others were sometimes required to work as many as eighteen hours a day at cane cutting."[28] French then contradicted his claim that African American workers refused to work for U.S. Sugar by advocating a ceiling on piece rates. He noted, "A very large number of Negroes (a majority of them, in the opinion of the growers), are not interested in making more money, but . . . in making the same money quicker."[29]

Unable to use force without federal interference and uninterested in co-operating with the federal government's domestic labor supply effort, U.S. Sugar signed on to vegetable growers' campaign for Caribbean labor. The harvest of 100,000 tons of "vitally needed sugar" was "menaced by the tight labor situation," warned Jay M. Moran, U.S. Sugar's general manager, and the problem was made "more acute by the consistently increasing amount of absenteeism on the part of sugar workers now employed." What U.S. Sugar needed, he noted in the *Clewiston (FL) News*, was labor from the Bahamas, Puerto Rico, and Haiti.[30]

The plan was not to replace African American workers but to put a fire under them by inserting competitors into the labor force. "We in this area," Al French wrote, "are still of the opinion that the only hope for harvesting the spring vegetable crop, barring Acts of God, is to import Bahamians on a strictly agricultural basis." "With a sufficient number of Bahamians in here," he continued, "it is believed resulting conditions *would force idle domestic labor to work also.*"[31] Bahamians would put African Americans back in their place.

Florida growers could in fact point to thousands of Bahamian workers who were desperately anxious to work in the United States and who were familiar with local conditions because the histories of Florida and the Bahamas had long been intertwined. Many white Bahamians were descendants of American loyalists who had departed eastern Florida with their slaves after the American Revolution. Many black Bahamians were descendants of those slaves. During the Civil War, Bahamians had prospered by smuggling Confederate cotton to English mills. In the late 1860s, white Bahamians had emigrated to the Florida Keys, complaining that emancipated blacks in the Bahamas had become too assertive. Black Bahamians followed them, attracted by high wages in Key West's cigar, sponging, and wrecking industries. By 1892, Bahamians (black and white) made up almost a third of Key West's population.[32] From there, black Bahamians moved north to the South Florida mainland, some working seasonally in agriculture, construction, sponging, and tourism, others bringing their families and settling permanently in Miami's "Colored Town" or in the new communities that sprung up along the route of the Florida East Coast Railway.[33] "All of our heavy laborers were Bahamian negroes," one early historian of South Florida remarked.[34] With legal migration blocked by the Literacy Act of 1917, the migration continued but at a slower pace. In August 1921, newspapers reported that the Immigration Service was looking into reports of "the smuggling of Negroes from the Bahama

Islands." The Immigration Service was apparently effective at blocking them because, by the 1930s, Miami's Bahamian population had declined by about a fifth.[35]

Florida growers who maintained their Bahamian connections knew that thousands of the Bahamas' 69,000 people were indeed anxious for work. What little topsoil there was on the archipelago's 700 coral islands was eroding, which spelled the decline of the sisal (used to make rope) and pineapple industries. Then in 1938, an underwater fungus caused the complete collapse of the natural sponge industry, putting an additional three thousand men out of work. The outbreak of war gave the embryonic tourism industry a small boost, as well-heeled refugees arrived to sit out the war in safety, but German U-boat activity brought a rapid halt to the tourist traffic. Some Bahamians found jobs building the U.S. naval and air bases on the Bahamian islands of Exuma and New Providence, but base construction wouldn't last forever.[36]

THE SUPERABUNDANCE OF LABOR POWER ON AMERICAN FARMS

Though Florida growers demanded Bahamians as early as 1940, and Bahamians were open to their overtures, U.S. officials in Washington remained unconvinced that foreign workers were necessary. The war, they concluded, had made little dent in what the U.S. Department of Agriculture (USDA) called the "superabundance of labor power on American farms."[37] In the first four months after Germany's invasion of Poland, they noted, U.S. average daily farm wages fell. The problem of homelessness among farmworkers was still so dire, in fact, that the Farm Security Administration continued to open permanent and mobile migratory farm labor camps for homeless farmworkers. The FSA had been building such camps in California for several years, but in 1940, East Coast construction had just begun and the ubiquitous Eleanor Roosevelt had only just returned to Florida to cut the ribbon at the FSA's first East Coast camp, a segregated facility in Belle Glade. There, FSA social workers taught migrants canning, sewing, and reading skills designed to help farmworkers escape the migrant stream.[38]

Elsewhere, migrant poverty was also very much in the news. The same year that the FSA began building migratory labor camps on the East Coast, John Steinbeck won the Pulitzer Prize for *The Grapes of Wrath*, and Darrell Zanuck's film based on the novel opened in theaters across the nation. In the U.S. Senate, the "Tolan Committee" held hearings on the "interstate migration of destitute citizens," at which Frances Perkins, the Secretary of Labor, publicly criticized the exclusion of agricultural labor from federal labor laws.[39] If there was a farm labor crisis, it was a problem of excess, not scarcity.

L. L. Chandler was nevertheless determined to secure Bahamians. The day after New Deal production restrictions were lifted in the summer of 1941, he wrote to his congressman, Pat Cannon, "relative to the idea of permitting negro farm labor from the Bahama Islands to enter this country under a waiver of the immigration laws." Warning that government projects, private industry, and the draft had "taken up the slack," he anticipated the arrival of only two- to three thousand of the eight- to ten thousand farm laborers that growers in his area would require by late fall.[40]

Cannon, who as a two-term congressman was best known for absenteeism, became Florida growers' staunchest supporter during the war. Opposing price controls on crops in a rare appearance in the House, he thundered, "The trouble is, there's none of you ever saw a damned bean field in the first place!" "Working out price ceilings is very beautiful on paper, but there's too much damned socialism in this country"; this was an ironic statement from a politician who had gotten elected by advocating the Townsend Plan, which would have guaranteed every senior citizen an income of $200 provided they spent it.[41]

Cannon sent Chandler's letter to Cordell Hull, President Roosevelt's Secretary of State, whose unenthusiastic reply noted the terms of the 1917 Immigration Act. Echoing the 1885 Foran Act, the 1917 Act specifically excluded immigrants who had been "induced, assisted, encouraged, or solicited to migrate" by "offers or promises of employment." Employers, in other words, were not permitted to recruit labor abroad. Hull noted, however, that there were two exceptions to that fifty-year-old rule: employers could petition for the admission of people with particular skills if residents with similar skills were not available, and under the ninth proviso of the act's third section, the Attorney General had the authority to admit otherwise inadmissible aliens on a temporary basis under conditions established by the Secretary of Labor. That latter provision was precisely what Chandler had in mind. Since it was up to the Immigration and Naturalization Service (formerly known as the Department of Justice's Immigration Division) to grant such a waiver, Hull forwarded Chandler's letter to the INS's director, Major Lemuel Schofield.[42]

Backed by U.S. Sugar and the head of the Florida Employment Service, L. L. Chandler went after Lemmy Schofield with unflagging determination. He started out gently enough: "Years ago," he explained to Schofield, "before it was against the law to do so, great numbers of negroes from the Bahama Islands came into this country during the harvesting season, helped harvest these crops, and the majority of them went home." Concerned, no doubt, about the minority that didn't, Schofield or an underling underlined that last bit in red. "We understand," Chandler continued, "that thousands of these negroes in the Bahama Islands are without employment, and it would really be a favor *to them* if permitted to simply fill in the slack."[43] Growers would not be able to guarantee the return of the Bahamians they imported, Chandler informed the INS, unless they were "allowed to protect themselves by holding the laborers behind an inclosure [*sic*] during their leisure hours."[44]

Chandler made little headway with Schofield, perhaps because the INS director was busy with his own affairs. Not only was he supervising the roundup, arrest, detention, and deportation of immigrants who had failed to comply with the 1940 Registration Act, but he was trying to prevent the detention of his lover, Princess Stephanie von Hohenlohe, a Nazi spy and confidante of Hitler (who was also a Jew, according to her biographer). Although she was "worse than 10,000 men," according to the FBI who had been tapping her phone, Schofield was enraptured. She had a diamond-studded swastika brooch with Hitler's signature on the back, a son by Emperor Franz Joseph's married son-in-law, and a royal title from a short-lived marriage. L. L. Chandler only had tomatoes.[45]

Eventually, however, Chandler would prove himself just as irresistible as von Hohenlohe. After his first ineffective message, he stalked Schofield like a spurned lover. He wrote to him frequently and traveled to Washington to meet him. Eventually, Schofield weakened. Since he could only waive the ban on recruiting abroad if he ascertained that there was indeed a labor shortage, he directed the Miami office of the Immigration Service to send two immigration inspectors to Goulds. The inspectors were not impressed. One met with Chandler, whose response was predictable, but a few days later another paid a visit to Chandler's neighbors while he was out of town. The latter inspector dismissed Chandler's claim of labor scarcity, reporting that he had interviewed a large independent grower, southeast of Goulds, who insisted that he "did not anticipate any great shortage, in as much as he had always maintained favorable working conditions and always paid the prevailing wage." While some farmers and packers predicted labor shortages ranging wildly from 10 percent to 50 percent, the inspector wrote, there was no consensus on the matter. Some growers were opposed to the importation of foreign labor, he noted, and those who offered good quarters and pay well "are not greatly alarmed." Indeed, he added, a freeze the previous year had thrown six thousand farmworkers out of work and onto local relief rolls. Satisfied that there was no crisis, Schofield dropped the matter. In the winter of 1941–42, another freeze in South Florida forced thousands of farm laborers out of work once again. Schofield felt vindicated.[46]

Chandler wasn't giving up. Unable to convince Schofield to authorize the importation of Bahamians, Chandler took matters into his own hands, opening international negotiations with none other than Edward VIII, Duke of Windsor, and former King of England, who had abdicated his throne to marry an American divorcée. Because of the scandal and his Nazi sympathies, Edward was appointed governor of the Bahamas to get him out of the way and out of the news. There on his Elba, the Duke and his controversial Duchess whiled away their time entertaining wealthy war refugees while the Bahamian unemployment crisis grew. In 1941, Chandler arrived with a delegation of Florida growers, who offered to take the Duke's unemployment problem off his hands. Chandler later admitted to an INS official that "this is a matter, when officially handled, that should be treated through diplomatic channels." That didn't stop him from broaching the matter unofficially.[47]

Back in the United States, federal officials were still unconvinced of the need for foreign labor, though they had begun investigating the matter more systematically. In 1941, the U.S. Departments of Agriculture and Labor formed a Coordinating Committee to consider the question of farm labor demand. The USDA directed its local agents to estimate farmers' labor needs, while the Department of Labor directed its Employment Service offices across the country to estimate labor supply. They then shared their findings. The coordinating committee concluded that while some growers were clearly in dire need, especially those near new military bases and on the outskirts of large cities, overall, growers' claims of labor scarcity were exaggerated. Comparing labor prices from county to county and state to state, the committee's report pointed out that the growers who were complaining most vociferously about labor scarcity and spiraling wages were the growers who paid the least, and Florida growers were among the worst offenders. The problem, the committee concluded, was not labor scarcity, but a maldistribution of labor, made worse by many growers'—particularly white southern growers'—unwillingness to recruit workers by paying attractive wages. Accustomed to a great "over-supply of workers" during the Depression, the Coordinating Committee concluded, farmers had "come to consider this over-supply as the normal supply, and to consider any reduction in the surplus supply as a shortage." Southern growers, in other words, had become so used to a glut of poor black labor that they had come to see it and the wages that came with it as normal and natural.[48]

In early 1942, after Chandler had made his first overtures to the Duke of Windsor, the federal government launched its own solution to uneven labor distribution. According to the plan, the Farm Security Administration would transform its migratory housing camps into farm labor supply centers, which would be located along the paths that migrant workers followed. To maximize the availability of labor, farmworkers would be directed and transported, if necessary, from areas of surplus to the areas of greatest need, just as the Freedmen's Bureau had done during Reconstruction. The program that resulted was just about as popular with southern planters.

Congress adopted the FSA's proposal and, by the summer of 1942, the FSA was operating eighty-nine permanent and mobile labor camps around the country, one hundred and forty new sites were under consideration, and workers were being shuttled from harvest to harvest. When in 1942, the USES reported that the Eastern Shore of Virginia needed nine hundred workers for its fruit, vegetable, and berry harvests, the FSA readied mobile camps for what it called "Migrant Soldiers on the Food Production Front." The USES then located workers in Florida who had been made superfluous by a flood, and moved them to Virginia. The USES kept track of every county and every crop, while the FSA moved, housed, and fed the workers and their families, babysat their children, and tended to their illnesses. Uncle Sam had become crew leader to the nation.[49]

From the vantage point of Washington, this labor supply system worked well. Wartime agricultural production increased even as the labor pool shrank. Small farmers seemed happy to be spared the expense and effort of securing harvest labor themselves, and farmworkers got more work and earned more money because officials helped rationalize their movements, saving them the time and expense of wandering in response to rumors of work.[50] But large growers in Florida were furious. They were willing enough to have labor supplied but were outraged when it was removed. When the USES recruited several hundred farmworkers in South Florida for work at Campbell Soup in New Jersey, Florida growers called it the "most high-handed act of labor piracy ever perpetrated in this state."[51]

Florida growers also tended to consider the FSA's operation of federal migrant labor camps an intrusion into their labor relations, which depended on their ability to evict uncooperative workers. When camps were first built in Florida in 1940, growers considered them a subsidy at best and a silly experiment in social engineering at worst. But as the labor market tightened, and the camps became bases from which African American farmworkers organized and struck, growers saw the camps as incendiary. In fact, FSA camp managers indirectly (but intentionally) supported workers' organizing efforts, by encouraging black residents, who were disfranchised outside the camps, to elect their own representatives, vote on camp rules, and meet in camp assemblies. FSA officials refused to evict farmworkers who rejected growers' wage offers, allowing striking residents to do chores around camp in lieu of paying their rent. Growers accused the FSA's liberal camp managers, some of whom were graduate students from the University of California at Berkeley, of coddling camp residents. Growers were already angry when they dropped the piece rate

FIGURE 2.5 Migrant workers relaxing outside a Farm Security Administration "permanent" camp in Belle Glade, Florida, 1941. Camps like these were sold to growers' associations for $1 each after World War II and later were turned over to local housing authorities (Marion Post Wolcott, State Archives of Florida).

for beans and the bulk of the Everglades Labor Supply Camp's 872 black workers refused to leave for the fields. They became furious when the FSA camp managers did not force them to leave the camp. "There is not a shortage of farm labor," a Homestead, Florida, farmer said tellingly in a telegram to Washington; "They just wont stay on the job long enough to do any work." "Such domestic labor as I have been able [to] procure only works part time," another stated; "Remainder they loaf gamble drink chase women, that is our American negro citizens illiterate no patriotism whatsoever."[52]

DEAREST PAT

Not interested in government-supplied workers who could demand higher wages and wait around in federal camps until they got them, Chandler continued to pursue black workers from abroad. He wasn't beneath a

FIGURE 2.6 Farmworkers' baby getting a shower in a Farm Security Administration labor camp in Belle Glade, Florida, 1941 (Marion Post Wolcott, State Archives of Florida).

little international diplomacy. In February 1942, he helped the Duke of Windsor secure a meeting with President Roosevelt in Washington. After broaching the idea of a migration scheme with the President of the United States, the former King of England stopped off in Miami to work out the details with the tomato farmer from Goulds.

According to Chandler, Edward contributed two "very good ideas" to the plan. Edward suggested first that, while in the United States, Bahamians should be confined to particular areas near their places of work, a notion he might have gleaned from British South Africa's system of closed labor compounds in the gold and diamond industries. Second, he suggested that a part of each man's pay be withheld and deposited in the Bahamas to guarantee his return to the colony.[53]

Buoyed by these meetings, Chandler redoubled his efforts to put pressure on the INS. Although growers rarely hired labor during Florida's blistering hot summer months, in July 1942, he wrote Congressman Cannon: "Dearest Pat . . . Farm labor is short in Florida now." Raising his estimates by as much as 15,000, he claimed local growers needed 15,000 to 25,000 workers. "If you can turn this trick," he promised Cannon two weeks later, "you will be a hero sure enough." Cannon, who was up for

FIGURE 2.7 Dance at an Elba, New York, Farm Security Administration labor camp, 1942. (John Collier, Library of Congress.)

reelection in November, forwarded the letter from "my very good friend, Mr. Luther Chandler" to Schofield, the INS director.[54]

By November 1942, Chandler had succeeded in turning the "labor crisis" in Florida into national news. According to the *Washington Post*, Florida's labor problem was caused in part by tire and gas shortages that left tireless jalopies jacked up around Georgia cabins. But it was also explained "by grinning Negro bucks taking their first look at kangaroos in the zoo at Sydney, Australia." In other words, black men were in the armed forces instead of the fields where they belonged.[55] The *Post* acknowledged that the federal government was supplying Florida farmers—and growers around the country—with domestic labor, but it explained that farmers do not "take kindly to the regulations attendant on the labor being transported by the Farm Security Administration." They balked at the 30-cent minimum wage that the FSA required them to pay the men and women it provided and opposed anything "that smacks of collective bargaining."[56] The only solution to the problem "was the plan for transporting some 40,000 Negro laborers from the Bahama Islands *to the mainland*," the *Post* reported, as though the Bahamas was the fifty-first state.[57]

Chandler knew, of course, that the Bahamas were not part of the United States. In fact, that was the key to Bahamians' appeal. "There is no way of forcing [domestic labor] to work either efficiently or regularly," he noted in a confidential memo to Governor Spessard Holland, a stalwart segregationist whom Chandler could trust with his true sentiments. Importing U.S. citizens from Puerto Rico would not work for the same reason, Chandler explained. "The vast difference between the Bahama Island labor and domestic, including Puerto Rican," he wrote, "is that the labor transported from the Bahama Islands can be deported and sent home, if it does not work."[58] The power to deport meant the power to compel.

Back in July, when Chandler was writing to Cannon that labor was short, Chandler's radio brought him news that southwestern growers had been successful in their campaign to secure Mexican labor. Secretary of Agriculture Claude Wickard had just flown to Mexico City and negotiated a recruitment program that would bring thousands of Mexican nationals to the United States to work as farmworkers and railroad trackworkers. The program, which would be run by the FSA, was to begin in August 1942. [59]

Although California growers began receiving Mexican braceros in the summer of 1942, Chandler continued to meet resistance from the INS. When Representative Cannon complained on Chandler's behalf, Schofield wrote a terse reply, which explained that Chandler's request for immigrant labor had been canceled after Chandler himself reported that local labor had proved adequate the winter before. By this time, Chandler's estimate of local labor had increased to thirty thousand, and he had added U.S. senators Claude Pepper and Charles O. Andrews to his list of correspondents.[60]

In the fall of 1942, Chandler's persistence finally paid off. U.S. State Department officials opened negotiations with a reluctant Oliver Stanley, the British Secretary of State for the Colonies, who was not a fan of Chandler's scheme. He feared that the migration program Chandler and Edward proposed would contravene International Labour Organization (ILO) conventions on the migration of indigenous workers, conventions that Britain had helped author. (The ILO was established in 1919 as an agency of the League of Nations, and had survived the collapse of the League.) Stanley objected in particular to the suggestion that workers would owe employers the cost of their fare and could be passed from employer to employer without their approval. To Stanley, the scheme sounded a bit too much like indentured servitude, a labor system that the ILO had been created to eradicate.[61] American officials simply noted that, as written, ILO conventions on migration concerned indigenous workers; black people, they noted, were not "indigenous" to the Bahamas. In any

FIGURE 2.8 Mexican workers recruited by the Farm Security Administration to harvest sugar beets, 1943. (Library of Congress.)

case, they pointed out, the United States hadn't signed the ILO conventions, so the United States could do what it wanted.[62]

Ultimately, after several months of negotiations, Stanley was persuaded to relent, not by U.S. negotiators, but by unemployment levels in the British Caribbean. In January 1943, he signed a memorandum of agreement with U.S. officials. "[I]n the interest of the war effort," he wrote, "His Majesty's Government" declined to press for modifications in the contract. The only ILO convention that the Colonial Office insisted on honoring was the ban against charging international labor migrants for their own transportation. The government of the Bahamas agreed to pick up the tab for workers' voyage from Nassau to Miami, and the United States later agreed to pay the greater expense of Jamaicans' transportation from Kingston. Together, the United States, the Bahamas, and the British Secretary of State for the Colonies allowed five thousand Bahamian men and women between the ages of twenty and forty to leave for the United States to do farmwork and to bring their families with them.[63] The practice of marking a red "X" in the passports of any workers who returned home

FIGURE 2.9 Bahamians arriving in Miami, Florida, for work in the United States, 1943. (State Archives of Florida.)

in less than six months, refused work, or committed a crime served as an informal blacklist.[64]

THE DEATH OF FARMWORKERS' NEW DEAL

Chandler had won, but he was just getting started. He immediately resumed his lobbying, complaining about the small number of potential recruits. The local labor supply would be "twenty-five to eighty-five percent" short during the coming winter harvest season, he now predicted.[65]

He also protested the terms under which federal officials secured Bahamian labor for him and his neighbors. Both Bahamians and Mexicans would be arriving with strings attached by the Mexican and British Colonial governments respectively. Like the U.S.-Mexican agreement on which it was modeled, the Bahamians' contract required that growers pay a minimum wage (which was set at 30 cents an hour in 1943) or the prevailing wage, whichever was higher. The contract also guaranteed them

FIGURE 2.10 Bahamian workers packing celery in Belle Glade, Florida, 1945. Women were soon banned from the program (Osborne, National Archives and Records Administration).

free transportation and free repatriation, and contained a "three-quarter guarantee" that ensured either work for three-quarters of the contract period or wages of $3 a day if work was unavailable. This was an unprecedented benefit for agricultural workers who frequently lost days and even weeks of work to cold snaps, droughts, or downpours. The FSA would provide housing free of charge in its camps or in approved grower facilities. Remarkably, the agreement also contained a non-discrimination clause.[66] U.S. officials would recruit and screen imported workers, have them examined by doctors, transport them on navy ships, house them in federal labor camps, feed them, and treat them when they were sick or injured. The United States would pay the salaries of Mexican "consuls" and Caribbean "liaisons," who would be sent to advocate on the workers' behalf. Most importantly, to ensure that the presence of foreign workers elevated rather than undermined the abysmal conditions under which domestic farmworkers labored, U.S. officials required that growers hiring guestworkers offer the same terms to American farmworkers. The United States had not simply waived immigration restrictions; it had launched the

first guestworker scheme in the world designed to protect foreign workers *and* elevate the condition of native-born workers. This, finally, was
farmworkers' long delayed New Deal, brought to U.S. farmworkers from
south of the border.[67]

Convinced that growers had gotten a raw deal, L. L. Chandler and his
neighbors were outraged. Fuming about the strings attached to the immigrant workers for whom they had so forcefully lobbied, and furious
at the fact that foreign workers would be under the supervision of the
hated labor-friendly Farm Security Administration, Chandler enlisted
other Florida farm employers in an effort to wrest control of the labor
importation program. Now president of the Dade County Agricultural
War Board, Chandler organized local War Board meetings, after which his
neighbors barraged the White House and executive branch offices with
angry telegrams.[68] I have "not struck nor sat down," one female grower
insisted, but her labor force had done so several times. "We've tried everything but holding a gun to their heads," another wrote tellingly.[69] The
Palm Beach County Farm Agent blamed "the Negro papers up North"
for "running articles written by Jews" that "stirred up" "the Negroes."
He hadn't had "any help" in his house for nine months and was expecting a riot, he wrote.[70] FSA-supplied labor was no help, growers' lobbyists insisted. In February 1943, Chandler testified before a Senate Agricultural committee, asserting that "orgies" took place in the fields among
workers supplied by the FSA. The federal government, he continued, gave
them "riffraff whites and Negroes" who had been "petted, pampered and
spoiled by the FSA."[71] The American Farm Bureau Federation proposed
that the whole labor camp program be turned over to the locally adminis-
tered Agricultural Extension Service.[72]

There was nothing growers could do about the contract that had been
negotiated on foreign workers' behalf; these were the conditions imposed
by the sending governments. But employer lobbyists did not want the
minimum wage and housing standards applied to *domestic* workers, who
would remain the vast majority of the workforce. They also didn't want
the liberal Farm Security Administration anywhere near the new program.
Before the guestworker programs had barely gotten under way, as a result,
growers mobilized to ensure that the protections guaranteed foreign workers would have little positive impact on domestic farm labor relations. By
doing so, they ensured that farmworkers' New Deal withered on the vine
even before Caribbean guestworkers had set foot on U.S. soil.

In April 1943—just as Bahamians were arriving—growers commandeered the federal government's labor supply program. That month, Congress passed Public Law 45, a remarkable bill that the nation's two most
powerful growers' lobbies—the American Farm Bureau Federation and
the Associated Farmers—had penned. Public Law 45 allocated $13 million

for the continued expansion of the farm labor supply program but banned federal officials from using those funds to improve the wages and conditions of *American* farmworkers. The federal labor supply system would continue to supply foreign workers to large farms or associations of farmers, but American farmworkers would be banned from quitting one farm job for another or from quitting a farm job for an industrial job. To change jobs, a right which had been the cornerstone of labor law for free workers since the early nineteenth century, an American farmworker would need the consent of his or her local county agricultural extension agent, who was likely a farmer himself. Federal officials would no longer have the authority to move American workers they deemed "surplus" to areas of scarcity, nor would American farmworkers have the freedom to quit one job for another. Foreign workers would get first dibs on berths in federal migratory labor camps. Moreover, the War Food Administration, which was dominated by officials from the rural South, would take over the operation of the program from the liberal Farm Security Administration. As a result of Public Law 45, in the last year of the war the War Food Administration transported fewer than 11,000 Americans to farm jobs, while it moved 122,000 POWs and 56,000 foreign workers to the employers who demanded them, no questions asked.[73]

New Deal liberals continued to run many of the migrant labor camps, and foreign workers' contracts still contained unprecedented protections—at least on paper. But growers had hijacked the guestworker programs, excluded domestic workers from those same protections and guaranteed that reformers would not use foreign workers to elevate conditions for domestic farmworkers. American farmworkers' New Deal was over before it had begun.

GOING TO SEE UNCLE SAM'S PLACE

For Caribbean guestworkers, the New Deal was just beginning. Expecting to earn three times more in the United States than they did at home, Bahamian men and women jammed recruiting stations in Nassau in the spring of 1943. According to one Cat Island woman, the only man left on the island was her husband, the local minister. "Even the bell boys in my hotel asked me to help them enroll," an FSA recruiter reported.[74]

Men weren't the only Bahamians to go, though they made up a majority of the migrants. Rufus Layton of Cat Island had been apprenticed to an English plumber in Nassau when he found work on one of the U.S. bases being built in the Bahamas. Although he was earning a princely sum as a plumber on the U.S. base, and although he had been offered a permanent job after the base was completed, he gave it all up for the chance to see the

United States. "[N]o man. I ain't being no maintenance plumber," he later recalled thinking. "I gotta go over there and see Uncle Sam's place . . . Hell you don't want to stay home and see everybody [you know]."[75]

Layton and other Bahamians worked all over the United States, not just in Florida as L. L. Chandler had hoped. Layton was first sent to Rehobeth Beach, Delaware, where he boasted that each Bahamian did the work of two Mexicans breaking corn. The work was simple but fast and dangerous. It required workers to break the corn off the stalks and throw them into the truck, while the truck rolled backward down the rows. The captain of the team told the drivers to keep the "bumpers on the heels of the workers," Layton recalled. From Delaware, he went by bus to Raleigh, North Carolina, where he harvested tobacco, and from there he flew to Wauseka, Minnesota, "to catch the August corn" and pick peas. Then onward he and other Bahamians traveled for four days and nights to Stokely Foods in Mount Morris, New York, but the crop there wasn't ready, so Stokely sent them to Caribou, Maine, where they picked peas for six weeks. From Caribou he went by bus to Charleston, South Carolina, where he boarded a plane for Nassau. He then signed a new contract, which took him to Feldsmere, Florida, where there was "nothing but cane as far as you can see." He averaged $4 a day cutting cane. At night he opted to work for 90 cents an hour in the sugar factory, which he called "stretching your money." He worked all day, then at the mill from 6 p.m. to midnight, slept a few hours, and then got to the mess hall by 5:30 a.m. The few hours Layton wasn't earning money, he was spending it. He was glad, in retrospect, that a portion of his pay had been deposited in a savings bank back home. "That made it a lot better . . . 'cause I can tell you the truth . . . I was so wild in the United States . . . I'd come back like how God leave the goat—with a short tail!" The men called the compulsory savings their "main money," though in fact it was only a quarter of their earnings.[76]

The most remarkable thing about all this is the fact that the INS never agreed to it, as U.S. immigration law required. As Bahamian contract workers began arriving in the United States, and as U.S. officials began negotiating with the British Colonial Office to import much larger numbers of Jamaicans, Joseph Savoretti, the Deputy Commissioner of the INS, reviewed the file. He noted ruefully that "the original request . . . came from a Mr. L. L. Chandler of Goulds Growers, Inc. in a letter dated September 9, 1941." "Since that time," he wrote, "through members of Congress and local agricultural boards, Mr. Chandler has pursued his application with force." Indeed, Savoretti continued, the migration scheme had been launched before the Board of Immigration Appeals had ruled on the case, though it was the only agency with the authority to consider such applications. "I think it is a dangerous thing," he warned, "to treat such matters in an offhand fashion."[77] In offhand fashion or not, the Caribbean guest-worker program had begun and there was no stopping it.

When tomato farmer L. L. Chandler died in Homestead, Florida, in 1962, he had a funeral befitting an elder statesman. One hundred and fifty local, state, and national dignitaries attended, but it was his honorary pallbear-ers who revealed most about the life he had led. Trailing the coffin on the way to the grave were U.S. Representative Dante Fascell, U.S. Senators Spessard Holland and George Smathers, and former Senator Claude Pep-per.[78] Born the humble son of a Florida rancher, Chandler had wielded power like a state leader. In his lifetime, he had negotiated an international trade agreement, received a medal of honor from Fidel Castro, influenced a former monarch, and won a guestworker program. What he never did was prove that he and his fellow growers needed one. Domestic farm-workers were militant, not missing. Ultimately, though, it didn't matter. What mattered was growers' fears of labor scarcity, their sense that they had lost control of their labor force, their fury that the Farm Security Ad-ministration encouraged African Americans' militancy, their confidence that Caribbean workers would help restore labor peace, and their power.

CHAPTER THREE

"Stir It Up"

Jamaican Guestworkers in the Promised Land

IN EARLY 1943, Oliver Stanley, the British Colonial Secretary, agreed to allow Jamaicans to join Bahamians in the United States, with one important caveat: Jamaicans would not be assigned south of the Mason-Dixon Line. Bahamians, Stanley reasoned, were accustomed to the sort of racial segregation they would experience in the Jim Crow South. They had labored in Florida for many years and the Bahamas imposed similar sorts of restrictions on black Bahamians' use of hotels, restaurants, and cinemas. But although Jamaica's cavernous class divide effectively separated the black majority from the white ruling class, black Jamaicans were unaccustomed to a formal system of segregation, and would chafe, Stanley was sure, at the imposition of Southern mores.[1]

By the summer of 1943, therefore, thousands of Jamaican men—and only men—went to work in northern communities from Iowa to Connecticut. They were welcomed by labor-poor farmers, fêted by rural communities, even taken to church by white people who were surprised and bemused by the sight and sound of black farmworkers with "almost Oxfordian" accents. Many farmers seemed willing to entertain the notion that Jamaicans were, if not quite their equals, an exotic and superior sort of "Negro," who required and deserved special treatment.

The Jamaican guestworkers who came to the United States during World War II were in fact an unusually worldly, educated, and articulate group of farmworkers. Most probably came to the United States like Leaford and Enoch Williams did, desperate for economic opportunities that were unavailable to them in Jamaica, but they were also imbued with the knowledge that they were war workers, sent by an allied country to do an essential job. Determined to be treated as the equals of whites, they boldly defied growers' expectations that they would be cheap, tractable, and submissive. They responded decisively to affronts to their dignity and violations of their contracts. They were British war workers and volunteers, and for a few months at least they were treated as such by U.S. officials and the liaison officers assigned to enforce the terms of their contracts. Those few months were the pinnacle of the U.S. guestworker programs; it would be downhill from there.

STARVING FOR HALF THE YEAR

Like Bahamians, Jamaicans were anxious to find work wherever they could. At the outbreak of war, the vast majority of Jamaicans (about a million people out of a total population of 1.2 million) still eked out a living in the countryside, though they owned little of it.[2] Half of all the cultivated land in Jamaica was divided among just 1,400 mostly foreign landowners, the bulk of them American and British corporations. The largest of these foreign-owned firms—the British Tate & Lyle sugar company—owned 60,000 acres and produced a third of the island's sugarcane. Two American banana companies—United Fruit and Standard Co.—controlled much of the rest of the island's best land.[3]

Jamaica was a society of have-nots. Those who continued to work on Jamaica's sugar plantations earned wages so low and suffered conditions so dire that they were forced to supplement their meager wages with food they grew themselves, just as their slave forbears had done. Hired farmworkers were outnumbered, however, by small farmers who worked tiny plots—usually two acres or less—that they owned or rented. The descendants of freed slaves who had fled to the mountains to get as far away from their former masters as possible, most had either settled in "free towns" established by missionary societies or procured land by buying it, renting it, or squatting on it. There in the mountains, where they could live far from white interference, rural families grew crops for their own use—yams, cassava, bananas, mangos—selling the excess to hagglers who took it to market. By the standards of a peasant society, they did well. By the start of World War II, Jamaica's small farms were producing most of what the island's people ate as well as some 25 percent of exports.[4]

In other ways, Jamaican society had changed little since emancipation. Jamaica did not have a rule-bound system of segregation. There were no sundown towns that black visitors had to leave by a certain time or residential covenants that barred them from particular neighborhoods. There weren't separate black and white school boards, or grandfather clauses to bar black Jamaicans from voting. But none were needed. The vast class differences separating the white elite from the black majority achieved the same ends. Property requirements for voting reduced the electorate to just 6 percent of the population, and since Jamaica lacked a free secondary school system until 1973, few black Jamaicans could afford the school fees that would have allowed their children to attend the island's secondary schools, let alone university in England. Haltingly in the nineteenth century, a middle class of mixed-race professionals and civil service officials did coalesce. But for the vast majority of Jamaicans, poverty and blackness were inseparable.[5]

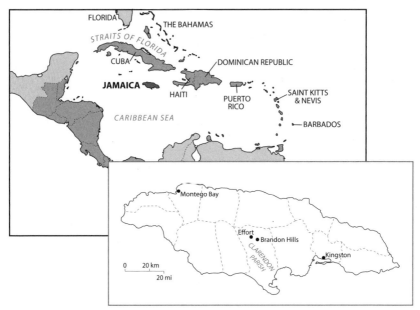

Map of the Caribbean and Jamaica

Those black Jamaicans who changed their fortunes often did so by leaving the island in search of work. Jamaicans began traveling for work and opportunity soon after emancipation, but by the late nineteenth century, leaving for offshore work had become almost a rite of passage. Jamaicans left to build the Panama Canal, to clear forests for railroads in Central America, to drill for oil in Venezuela, to work on sugar, coffee, banana, and sugar plantations in Cuba, Colombia, Nicaragua, Honduras, Guatemala, and Costa Rica, and to take all manner of jobs in the northeastern United States. Between 1911 and 1921, 9 percent of Jamaica's population left, with thirty thousand people heading to the United States and ten thousand to Cuba each year.[6] Few, if any, ventured into the U.S. South.

In the 1920s and '30s, however, the doors to opportunities abroad began to slam shut. With the canal completed in 1914, Panama did not want any more West Indians and even expelled some. A decade later, the United States passed the Johnson-Reed or Quota Act, which reduced the flow of U.S.-bound immigrants to a trickle. The Quota Act of 1924 is better known for curtailing U.S.-bound immigration from Southern and Eastern Europe and for barring Asians from anywhere in the world, but it had an enormous impact on the West Indies as well.[7] While it set no limit on the number of immigrants who could enter the United States from Western Hemisphere countries, it restricted colonies to one thousand immigrants each, effectively reducing Jamaican migration by 97 percent. Concerned, perhaps, that Caribbean migrants blocked from the United States would turn to Latin America, Panama and Venezuela banned West Indians entirely. The Great Depression made matters worse. In 1935, ten thousand Jamaican migrants returned home from Cuba.[8]

Depression-era Jamaica became a pressure cooker. As was the case elsewhere in the Caribbean, returning migrants brought mouths to feed but also trade union experience, nationalist ideas, and even revolutionary sentiments. In 1938, on the heels of mass strikes in other parts of the British Caribbean, Jamaican plantation workers, dockworkers, and the urban unemployed launched full-scale rebellions for pay hikes, collective bargaining rights, and the franchise. Their protests were quickly and violently crushed—labor leaders were thrown in jail for months and even years at a time—but news of the uprisings and the repression that followed strengthened anti-colonial forces in England. The result was the 1940 Colonial Development and Welfare Act, which, among other things, required colonial governments to legalize trade unions before becoming eligible for imperial assistance. Jamaica's newly legal unions soon spawned two political parties—the Labour Party and the People's National Party (PNP)—both of which called for more reforms and, in the case of the PNP, independence.[9]

Buoyed by this rapid change, black Jamaicans' expectations rose, but their hopes were soon dashed by the outbreak of war. In the United States, World War II lifted the economy out of depression. In Jamaica, the interruption of commercial shipping devastated what was essentially an export economy. The British government purchased the entire British West Indian sugar, coffee, citrus, and cocoa crops—a measure that salvaged the fortunes of Jamaica's plantation owners—but it prohibited the use of scarce ships to transport bananas, which was the principal export crop of the island's peasant farmers.[10] The coming of the war meant Jamaicans had to buy goods at inflated wartime prices with decreasing earnings.[11] "We were small farmers," one Jamaican explained to an American reporter, "but we were dumping our bananas because we had no market for them. There is no export now." A Jamaican seaman, who arrived in London in time for the first blitzkrieg after his ship was torpedoed said as much: "There is no shipping . . . so we had to find other work." "Conditions there are terrible," a third lamented, "the government is not interested in the poor man."[12]

Jamaica's government was, in fact, far removed from the cares of "the poor man." The tiny electorate, which represented whites and the small "brown" middle class, chose only half the members of Jamaica's legislative council, who were known as "electives." The remaining "officials" were appointed by Jamaica's white governor, and only "officials" served on the governor's executive council, which saw its job as preserving the interests of its members' class.[13] In 1942, the government's response to the wartime economic crisis was to restore public flogging for men caught stealing vegetables and fruit. It invoked the new statute nearly seven hundred times over the next three years.[14]

The writing was, nonetheless, on the wall. The appointment of Oliver Stanley as Secretary of State to the British Colonies signaled more reforms to come. A Tory and an imperialist, Stanley nevertheless believed that reform was essential to the survival of the empire. In the case of Jamaica, he demanded constitutional amendments requiring secret balloting, universal suffrage, and an increase in the number of elected seats on the legislative council. When these reforms went into effect in 1944, as Jamaica's oligarchy knew well, universal suffrage would increase Jamaica's electorate from 70,000 to 750,000, and those new voters would owe Jamaica's white rulers nothing.[15]

That prospect made Jamaica's political elite positively gleeful at the prospect of temporarily exporting as many as 100,000 unemployed black workers (that being the number suggested by U.S. negotiators). Oliver Stanley may have been reluctant to sign on to the idea of sending British subjects to the United States on temporary labor contracts, but Jamaica's electives, who were hanging on to power by the skin of their teeth, jumped at the idea of relieving Jamaica's growing social pressures without bringing lasting change. The migration scheme appeared to be an ideal way to curry favor with the soon-to-be black electorate. Thus in a last ditch effort to hold on to political power, Jamaica's oligarchy formed a party, disingenuously named it the Jamaican Democratic Party, and began courting the affections of Jamaica's black majority by personally distributing the tickets that entitled the holders to apply for farmwork in the United States.[16]

Not everyone in Jamaica was sanguine about the migration scheme. The Colonial Governor worried about the impact the migrants might have on Jamaican society at the end of their stint in the United States. "What," he wrote to an official in the Colonial Office in March 1943, "will happen when these highly paid gentlemen return from the States God only knows." Some planter-members of the Legislative Council were concerned at what they saw as competition for their labor supply. Facing reelection in 1944, however, they couldn't resist the opportunity to export trouble and plant the seeds of patronage. The Legislative Council approved the scheme but limited the number of recruits who could leave in any one year to ten thousand.[17]

ARE YOU GOING TO AMERICA?

As news of the "U.S. farmworker programme" spread by newspaper, radio, and word of mouth in the spring of 1943, thousands of Jamaicans began sending letters of inquiry to the Jamaican Department of Labour and to the United Fruit Company, whose president, Samuel Zemurray, had been asked by U.S. authorities to organize the screening of the recruits.[18] Even in Maroon Town, where descendants of escaped slaves still lived in isolation from the rest of Jamaican society, a delegation called for the inclusion of two hundred Maroons in the migration scheme and the construction of a road to make it easier for recruiters to get to them.[19]

Instead of distributing the tickets by some equitable system when they became available in April 1943, the elected members of Jamaica's Legislative Council doled them out themselves, hoping that a ticket-holder's gratitude might later translate into a vote. Because the "Farmworker Programme"—as the U.S. recruitment program was called in Jamaica—was founded as a patronage system, getting a ticket depended on one's connections and professed loyalties. The Electives traveled their parishes, avoiding active members of the opposition parties, experienced sugar-cane cutters (who were likely to be union members), and men employed by members of their own party. Women were not invited to participate, though they did all manner of fieldwork in Jamaica and were clamoring to be included. No reason was given but U.S. officials' experience with Bahamian women accounted for the ban.[20]

U.S. officials also excluded Jamaicans of South Asian descent because, since 1924, U.S. immigration policy had banned all Asian laborers from entering the country, no matter where they were born. "East Indians" had been "deprived of serving" on Panamanian bases for the same reason, according to the *Daily Gleaner*. The United States relented after the president of the East Indian Progressive Society protested the policy, cabling Franklin D. Roosevelt, Winston Churchill, and Sir G. B. Bajrpai, the Agent General for the Government of India in Washington. As a compromise, recruiters were instructed to consider only East Indians born in the Americas.[21]

Besides having to be male and not Asian-born, prospective recruits required no prior experience or qualifications. All they had to do was hold out the promise of patronage and, on occasion, grease someone's palm. The leaders of the People's National Party and the Labour Party complained of a brisk trade in black market recruitment tickets.[22]

This highly politicized and sometimes corrupt ticket distribution system resulted in an unusual group of farmworkers, as tickets tended to go to the men or sons of men whose favor the electives particularly wanted. Although American growers might have expected the recruits to be strapping farm boys, the men who got or bought tickets were on the whole an urban, worldly, and eclectic group, definitely not typical of Jamaica's rural majority. Among the men sent to the United States during the war were masons, machinists, dock and railroad workers, seamen, tailors, carpenters, clerical workers, a typesetter from the staff of the *Daily Gleaner*, and the son of Jamaica's first car dealer. Jamaican men sent to Connecticut in 1944 included a cycling champion, a welterweight champion (Kid Axle), a well-known sprinter, and a highly rated soccer player. Fully 10 percent of the Jamaicans who served as farmworkers in the United States in 1945 were war veterans, nearly half of them members of the Royal Air Force.[23]

The recruits were also better educated than average Jamaicans. As late as 1960, only 60 percent of children aged seven to fourteen attended school at all. Yet, of the two hundred Jamaican guestworkers in Connecticut interviewed by a minister from the Connecticut Council of Churches during World War II, two-thirds had completed elementary school, and several had completed some college coursework. Many Jamaican guestworkers enrolled in correspondence courses in the United States.[24]

Jamaican guestworkers were also likely to be better traveled than American farmworkers, or at least related to Jamaicans accustomed to conditions abroad. Sidney Barnett had worked four years as a crane operator on the Panama Canal before being sent to Connecticut to do farmwork. He had led the good life in Panama, buying Creme serge suits, Florsheim and Placard shoes, and Arrow and Van Heusen shirts. A week after he returned home from Panama, he departed for war work in the United States. Unlike Barnett, most of the recruits were too young to have worked overseas, but like many Jamaicans, they had well-traveled parents or relatives. Alphonso James, who also worked in Connecticut, had a grandmother from Panama and a grandfather from Cuba. The first thing Alfred Chambers did when he got time off from harvesting shade tobacco near Hartford was to look up his grandmother, who had been living in New York since 1922.[25]

It Is Just Like a Honeymoon to Me

Recruits gathered in late spring at the port in Kingston to await the naval vessels that would take them to the United States. Reginald Leslie remembered getting a mug fashioned out of a Vidal oil can. "We got our nice tea," he recalled, and boarded the SS *Shank*, which was the first vessel to depart for the United States bearing Jamaican farmworkers.[26] At that point, everything that could go wrong did go wrong. A U.S. troop transport vessel, the *Shank* had been built to hold 1,800 men, but 4,000 recruits were crammed aboard. The ship was so overcrowded that the recruits had to arrange shifts for meals, water, toilets, and bunks. George Pitt, a machinist from Spanish Town, wrote home that men had to wait in line for hours to eat and were treated like prisoners by the military police guarding the vessel. On their third day at sea, he and other observers reported, MPs turned a fire hose on the recruits. One man died on the voyage—by his own hand, according to the Jamaican official who investigated the incident; by accident, according to the U.S. Department of State; and at the hands of MPs, according to Jamaicans on board. Whichever report was true, it was an inauspicious beginning.[27]

Even on less crowded ships, the voyage was exceedingly dangerous. With German U-boats patrolling the Caribbean Sea, Leaford Williams' ship left Kingston with an escort of three destroyers and a blimp. From the deck of a luxury liner leased to the U.S. Navy for the duration, other Jamaicans watched as German torpedoes struck and sunk freighters in their convoy.[28]

Because of the dangers of wartime sea travel, the ships transporting Jamaicans to the United States docked in the first U.S. port they could reach. This meant that guestworkers disembarked in the South, whether the Secretary of State for the Colonies liked it or not. Arriving in New Orleans, Miami, or Norfolk, Jamaicans were fearful of white Americans and mystified by their interactions with African Americans, whom the recruits found difficult to understand. Though Sydney Barnett had worked under Americans in Panama, he had been warned by an elderly Jamaican man that he "would not survive" in Florida and that some "people up north thought we were monkeys and that we had tails." He was therefore horrified to discover that he was not only landing in Miami but was being taken by truck to a place called Monkey Jungle.[29]

Disembarking in New Orleans, Leaford and Enoch Williams were taken to Camp Pontchartrain on the outskirts of the city, which was a staging area for African American army personnel shipping out to join the nation's still segregated military. Leaford recalled seeing no white soldiers during the two weeks he spent there, but neither did he feel at ease with the "black men in woolen uniforms" who populated the camp. He watched them play baseball and horseshoes, and run races, but could not understand anything they said. Even the food was alienating. Accustomed to ackee and codfish, breadfruit, and boiled green bananas in the morning, he loathed the scrambled eggs they were served and did not recognize the corn flakes as food. He and his brother thought the hotdogs in their almost daily diet of pork and beans looked like giant earthworms.[30]

Upon their arrival in New Orleans, men were processed and fingerprinted before being sent north by train. Each recruit left with a pamphlet written by J. Harris, Jamaica's Labour Adviser, and Herbert MacDonald, chief of the liaisons sent by the Jamaican government to look out for the men in the United States. Though Harris and MacDonald assured the recruits that they would be "among a friendly English-speaking people," the brochure warned them to expect habits and customs "somewhat different" from their own. "In the United States the word 'Negro' is not used to offend," the pamphlet explained, "but is used and accepted in the same way as the word 'coloured' in Jamaica." "Respect the 'Star Spangled

Banner,'" it admonished, and "try to recognize it whenever it is played . . . remember it is as sacred to Americans as 'God Save the King' is to us."[31] Whether "God Save the King" was in fact "sacred" to Jamaican workers abroad, they would use their Britishness to protect themselves as they fanned out across the country.

From the points at which they disembarked, the recruits were shipped out in alphabetical order. Leaford and Enoch Williams both went to Michigan, while their cousin, Victor Tomlinson, was sent to Connecticut. They never saw him again.[32] Their train took them east to Macon, Georgia, where one of their countrymen received an angry response from a white man on the platform when he leaned out the window of the train to ask where they were.[33]

The sheer breadth of the country amazed everyone. On their way to Michigan, Leaford and Enoch had a friendly conversation with a black porter in the dining car, who to Leaford's ears said, "Dis hiya is Cinci-natta," and that they would arrive in "Sag-I-naw Mith-chi-gan" the following morning. This astonished everyone on the train, Leaford recalled. Had they been traveling that long in Jamaica, they would have already made four round trips from one end of the island to the other.[34] J. C. Green wrote his family that he had passed "through a lot of beautiful cities which I do not have tongue to explain" on his way from New Orleans to Bridgeton, New Jersey.[35]

Although Jamaicans' early days in the U.S. South were alienating and a little frightening, their first experiences in the North far exceeded their hopes and expectations. Most Jamaican guestworkers who left a record of their arrival in the North recalled the thrill of those first encounters. Rupert Holn wrote from Burlington, New Jersey: "We have found the Americans a very fine lot. I am feeling very homely and would not mind if stay could be for all times . . . the experience that I have gathered could never be bought in a lifetime in Jamaica." Another recruit wrote his relatives from nearby in Bridgeton that he and the other men on the boat "got over safely and have started to work. We are now in a place where the people are very fine and courteous to the Jamaicans." They had been "treated royally" on their voyage from New Orleans to Bridgeton, one man remarked, adding hyperbolically that Uncle Sam provided them beer to drink "every hour of the day." Upon their arrival in Randolph, Wisconsin, in May 1943, Ernest Pendley and his thirty-four compatriots were surprised to be greeted by a military band and offered full use of the Randolph Country Club for as long as they were in the area picking peas that had been planted on the golf course's fairways and greens. They were even more amazed that townspeople invited them to attend their churches the following Sunday. Obviously expecting white Americans to be hostile, C. W. Creightney reported with surprise that white locals were willing to

Figure 3.1 A group of men from Manchioneal, Jamaica, getting instructions from an apple grower in New York, 1943. (National Archives and Records Administration.)

"come from miles with their cars to take us around and show us a good time." "They were not expecting us to be such fine fellows," he noted, and "we never expected to rub shoulders" with them in restaurants and stores. Expressing similar surprise, David Bent wrote a former teacher that his Wisconsin boss was a "gentleman." Samuel Gayle only wished he had come twenty years earlier. "It is just like a honeymoon to me," he wrote home, "Please tell them that life is given away in United States."[36]

Jamaicans were particularly struck by the efforts white Americans made to welcome and even entertain them. The Connecticut Council of Churches, which helped organize recreational activities for guestworkers on Connecticut farms, linked up Jamaican singers with "other Negro singers" who had been recruited in the South for northern farmwork. The result was a series of seven choral performances aired on a Hartford radio station.[37] On their arrival in Michigan, Leaford and Enoch were taken by truck from the railway station to a place called Reece, which was much larger than their village of Mulgrave but had no black people, Leaford noted, and only a few American Indians. The Jamaicans were each given the princely sum of $100 as a cash advance, from which they bought supplies in town, five miles away. Sometimes in the evenings, Leaford recalled, they hiked to town with an entourage of locals who pressed them for information about where Jamaica was and what it was like. "Their lack of knowledge" made him feel less ignorant for knowing little about "Merika," he noted.[38] He was pleased to find that he understood the farmers in Michigan better than the white man in Georgia or the black porter on the train.[39]

Cities with established West Indian communities went to even greater lengths to welcome Jamaican guestworkers. On Labor Day, four hundred Jamaicans working in New York State were treated to a tour of Manhattan and a cricket match between the best cricket players among them and a team made up of West Indian New Yorkers (the New Yorkers won). After the game, they were treated to a Jamaican-style dinner, during which public officials and members of New York's many West Indian civic organizations welcomed them to the area. The assembled guests sang both the American and British anthems, and the whole affair was broadcast on Jamaican radio stations. The Brant Labor Camp, near Buffalo, New York, held a celebration on August 1 to commemorate the abolition of slavery in Jamaica 105 years earlier.[40]

Not all recruits were content with the conditions they found on northern farms and in hastily built farm labor camps. Disembarking the SS *Shank*, which he called the "hell-ship," George Pitt enjoyed the long but "pleasant train trip" from New Orleans to Hebrant Camp in New Jersey. But once there, he worked for three different employers, only two of whom paid him despite his protests. After a week the FSA moved him to Swedesboro, which was even worse. There, guestworkers worked overtime (without overtime pay, he noted), and then the work slowed, until there was only enough work for fifty of the four hundred men. Food and water supplies dwindled. Their contracts guaranteed them pay for three-quarters of their contract time, but since they regularly shifted from one employer to another, it was never clear who was supposed to pay them for their down time. In Michigan, 1,450 workers had a similar experience. They lived off food bought on credit from the camp store or demanded relief at police stations while they waited a month for work. "State of affairs . . . is deplorable and fraught with danger," the Jamaican governor telegraphed to Oliver Stanley. When they were finally put to work the following week, the men complained that they were paid less than prevailing wages and were victims of racial prejudice stemming from the recent race riots in Detroit. In all, 160 men insisted on returning to Jamaica.[41]

While some angry, disappointed, or homesick men opted to return home early, no Jamaicans were involuntarily repatriated from northern states for refusing to work under the conditions proffered in those first months. Rather, when War Food Administration officials couldn't get

Figure 3.2 Jamaicans arriving in Michigan for work on local farms (c. 1943). (Photo courtesy of the Library of Congress.)

growers to redress conditions, they would move guestworkers to new locations. On one such occasion, one hundred Jamaicans were relocated to prevent problems. After an unusually long voyage to Norfolk, Virginia, during which a German submarine chased their ship and the delay caused the food on board to spoil, a group of Jamaicans arrived in Centerville, Maryland, so hungry that "they broke into a neighboring orchard and consumed large quantities of green apples." The farmer, who had been unprepared, soon got his mess tent up and running, and the men worked for two weeks, during which "the farmers on the Eastern Shore of Maryland [were] very pleased." By that time, however, the Colonial Office had discovered that Centerville was well south of the Mason-Dixon Line, and all the men were quickly sent north.[42] U.S. officials, in other words, willingly intervened and redressed workers' concerns.

Generally, Jamaicans were pleasantly surprised by their northern hosts, and the feeling was usually mutual. Leaford Williams recalled that he'd "get 50 cents a week in Jamaica and that was big money. Here I was able to get 50 cents an hour." He had $3,000 saved by the end of the war.[43] Reginald Harris of St. Elizabeth "enjoyed every minute" of his time working in

FIGURE 3.3 Jamaican men imported by the Farm Security Administration for work in New Jersey and Connecticut, 1943. (Photo courtesy of the Library of Congress.)

New Jersey and Connecticut.[44] Wisconsin's Richland County Emergency Labor Assistant was effusive in his report on the twenty-five Jamaican men who worked on fifty-four Richland County farms in the summer of 1944. "While we sincerely hope the [S]econd World War is at such a stage that . . . it will not be necessary to import labor" for another crop season, he wrote, "the Jamaicans proved themselves capable of learning and performing our work under our conditions." He recalled "their 'yes boss,' 'everything is quite okay,' their souvenirs of ginger, nutmeg, and stamps, and their stories," which, he said, brought back "thoughts of a summer of hard work mingled with pleasant memories." It was an experience he "would not have wanted to miss."[45] Mrs. Virginia J. Krelling of Briston, Pennsylvania, sent a letter to the manager of King Farms, after encountering two of the three hundred Jamaicans working on his Morrisville farm. "While riding on the bus line connecting our towns," she wrote, "I have encountered your young workers from Jamaica. I have been so impressed by their quiet mannerisms and cleanliness that I felt you people would appreciate knowing how the public has been impressed. Last evening two of those young men sprang to their feet to offer me their seats when I had to stand before them due to an overcrowded bus . . . Tell them my husband and I welcome them to America." Giving the letter to Herbert MacDonald, the farm manager added: "We have had only one serious complaint . . . about one of our boys." The "boy" had earned $23.00 in one day, blocking beets. "He is a real good boy; but he works too hard," the manager said jokingly.[46]

The reference to a Jamaican man as "a real good boy" notwithstanding, Jamaicans clearly challenged white northerners' preconceptions about black workers. The white press, in particular, could not resist comparing the recruits favorably to African Americans. Arriving in Swedesboro, New Jersey, *Waterbury Republican* reporter Sigrid Arne remarked on the "queer sound" that could be heard coming from a long building that looked like an army mess tent. "Dominoes," explained the FSA official who showed him around. "They play dominoes with a fine fury." Writing for a local population that had been hiring African American migrants from the South for sixty years, Arne explained, "The Jamaicans come from a Negro country," a place "without color prejudice." "It's a British colony," he noted, "a fact which lends to amusing situations when the Jersey farmer runs into his first Jamaican. Many of them have clipped, British accents that are quite surprising coming from a Negro field hand." "I was talking to one," he continued, "who told me, 'we're rather fond of cricket, you know. But we're having extreme difficulty acquiring the gear.' I could have closed my eyes and thought I was in a Park Avenue drawing room."[47]

Like Arne, white journalists took it upon themselves to point out the differences between Jamaicans and African Americans. In a story that found its way to Kingston's *Daily Gleaner*, the Humboldt, Iowa, paper described Humboldt's visitors as "happy men" who sang as they worked. "Sometimes, while they wait to start along the rows, they break into a soft shoe dance." "The only language the Jamaicans know is English," the paper noted. "However, among themselves they speak in rapid vernacular which no midwesterner ever could follow. But in talk with visitors, some become almost Oxfordian." "In physical appearance," the reporter explained, "the Jamaican resembles the American Negro of the deep south. But they have enjoyed generations of equal social rights with white men in Jamaica . . . There are no Jim Crow laws in Jamaica and some of the men, encountering racial prejudice for the first time in their lives, have been deeply hurt in several instances." Jamaicans, the Humboldt paper seemed to suggest, only looked like black people. "Their employers," the paper noted, were "defending Jamaicans loyally."[48]

Jamaicans interviewed by the American press were equally quick to note their British citizenship and to imply that they were unfairly lumped with black Americans. In an open letter thanking the people of Humboldt for their "kind hospitality," three Jamaican men introduced themselves: "I suppose you all must have heard about us. We are from a British West

Indies Island, a peaceful and law-abiding country as you are in Humboldt City." "[T]he people of Humboldt City have been just too good to us, but we know why," they wrote, implying that they expected to be treated as poorly as African Americans. "[T]hey had something on their minds about us," they continued, "but we have erased that by our actions in this city." They assured their readers that when they got back to their "sunny Jamaica homes," they would "always remember America, especially Humboldt City where you have treated us so good that the only difference between us is colour and that's nature's work . . . Men are judged by their minds." "We are made from the same clay," added Gerald Johnson, a cook from Port Antonio.[49]

Stanley Amritt, a self-appointed spokesman for the Jamaican guest-workers of Le Sueur, Minnesota, insisted that Jamaicans had come to the United States because of their patriotism, not their destitution. "[O]ur income in normal times is in most cases equal to the wages we earn in the United States," he wrote to the *Minneapolis Sunday Tribune*, though the war had caused "some economic stringency" which made it necessary to "seek work in your country." Still, he insisted, "it should always be borne in mind that we are induced to come here to do our part in the war effort. Hence we are willing to live under conditions that we have never been used to. We are happy to make the sacrifice if it hastens the victory which every loyal Britisher longs for."[50]

Some Jamaicans took particular pride in the fact that they overcame prejudices they believed African Americans tolerated. Renford Glanville, who arrived in the United States in 1943 at the age of nineteen, recalled years later that he had worked for a year alongside black and white Americans at Seabrook Farms, New Jersey, loading and unloading cartons of asparagus for 50 cents an hour, ten hours a day. The Americans had a union and the Jamaicans did not, as they "were foreigners and on contract." "Still," Glanville recalled, "we were treated nicely."[51] On one occasion, however, he and other Jamaican guestworkers encountered the America they had feared and expected. They stopped at a local restaurant on their way home from working in the fields, as they "had worked all night, and some of the fellows wanted to get something to eat before we went home." At first, Glanville and his co-workers waited politely, but eventually they realized that the restaurant staff had no plans to serve them. "They served all of the other people before us," Glanville recalled. He and the others "kept sitting there," until finally "some of the boys got mad." The "boys" "jumped over the counter and started breaking up the dishes, tearing up the place. All for one and one for all, you know." Not knowing what to do, the restaurant staff called John Seabrook, the manager of Seabrook Farms, whose response, according to Glanville, was: "Feed them. You better feed them." "So, that," he noted with satisfaction, "was that."[52]

Insisting that "[m]any of the discrimination barriers were broken down by us," George Hudson recounted an incident in Connecticut in which a theater called the Strand refused to admit him and other Jamaicans. "[B]ut we showed up in force," he recalled, "sometimes ten to fifteen of us, and demanded they let us in . . . The Americans (blacks) were scared to challenge these places," he insisted, "but because we had numbers of us who traveled together we were not afraid." He also reported that a group of Jamaican farmworkers, having heard that bartenders would break any glass used by a black person, began going to bars en masse. "When the owners found out that they were breaking forty to fifty glasses a night, they then stopped the practice."[53]

While Hudson's stories have the ring of urban legend, Jamaicans clearly used their foreignness as a weapon. Some of this militancy can be attributed to the participation of urban Jamaicans from relatively privileged backgrounds, but even Leaford Williams, the eighteen-year-old farmer's son from tiny Mulgrave, remembered standing his ground with a gruff employer. Having injured his back harvesting cranberries, which involved stooping for hours at a time, Leaford says he "told" the foreman at the Central Cranberry Company in Cranmoor, Wisconsin, to give him a job in the drying yard. Not accustomed to letting farmworkers make management decisions for him, the foreman's face turned red, Williams recalled. Nonetheless, Williams stared him down and got the lighter job. Learning to drive by watching others do it, he was soon driving boxes of cranberries to the drying yard. By the time he left Wisconsin for Florida, Williams later wrote in his memoir, he was custodian of the drying yard and spokesman for the Jamaican farmworkers at Cranmoor.[54]

Williams and his compatriots were remarkably willing to stand up for themselves, at least according to their recollections, but what they failed to note is that they were privileged in ways that African American farmworkers were not. Unlike American farmworkers, they were protected by labor contracts signed and enforced by U.S. officials, and they could report problems to Jamaican liaisons, who had been sent to advocate for them and whose salaries were paid by the U.S. government. If their employers treated them with less than "a fair degree of cordiality," as Leaford Williams put it, they could count on their liaisons and War Food Administration officials to intervene.[55] Jamaicans clearly played up their Britishness for effect, and indeed, as long as they remained exotic outsiders to the press, their foreignness worked to their advantage. Jamaicans seemed unassailable.

The fact that Jamaican farmworkers were being treated with more consideration than African American farmworkers was not lost on African American observers. While white reporters emphasized the difference between black Americans and Jamaicans, African American reporters presumed a kinship with Jamaican guestworkers. They reported news of the program regularly and protested cases of mistreatment with vigor. Yet they keenly observed the special treatment accorded Caribbean workers, treatment they attributed to the guestworkers' citizenship, not to any innate or cultural superiority. Roy Wilkins, the editor of the NAACP's magazine, *Crisis*, writing for New York's *Amsterdam News*, noted that, when the government brought several thousand Jamaicans here to work as farm laborers, "it was careful to explain that these people were not accustomed to racial discrimination and must be handled accordingly." "But for its own Negroes . . ." Wilkins complained, "the War Department says not a word." "Fair Wages Should Begin at Home," began a similar editorial in the (Norfolk, Virginia) *Journal and Guide.* The author noted that West Indian laborers had been guaranteed a minimum wage of 40 cents per hour and adequate housing, "which is much more than any U.S. Negro farm laborers are assured of making." "A minimum wage has been denied Negro or white farm labor in the United States," the author continued, though "the experiment points up what the farmers can do, and what our government can do when necessity demands that something be done."[56]

The first few months of the Emergency Farm Labor Importation Program did indeed reveal what governments could do to guarantee farmworkers decent conditions and fair treatment. In the northern communities where they worked, Jamaicans were amazed at the receptions they received. Some communities greeted arriving farmworkers with marching bands; others offered them the keys to the city. Jamaicans were invited to church by white people and driven to town by farmers' daughters. Reporters from white newspapers eagerly introduced them to white readers as alien oddities: black men with British accents. Reporters for black newspapers were quick to report any mistreatment that befell them. As long as the program placed Jamaicans only in the North, and as long as Farm Security Administration officials and Jamaican liaisons responded promptly to workers' complaints, the scheme seemed useful to all concerned, and at least to some, a promising experiment in interracial cooperation. However, once the War Food Administration forced the British Colonial Secretary to abandon his decision to boycott states south of the Mason-Dixon Line, the program's high standards began a rapid decline. For a few months, the Colonial Secretary held fast to his ban on the Jim Crow South, but before long, Jamaicans would be on their way to Florida, to Big Sugar, to the land where a black man with a funny accent was still nothing but a black man.

CHAPTER FOUR

John Bull Meets Jim Crow

Jamaican Guestworkers in the Wartime South

AFTER SPENDING FIVE months in communities all over the U.S. north, where they were treated more like allied soldiers than black farmworkers, Jamaican guestworkers began arriving in Florida in the fall of 1943. Entering the hot, squalid barracks built to house them in Clewiston, the home of U.S. Sugar, Stanley Wilson and fifty-eight other Jamaican men discovered that they were expected to sleep on bare mattresses, without sheets, pillows, or blankets. When they complained, the camp superintendent's response was: "Pillows! . . . you aren't serious! This is the first time in my life that I ever heard niggers slept with pillows, too." Mosquitoes, flies, snakes, and "deadly insects" plagued the camp, Stanley Wilson wrote home to *Public Opinion*, the Kingston newspaper published by the democratic socialist People's National Party. Their living quarters were "absolutely intolerable," he reported, and the latrine was in an "unimaginable" state of filth. The latrine not only adjoined their barracks; it stood directly across from the mess hall, so swarms of flies "trafficked regularly between the food served to the workers and the deposits in the convenience." While hard at work cutting sugarcane, moreover, men were given rank water to drink. If they wanted the same water that the company's white millworkers drank, Wilson wrote, they had to pay 35 cents a gallon for it—almost an hour's pay. "Workers made the strongest representations" against these conditions, Wilson reported, "but could secure no redress." Instead, Wilson and the others who refused to tolerate this treatment were loaded onto a truck and taken directly to jail, where they spent the next three weeks awaiting passage back to Jamaica.[1]

Transferred from northern farms to Clewiston, Florida, to cut sugarcane for U.S. Sugar, Jamaicans were greeted, not by marching bands and curious townspeople, but by gun-toting labor bosses who treated them much like they had treated African American workers before them. Jamaicans weren't forced to stay at U.S. Sugar—as African Americans had been—but if they objected to the terms of their employment, their choice was to lump it or leave the country. In Florida, a negro laborer was a negro laborer, funny accent and British citizenship not withstanding. No longer were Jamaicans told to expect "a friendly English-speaking people," with habits and customs "somewhat different" from their own. In Florida, they were warned to adapt to the dictates of "the Jim Crow Creed."[2]

It's hardly surprising that Jamaicans encountered a more virulent variant of racism in Florida than they had in Wisconsin or New York. What was surprising was how quickly federal officials abandoned them to it, despite the non-discrimination clauses included in guestworkers' contracts and despite some U.S. officials' hopes that the importation of foreign workers on decent contracts would elevate conditions for all farmworkers. The guestworker program didn't elevate conditions in Florida. It pitted West Indian and Bahamian workers against African Americans, undermining both domestic *and* foreign workers' militancy. By the end of the war, federal negligence and employer recalcitrance had begun to fashion the perfect immigrant, Jim Crow style: the sort of immigrant who knew from day one that deportation was the price of protest.

BIG SUGAR

World War II had come as a mixed blessing to the managers of Big Sugar. Congress lifted the federal production quotas it had imposed during the Depression, which allowed U.S. Sugar to expand its acreage as never before, but the boom only exacerbated the company's labor troubles. Louisiana sugar growers dealt with the same problem by mechanizing their sugar harvest but in Florida harvesting machines sunk into the soft muck soil, causing their blades to cut the base of the cane stalks so low that the perennial plants didn't always ratoon (grow back).

Instead of turning to machines, U.S. Sugar banked on Caribbean labor and a new management style. To clean house after the embarrassing peonage indictment, U.S. Sugar's CEOs hired Fred Sikes, formerly of the Department of Labor's Wage and Hour Division, to head a new personnel department. To fill the role of chief harvest labor recruiter, Sikes brought in Earl Morrison, a college-educated Mississippian, who had been training Royal Air Force pilots in Florida.[3] Together, Sikes and Morrison crafted a transnational solution to U.S. Sugar's labor problem.

To Morrison, the problem with U.S. Sugar's past labor practices wasn't so much their immorality but their impracticality. "There was no way you could lock [workers] up or anything else; they were free people," Morrison admitted decades later. Yet, he complained, "They'd come and we issued them clothing, shoes, boots, cane knives, leg guards, hand guards, caps, jackets." "When you outfit a man it cost about one hundred dollars. Then he walks out with the clothes on and goes on down the road." There was nothing managers could legally do, Morrison explained, "You just got to let him go." "What are you going to do? Lock him up or have the sheriff do it? Then they'd charge you with peonage and all other kinds of stuff. It was simpler to let him go and write off your loss."[4] The use of force was too risky; lack of force too costly.

Black workers from abroad offered a legal way to use bound labor. Caribbean men came freely, of course, but they risked deportation if they tried to switch employers on their own or refused work at the contractual wage. To U.S. Sugar, then, Bahamians seemed like the perfect solution—that is, until they arrived.

The Bahamians made available to U.S. Sugar in early 1943 "were very unsuccessful in cane," as Morrison put it. Morrison attributed this to the Bahamians' lack of experience as cane cutters—sugar is not produced commercially in the Bahamas—but few of the Jamaicans who later monopolized Florida's sugar harvesting jobs were experienced cane cutters, either. More likely the problem was that Bahamas knew Florida, and they knew that easier, less dangerous, and much better paying work was available on nearby vegetable farms. According to Morrison, "[If] anything is hard work, they are going to avoid it . . . [s]o they were just never adaptable to cutting cane."[5] What he failed to mention is that U.S. Sugar paid Bahamians the minimum wage of 30 cents an hour or $3 a day for a ten-hour day planting sugarcane, as required by the U.S. agreement with the governor of the Bahamas. Bahamians on Florida vegetable farms were earning more than $8 a day harvesting vegetables. Whether U.S. Sugar rejected the Bahamians or vice versa, after 1943 most Bahamian guestworkers worked exclusively in fruits and vegetables. U.S. Sugar's managers demanded Jamaicans instead.[6]

Boycotting Dixie

Hiring Jamaicans seemed the obvious solution to U.S. Sugar's problems. Like Bahamians, Jamaicans spoke English, but unlike Bahamians, they came from an island whose principal crop was sugar. There were also far more of them and few, if any, would have any knowledge of Florida. Better yet, Jamaican guestworkers would run out of work on northern farms just as Florida's six-month winter sugar harvest was about to begin. All Sikes needed to do was break Oliver Stanley's boycott of the U.S. South.

U.S. Sugar enlisted the help of the War Food Administration (WFA), whose officials dangled the prospect of 100,000 jobs in the U.S. South under Stanley's nose. When that didn't work, the WFA blackmailed Stanley into relenting by announcing that Jamaicans would have to work in Florida or face repatriation and the cancellation of the program. Thus in

May 1943, just as the first Jamaican recruits were arriving in the United States, the WFA suspended the distribution of new recruitment tickets in Jamaica and stopped transporting Jamaicans to the United States. Men already holding recruitment tickets were left stranded in Kingston, while U.S. officials waited for the British Secretary of State for the Colonies to change his mind.[7]

As it got colder in the North, Jamaican officials tried and failed to find alternative places for Jamaicans to work in the United States. "In avoiding districts like Delaware and Maryland in the Northeast and the 'deep south' . . . where a rigid colour bar exists," Jamaicans would soon run out of crops to harvest, worried J. Harris, Jamaica's Labour Advisor. "We tried hard . . . to have numbers of the men sent to California," he noted, "but this State is worked almost entirely by Mexicans."[8]

For four months, the Colonial Secretary held his ground, leaving Jamaican recruits gathered in Kingston "in a state of despondency."[9] The Jamaican press published heartbreaking tales of men who had secured recruitment tickets and spent what little money they had to travel to the port at Kingston for departure, only to discover that the program had been called off. Even the PNP, whose party organ *Public Opinion* had kept up a steady barrage of criticism against the program over the previous months, could not help but note how important it was as a relief measure. *Public Opinion* reported that workers still in the United States had sent home remittances in the amount of £20,000, or $100,000, in the month of June alone. The *Daily Gleaner* editorialized about the "real and serious difficulty" of sending Jamaicans to the U.S. South because they were "bred and reared in an environment of flexible and subtle but illegal discrimination[, and] may react to ironbound racial discrimination in a variety of ways, some of them unpleasant or even alarming." But, the *Gleaner* reasoned, "if the men who volunteer for such a trial are made fully aware . . . of the realities of 'down South' conditions . . . the experiment might end satisfactorily." "Perhaps, too, as a racial experiment," the *Gleaner* added, "it may prove instructive, certainly enlightening."[10]

While Jamaicans debated the implications of sending their countrymen to the U.S. South, U.S. officials, presuming correctly that the Colonial Secretary would relent, prepared for Jamaicans' arrival in Florida. Some U.S. officials shared Stanley's concerns. "It may not be advisable for us to encourage the placement of these workers in the areas of our country which customarily employ American negro labor," noted George Hill, assistant director of the War Food Administration's Office of Labor. Jamaicans had "a set of mores and social patterns radically [different] from those of the [American] Negro," and the "States' Negroes," he wrote, were "more amenable to acceptance of the traditional local racial differentials," though of course African Americans had been protesting their treatment at U.S. Sugar for years. The War Food Administration's response was to house "Jamaicans and the negro migrants" separately so that the Jamaicans' militancy wouldn't influence an African American population supposedly resigned to segregation.[11]

The pressure on Stanley continued to grow. Not only were Bahamian guestworkers already laboring in Florida under a separately negotiated contract but, Stanley learned, Puerto Ricans, who also hailed from a sugar-producing island, were clamoring to be included in the temporary importation scheme. Concerned that failure to comply with the U.S. demand might mean the loss of all opportunities for Jamaican guestworkers in the United States, Stanley relented in September 1943. He allowed officials of the Colonial Office to meet secretly with Jamaican and U.S. officials to negotiate an agreement under which Jamaicans would be allowed "to proceed south" to Florida's sugar plantations.[12]

Instead of emphasizing the non-discrimination clause in Jamaicans' contract, however, Stanley followed the *Gleaner*'s advice that the Jamaicans sent to the South had to be made aware of and accept local customs. Under the revised rules, only those recommended "for character and efficiency" would be allowed to stay in the United States for winter work in Florida, and those who chose to remain would have to be fully informed of the "racial and other conditions prevailing in the Southern States." To start, Jamaicans' work in the South would be restricted to Florida, where they would labor under the supervision of an expanded staff of Jamaican liaisons. Most importantly, the new contract gave the U.S. government the authority to "immediately" repatriate any worker for "indiscipline," a term the contract left undefined.[13]

THE JIM CROW CREED

Although northerners had been warned to adapt to black workers from Jamaica, and most had seemed willing to do so, white Floridians were assured that Jamaicans would adapt to them. The U.S. War Food Administration and Herbert MacDonald, the white chief of the all-white staff of Jamaican liaison officers, prepared to isolate Jamaicans in federal labor camps and deport those who made trouble. The camps would be segregated by color and citizenship. MacDonald announced in press releases that Jamaicans were "good workers," "and only those who have made excellent records" would be given contracts for work in Florida. "These men *want* to abide by the customs of the South," he assured white readers. "They are not arrogant and do not wish to get out of bounds." "If one should enter a restricted place," MacDonald promised, "it will be through a lack of knowledge of Southern customs, and he will leave immediately when he is reminded."[14]

Florida newspapers apparently got the message that Jamaicans could be treated just like black southerners. While northern papers usually referred to the recruits as Jamaicans, noting that they were British citizens and different from African Americans in many respects, Florida papers simply referred to them as "Negroes," "West Indian Negroes," or in one case as "alien negro laborers." In Florida, race trumped citizenship.[15]

To ensure that the first eight hundred Jamaicans shifted southward did in fact abide by the customs of the Jim Crow South, the Chief Liaison insisted that the men agree to what New York's *Amsterdam News* dubbed the "Jim Crow Creed." "A distinction is made in Florida with colored people," MacDonald informed Jamaicans on their way to Florida, "and you must be careful and endeavor to help the position, as by your conduct you will be judged." "It is well to tell you for the sake of general information," he continued, "that there is a law in many Southern States, including Florida, which makes the offense of rape punishable by death. This, of course, is a very serious offense anywhere, but down there it is viewed even more seriously." Making clear that his intent was to warn the workers against interaction with white women, he noted: "There will be ample opportunity for you to make friends among the colored people, as every city, town and village has its colored section." "You are free to purchase wherever you wish, but there are certain places of amusement, restaurants and bars where you will not be allowed." MacDonald also informed the men of the new "misconduct and indiscipline clause," which gave the U.S. government the right to terminate the contract "if the worker misconducts himself." He exhorted the arrivals to "behave themselves" because there was "a slight possibility that the success of the Florida venture might well influence any future recruitment in Jamaica." Those who refused to behave, he said in conclusion, would be turned over to the INS for "repatriation."[16]

To induce Jamaicans working in the North to shift to the South, recruits were given an ultimatum: cut cane or go home. Fitzroy Parkinson, who had been harvesting potatoes in Long Island with other Jamaicans, noted, "We had heard about Florida and the segregation, so we were scared, but a bunch of us said we would try Florida and if anything happened we would go home from there."[17] Leaford Williams was equally apprehensive as he rode the rails toward Florida alone, his brother Enoch having opted to return to his new wife in Mulgrave.[18] Leaford's apprehension only increased when the train passed a "herd of black men chained together," guarded by white men armed with shotguns. Arriving at Belle Glade's train station, there was no marching band to greet him, no dignitaries ready to present the new arrivals with the keys to the city. He found the waiting white men "distant and unfriendly." One carried a swagger stick, which later proved to be a folded whip. "You boys come on over heya," Williams recalled the man saying, his neck "bloody red . . . with wrinkles like deep trenches."[19] On their first day of work, the red-necked man told the Jamaican men to keep their noses clean. "I am trouble," he warned them.[20] "We had just met our enemies," Williams later wrote. "We were just a few more 'negras' joining farm hands on the sugar plantation."[21]

Tent cities and squalid, cement-block dormitories surrounded by barbed wire–topped fences made the new arrivals even more nervous. Here finally were the fenced compounds that the Duke of Windsor had proposed. In some camps, men discovered they needed passes to leave, and bells summoned them to daily roll calls. The parallels to slavery were hard to miss. Those aware of the apartheid system developing in South Africa may have found the similarities between the controls on their movements in Florida and the pass system there equally striking.[22]

The first arrivals reacted with all the passion of a slave uprising. Stanley Wilson and the fifty-eight workers with whom he arrived were not the only Jamaicans who refused to "abide by southern customs." In October 1943, ninety-three Jamaicans "refused to get off the busses," according to Herbert MacDonald, and when they did, "they refused to carry their own luggage." When they got to the mess hall, "they scraped their food on the ground & trampled on it . . ." and "abused everyone & everything in sight." The men were quickly shipped off to the Dade City jail to await deportation. Within two weeks of their arrival, the number of Jamaicans sitting in Florida jails had risen to seven hundred. "I must advise caution as they are in an ugly mood," MacDonald warned Jamaica's Labour Advisor.[23] The *Pittsburg Courier* reported that in October, eight hundred to nine hundred Jamaican workers were taken to INS offices and later transferred to common jails in Miami, Tampa, and Raiford, Florida for refusing "to sign the Jim Crow agreement forced upon them."[24]

Those slated for repatriation were quickly replaced by new Jamaican transfers from the North, however, and in 1944, Jamaicans harvested 65 percent of Florida's sugarcane. Those who stayed were not necessarily content with the treatment they received or resigned to it, but they stuck it out nonetheless. Leaford Williams was among those who remained, though he no longer stared down local field bosses or mouthed off to managers. He recalled the story of a Jamaican who was woken from a nap in the cane fields by a foreman's whip. Startled, the Jamaican struck back impulsively with his machete and cut the foreman above his riding boot. Coming to his senses, the Jamaican fled into the canefield. Men complained to each other and to family and friends back home. "Rass mon!" Williams recalled a man in his barracks saying, "No mon beat mi wit no whip! Mi kill him

mon!" One worker wrote to Jamaica's Legislative Council reporting mag-
gots in the food, inept liaisons, and conditions that only got worse when
men complained.[25] Having heard rumors of Jamaicans being taken away
in pick-ups and whipped, Williams recalled, "We formed a union" and
decided that "no . . . Jamaican would go with a white man anywhere on
the plantation alone. Whenever a Jamaican was called to go anywhere, we
moved in pairs."[26]

As in the North, Jamaicans occasionally went on strike, but with very
different results. Fitzroy Parkinson recalled that when a white supervisor
threatened to kick "one of our boys," "everybody said no and everybody
stopped working." They demanded that the head liaison officer come
down from Washington, DC, asserting that the supervisors "could not
treat the Jamaicans as they treated the natives." Instead of resolving the
conflict, however, the liaison told the men that nothing would be done.
Once the sugar crop was in, they could go home or go north.[27] Indeed,
despite Jamaicans' continued militancy, there is no evidence that their
complaints in Florida were ever redressed. A liaison would be summoned
if one were available, but U.S. Sugar's field bosses were not accustomed
to negotiating with black workers or their white representatives, and they
weren't about to start. The liaison officers had little clout beyond the force
of Chief Liaison Herbert MacDonald's personality, which was considerable, but it only got the men so far. "Herbert MacDonald was one of the
characters of the century," Earl Morrison recalled, but he also "didn't have
much patience for workers." "Herbert would call up and raise hell, saying
"I'm going to take these damn people out of here," but when Morrison got
his "dander up," and replied angrily, McDonald would back down. He'd
say, "Oh, what's the matter here, Mr. Morrison, can't take a few jokes?"
Morrison recalled, imitating McDonald's accent. Ultimately, McDonald's
only real power was to remove men from a particular farm, which was
nearly impossible to do when one farm employed nearly all the Jamaican
guestworkers in the country. You couldn't shut down a $50 million fac-
tory, as Morrison put it, because an employer violated his contract.[28]

Nearly all Jamaican guestworkers worked at U.S. Sugar in the winter
of 1943–44, but when the importation program expanded to include other
southern states and other southern employers in early 1944, Jamaicans
discovered that conditions weren't better elsewhere in the South. After
arriving at a labor camp in Louisiana, George Hudson recalled walking
down the road "to look at the place." A policeman stopped him, saying,
"Boy, where are you going?" Hudson replied that he was "just walking,"
but the officer told him to "Get back where you belong." After staring
at the policeman angrily for a moment, Hudson turned back because he
"did not know the customs and . . . did not want to cause any trouble."[29]
Nathaniel Allen wrote his mother from Delaware that work was scarce

and dust plentiful: "No Latrines, no water to bathe, no beds to sleep in, no lights to sleep with and see at nights [*sic*] and worse than all, no work to do." The most he had earned so far was $2.50 a day, out of which $1.00 was deducted for meals and $.50 for rent. Since another dollar a day was withheld as "voluntary" savings, he received no money at all. He was sleeping "on a bit of board on the floor with only a blanket to put on it." "What this thing is going to lead up to I don't know," he wrote, "but what I can tell you is that every one is getting panicky." "Mam, you can't imagine," he wrote in closing, "This is a one man's place. Every where you look belongs to no one else but him, so then he runs the place and fixes the rates the people must work for. . . . I am not working because working here is only putting money in some one else's pocket."[30]

Some Jamaicans tried to subvert the racial order as they had in the North, still assuming that they were more courageous and defiant than African Americans. Sidney Barnett recalled leaving "Monkey Jungle" as a group to spend the advance of five dollars they got on their arrival. "The black natives warned us" to go to the back of the local store to be served, he recalled, but "We went in a large group and stormed through the front door." Proud to have been more assertive than the "American blacks," whom he described as "outside shivering," Barnett admitted that the "whites did not do anything to us because they must have heard that we were coming and they knew we would not be there for long."[31] Alphonso James remembers a shopping trip to West Palm Beach in which he returned to the bus to find the driver and a group of whites waiting at the bus door, while a couple of Jamaicans sat in the middle of the bus, instead of in the rear seats, where local custom dictated black riders should sit. When the sheriff arrived, he didn't arrest the Jamaicans or eject them. He told the bus driver to take them back to the camp but he made clear that the driver was not required to pick them up in the future. Turning to James and his compatriots, the sheriff remarked: "We hate you boys more than we hate the Japanese because you come to this country and stop the people from having manners."[32] By "the people," the sheriff didn't mean the bus driver or his white passengers, of course; he meant local black southerners who might be tainted by Jamaicans' behavior.

Jamaicans' attempts to assert themselves elsewhere in the South were no more successful than they had been in Florida. In the Vienna, Maryland, labor camp, Jamaicans objected to the daily "shape up," whereby workers were expected to gather at dawn and then wait to see which of them the growers would pick for the day's work. Those lucky enough to be chosen waited in the fields without pay until the farm manager declared the fields dry enough for picking. Workers complained and attempted to renegotiate wages but were immediately rebuffed.[33] "The Jamaican workers are reluctant to be treated as the domestic colored people are in this area," the Hebron, Maryland, labor camp manager reported when one of the Jamaicans tried attending a white church in Hebron. "It is hard for these workers to realize that they can have only the privileges of the local colored people."[34]

For African Americans and Jamaicans alike, organizing was virtually impossible. African Americans who tried to act collectively faced threats, violence, or replacement by foreign contract workers.[36] Foreign workers' organizing attempts were aborted by arrest and deportation. When a white camp manager reported Jamaican James Morrison to the local police as an "agitator," he was arrested and held at the Vienna, Maryland, police station, without so much as a warrant or a hearing. Though he was eventually released, he noted that two other Jamaicans had been deported as "trouble-makers."[37] "The workers as a whole have willingly performed their jobs[,] most of which were picking beans because of the short crop and higher wages," George Winston reported from the Pahokee Labor Supply Center in Florida in April 1944. "Approx. 75 workers held a strike at one celery packing house demanding 75cents/hour against the 50cents/hour paid them which was the prevailing wage at that time." But the "strike was caused by 3 workers only," he wrote, so after "a hearing was held for the 3 workers involved . . . they were turned over to the Border Patrol for deportation." No other trouble had occurred since, he noted tellingly.[38]

Aliens or not, Jamaicans were encountering precisely the same conditions African Americans had long faced as agricultural workers in the American South. But while black Americans might simply have left, Jamaicans were stuck. Their only choice was to demand repatriation, and even that took a while because ships were scarce. Those who tried to switch employers or who protested wages or conditions would be ordered deported by the INS, isolated from other guestworkers in a federal holding facility, and shipped home on a U.S. vessel.[35]

MUTINY

Federal authorities did their best to squelch information about Jamaicans' protests, and censored news of Jamaicans' November 1944 "mutiny" on the S.S. *Bienville*, which had come to take men awaiting repatriation back to Jamaica. "From the beginning of the voyage," U.S. officials later reported, "the workers seemed restless and anxious to return home as quickly as possible." But the ship needed repair and could only travel at 6 knots per hour. As the trip dragged out, food supplies ran low. The crew told the farmworkers to clean their quarters. But the farmworkers, who knew they were paying passengers since the cost of their return voyage was being withheld from their pay, told the crew to "go to hell." On November 13, twelve days after it left the United States, the *Bienville* limped into Guantanamo Bay. During mealtime the following day Jamaicans stormed the galley, overwhelmed the crew, and took possession of the ship. A detachment of thirteen marines and two officers had to be sent from the naval base to reclaim it.[39]

The behavior of the marines on the *Bienville* was consistent with the behavior of U.S. officials throughout the South. In Florida, federal officials acted not as defenders of foreign war workers, as they had just a few months earlier, but as suppliers of labor and enforcers of workplace discipline. Though U.S. officials were supposed to ensure that guest-workers were never brought to an area that had ample domestic labor, they approved growers' requests for immigrant workers without question. According to Fred Sikes, U.S. Sugar's personnel director, "during the War Administration Period we just placed an order and the government took it from there. They handled everything. There was no limit on how many men you could request and no justification for the request was required. You just asked and the government supplied."[40] The WFA blacklisted those accused of "indiscipline," and the INS took responsibility for apprehending and repatriating guestworkers who tried to change farms or leave farmwork altogether. "We have had quite a few workers go A.W.O.L., leaving one camp and going to another and being taken in w/o official transfer from either ext. or management of the area from which they go," reported Roy Litchfield, the manager of the Goulds, Florida, Federal Labor Camp in January 1944. "In this area," he noted, "we happen to be fortunate in having immigration officers to help us out on this problem."[41] Workers turned over to the INS were supposed to be granted a hearing before they could be repatriated, but there are scant references to such hearings and no record of their proceedings.[42]

Although U.S. officials apprehended and blacklisted guestworkers, officials no longer enforced contracts or investigated workers' complaints. With thousands of men and women in the Caribbean still clamoring to come to the United States, and with the power to repatriate those who complained, it was simply easier to replace "trouble-makers" than it was to identify and eliminate the cause of the trouble. Likewise, while Jamaican liaisons ran themselves ragged traveling from farm to farm trying to arbitrate conflicts, Jamaican officials at home were more concerned with expanding the program and creating jobs than they were with the welfare of recruits already in the United States. The fact that Jamaicans were sending more money home than ever fed the program's popularity, no matter how bad the reports from the United States got. So many men were trying to get into the program that, in April 1944, "bedlam, and minor damage to property" were the result when police used batons to beat back three thousand people trying to get the 180 available tickets at the Port Maria recruiting station in Jamaica. Even public outrage that American doctors were requiring recruits to strip naked on Kingston's pier for venereal disease examinations failed to dampen public enthusiasm for the program.[43] In August 1944, *Public Opinion* reported that Jamaicans had sent home nearly $1 million, or £200,000, in the previous two months.[44] "It is unprecedented, the amount of money which our workers are sending back to the island," a post office official declared in September. "We expected that there would be a lot this year, but nothing quite like this."[45] In all, Jamaicans remitted £1.6 million (then $6,464,000 in U.S. dollars) in compulsory and voluntary savings combined in 1944.[46]

Bedlam

Given those sorts of returns, it's not surprising that unemployed and underemployed Jamaicans were desperate to try their hand at farmwork in the United States. Groups excluded from the first round of recruiting insisted that they be offered tickets in 1944. Residents of Kingston, many of whom were passed over in 1943, found that if they volunteered specifically for work in Florida's sugarcane fields, they could get tickets readily. By May 1944, the Kingston Employment Bureau was interviewing four hundred applicants a day for cane-cutting jobs in Florida. Also barred completely from the first wave of recruitment, Jamaicans of East Indian descent won themselves a quota of 150 out of the three thousand tickets available in July 1944. Three light-skinned men complained that American officials on board a transport vessel had rejected them on the grounds that they were "too white" to be agricultural workers.[47]

Jamaican women also continued to appeal for jobs in the United States, though with less success. The leaders of the Democratic Party reported that they were being "deluged with anxious inquiries from women all over the island as to the progress of the proposal." In response, they sent telegrams to Eleanor Roosevelt and the U.S. Secretary of Labor, asking for help in fulfilling the desire of Jamaican women to serve in the United States as "domestic helps." In April, the First Lady heard their appeal, and after completing a 14,000-mile tour of the Caribbean by army plane, she promised to investigate the possibility of bringing Jamaican women to the United States as domestics. By the time the war ended, however, the question of importing Jamaican women still had not been resolved.[48]

Given the program's enormous popularity at home and the fact that they stood to gain personally from the program, Jamaican officials were reluctant to rock the boat. The year 1944 brought Jamaica a new constitution, universal suffrage, and, therefore, the first democratic elections in its history. The Jamaican Labour Party, the political wing of the Bustamente Industrial Trade Union (BITU), swept the polls, completely unseating the Democratic Party and winning twenty-two seats to the PNP's five. The Labour Party readily assumed control of the ticket distribution system established by the Democratic Party. In May 1945, four PNP members in Jamaica's House of Representatives challenged this patronage-based system, arguing that non-elected officials should distribute the tickets. After a rancorous debate, the motion was defeated twenty to four and the migration program and the patronage system it spawned became permanent features of Jamaican political life.[49]

In their first year, the guestworker programs remained restricted to Jamaicans, Bahamians, and Mexicans, but citizens of other Caribbean colonies demanded to be included in the migration scheme. Governor Grattan Bushe had been trying to secure a similar agreement for Barbados since the start of the program, but the War Food Administration expressed little interest in Bajan men because of the island's much greater distance from the United States. In June 1944, seven thousand people gathered in Bridgeton to protest Barbados' exclusion.[50]

A few U.S. growers offered to shoulder the extra travel costs, but there was a bigger obstacle that could not be discussed publicly. U.S. officials had nothing against Bajans, despite their distance from the United States, but they wanted to exclude Puerto Ricans from the program because, as U.S. citizens, they couldn't be deported for "indiscipline." That was precisely the reason L. L. Chandler and U.S. officials had given for passing over Puerto Ricans in the first place. "As they are United States citizens," the American co-chair of the Anglo-American Caribbean Commission had explained in a letter to Oliver Stanley, "they could not be sent back to Puerto Rico against their will." "This cannot, of course, be stated," he added, so the "reason given is lack of shipping facilities." If workers were brought from Barbados or elsewhere, the "falsity of the reason given would be apparent." U.S. officials believed that the power to deport outweighed other concerns, including the needs of U.S. citizens willing to fill U.S. jobs.[51]

In the spring of 1944 the point became moot, however, as farm employers in particularly labor-scarce areas like New Jersey began importing Puerto Ricans on their own. The importation of Bajans thus began immediately, and once the logjam broke, the governors of St. Lucia and the British Honduras insisted that their people be included as well, citing protests at home.[52] In the last year of the war, 38,000 Jamaicans, Barbadians, British Guyanans, St. Lucians, and British Hondurans labored in the United States alongside almost 62,000 Mexicans, 5,800 Bahamians,

120,000 POWs, and an undisclosed number of Puerto Ricans. Instead of just representing Jamaican farmworkers in the United States, Herbert MacDonald would soon supervise all British West Indian guestworkers as head of the newly formed British West Indies Central Labour Organisation (otherwise known as WICLO).[53]

GOOD OLD CRACKER STYLE

In the last year of the war, the U.S. War Food Administration transformed itself into an enforcer of workplace discipline. In December 1944, the WFA turned the military base at Fort Eustis, Virginia, into a repatriation center that would only house workers awaiting boats back to the Caribbean. Detention was not meant as a punishment, though imprisonment certainly had that effect. Its purpose was to quarantine angry migrants awaiting their return to Jamaica from newly arrived recruits, who had no experience in the United States with which to compare conditions at U.S. Sugar. The Fort Eustis center was soon replaced by a repatriation facility at Camp Murphy in Florida. There, men who refused work or who simply wanted to go back to Jamaica spent their savings on food and necessities while waiting impatiently for ships to take them home.[54]

The guards at Camp Murphy and the problem of securing transportation back to Jamaica were sources of discontent for the remainder of the war. The *Christian Science Monitor* attributed a riot of 250 workers at Camp Murphy in August 1945 to "the Negroes [*sic*] unwillingness to return to their comparatively drab former existence after sampling the high wages and luxury goods during their employment in the U.S." In fact, the "riot" was a fight between Bajans and Jamaicans over which group would get to leave first. According to the *Palm Beach Post*, the rioters were handled in "good old cracker style" by Palm Beach police.[55]

Discontent among Jamaicans in northern camps had sent managers scrambling to find cricket equipment and Jamaican-born cooks; the managers of Camp Murphy scrambled for their guns. A week after the Camp Murphy riot, a white camp employee named Lacey A. Griffin fired his weapon while chasing a Jamaican who had urinated against a building. When Griffin lost his quarry, he was taunted by a group of men, who dared him to enter their barracks. Griffin went for help instead, telling the camp's manager, Captain R. G. Ray, that he would quit before he took "such talk off of these men any further." Ray, Griffin, and two other camp employees returned to the barracks armed. Entering the building, they screamed at the men to stand up, and beat those who moved too slowly with billy-clubs. "If we did not behave ourselves," one worker reported,

Ray said he would "shoot us and throw us in a hole." To reiterate the point, Ray shot his gun toward the floor. Griffin fired his through a window, accidentally hitting a man in the leg in another building. In the aftermath of the incident, Ray, Griffin, and the other camp employees were fired or transferred. Although the Military Police sent to replace Ray and Griffin were "well received by the men," according to Herbert MacDonald, a month later, an MP shot another worker.[56]

The more Jamaicans soured on the southern "experiment," the more workers' distaste for working and living conditions seemed to spread northward. And the more dissatisfied workers were, the more frustrated they became with chief liaison Herbert MacDonald and he with them. In November 1944, after quickly settling a Wadsworth, Ohio, strike over the phone, MacDonald remarked, "As far as I can see, the only reason these men had for striking was to keep in practice for the day when they return home." He reported in March 1945 that a worker had punched a Cleveland camp manager in the face "and got away with it." "I told the Camp Manager," MacDonald noted, "that he should have reported this and I would have taken responsibility [for] removing the man. Subsequently another worker abused him shamefully and was removed. The effect of this," MacDonald lamented, was that "the workers are under the impression that it is safer to punch the Camp Manager than to abuse him." "Men write home or go home and say they have never seen me," MacDonald added two months later; "that is their theme song." But, he estimated, it would take him nearly four years to visit every man.[57] MacDonald and his staff would, of course, have been hard pressed to attend to every grievance made by their far-flung compatriots. However, with U.S. immigration authorities ready to deport importees who contested their wages and treatment, what efforts they did make had little impact. By 1944, the federal government was carrying the swagger stick.

OUR OWN NATIVE MIGRANT LABOR

Repatriations helped to neutralize the effects of West Indian workers' protests, while guestworkers' presence undermined African American workers' militancy. Denied the higher standards guaranteed foreign workers and no longer protected by assurances that foreign workers would only be used where American workers were truly absent, domestic farmworkers found themselves workers of last resort. Bahamians arrived at the Okeechobee, Florida, labor supply camp in 1943, though the federal labor camp manager had reported that "the farmer had more than necessary labor." "[D]aily we turn down hundreds of applicants who are so anxious to call this their home," he noted. Even where domestic workers did find employment, employers were able to play foreign and domestic workers off each other.[58] Bahamians arrived at the Okeechobee Camp in 1943, although the camp's staff thought that the domestic labor supply had been adequate the previous year. "The farmer had more than necessary labor" in 1942, one staff member noted. With the addition of the Bahamians, "many farm laborers were without day work," she added. The War Food Administration reserved many federal labor camps for importees only. After a visit to the Swedesboro, New Jersey, camp, an official of the Division of Farm Population and Rural Welfare reported that all but twenty-five of the three hundred residents of the camp were Jamaicans. The African American migrants who had come to the camp in family groups early in the year "were permitted to stay," but no new native families were accepted. The "Jamaican and Negro migrants" were housed separately, he noted. Domestic workers' children simply took up space, remarked one federal official, by way of explanation. During the previous year's peak season, the Pahokee, Florida, camp had only housed 213 workers old enough to work, he noted. If it was reserved for Bahamians only, it could house at least eight hundred "easily."[59]

Barred from their berths in federal labor camps, African Americans also found that they were hired only as a last resort. Growers in the Fort Pierce area preferred Bahamians, whom they found "*very satisfactory.*" The camp manager there noted that most employers "considered Bahamians, all things considered, as superior to native American workers," adding that "in some instances, the Bahamians have out cut the domestics who have been cutting fruit all their lives." To him, this was a question of innate character, not the work ethic produced by guestworkers' knowledge that they had a brief time to make good. "[M]ost of the Bahamians were quite contented and happy," he observed. "It is said that they are that way by nature anyway."[60] "FSA now runs the camps with food administration money," the Waterbury, Connecticut *Republican* reported, which meant that foreign workers had dibs on berths in federal labor camps. "So our own native migrant labor had to go back to the new houses, shacks, and barn floors provided by the farmers." "[D]omestic labor still outnumbers the imports," the paper noted, but African American workers were last in line for jobs and housing. "That could have led to explosive riots," but, fortunately, the paper added, "the southern Negroes took it in good grace."[61]

Not surprisingly, the "southern Negroes" did not always take the presence of Bahamians and West Indians with good grace. Hostility between Caribbean and African American workers occasionally flared into violent confrontations, despite the practice of housing them separately. One Jamaican reported that after a movie shown jointly to Caribbean and African American workers in March 1945, an American worker backed his car into a crowd of Jamaicans, saying, "Kill these damn Jamaicans." His action set off a brawl during which one Jamaican was shot. The same man insisted that African Americans lined up in the streets with guns, waiting to shoot passing Jamaicans.[62]

Such hostility ultimately benefited growers. The Reverend David Burgess, sent by the Southern Tenant Farmers Union to minister to migrant farmworkers, noted that West Indians and African Americans were housed in two separate Belle Glade camps, about a mile apart. Growers, he recalled, would drive from one to the other, forcing wages down by telling each group that the other had underbid it. There was no shortage of labor, Burgess insisted; the importation program was simply a means to break strikes and depress wages.[63]

Indeed, by the end of the war, the foreign worker program had served its primary purpose: it had reined in domestic workers, undermining those who had taken advantage of the war economy to agitate for better wages. The Homestead Farm Labor Supply camp manager reported in 1945 that, "The Domestic colored did a swell job in harvesting the vegetable crop. They never once asked for higher prices than prevailed in the area."[64] In fact, knowing that their time in the United States was limited, the Jamaicans had cut cane so fast—nearly a ton an hour to the American's half ton—that instead of making the minimum wage of 40 cents an hour that their contracts guaranteed, they had averaged 80 cents an hour. U.S. Sugar didn't reward their efforts with Emancipation Day celebrations, however; it responded by reorganizing its payment system so that Jamaicans earned half as much.[65]

Instead of paying gangs of cane cutters for every ton they harvested, Fred Sikes of U.S. Sugar began assigning individual workers "a cut row" of sugar cane, which meant two side-by-side rows, each a quarter-mile long. Men were then paid by the cut row rather than by weight or by the hour. Ostensibly because some rows were harder to cut than others—depending on factors such as the variety of cane, how upright it grew, whether the fire set the day before had burned off the leaves—rows were priced individually. The result was that men began cutting cane each morning without knowing what they were being paid for their row. The first time Sikes implemented this system, he based his row prices on the old tonnage rate. But Jamaicans continued to earn twice as much as the minimum wage their contracts required. The following season, Sikes cut the row prices in half, which meant that the Jamaicans got the 40 cents per hour that their contracts demanded, but few earned more than that. African Americans' average earnings fell to 20 cents an hour, far below any conceivable subsistence level. Not surprisingly, U.S. Sugar's remaining African American workers quit, leaving U.S. Sugar with an all West Indian-all guestworker harvest labor force.[66]

Jamaican men lined up to come to the United States in 1943 seeking opportunity, adventure, and much needed cash. Wherever they went in northern states, they were surprised by the friendliness of American whites. Testing Americans' notions of blackness, they used their foreignness and Britishness to protect themselves against racist abuse and to distinguish themselves from the African American farmworkers with whom they were inevitably compared. U.S. officials rushed to accommodate them and address their concerns. All this changed, however, when U.S. officials decided that Jamaicans would work in Florida or they would not work at all. In Florida, Jamaicans did not stir up white southerners' notions of blackness, try as they might, but they did succeed in stirring African Americans right out of the cane-cutting jobs they had held seasonally since the 1930s. By the end of the war, Caribbean workers—with Jamaicans still in the vast majority—had supplanted U.S. Sugar's traditional labor force, cementing Florida's dependence on guestworkers and insuring that corporate growers would agitate for the program's persistence in the decades to come.

The fact that Caribbean workers were represented by liaison officers, their home governments, and the British Colonial Office made little difference. Even when workers' representatives tried to take a hard line with growers, there seemed to be little they could do to improve conditions for guestworkers, short of removing all Jamaican workers from the principal industry that employed them. In April 1946, the British colonial office and Jamaica's new Labour government tried to do just that, responding jointly to Jamaicans' complaints of racist treatment in Florida by withdrawing all Jamaican contract workers from the state until the problem was redressed. However, the government of Barbados quickly offered to take up the slack, ending the Jamaican "strike" before it began. Their bluff called, Jamaicans went back to work.[67]

Jamaicans kept "their" jobs in Florida, but their near monopoly over the Caribbean guestworker program was a dubious achievement. They were not free to change employers or switch to other employment. They were not free to travel in their spare time, and they faced blackjack and gun-toting labor camp bosses or American military police who treated them more like convict laborers than allied war workers. While in northern states Jamaicans had been protected by their foreignness; in the Jim Crow South it just made them deportable. More importantly, the federal officials who had watched their backs in conflicts with employers in northern states became enforcers of workplace discipline. In the South, "the Jim Crow State" was far more powerful than the Welfare State.

Within months of their arrival in the United States, therefore, Jamaicans' status sank from exotic British war workers to "alien negro laborers," and neither their citizenship nor U.S. officials proved to be protection from the perils of farm labor relations in the southern countryside.[68] In Florida, guestworkers' foreignness provided employers with a new and effective weapon in the arsenal of labor discipline: workers who protested their treatment now faced detention, repatriation, and blacklisting. In this new era of transnational labor, the threat of deportation became the new whip.

CHAPTER FIVE

The Race to the Bottom

Making Wartime Temporary Worker Programs Permanent and Private

WHEN NEWS OF Japan's surrender reached Jamaican farmworkers at "old John Kirby's Farm" in Harrisonville, New Jersey, Leaford Williams put on one of his best "double-breasted 'zoot-suits'," hitched a ride with John Kirby's daughter, and headed for Philadelphia to join in the celebrations. The revelry failed to meet his expectations. Not only did women neglect to "grab and kiss" him as they did American soldiers, but the U.S. government failed to recognize his and other Jamaican workers' contributions to the allied war effort by offering permanent U.S. residency to those guestworkers who wanted it. Returning dejectedly to Kirby's farm in time to harvest asparagus the following morning, Williams prepared to go home.[1]

If he had to abandon what he considered a profitable adventure as a war worker, Williams determined that he would "be the best dressed man" in his little village of Mulgrave. Having bought two steamer trunks worth of suits, shirts, shoes, and hats, he returned home in triumph, arriving in Mulgrave to shouts of "Leaford come — Leaford come." "Wearing a light-blue suit, white shirt, red-and-white tie, black shoes and a grey hat," the eighteen-year-old Williams felt "a bit ashamed" of the contrast between his finery and his waiting family's bare feet. He was struck, moreover, by the folly of his new wardrobe; in Mulgrave "there was no where to go" but church.[2]

That night at home, Williams's family stayed up late to talk and pray, singing "On Christ the solid rock I stand, all other ground is sinking sand," and listening to his father read scripture about the return of the prodigal son. But Williams had no intention of staying to work the family plot, as his father hoped. Too little had changed in his absence. A few old people had died. One young woman was in nursing school in England. But in 1945 Mulgrave, there were no wages, no educational opportunities, and few prospects for a young man with ambition. Having already made it, if not from rags to riches, then from home-made shirt and valise to suit, tie, and steamer trunks, Leaford determined to return to the United States. With an uncle who was an AME bishop in New York ready to sponsor him and $3,000 in savings, he went to the American consulate in

Kingston to apply for a visa. The American consular official refused him, predicting that he would become a public charge, a presumption that still stung half a century later. Boldly, Williams tried to hire Michael Manley, one of Jamaica's leading attorneys and its future Prime Minister, to help him press for readmission, but Manley told him he did not have enough collateral.[3]

In fact, whether Williams was the "right sort" mattered little to U.S. immigration officials. Permanent Jamaican immigration to the United States was still limited to one thousand applicants a year, and the gate would soon shut even further. Many Americans were fearful that an avalanche of European refugees would blanket the United States. Not even Jews liberated from concentration camps were welcomed. No exception would be made for poor black men from the Caribbean, whatever their wartime service.

Some Caribbean war workers remained in the United States after World War II by virtue of the fact that they had married American women. Others stayed without authorization, blending into families and Caribbean communities already in the United States and trusting in the apparently reliable rumor that if they lasted seven years without discovery and without causing trouble, the INS would grant them permanent status. Already back in Jamaica, Williams didn't have these options. In 1947, stymied in his effort to reenter the United States, twenty-two-year-old Leaford Williams shipped out on a banana boat bound for "somewhere in England."[4]

Like many other people looking for work in the post–World War II world, Leaford Williams had run up against barriers erected by twentieth-century states in their attempts to bolster their authority and security. Leaford made it to England, as many West Indians did in the postwar period, but England's parliament would soon bar nonwhite migrants from its former colonies. After the war, Congress voted twice to put a moratorium on all postwar immigration, though neither bill became law. West Germany persisted in limiting citizenship to ethnic Germans, despite the horrific consequences of its national chauvinism during the war. The Soviet Union stopped all passage in and out of its zone of occupation. In other words, instead of responding to the horrors committed in the name of national purity by returning to the liberal immigration policies of the nineteenth century, postwar governments tightened their borders and cleaved to narrow definitions of citizenship.

Though the permanent immigration status Williams sought became more difficult on both sides of the Atlantic after the war, the temporary status he had experienced became increasingly common. In the quarter century after the war, 30 million guestworkers shifted from Europe's periphery to its center, providing labor for the continent's reconstruction and the rapid recovery of its industry. In postwar Europe, guestworkers labored in construction, mining, manufacturing, and agriculture. They rebuilt Europe's infrastructure and industries and then kept them running. Two-thirds of the 30 million European guestworkers worked in France and Germany. In Switzerland, guestworkers made up fully 30 percent of the workforce.[5] In the United States, there were 95,000 guestworkers on U.S. farms at the end of the war. By the early 1960s, nearly half a million would enter the United States every year. In the aftermath of the war, in other words, international "temps" became the immigrants of choice.

It is easy to understand why European nations promoted the use of guestworker schemes in the postwar period: some 50 million Europeans had perished during the war and whole cities and industries had to be reconstructed. Explaining why the United States retained its wartime guestworker programs after the war is a bit trickier. The United States also lost citizens—nearly half a million in all—but Americans had no cities to rebuild, no industries to recreate from the ground up. Indeed, U.S. officials presumed that guestworker programs would end immediately, and within weeks of the war's end, the War Manpower Commission had repatriated all the guestworkers who had been placed in industrial jobs, including 68,000 Mexicans employed by U.S. railroads, and 16,000 Jamaicans and Bajans working in northern war industries. Only agricultural guestworkers were allowed to remain.

Farm labor scarcity does not explain this agricultural exceptionalism. The Mexican and Caribbean guestworker programs persisted after the war, not because there was a labor crisis in agriculture, but because farm employers had come to appreciate the certainty, flexibility, and authority that deportable workers afforded them. Employers of migrant and seasonal farmworkers—a tiny fraction of the nation's farmers—had become hooked on the nicotine of guestworkers.

GASTARBEITER

Both the United States and Europe imported large numbers of guestworkers after World War II, but that is about where the similarities ended. Because guestworkers in Europe were originally imported for reconstruction work and to restart industries that had been flattened (sometimes literally) by the war, they labored at all kinds of work, including in highly paid and highly unionized industries. Thus members of Europe's most powerful unions worked alongside guestworkers. Unions increasingly advocated on guestworkers' behalf, if only because guestworkers would undermine them unless they were paid equally for equal work and enjoyed the same right to organize and strike. Thus unions in Germany, France, Switzerland, and England put time and money into organizing foreign workers, opening offices to address foreign workers' legal, social, and personal problems, publishing foreign language labor newspapers, and offering language and literacy classes.[6]

In the United States, in contrast, guestworkers were limited to the nation's poorest paying and least unionized industry. In fact, Caribbean guestworkers were far more likely to have been members of labor unions at home than in the United States. In the United States, guestworkers labored alongside workers still excluded not only from collective bargaining law but from minimum-wage and overtime regulations, from unemployment insurance, workers' compensation, child labor laws, and even social security. To the extent that American labor unions were involved at all in the affairs of guestworkers, as a result, they struggled to ban guestworkers from the country altogether. They had little choice in the matter. Contract workers were not always cheaper than domestic workers, but they made up a highly contingent workforce that could be deployed on short notice to undermine domestic workers' all too infrequent attempts at organization.

There were other differences as well. Conditions for guestworkers in Europe varied from country to country and even within countries, but in most European countries guestworkers received separate work and residence permits, so losing one's job did not necessarily mean losing one's right to stay. Governments, not employers, controlled who could enter and who could be made to leave.[7] And in Europe, guestworkers could generally renew their contracts year after year, and millions were eventually allowed to settle and bring their families. None of this meant that guestworkers were warmly welcomed in Europe, but guestworkers on the continent generally enjoyed more rights and protections than they did in the United States (and in South Africa), where guestworkers were cycled in and out of the country and explicitly denied the right to convert their status from "temporary, non-immigrants" to "resident aliens."[8]

The gulf between European and American guestworker programs also widened over time. Pressured by unions, Europe moved in the direction of more pervasive state management of guestworker programs, while American growers fought federal management tooth and nail. In the postwar United States, federal officials largely withdrew from the day-to-day affairs of the American guestworker programs, leaving employers with nearly sole control over the men they imported. Increasingly, employers chose the particular Caribbean and Mexican men they wanted (all but a few Bahamians were men at this stage). After selecting their workers, growers advanced the cost of their transportation, paid their return fare if they lasted the season, and housed them in company-owned labor camps. Workers labored under "no-strike" contracts and faced repatriation for "indiscipline," a term defined unilaterally by employers. And because employers, not federal officials, wielded the right to repatriate, guest-workers in the United States had little recourse when conditions were intolerable, despite the protections guaranteed in their contracts and the presence of "liaison officers" or "consuls" sent by their home countries to advocate on their behalf.

Pressured by Mexico, U.S. officials accepted responsibility for the enforcement of employers' contracts with workers, but federal oversight of the Bracero Program was more theoretical than real. The Bahamian and West Indian programs were not regulated by U.S. officials at all. Bahamian and British West Indian liaison officers continued to advocate for men on contracts (as did Mexican consuls), but they worried as much about sustaining the programs and the remittances they generated as they did about the welfare of their countrymen.

And although in Europe the treatment of guestworkers generally improved over time, the opposite was true in the United States. European states competed among themselves for the same pools of labor, and were thus forced to offer guestworkers more favorable terms. Unlike Europe's programs, in other words—but much like the system by which South Africa's mine companies still recruited contract labor from north of the border—American guestworker programs operated with federal sanction but little federal oversight. Like materials shipped to "free trade zones" for assembly, Mexican and Caribbean guestworkers in the United States increasingly worked in labor regulation–free zones. And, like commodities imported for sale, they competed against each other and against their domestic counterparts in a mad race to the bottom.[9] The Depression was over, the war had ended, the economy was booming, and, in the richest country in the world, farmworkers got poorer.

The Forgotten People

When World War II ended in 1945, the United States' Emergency Labor Importation Program was supposed to end with it, but the nation's largest producers of fruit, cotton, vegetables, and sugar were not prepared to give it up. "It would be very disastrous to abandon this program now," the president of the American Farm Bureau Federation insisted in a letter to President Truman two months after the surrender of Japan.[10] "A serious labor shortage" would result, wrote Frank Seymour of the Florida Growers Administration Committee, "unless Bahaman [sic] and other foreign workers can supplement the inadequate local supply."[11]

In the fall of 1945, Congress heeded farm employers' warnings, extending the farm labor importation program for another year, granting farmers a two-year price guarantee, and maintaining ceilings on farm wages to keep them from rising. A year later, lawmakers extended the farm labor supply program yet again. And although the war had ended, the number of guest-workers in agriculture grew. Within two years of the war's end, there were some 220,000 Mexican guestworkers in the United States (up from 62,000) and some 50,000 British West Indians and Bahamians (up from 43,800), all assigned to agricultural employment. Perhaps to preclude a second Jamai-can strike against Florida employers, in 1948 U.S. Sugar supplemented its pool of Jamaicans, Barbadians, St. Lucians, British Hondurans, and British Guyanans with workers from the Leeward Islands of Antigua, St. Kitts, and Montserrat.[12]

That Congress extended the guestworker programs beyond the war's end is hardly surprising. Lawmakers had no way to know whether the farm economy would continue to expand or collapse as it had after World War I. They didn't know whether veterans would turn their swords back into plowshares or abandon the farm for the city. And they could hardly have missed the news that black, white, Latino, and Filipino farmworkers had gravitated to war jobs in cities in the North and West. But the fact that lawmakers thought there might be a farm labor shortage doesn't mean there was one. In fact, if there was a farm labor crisis in agriculture, it was once again a crisis of oversupply.

The nation's farms required less labor than ever after World War II, yet farms weren't shrinking. In what became known as the "Green Revolu-tion," farms got bigger and, as a result of chemical fertilizers and pesticides, more productive. They were also the beneficiaries of big subsidies, devised during the New Deal and continued long after the Depression ended. In general, farm owners, many of whom had been on the verge of bankruptcy before the war, either got big or got out at the war's end. Those who re-mained enjoyed the bounty of state and federal electrification projects, trading their washboards for washing machines, their iceboxes for Frigid-aires, and their year-round farm hands for machines.[13]

Farms got bigger on average, but there were fewer of them. They also demanded less labor as tractors replaced workhorses, six- to eight-row drills supplanted single-row planters, and picking machines reduced the "man-hours" required for producing cotton from 150 to just 25 per acre. Soaring yields rendered many farmworkers superfluous. Within a few years of the war's end, small grains were harvested entirely by combines, and human hands were rarely needed for haymaking, milking cows, or harvesting corn.[14]

Mechanization led to specialization because there was no point invest-ing in a massive piece of equipment if you only grew a small crop. And when growers in particular regions produced the same crop, they could also share processing, shipping, and marketing costs. This sort of regional specialization made Sanford, Florida, the "celery capital of the world,"

Zellwood, Florida, the source of the best sweet corn on Earth, and New Jersey famous for blueberries. It also meant that farm employers needed lots of labor for short periods of time, and then almost none at all.[15]

This Green Revolution allowed farm owners to reduce their demand for labor by 26 percent in the 1940s, 35 percent in the 1950s, and by almost 40 percent in the 1960s. "Fifteen years ago the farmer, his family and local workers did 90 per cent of the harvest," remarked the director of Rochester, New York's State Farm Placement Bureau in 1960; "Now they handle maybe as little as 25 per cent and they need migrants for the rest."[16]

Because farm owners needed less year-round labor, they spurned long-term sharecropping and tenancy arrangements in favor of short-term contracts or day labor. As a result, the rural population as a whole shrank but the seasonal and migratory work force grew. By 1950, only 14 percent of the approximately 5.5 million Americans who did waged farmwork labored more than six months on any one farm. Farmwork was never steady work, but in the postwar period there was less of it and it was harder to find. The average hired farmworker found 113 days of work in 1946 but only 90 days in 1949.[17] "If you don't get no work in the summer," a Palmetto, Florida, woman told a reporter in Cranbury, New Jersey, where she was digging potatoes, "the rent man's going to shut you right out the door."[18]

Only a small minority of farmworkers migrated long distances, but those who did ventured farther afield than ever before, often traveling with their children. In 1952, William Metzler interviewed 1,866 migrant farmworkers in Belle Glade, Florida, of whom one-third were younger than fourteen years old. Between them, they took 325,000 jobs a year, or six each, and traveled an average of 2,000 miles a year to find work, often standing upright in the bed of a crew leader's truck.[19] One *New York Times* reporter described eighty "grown-ups and twenty children" arriving in New York from Lake Okeechobee, Florida, "in five battered, stake-sided, tarpaulin-covered trucks." The trip had been broken by a few weeks picking potatoes in North Carolina, but on the road they paused only to eat and stretch. "[N]either in the segregated South nor in the North could they find or afford a night's lodging."[20]

Farm owners made record profits while continuing to enjoy the largess of the welfare state, which included federal price support programs, federal surplus commodity storage programs, and the research know-how of federally supported agronomy departments at universities around the country. Farmworkers got nothing. The New Deal experienced by other workers had passed them by. Congress expanded the Social Security system in 1954 to include farm employees who earned more than $100 on a single farm, but that just encouraged farmers to hire fewer long-term farmworkers. In New York in 1959, only three out of forty farm labor camps even kept the payroll records required by law that would have verified whether a worker earned more than $100. Farmworkers, reporter Paul Jacobs wrote in 1959, are "the unorganized debris of an unorganized society. They are . . . the forgotten people."[21]

ALMOST UNBELIEVABLE

Federal officials were not oblivious to the growing crisis in the countryside. Concerned officials in multiple agencies—the Bureau of Agricultural Economics, the U.S. Employment Service, even the Interstate Commerce Commission—counted heads in the countryside in the postwar period, and came to the same conclusion: the seasonal labor force was growing.[22] Concerned that migrant poverty had proved remarkably resistant to the wartime boom, these officials convinced President Harry S Truman to let them form a Federal Interagency Committee on Migrant Labor.

The committee's 1947 report was a passionate indictment of governmental negligence. "A sizable segment of our population" had been "robbed . . . of many normal American and human rights" through community and State neglect, the report stated categorically. Farmworkers' marginalization was "almost unbelievable." "Child labor, substandard living, and a padlock against education," it continued, "destroyed the rights of children and drastically disturbed the integrity of family life among migrant workers."[23]

The report called for federal and state legislative standards for housing, wages, child labor laws, and transportation, as well as the extension of state workers' compensation laws and the Social Security Act to farm laborers. Instead of arguing for the cancellation of the guestworker programs as unfair competition, however, the report suggested that the wartime guestworker programs had proved that it was possible to regulate conditions in the countryside. During the war, the report noted, foreign contract workers had "enjoyed guarantees far more liberal than those provided domestic workers."[24] Though it had little immediate impact, the report was a blueprint for the reforms Congress would adopt a quarter century later.

The inquiry did have one result: after the report's publication, the federal Farm Placement Service launched an "Annual Worker Plan," in the hope of rationalizing farmworkers' movements as the USES, FSA, and later the War Food Administration had done during the war. Its goal, though, was less to maximize production than it was to maximize workers' earnings. Even that minor effort was controversial, however, because by providing migrant workers with information on harvests, the Placement Service sometimes inspired them to abandon ongoing harvests when pickings started to get thin. "Southern Migrants," F. A. Curry, the personnel manager of Birds

Eye Vegetables in New York State complained to his senator, were "a con-
niving bunch of people who cannot be depended upon to do the work in
question." "I have seen these people pick up and leave whenever the occasion suited them irrespective the crops that were lost by their action, or the
hardships that it created for the company." "We do not wish, nor intend,"
he made clear, "that these people be the main source of our labor supply."[25]
The more domestic farmworkers acted rationally by moving to where they
could maximize their earnings, the more growers saw them as shiftless and
irrational.

In the protracted struggle over farmworkers and guestworkers that followed the war, Curry clearly came down on the side of guestworkers, and
he wasn't alone. No matter how many unemployed domestic farmworkers there were, foreign farmworkers bound by contracts were the object of
growers' desire, and growers were organized.

A tiny number of large and influential growers—perhaps 2 percent of
commercial farmers—employed the bulk of hired farm labor in the United
States. They came out of the war more powerful than they had gone in,
in part because they had been encouraged by the federal government to
form cartels in the name of wartime efficiency. To justify the high cost of
transporting workers from abroad, the War Manpower Commission had
required growers to hire foreign workers in large groups and promise a
minimum of thirty days' work. Since only big growers or consortiums of
growers could afford to do so, the Manpower Commission encouraged
and, in some cases, required smaller growers to enter into cooperative
agreements.[26] As a result, farm employers had formed associations, which
handled the logistics of recruiting workers and assigning them to member
farmers as needed. In the last year and a half of the war, the Extension
Service came to rely on these organizations, not just for calculating growers' labor needs, but also for estimating "prevailing wages" in particular
locales. Thus employer associations functioned as trusts: fixing wages locally, discouraging members from paying above the agreed upon "prevailing wage," pressing for the "certification" of their need for foreign
workers, and opposing unionization efforts. They did so, moreover, with
the federal government's blessing and encouragement.[27]

By the late 1940s, there were some four hundred of these agricultural
pressure groups, some of which united producers of the same commodity, like the National Cotton Council of America, and some that united
growers in particular regions, like the Florida Fruit and Vegetable Association, headed by L. L. Chandler. They wielded enormous clout in state
houses and in Washington, where rural lawmakers with years of seniority
dominated the House and Senate Agriculture Committees.[28] And they uni-
formly backed the extension of the wartime guestworker programs.

Reinventing Non-immigrants

In 1945, the only group that actively opposed the extension of the wartime programs was a ragtag but outspoken outfit called the National Farm Labor Union (NFLU), the postwar incarnation of the Southern Tenant Farmers Union.[29] The charismatic socialist H. L. Mitchell had formed the interracial Southern Tenant Farmers Union in 1934 to protest the displacement of the South's sharecroppers and tenant farmers by the New Deal's crop reduction policies.[30] But there weren't many sharecroppers or tenants left by the war's end, most having been transformed into landless laborers by New Deal crop reduction programs and mechanization. Mitchell thus shifted the union's orientation from building an organization of the nation's poorest farmers to building a national union of its farm workers.

By the end of 1945, the union reported 20,000 members, but its grassroots campaign was no match for well-organized and well-connected farm employers. Between poll taxes, grandfather clauses, literacy restrictions, white primaries, and residency requirements, the union's faithful could rarely vote, let alone shape policy. And the union certainly didn't have the kind of budget that could influence political campaigns. Ironically, it would eventually cultivate more powerful allies as the balance of power in Congress gradually shifted to urban congressional districts—where lawmakers had little to lose by defending the rural poor. In the meantime, the NFLU waged a lonesome campaign against imported farmworkers.

In early 1946, the NFLU affiliated with the American Federation of Labor and hired Ernesto Galarza—a Mexican immigrant and former farmworker with a Ph.D. in Political Science from Columbia University—as its Director of Research and Education. Together Mitchell and Galarza railed unsuccessfully against the second extension of the wartime guestworker programs. In January, Mitchell reported in the *Farm Labor News* that Ed O'Neal, "the Alabama cotton planter who heads the Farm Bureau," was in Washington, D.C., lobbying for a law that would appropriate $14 million "to continue importing foreign workers for exploitation this year on the big farms and plantations of the nation." Hundreds of thousands of underemployed farm laborers in the South would be happy to take jobs in other areas of the United States, Mitchell insisted. NFLU members sent telegraphs to President Truman from their annual convention, suggesting, whimsically, that the government seize and distribute large plantations and commercial farms in the United States, "just as General MacArthur was doing in Japan."[31] Not surprisingly, they got no response from Truman.

At first it seemed as though Mitchell's volley of press releases had no effect whatsoever. "Just before Congress adjourned for Christmas, the bill was slipped in as an amendment to the agricultural deficiency appropriation," Mitchell wrote angrily. "It was passed without debate and signed by the President. No one realized what had been done except the slick Farm Bureau lobbyists in Washington." Guestworkers were not cheaper than domestic workers, Mitchell insisted. The program would cost taxpayers $347 for each farmworker imported, although the average cost to transport a domestic farmworker a thousand miles round trip [by bus, presumably] was only $75.[32] The extension's purpose, according to Mitchell, was to depress domestic workers' wages. Congressmen and senators "elected from agricultural areas" were "[t]he most powerful and reactionary enemies of the working people of America," according to the NFLU.[33] "Big Farmers Plot[ted] to Flood Nation With Cheap Foreign Labor," Mitchell warned.[34]

Then, for a few short days in 1947, it seemed as though the NFLU had won. To Mitchell and Galarza's glee, Congress voted to dismantle the War Food Administration and, with it, the Emergency Labor Importation Program. The Caribbean and Mexican guestworker programs both seemed to be dead.[35] The NFLU celebrated, though Mitchell noted soberly that Congress simultaneously cut the migrant health, housing, and educational programs that had served both foreign *and* domestic farmworkers in federal labor camps during the war.

Mitchell and Galarza soon discovered, however, that the labor importation programs were not dead but transformed. Congress had not voted to suspend the importation of foreign farmworkers; it had simply banned the federal government from footing the bill.

It was U.S. Sugar that had saved the Caribbean guestworker program from extinction. In the summer of 1947, Fred Sikes and Earl Morrison, who represented the only company that was by then completely dependent on guestworkers for harvest labor, visited INS headquarters in Philadelphia. "We were concerned," Sikes later recalled, "that even though the war was over we would not find sufficient American labor to harvest the crops, so we began to explore ways to continue the program on a private basis."[36] There they met the U.S. commissioner of immigration, who informed them that the "ninth proviso" of the 1917 Immigration Act continued to give the INS authority to admit "otherwise inadmissible" foreigners on a temporary basis. According to Earl Morrison, the immigration commissioner "showed Fred all the laws that would permit a private program with a foreign country. He told us how to go about doing it, everything about it. He told us all the people to see."[37] As long as the secretary of labor gave his assurance that local workers were unavailable and employers were prepared to put up bonds to insure that foreign workers' stay would indeed be temporary, the commissioner general of immigration could admit unlimited numbers of foreign workers. Thus the INS, the agency so resistant to the creation of the Caribbean guestworker program during the war, orchestrated its rebirth.[38] Jubilant, Sikes and Morrison shared the good news with apple, tobacco, and other producers who relied on large numbers of Caribbean workers, and together they relaunched the West Indian and Bahamian guestworker programs on a privately run but federally sanctioned basis.[39]

That summer, the federal government disposed of the fifty-two permanent and seventy temporary migrant labor camps it had built to house domestic workers during the Depression and war, selling them to growers' associations for just one dollar a piece. The NFLU called the sale of the camps "one of the blackest marks on the record of the Congress of the United States." "[A]ll of the farm labor camps built by the government for the use of farm workers and their families, is [sic] now in the hands of the big farmers," the NFLU noted in the *Union Labor News*. As a result, "rents have greatly increased, health and sanitation services have been abolished, and all child care services are at an end."[40] The NFLU, which might have purchased the labor camps itself, didn't learn of the clearance sale until it was over.

In December, federal officials stopped recruiting and transporting foreign workers, washing their hands of responsibility for negotiating, signing, or guaranteeing the terms of foreign workers' contracts. In their place, growers' associations now bargained directly with foreign governments, who recruited workers for them. Instead of being contracted by the federal government, guestworkers were now bound to the particular employers or employer associations who advanced their fares, just like nineteenth-century debt migrants. The difference was that at the end of their contracts indentured servants could stay in the country or colony that had recruited them; postwar guestworkers were classified as "non-immigrants," who had no right to stay or be reclassified as permanent immigrants. Temporary workers would be permanently temporary.

DOOMED IN ADVANCE

The NFLU soon discovered what privatized guestworker programs would mean for the fortunes of organized labor in agriculture. The same year that the guestworker programs lost their federal funding, Mitchell and Galarza launched organizing campaigns among fruit harvesters in California and Florida, the two states where seasonal farm laborers worked most often. As soon as the union began to make headway, it found guestworkers from the Caribbean and Mexico in direct competition with its members.

In California, the NFLU targeted the DiGiorgio Fruit Corporation's 1,100-acre Arvin Ranch, where half the workforce consisted of Anglo workers who had been there since they were brought in to break Mexican workers' strikes during the Great Depression. Once the union signed up members, its leaders made overtures to DiGiorgio. When they were rebuffed, the union called a strike. On the first day, two-thirds of the workers walked out. The NFLU pioneered a strategy, dubbed "the world's longest picket line," which consisted of a long caravan of cars and trucks bearing strikers. Twenty-one-year-old Cesar Chavez was on that picket line. The NFLU also urged supporters to boycott companies that sold DiGiorgio's products, a strategy that the United Farm Workers would expand on dramatically in the 1960s. Most remarkably, all the Braceros on the farm joined the strike.[41] After a week, however, the Mexican consul ordered the Braceros to return to work, although the use of Braceros during a labor dispute violated the U.S.-Mexican agreement. Instead of removing the Braceros, as the bilateral agreement required, the U.S. Department of Labor authorized hundreds of additional contract workers and DiGiorgio's lawyers secured an injunction against union pickets. The union got the injunction cancelled seventeen months later, but by that time the strike was long over.[42]

To finish off the union, DiGiorgio filed and won a libel suit against the NFLU for a film the union had produced, called "Poverty in the Valley of Plenty." The judgment forced the union to find and destroy every copy of the film, which had been distributed widely by allies in the labor movement. Over the next decade, the company sued anyone who showed a copy of the film.[43]

Meanwhile, in Florida the NLFU launched a campaign to organize Florida's 70,000 citrus packinghouse workers, who were mostly white and local. Because they were packinghouse workers, not fieldworkers, they enjoyed the right of collective bargaining and could call for National Labor Relations Board elections.[44] By April 1947, two hundred NLFU members had won a collective bargaining agreement, which, according to the union, would mean an "excellent" piece rate, overtime pay (unheard of in agriculture), a maintenance-of-union-membership clause (so the union contract would remain in force if the company was sold), and a grievance procedure. A month later and nearly twenty years before the UFW began to win union contracts in California, the NFLU won twenty-two out of twenty-four NLRB elections among citrus workers in Florida. There would be no Cesar Chavez in the Sunshine State, however, no social movement of national import. By the time H. L. Mitchell was publicizing the union's victories, it had become clear that citrus industry officials had merely agreed to concessions in their rush to get their crops in. Once the oranges were picked, packed, and shipped, citrus industry officials scrambled to secure Bahamian guestworkers, who had no collective bargaining rights and could be deported for striking. With their members supplanted by guestworkers, the NFLU quit Florida altogether.[45]

The NFLU went on to lead nine more strikes in California over the next few years, some of which led to concessions, but ending growers' access to immigrant workers—whether in the United States on contracts or without authorization—became the NFLU's obsession. As long as growers had direct access to foreign workers, Galarza quickly concluded, unionization in agriculture was "doomed in advance."[46]

GOING PRIVATE

Any hope that the guestworker programs would help to uplift conditions for domestic farmworkers in the United States died with the rebirth of private recruiting. With Uncle Sam out of the foreign labor supply business, growers negotiated new contracts that passed costs formerly paid by the U.S. government on to the workers themselves. Instead of traveling to the United States on navy ships at U.S. taxpayers' expense, Caribbean men now came to the United States on chartered planes, and worked off their fare in the fields. Employers paid workers' return fare, but only if they completed the season without incident, which made airfare a tool of labor discipline. Housing was no longer free, either. Growers made payroll deductions for housing and food, plus 3 percent for medical insurance, and another 3 percent to pay the salaries of the Caribbean liaisons and to defray employers' recruiting and management costs. An additional 10 percent of workers' pay was withheld for them in government banks at home to encourage the workers to return at the end of their contracts, as Edward, former king of Great Britain and governor of the Bahamas, had recommended. Jamaican men collected their money with great difficulty, since their government wanted to hold it as long as possible, and the government, not the workers, earned the interest on it.[47]

Caribbean guestworkers were not party to these new terms, and they were not happy with them when they learned of the new contract's contents. George Winton, the federal manager of the Clewiston, Florida, camp, noted in one of his final reports that "The Jamaican workers are very anxious concerning their new contract, a copy of which has been read and explained to them by supervisors in each camp. There has been a great deal of discussion of this matter," he added, "the general feeling being one of dissatisfaction as to contents of the contract." Some Jamaican sugarcane cutters went on strike to protest the new contract; others jumped their contracts and took their chances as unauthorized immigrants. "It is my opinion," Winton concluded, "that if this document is presented in its present form there will be a wholesale movement of Jamaicans being repatriated who might otherwise remain and work."[48]

Winton underestimated just how much Jamaicans needed the work. Jamaican guestworkers continued to signal their bitterness over having to pay for the services of the liaisons—services they considered woefully inadequate—by dubbing the new payroll deductions the "MacDonald money," after Herbert MacDonald, the chief liaison. But if some men quit and returned home in protest, there were always others waiting to take their place.[49]

Not all growers were thrilled about the privatized labor supply system, either. The new contract passed transportation, recruitment, and housing costs on to the workers, but growers had to be willing to advance those costs. To growers who were accustomed to hiring workers at the gates of labor camps or at street corner "shape ups," and who generally paid farmworkers in cash, the process of advancing fares, applying for permission to import labor, recruiting overseas, arranging visas and transportation, building appropriate housing, paying workers by check, and wiring a portion of their pay to overseas banks was far too much trouble. Some growers joined together to share these costs and responsibilities; the Florida Vegetable Committee that L. L. Chandler chaired during the war became a labor supply cooperative called the Florida Fruit and Vegetable Association; U.S. Sugar organized the Florida Sugar Producers Association, which recruited for U.S. Sugar and several smaller companies; and northern importers of Caribbean guestworkers formed the Labor Users' Association. But most small growers found it easier to switch back to domestic labor. As a result, the British West Indian and Bahamian programs shrunk from about 50,000 workers in 1947 to just 5,000 in 1950.[50]

Though most growers dropped out of the newly privatized scheme, the small minority of growers who continued to use West Indian and Bahamian labor became faithful converts to privatization. After 1947, most Caribbean contract workers were imported by the three employer associations. The members of these three organizations benefited from the fact that they could now re-request or, as they put it, "predesignate" workers who had worked well and without complaint in the past. Indeed, by 1950, virtually all of the remaining five thousand West Indians coming to the United States annually had been predesignated. When Jamaican authorities protested that it was politically untenable to let a few thousand men reap the benefits of the program when so many Jamaicans were under-employed, U.S. employers agreed to negotiate the percentage of recruits that would be predesignated each year. In exchange, growers insisted on a greater role in selecting new recruits and on West Indian officials' collaboration in maintaining a registry of troublemakers, which was dubbed the

"U-list" or "Undesirable list" after grower representatives explained that the word "blacklist" was frowned upon in the United States.[51]

Growers used their new control over the recruitment process to avoid the sort of men likely to cause trouble. They didn't want sugarcane cutters from Jamaican plantations, because they had a standard of comparison and were likely to be union members. They certainly didn't want any more sailors, typesetters, tradesmen, or sons of car dealers. They turned up their noses at construction workers back from Panama or Cuba. In fact, anyone with a stamp in his passport showing that he had been somewhere other than where guestworkers went would be rejected outright.[52]

Growers' ideal recruits were peasant farmers from postage stamp-sized plots in Jamaica's lush hills and mountain villages, where farms were so steep that goats and cows sometimes fell to their deaths. There in the mountains, there was little competition from Jamaica's sugarcane plantations or its budding tourist industry. Recruiters could find hardworking men who scratched out a living growing yams, cassava, dasheens, mangos, breadfruit, corn, red peas, coffee, pimento, often twenty crops or more on an acre or two. There they could find men who had few if any opportunities to earn spare cash at home; men with calloused hands, strong backs, and families to return to, in many cases more than one.[53]

With Jamaica's population swelling by 30 percent between the census of 1943 and the next in 1960, the countryside was crowded with willing recruits. Many rural people were migrating to Kingston and its urban environs, looking for work in construction, new assembly plants, or domestic service, and hoping for amenities like running water and flush toilets. Still, most "country people" lived in the parish of their birth and most had only a few years of formal education, if any. Their prospects of earning enough money to pay their children's school fees, buy more land, or a few farm animals was slim. Nearly half of all men working in agriculture earned less than £50 a year (approximately $250). More than 90 percent earned less than £200 ($1,000).[54]

It's no surprise, then, that when radio stations announced that U.S. recruiters were coming to a regional recruitment center on a specific day, ten men would arrive for every job available, and those were just the men who had managed to secure recruitment tickets from a local MP (or buy one from someone who had). Once inside, each recruit would be sent to a man sitting behind a table, who would ensure that his name didn't appear on the "U-list." As a U.S. Sugar official put it: "we . . . check our black book to see if a man has breached."[55] If the applicant made it past the U-list, he'd be sent over to be examined by an American or West Indian recruiter, who would look in his mouth, feel his hands for callouses and his arms for strong muscles. He might be told to turn around and bend all the way forward, while the recruiters felt his spine and back muscles. All the while he would try to answer questions — "Are you ready to work hard?" "Can you follow instructions?" "Do you eat pork?" "Will you work on Sundays?" — questions designed to determine his attitude and his ability to follow instructions in American English as opposed to Jamaica's rapid-fire patois.[56] Men quickly learned to tell recruiters what they wanted to hear.

A shake of a recruiter's head would send a man back out the door. A nod meant he was on to Kingston at his own expense for a medical exam, which involved X-rays, tests for infectious diseases, and, oddly, a prostate exam, most likely the first for most recruits. (One can only wonder what men thought of the United States, where having another man's finger inserted up one's anus seemed to be a prerequisite for farm work.)

Not even that deterred Jamaican men from applying. In 1960, one in forty Jamaican men between the ages of eighteen and thirty-nine headed for the United States through the "farmworker programme," a far cry from the one in six who came during World War II. But out in "the country," the program's impact was even more profound. Perhaps one in twenty Jamaican *agricultural workers* spent part of 1960 in the United States under contract, and fully half of all Jamaican farmworkers lined up for a chance to go.[57] For rural Jamaicans, the farmworker program was their best hope of getting a little ahead, of earning wages three times higher than they could make at home doing similar work, of "paying some smalls," as one man put it.[58]

RACE TO THE BOTTOM

In the United States, Jamaican farmworkers found themselves in competition with domestic workers, the white, black, Mexican, Puerto Rican, and Native American men and women who made up the vast majority of the agricultural workforce. They also vied with other guestworkers: Mexican Braceros; vegetable workers from the Bahamas; experienced sugarcane cutters from the unionized islands of Barbados, St. Kitts, Nevis, and Antigua; and British Guyanans from the South American coast.[59] Leaford Williams wrote that Jamaicans working in Stevens Point, Wisconsin, worked alongside Mexican laborers who always seemed to be sitting around. It didn't occur to him that the Mexicans might have been conducting a work stoppage, though he noted that they seemed to be singing "We Shall Overcome" in Spanish, a tune that had been written during the Gastonia textile strike of 1929 and probably traveled west with UCAPAWA, the United Cannery Agricultural Packinghouse and Allied Workers Union, which organized Mexican cotton workers in California. "American farmers were delighted with the Jamaican farm workers," Leaford wrote; "the farmers had used Mexicans the year before . . . and [i]t was a fiasco." He noted, at the same time, that Mexicans received inferior treatment.[60]

Workers were sometimes divided among growers who preferred one group over another, based on growers' presumptions about national character. "I kid the Jamaicans and tell them I know where the lost tribes of Israel wound up," remarked Fred Sikes of U.S. Sugar. "The Jamaican is excitable and a born griper. He doesn't give a damn if you do anything about his complaint as long as you listen to it. Just build a wailing wall in each housing camp and you'll have no problems." "He's also the most group minded and is easily lead," he added. In contrast, Barbadians were individualists and more thrifty and proud than Jamaicans, according to Sikes. William Anderson, Jr., of the Florida Fruit and Vegetable Association, thought Jamaicans were more individualistic and Barbadians more excitable. These sorts of preconceptions led some growers to try to mix workers by nationality to prevent workers from organizing and others to choose one group over another.[61]

Race, nationality, and sex seemed to dictate who did what. In Florida, only West Indians harvested sugarcane, but African Americans, including African American women, were hired to plant it. Corn, celery, and beans were black crops; white workers got preference in citrus. Packers and processors seemed to prefer women. The segmentation of the labor force may have given groups of workers a sense of entitlement to certain kinds of work and heightened competition among groups, but it also divided them. Workers of the world generally did not unite.[62]

The agricultural workforce was further divided by the terms under which farmworkers labored. Mexicans, West Indians, and Bahamians signed different guestworker contracts. Puerto Rican farmworkers also came to the mainland on contracts, but could not be threatened with deportation if they broke them. Citizen workers had no contracts to bind *or* protect them.

Then there were the unauthorized immigrants from Mexico—commonly called "wetbacks" by their detractors—whose numbers rose dramatically as the Bracero Program grew. In 1949, the INS reported that it had "located" almost 280,000 unauthorized immigrant farm laborers at a time when there were just 107,000 Braceros in the country. The following year, the number of Braceros was only 67,500, while the total number of "wetbacks located" had reached almost half a million. By 1954, the number of "known" unauthorized immigrants exceeded one million, outnumbering Braceros threefold.[63] Unauthorized immigrants had the worst of both worlds. Like domestic workers, they had no job security and no contractual guarantees, and they often depended on rapacious crew leaders to find them work. But, like guestworkers, they could be threatened with deportation. On the other hand, an unauthorized immigrant could often walk away from a particularly abusive grower; if a guestworker did the same, he instantly became an unauthorized immigrant.

As these diverse groups fanned out across the country in search of work, they came in increasing contact and competition with each other. The number of Braceros exploded in Texas in the 1950s, forcing Tejanos to leave in search of less crowded fields. The Tejanos headed north along well-worn routes to the Midwest and East, but also East to the Atlantic coast's "migrant stream," appearing in Virginia and Florida fields in the early 1950s.[64] Jamaicans and other British West Indian guestworkers monopolized sugarcane harvesting but also pushed white "fruit tramps" out of the apple orchards from Virginia to New York.

Although particular groups tended to monopolize particular tasks in particular industries, growers' ability to switch workforces rapidly served as a form of labor discipline, as when growers chased the National Farmers Labor Union out of the citrus industry by hiring a couple of thousand Bahamians guestworkers. History repeated itself in 1951, when Bahamians were used a second time to undermine a union campaign.[65]

In most cases, however, it wasn't so much real competition as the threat of competition that gave growers the upper hand in negotiations with sending governments and individual farmworkers. In 1953, for example, A.G.H. Gardner-Brown of the Colonial Office of the Bahamas reported that growers responded to his efforts to negotiate on behalf of Bahamians by pointing out "the ease of getting labour from Puerto Rico."[66]

This sort of national competition undermined the ability and willingness of individual state actors to advocate for their countrymen. West Indian liaisons began to spend at least as much time trying to protect West Indians' jobs as they did advocating for their rights. In May 1952, Herbert MacDonald reported gleefully that "the experiment to use Puerto Rican workers in Connecticut was . . . backfiring. Over twenty of these workers have gone AWOL within the last few days, and they have called a strike and have demanded hot lunches." "We shall be watching this with much interest," he added.[67] It didn't seem to occur to MacDonald that he might have demanded hot lunches for West Indian workers too. Liaison J. L. Meagher reported that, "Owing to the Puerto Rican workers' entrance into Tobacco Valley the requirements for BWI workers have been cut by 300 men." "All our workers were called to meetings during this month to have explained to them the very serious menace that this competition means," he noted. "Our workers are inclined to dismiss the Puerto Ricans as poor workers. I hope I have disillusioned them. These Puerto Rican workers were specially chosen. They are intended as an advance guard to oust us from the work we have done here since 1943. I have requested our men to treat them courteously in Camp, but to outdo them at work. Already foremen are saying that the Puerto Ricans show more willingness than our men. The new brooms are sweeping clean at the moment. This is serving to rouse our workers to surpass them." "It is hoped, however," he noted in closing, "that the Puerto Ricans will soon discover that as U.S. Citizens they can obtain more lucrative work outside than any in the Tobacco fields."[68]

In 1951, the various British West Indian governments closed ranks to improve their bargaining position vis-à-vis growers. After the Windward Islands—Grenada, St. Lucia, St. Vincent, and Dominica—joined the farmworker program that year, the sending governments of the British West Indies organized a Regional Labour Board charged with representing British West Indian colonies collectively in negotiations with American employers.[69] It was then that they consolidated the various liaison services into one British West Indian Central Labour Organization (WICLO). Instead of each government going its own way and trying to secure more jobs for its citizens by underbidding the others, the Regional Labour Board negotiated one contract for all and divvied the jobs among the sending nations, based on an agreed-upon formula (as the most populous country in the British West Indies, Jamaica received 80–90 percent of the total).

The advent of the Regional Labour Board prevented British West Indian nations from undercutting each other, but the problem of competition among farmworker groups persisted. The Bahamas, which is not in the West Indies, remained outside the Regional Labour Board's "trust," as did Puerto Rico and Mexico, the colossus among guestworker-sending nations. Thus growers' ability to play off one national group against another remained long after the Regional Labour Board's formation. In 1952, when an employer refused to dismiss two white supervisors on a Florida farm for assaulting some guestworkers, Brigadier Buxton Randall, the head of the Bahamian program, withdrew all the Bahamians employed by that grower and refused to send more. Instead of apologizing and promising better behavior, the grower simply contacted Herbert MacDonald, who sent West Indians in their place. When Randall complained to MacDonald, and insisted that he withdraw the West Indian workers, MacDonald refused, arguing that the employer had "no doubt" learned "his lesson." Though MacDonald noted in his report that he regretted the incident, he could not help bragging that "our B.W.I. workers are . . . superior workers to the Bahamians."[70]

Like MacDonald, the liaison officers under him got into the spirit of competition and spent an increasing amount of time trying to get their charges to work harder and more efficiently. In 1951, liaison G. H. Scott accompanied fifteen West Indians—representing four different colonies—to Sugar Land, Texas where he realized, after watching them work, that they needed to "become adapted to cotton picking." To ensure that they compared well to more experienced cotton harvesters, Scott drove to neighboring fields "where they had natives picking." He watched how they did it, and then returned to his own charges to demonstrate what he had learned.[71] Liaison Charles Browne found the 340 men at "Mr. Hoyt's" in Leachville, Arkansas "in high spirits," but when Hoyt complained that "the men were not making an effort to learn to pick cotton," Browne checked the payroll records and determined that the men were marking time until their transfer to Florida." To get them to work harder, Browne suggested that Hoyt send the best pickers to Florida first, so as not to reward the slackers. "This notice caused an immediate jump in production the following day," he reported with satisfaction.[72]

Fear of losing "West Indians' jobs" to competing groups of workers made the liaisons desperate to settle disputes, even if that meant settling them in employers' favor. In 1952, Joffre C. David, the general manager of the Florida Fruit and Vegetable Association, wrote to Herbert MacDonald, thanking him for resolving "the incident" at the Harlem Heights Labor Camp in Winter Garden, Florida, "before the CIO or other opponents of the foreign labor program could capitalize on it." There would always be a "small number of workers . . . temperamentally unfit or emotionally unstable" who will "create trouble," David remarked, so it was "important that these men be weeded out as soon as they are found, because they are the ones who aggravate the employers or their foremen and who create dissatisfaction among the other workers." "It has been our experience," he continued, "that the longer these types of individuals are permitted to remain among the rank and file of workers, the worse the situation gets, and their removal invariably clears the atmosphere and everybody is happy again." Listing the four men "properly repatriated for cause," David reminded MacDonald that they were to be barred "forever" from future recruitment for work in Florida.[73] Rather than supporting workers' militancy, West Indian liaisons had also become enforcers of labor discipline.

The more liaison officers had to defend their charges' jobs against encroachment, the less inclined they were to take on growers who were abusive or who violated workers' contracts, though the workers were paying the liaisons to do precisely that. The liaisons could have withheld offshore workers from growers who behaved badly, but this almost never happened. Interviewed in 1966, Herbert MacDonald's replacement, Harold Edwards, could recall only three occasions in which WICLO withdrew workers from particular employers (two of which involved growers threatening workers with guns). WICLO did sometimes ask growers to remove particular foremen, but if WICLO did not take a worker's side in a dispute, he had no other avenues of appeal.[74]

As a result, the liaisons quickly lost what little credibility they had with workers, an advent growers happily abetted. Employers never involved liaisons in disputes unless the employers knew they, the employers, were in the right, explained a section foreman for the Sugar Cane Growers Co-operative in 1966. "The liaison officer is the worker's man, but he has no choice except to back us in disputes," he noted. "If we've messed up, we won't call him. Since he's got a contract to uphold, the liaison officer ends up backing us." As a result, workers tended to see the liaisons as company men. "Most of the workers we employ won't deal with a liaison officer," the foreman continued, "because they know when he comes he's going to back us. The liaison officer is a man caught in the middle."[75] Workers tend to put it more starkly: "the liaison officer, who . . . should . . . stand by your side . . . them do not care."[76] Workers assumed that the liaisons' loyalties had been bought by employers, an allegation liaison Walter Comrie said was true in some cases. "The liaisons," as one man put it, "were just for themselves."[77]

The liaisons weren't all for themselves, however. Despite his efforts to market Caribbean workers, Herbert MacDonald also advocated for them, and he was a constant thorn in growers' sides. According to Liaison Officer Walter Comrie, employers became "openly disenchanted" with MacDonald by the early 1950s. By 1955, they refused to work with him, "forcing him to resign."[78] Comrie, who arrived a few years later, felt intense pressure to ignore abuses but did not. Fred Sikes went out of his way to try to "buy [him] over," he recalled, even giving Comrie his key to the Playboy Club and building a fishpond in his yard. When Sikes's bald efforts to corrupt Comrie failed, Comrie recalled, "he had me transferred."[79]

Yet MacDonald's successor in 1955 was more than willing to live in the world growers had made. Indeed, if growers could have handpicked a chief liaison, they couldn't have done better than Harold Francis Quinn Edwards. Born in Kingston, Edwards was the first black chief liaison, but his race did not make him any more inclined to advocacy. He was charming, articulate, and so beloved by growers that Ashton Hart of the Valley Growers [Apple] Co-op wrote a tribute in verse on the occasion of Edwards's 1984 retirement party (after which he ended up working another decade). Besides citing "Harry's" enormous love of brandy and his even bigger ego, the verses ended with:

> His years of good service we most heartily savor
> For we apple folks are the fruit of his labor!
> Suffice it to say—and here I will stop—
> "Harold Francis Quinn Edwards"
> You're the pick of the crop!

Farmworkers wrote no such testimonial.

By the mid-1950s, when Harold Edwards became chief liaison, the only direction guestworkers in the United States could go was down. By then, farm employers enjoyed a sort of international shape-up, where if one nation's workers refused to get on the back of growers' truck, another one would. Each group of workers—Braceros, unauthorized immigrants, West Indians, Bahamians, Puerto Ricans, and domestic workers—competed against the others, all in a race to the bottom.

While Jamaican guestworkers were stuck in a no man's land between nations, a tiny number of Jamaicans won the right to remain in the United States permanently and strive for the sort of gains guestworkers could no longer even imagine. Leaford Williams was one of them, and his return to the United States as an immigrant, rather than as a "non-immigrant" temporary worker, demonstrates what permanent immigration status made possible and what was virtually impossible without it. Arriving in London after World War II, Leaford got a room in a hostel and soon started receiving a welfare check in the amount of £3 a week. While he studied for the civil service exam, he got a job at a cafeteria and then another at a post office. A few months later, he landed a job at the Ministry of Education based on a friend's recommendation. Despite his success in London, Williams was still determined to return to the United States.

After a year in England, the INS allowed Williams to enter, not as a guestworker but as a permanent resident, under the sponsorship of his uncle. Leaford then earned bachelor's and master's degrees in international relations at Georgetown and American University, respectively, specializing in Far Eastern and South Asian Affairs, after which he joined the U.S. Air Force. He was sent as a clerk to Okinawa, where he rapidly learned Japanese. He returned home to the United States in May 1950, a month before the start of the Korean War. Suddenly, his obvious talent for language was in demand. The U.S. Foreign Service rushed him to its language school in Monterrey to learn Korean and, because only citizens could attend, he was hurriedly naturalized. He later served as a translator during the peace negotiations that ended the war.[80]

Looking back at his life in his memoir, *Journey into Diplomacy: A Black Man's Shocking Discovery*, Leaford Williams was obviously proud of his achievements but not romantic about his American journey. In fact, his memoir largely concerns his struggle to overcome racism in the U.S. Foreign Service. Yet Williams is the American Dream personified. He lives in a modest home in Washington, D.C., and he and his African American wife have three successful children: a daughter who works for the navy in Florida, another who is director of admissions at Howard University, and a son who teaches high school. Now retired, Williams lives part time at "Fort Leaford Villa," his Jamaican guesthouse, which sits above the road he took to Montego Bay, bouncing along in a flatbed truck, all those years before.[81] None of this would have been possible had he remained a guestworker in the United States. His success is largely due to his hard work and obvious talents, but none of that would have mattered had he been forced to keep cycling back and forth between his family's tiny Jamaican plot and the cane fields of Florida. Only permanent residency and later citizenship allowed Williams to put his obvious abilities to use, to avail himself of every opportunity, and to transform his own life and his children's possibilities. Leaford's success depended on his escape from guestworkers' race to the bottom.

CHAPTER SIX

A Riotous Success

*Guestworkers, "Illegal Immigrants," and the Promise of
Managed Migration*

IN 1949, prospective Braceros gathered in Juárez, just south of the El Paso
Immigration Station. There they waited for an opportunity to pick cotton in Texas, as U.S. and Mexican officials haggled over the terms of a
new bilateral agreement. Under the old 1947 agreement, U.S. employers
had been required to pay the "prevailing wage," which the U.S. Department of Labor determined by asking committees of growers what they
planned to pay in the upcoming season. Under this system of government-
sponsored price-fixing, the prevailing wage had been set at a paltry $1.50
per hundred pounds of cotton, or approximately 25 cents an hour for a
twelve-hour day, substantially more than the rate paid during the Depression but about the same as that paid forty years earlier, in 1909. In reality,
most farmers paid far less. Mexican officials demanded that the official
wage rate for Braceros increase to $3.00 "per hundred" and demanded that
this minimum be specified in workers' contracts. Negotiating on behalf of
growers, U.S. officials refused. They countered with an offer of $2.50 per
hundred but patently refused to specify this or any wage in workers' contracts. When Mexican authorities rejected this offer, negotiations stalled,
the bilateral agreement lapsed, and the recruitment of Braceros stopped.
Mexican men gathered at border stations across the Southwest to await a
resolution. Eventually, U.S. officials decided to recruit Braceros "unilaterally," without Mexico's approval. After months of delay, the INS opened
the border at El Paso to thousands of Mexican farmworkers who waded
across the Rio Grande "in sight of the Border Patrol," Ernesto Galarza
recalled. The INS then "herded them into temporary enclosures and immediately paroled them to cotton growers who trucked the men at once
to the fields," putting them to work at $2.50 per hundred. The INS called
this process "drying out the wetbacks." Over the next five days, some
six thousand men crossed the border. With ample labor secured, growers
dropped the picking price back to $1.50. Mexico's officials had little choice
but to sign the agreement on growers' terms.[1]

There was no Jamaican equivalent of the border conflict of 1949 or
of the nearly identical events of 1954. Still, this southwestern story is

pertinent to the history of the Caribbean guestworker program because it was U.S. officials' high-handedness at the U.S.-Mexican border that eventually turned popular and congressional sentiment against guestworker programs in general. In 1964, the Bracero Program finally would succumb to a hail of controversy. The H2 Program lived on, though severely constrained by official reforms.

More importantly, perhaps, the border wars of 1949 and 1954 reveal the intimate and early relationship between illegal immigration and authorized guestworker programs, a relationship that continues to this day. Guestworker programs survived and grew in the postwar period precisely because Americans who feared "illegal immigration" believed that guestworker programs offered a manageable alternative to unregulated migration. Manageability proved illusory, however; growers regularly disregarded the promises they made in the labor contracts they signed; dissatisfied guestworkers jumped their contracts and went back to being "illegals"; immigrants kept crossing the border without authorization, encouraged no doubt by the fact that the worst that would happen is that the INS would transform them into Braceros.

To the extent that this was managed migration, it was managed to benefit the nation's largest farm employers, not to benefit farmworkers. Managed migration was a success from growers' perspective, precisely because the Caribbean and Mexican guestworker programs kept wages low and labor plentiful. From policy makers' perspective, the guestworker programs seemed like sensible and legitimate ways to keep the border open. Temporary worker contracts and guestworkers' deportability added a patina of legality to what was, in essence, a grower-dominated labor recruitment scheme.

"Drying out the Wetbacks"

The idea of transforming unauthorized immigrants into legal but temporary contract workers was almost as old as the guestworker programs themselves. When the government-run program first began during World War II, Mexico had imposed a boycott of Texas in response to the Lone Star State's history of anti-Mexican discrimination, mistreatment, and even murder.[2] But Mexican farmworkers crossed into Texas anyway, creating a crisis for the INS. Mexican migrants were pushed northward by a devastating drought in northern Mexico, which killed nearly 400,000 cattle in the state of Durango alone. They were pulled by wages that were on average five times higher than those available at home. Disregarding their government's boycott, Mexicans came to Texas by the thousands, making their own bargains with growers.[3] In 1947, the INS dealt with the growing presence of these unauthorized migrants in Texas by legalizing 55,000 of them, not as permanent residents, but as Braceros. It then expanded that policy to the whole region. By 1950, the number of Braceros who had been legalized and "paroled" outnumbered those recruited in Mexico five to one.[4]

The "drying out" process made the Bracero Program boom in the postwar period. There was no comparable boom in the Caribbean guestworker programs because there was no comparable illegal immigration problem. Caribbean guestworkers did sometimes jump their contracts and remain in the United States without authorization, but they did so at much lower rates than Braceros, probably because they had no easy way to return home to visit their families and reenter the country. The ocean saw to that.

The fact that Braceros walked away from their contracts so much more often than West Indians and Bahamians is particularly ironic since, after 1947, only the Bracero Program was governed by a bilateral government-to-government agreement. And Mexican leaders, far more than Caribbean workers, made an effort to bargain on behalf of U.S.-bound workers. Unlike the Caribbean programs, which received little media attention in Jamaica once the war ended—except to announce recruitment dates—the Bracero Program was regularly under fire in Mexico. Mexican media reports described discrimination, physical abuse, egregious contract violations, an ineffective grievance procedure, and deportations of men who complained of mistreatment. Particularly damaging were reports that the U.S. Border Patrol served at the pleasure of American agribusiness, suspending its deportations of illegal immigrations during the harvest and sometimes resuming them just before payday. As far as Mexican officials could tell, Braceros seemed little better off if not worse off than Mexican migrants who crossed the border without authorization.[5]

Mexican officials were also upset at U.S. officials' unilateral recruiting, which seemed to encourage unauthorized border crossings, led to the rise of shantytowns of would-be migrants at the border, and created labor shortages in northern Mexico. Moreover, unilateral recruiting undercut Mexican officials' bargaining power on behalf of Braceros (and their ability to collect bribes from prospective Braceros, an oft reported problem).[6]

Farmworkers Both Alien and Domestic

Mexican officials' complaints and INS reports on the rising number of unauthorized immigrants in the Southwest led to the first official reconsideration of the justice of maintaining guestworker programs when conditions for domestic farmworkers—still the vast majority of the workforce—were so poor. Both the Mexican and Caribbean programs came under scrutiny. The investigation began behind closed doors with a secret study of the border region commissioned by President Truman, which concluded that a large portion of the unauthorized immigrants in south Texas were dissatisfied Braceros who had jumped their contracts. Truman was concerned enough to sign an executive order creating the first President's Commission on Migratory Labor, which he charged with investigating the problems and conditions of migratory farmworkers, "both alien and domestic."[7]

The commissioners held twelve hearings around the country in 1950. The resulting testimony was typical of farm labor hearings before and for years after. On the one hand, farm labor advocates testified that there were too many domestic workers, not too few. Americans would be available to do farmwork, they insisted, when growers paid decent wages and when farmworkers enjoyed the same legal rights as other Americans.[8] The National Farm Labor Union complained that guestworkers were undermining unions' ability to organize. The NFLU's campaign to organize agricultural workers in Connecticut "got nowhere," Roland Watts of the Workers Defense League insisted, "because the Jamaican worker had no right to be represented by a union. If he incurs the displeasure of his employer he is returned to Jamaica and loses the benefits of his contract." Even more damning was the testimony of an INS official who confirmed that the Border Patrol had been instructed not to detain illegal immigrants during harvests.[9]

On the other hand, growers insisted that American workers would not work. "Migrant workers "could earn $20.00 a day," testified LaMonte Graw, a grower and chair of the Florida Farm Labor Advisory Committee, "but they didn't want to work hard enough to earn more than $20 a week." No amount of money would induce "the average migrant worker to accept steady employment," he continued, repeating what had become over the years the farm employers' mantra: "[T]he payment of higher wages is usually an incentive to loaf, *not* to work."[10]

The same arguments and counter-arguments would be repeated at periodic hearings over the next fifty years. This was the first time, however, that a federal commission came down unequivocally on the side of U.S. farmworkers, dismissing out of hand growers' claims that they had to have foreign laborers and documenting growers' manipulation of the Border Patrol.[11] "We have failed to adopt policies designed to insure an adequate supply of . . . [migratory] labor at decent standards of employment," the commissioners asserted. "Actually," they went on, "we have done worse than that. We have used the institutions of government to procure alien labor willing to work under obsolete and backward conditions and thus to perpetuate those very conditions. This not only entrenches a bad system, it expands it."[12]

Although the commissioners condemned the INS's practice of recruiting Braceros from among unauthorized immigrants and recommended that employers who hired illegal immigrants be penalized, they did not insist on an immediate end to the guestworker programs. On the contrary, after extensive testimony from both growers and farm labor advocates— though none from farmworkers, foreign or domestic—the commissioners concluded that the solution to foreign competition was not to eliminate the Mexican and Caribbean guestworker programs but to restore federal oversight of them. "For the Mexicans, who still insisted on a government-to-government agreement," the Commissioners complained, ". . . we virtually abandoned effective scrutiny and enforcement of the Individual Work Contracts." "For the Jamaicans and Bahamians whose governments did not insist on intergovernmental agreements," the report continued ". . . we have given no official scrutiny . . . In these instances, our authorities have permitted the entry of contract alien labor on whatever terms these foreign governments were able to secure in negotiations with private employers of the U.S." The result for Caribbean workers in particular, the report concluded, was "for all practical purposes, the abandonment of rules and conditions" governing living and working standards.[13] The report thus put its faith in managed migration, reaffirming the notion that federal officials could control and supervise the importation of farmworkers if they put their minds to it. "No employer, employer's representative or association of employers, or labor contractor," the Commission argued, "should be permitted to contract directly with foreign workers for employment in the United States."[14]

The National Farm Labor Union called the Commission's report "the most important document issued by the United States government since the Emancipation Proclamation," though it didn't make quite the same splash. By the time it was published, the Korean War was under way, and growers' renewed warnings of wartime labor scarcity drowned out reformers' insistence that guestworkers and undocumented immigrants represented unfair competition to underemployed domestic farmworkers. Truman made an effort to keep the border issue alive, at least as a security measure, requesting a $6.5 million supplemental appropriation for Border Enforcement. But despite a Democratic majority, the House reduced the enforcement subsidy to $4 million in committee and then eliminated it altogether in 1951.[15]

In the end it was Mexico's government that saved the report from the compost heap. Embarrassed by public testimony about the mistreatment of Braceros and their harmful impact on American farmworkers, Mexican authorities refused once again to sign a new agreement with the United States unless changes were made. Recognizing that the bilateral agreement was meaningless without enforcement, they demanded that the United

States do what its President's Commission had recommended: resume full control of the program so it could guarantee the terms of Braceros' contracts; penalize employers who hired unauthorized Mexican immigrants; police its borders; discourage illegal crossing by recruiting from the Mexican interior instead of at the border; and cease encouraging illegal migration by recruiting Braceros from among undocumented Mexican laborers already in the United States.[16]

Mexican authorities could not really enforce a ban on taking work in the United States—that much had been made apparent by the border war of 1949—but they hoped nonetheless that U.S. officials would want to avoid another embarrassing diplomatic incident at the border. Indeed, Mexico's 1951 ultimatum sent U.S. lawmakers scrambling to devise a solution that would satisfy Mexican officials. The result was two bills, either of which would have expanded federal involvement in the Mexican program, though to very different degrees. The question, in other words, was not whether there should be guestworker programs or whether the federal government should be more involved in them, but rather how involved it should be.

One bill, sponsored by Sam Yorty, a freshman Democratic senator from Los Angeles, proposed a return to the sort of federally run recruitment, transportation, and housing program employed during the war. It called for the creation of a National Farm Labor Board made up of industry, labor, and public representatives to determine whether foreign workers were truly required in particular locales and what wage rates really prevailed. The bill would have required growers to search for domestic workers nationwide—even in Hawaii, Puerto Rico, and the Virgin Islands—before the Department of Labor could certify the existence of a labor shortage. It also would have authorized the construction and repair of labor supply centers, childcare centers, and health-care clinics, as in the days of the Farm Security Administration. Finally, and most importantly, the bill responded to the allegation that contract workers were better treated than domestic workers by requiring growers to offer domestic and foreign workers the same wages and conditions.[17] Yorty's bill, in essence, would have meant re-nationalizing the farm labor supply program and reviving farmworkers' welfare state. It had about as much chance of passing as the NFLU's proposal to break up large farms and distribute them to sharecroppers.

W. R. Poage, the Democratic cowboy-cattleman-congressman, who had been representing Texas in the House of Representatives since 1937 (and who would serve forty years more), sponsored the competing bill, House Resolution 3048. It aimed to involve federal authorities just enough to win Mexico's approval and not an iota more, while shifting the costs of the Bracero Program from growers to taxpayers. The

Poage-Ellender bill looked like a guestworker's fantasy in many ways. It restored worker protections that had been abandoned in 1947, clarified those that had been buried in the English-language bilateral agreement, and required that all protections be spelled out in Spanish in the contracts workers saw. Under the bill, the U.S. Labor Department retained responsibility for contracting Mexican workers and enforcing their contracts. The bill authorized government funding for farmworkers' transportation, housing, emergency medical care, and burial expenses, but for Braceros only. Employers did not have to pay a specified minimum wage, but they did have to stipulate in writing whatever wage they were offering, and guarantee that wage for three-quarters of the contract. Growers had to provide insurance coverage, supply tools and housing free of charge, and pay workers' *round-trip* transportation. Domestic workers were promised none of this. Unlike Caribbean guestworkers, moreover, Braceros had the right to choose and reject employers and elect their own representatives. Finally, although the United States was not party to workers' individual contracts (as it had been during World War II), it was clearly identified as the guarantor that growers' contract obligations would be met. From the perspective of workers, the Braceros agreement seemed better than ever.[18]

Significantly, though, the bill would let local rather than national authorities determine whether labor shortages existed, and it expanded the legal definition of "agricultural laborers" to include packing and canning workers, which would have the effect of bringing Braceros into competition with unionized workers. Finally, it allowed the INS to continue the process of "direct recruiting" of Mexicans, a polite euphemism for the offensive euphemism "drying out the wetbacks."[19]

In the House Agricultural Committee, which got first crack at the two bills, the outcome was assured. Committee members thought Yorty's bill was a joke. The committee was chaired by Harold D. Cooley, a North Carolina Democrat with seventeen years of seniority, and vice-chaired by Poage himself. Committee members lampooned the idea of federal management of the farm labor supply, ridiculing anyone, including Department of Labor and Agriculture officials, who testified in support of the idea.[20] Not surprisingly, Poage's bill passed as did the Senate equivalent, which was sponsored by the sugar planter and senate veteran, Allen J. Ellender of Louisiana. The Poage-Ellender bill became Public Law 78 in July 1951. The new law ensured the continuation of the Bracero Program without ensuring that domestic workers received the same contractual guarantees as Braceros. Plus growers got the last laugh: the new U.S. and Mexican agreement that followed cynically stated that Mexican farmworkers would be entitled to all the rights and benefits American farmworkers enjoyed, without mentioning that U.S. farmworkers enjoyed none.[21]

The debate over Public Law 78 further distinguished the West Indian and Bahamian guestworker programs from the Mexican one. Though the private recruiting of Caribbean workers suffered blistering attacks during the President's Commission's hearings a year earlier, the 1951 debates over the Yorty and Poage bills hardly mentioned guestworkers from the Caribbean. Despite some growers' fears, this silence signaled the power, not the weakness, of the growers who hired Caribbean labor.[22] The Bahamian and West Indian programs were not discussed because leading employers of Bahamians and British West Indians didn't want them discussed. "So far as the agricultural interests of Florida are concerned," Florida Senator Spessard Holland explained, "they much prefer not to have any subsidy from the Government in this connection, not to have the Department of Labor serve as an official agency for recruiting offshore laborers." If the price of federal funding was federal interference, they preferred to go it alone. And since Florida growers were already charging Caribbean farmworkers for their recruitment, in-bound flights, housing, and food, they had little to gain from taxpayers' support.[23]

Thus when State Department officials approached a Caribbean delegation to the President's Commission about the prospect of restoring federal oversight over the West Indian and Bahamian programs, West Indian officials demurred, having been warned by U.S. employers that they would not abide a federally run program. Later, in 1951, a delegation of West Indian officials flew to Washington, eager to testify to the importance of the farmworker programs to their domestic economies, but growers warned them away, preferring to keep the Caribbean programs off the agenda and out of the limelight.[24] As of July 1951, the Mexican Program fell under the rubric of Public Law 78 and renewed public control; the Caribbean Programs continued unchanged.

Making Temporary Worker Programs Permanent

A year and a half after the passage of the new, improved Bracero Program, which reauthorized the temporary recruitment of guestworkers on a grand scale, Congress passed the most restrictive immigration legislation in U.S. history. The 1952 omnibus Immigration and Nationality Act, better known as the McCarran-Walter Act, drastically reduced the number of immigrants who could enter the country (reducing the flow of permanent Jamaican immigrants, for example, from 1,000 a year to just 100).

McCarran-Walter was the result of a long, intense struggle between liberal Democrats on the one hand and Republicans and rural Democrats on the other. Liberals wanted to modernize American immigration law, which to them meant abandoning the nation's embarrassing racial restrictions on naturalization and offering sanctuary to Jewish survivors of Nazi concentration camps and other European refugees. Republicans and Democratic conservatives favored a drastic reduction in the number of permanent immigrants to the United States. Within that debate, however, was a secondary conflict over temporary labor migration. Liberal Democrats allied with the resurgent labor movement were increasingly concerned about what they called "the wetback problem." They proposed an increase in the Border Patrol's appropriation to block unauthorized migration from Mexico. Republicans and conservative Democrats fought to guarantee agricultural employers continued access to foreign labor.

The legislation that resulted from this clash of ideas was, not surprisingly, a hodge-podge. In deference to the liberals and in the name of the Cold War goal of courting the allegiance of newly independent nations around the world, the McCarran-Walter Act removed the whites-only naturalization rule that had been in place since 1790. Conceding to conservative sentiment, however, it decreased the number of immigrants who could gain entry to the United States and preserved the old quota system that privileged northern and western European immigrants over their poorer, swarthier, and now sometimes communist counterparts in southern and eastern Europe. Although it finally allowed Asians to be naturalized, it capped their entry at one hundred immigrants per country. Western Hemisphere nations like Mexico remained exempt from quota restrictions, but lawmakers applied the hundred-person cap to colonies, thus blocking many prospective immigrants of color. Thus Jamaica's potential share of the British quota shrunk from one thousand to one hundred.[25] The result was the most restrictive immigration policy in U.S. history, topped with a patina of racial liberalism. President Truman and the liberal wing of the Democratic Party considered it an international embarrassment. Congress passed it over Truman's veto.

Permanent immigrants were out but guestworkers were in like flint. McCarran-Walter drastically reduced permanent immigration from places like Jamaica, Barbados, and the Bahamas but simultaneously reaffirmed the legality of temporary labor recruiting from those same places, replacing the 9th proviso of the now defunct Immigration Act of 1917 with subsection (h) (ii), which allowed for the admission of "non-immigrants" "coming temporarily to the United States to perform temporary services or labor, if unemployed persons capable of performing such service or labor cannot be found in this country."[26] From this point forward, non-Mexican guestworkers entered the United States with "H-2 visas," and were known as "H2 Workers" or just "H2s."

The act reauthorized the temporary admission of "nonimmigrants," but it made no provision for the immigration of foreign farmworkers on a permanent basis, despite growers' insistence that they needed farm labor.

Creating a simple preference system, McCarran-Walter ranked highest the applicants for permanent admission who had "high education, technical training, specialized experience, or exceptional ability."

They were allotted 50 percent of the permanent spots. The other 50 percent went to the immediate relatives of citizens and lawfully admitted aliens. Farmworkers could have been admitted as people with "specialized experience," but weren't. The unskilled, the category into which farmworkers were regularly lumped, appeared in a long list of excluded categories, below psychopaths, drug addicts, lepers, professional beggars, polygamists, prostitutes, and convicts. Immigrant farmworkers would enter temporarily or not at all.[27]

While reauthorizing temporary immigration, McCarran-Walter also assured growers' continued access to unauthorized immigrants. The bill made it a crime to harbor and conceal immigrants who had entered the United States without authorization, but rural lawmakers defeated an amendment that would have made it a crime to *hire* an illegal immigrant, despite Mexico's support for the amendment. The act also prohibited citizens' arrests of unauthorized immigrants, a measure aimed not at right-wing "Minute Men" but at the members of the National Farm Labor Union, who had been making citizens' arrests of illegal immigrants at the border.[28] In the months that followed, lawmakers from border states convinced Congress to *cut* funds earmarked for the Border Patrol.[29] Thus the same Congress that nearly shut the door to permanent immigration gave growers potentially unlimited access to temporary contract workers as well as immunity from prosecution if they passed up Braceros and domestic workers for unauthorized immigrants.

Unsuccessful in their attempt to criminalize growers' access to illegal immigrants, liberal Democrats tried attaching new regulations to growers' use of guestworkers. The rules they proposed, which were issued by the Attorney General's office, aimed to minimize the effect of the guestworker programs on American farmworkers by requiring growers who wanted foreign workers to submit a form, called a clearance order, for each foreign worker an employer wanted to hire. On the form, employers would have to specify the terms of employment, terms that had to meet or exceed standards specified by the U.S. Employment Service. The jobs would have to be offered first to American workers on the same terms. The draft regulations required a statement from "an appropriate representative of any labor organization" as to whether domestic workers were available, what it thought prevailing wages were in the region, and whether it "had any objection to the proposed importation." This was Yorty's bill risen from the grave. Employers, according to the proposed rules, would no longer unilaterally determine whether they needed foreign workers and what they would pay them.[30]

The draft regulations never went into effect. Like all previous farm labor reform efforts, this one died a swift death by lobby. Before the proposed regulations had even been published, growers' protests had convinced the Attorney General that they had to be "reconsidered and revised." The final regulations made no mention of any need to consult area labor unions, nor did they require employers to provide evidence of the effort they had made to locate local labor. Employers could file a single petition for all the foreign workers they sought and pay one $10 fee for the whole group instead of $10 per worker as the draft regulations had required. The private recruiting of guestworkers continued pretty much as before.[31]

Lumber Jacks and Taxi Dancers

Together, Public Law 78, which reauthorized the Bracero Program in 1951, and the 1952 McCarran-Walter Act, which reauthorized private recruiting of "otherwise inadmissible aliens," reaffirmed the legality of guest-worker programs. The result was an immediate spike in temporary foreign worker recruitment. The Bracero Program swelled to five times its World War II size; the West Indian and Bahamian programs tripled.[32] According to Ernesto Galarza, by 1957, Mexicans under contract had increased from 12 percent of the seasonal hired labor force in California to 28 percent.[33] Texas became the biggest importer of Braceros, despite Mexican officials' persistent reservations about working conditions and attitudes there. Not coincidentally, perhaps, Texas wage rates for picking a hundred pounds of cotton fell from $1.50 in 1949 to $1.25.[34]

While farm employers increased their use of Mexican and West Indian contract workers, others mined new sources of foreign labor, and not just in agriculture. In 1952, Vermont foresters and farmers imported ten thousand Canadian woodsmen and farmworkers on H2 visas, instead of informally as they had done in the past.[35] Southwestern growers imported several thousand Japanese H2 workers, not because they offered any sort of special skills, but because they were useful as a threat in upcoming negotiations with Mexican authorities. If Mexican officials didn't bend, in other words, growers would find "Braceros" elsewhere.[36] Likewise, in 1953, California citrus growers who were dissatisfied with the new Bracero Agreement paraded Caribbean officials, Herbert MacDonald, the British Consul General, and reporters through local orchards in an obvious attempt to threaten the Mexican consul with a switch.[37] New England hotels began importing Canadians in the summer, with at least one hotel illegally laying off American workers in the process.[38] Even the Defense Department brought nine thousand Filipinos to Guam as H2 construction workers. Over the next thirty years, guestworkers came to dominate the construction industry in Guam (though the Defense Department's application for "taxi-dancers"—ballroom dancers paid by the dance—was denied).[39]

Employers anticipated that workers imported on short-term contracts would be more motivated employees than American workers or permanent immigrants. The California Range Association and the National Wool Growers Association, for example, had successfully petitioned to have Basque sheepshearers admitted to the United States as permanent residents; but after the passage of McCarran-Walter they quickly canceled their request and applied instead for Basque sheepshearers on temporary contracts. The Department of Labor objected, arguing that the application was "an effort on the part of the sheepherding employers to obtain captive labor," but General J. M. Swing, the Commissioner of the INS, approved the amended request. The INS then alerted regional commissioners not to approve any more requests for permanent visas for sheepherders from Spain. Basque sheepherders would come to the United States as H2 workers or not at all.[40]

Why so many employers happily switched to guestworkers is no mystery. Motivated by the power of poverty and the knowledge that their opportunity to earn was temporary, guestworkers worked hard. "Even if we did attract the average domestic," argued E. S. Williams, president of the huge C. S. Williams Packing Company in Fremont, California, "it would take ten of them to do the work of one bracero in the lettuce field."[41] But although temporary workers' work ethic may have helped make them attractive, the key to their popularity was employers' ability to import them in sufficient numbers precisely when they wanted them and deport them if they caused trouble. "Due to his shaky economic life back home," Earl Morrison explained to a reporter after supervising the importation of West Indians for the U.S. Sugar Corporation for some twenty years, "the British West Indian is motivated to perform any work offered him with greater enthusiasm than the U.S. worker, who is always aware that if he doesn't like what he's doing he can go somewhere else and find an easier job . . . The offshore knows he is bound by his contract and that he has to please to stay." Morrison's boss, Fred Sikes, concurred: "[I]f I had a remedy comparable to breaching [firing and repatriating] an unsatisfactory worker—which is allowed under the West Indian contract—that I could apply to the American worker, he might work better, too." James Paulk, a section foreman for the Florida Sugarcane Growers' Cooperative, hammered the point home: "We bring the Jamaican here under contract. If he violates his contract we can send him home. So we've got leverage over that West Indian that we don't have over American workers. When that offshore comes in here, he's either going to cut cane or get sent home—or if he violates his immigration status and runs away from his employer, the law will get him."[42]

The liaisons or consuls sent by home governments to protect workers' welfare did little to undermine employers' use of deportation as a tool of labor discipline. Caribbean workers were entitled to hearings with liaisons in attendance before they could be repatriated, but what little evidence there is of these impromptu meetings suggests that, when they occurred, workers were not allowed to speak in their own defense. If liaison officers ever refused to repatriate a worker, there is no evidence of it. Criticized by a field foreman in 1956 for cutting cane incorrectly after only four days in the United States, Samuel A. Levy of Port Royal, Jamaica, snapped back that he had been cutting cane before the foreman was old enough to cut grass. For that, he said, he was beaten around the neck and back with a stalk of sugarcane, and sent back to the camp for a repatriation hearing. A liaison officer was present, Levy noted, but "[t]hey never gave me a chance to tell them about what happened." Learning that he was going to be sent home, Levy "ran off . . . sleeping in box cars at night and picking beans during the day." The INS apprehended him a few weeks later. Asked by an INS officer why "so many boys" were going AWOL from the sugar company camps, Levy replied, "Because the foreman is mistreating the boys and curseing [sic] at them and they don't like that."[43]

Though the INS caught Levy, going AWOL was still a better risk than speaking up for oneself, and some guestworkers went that route. The INS reported some two hundred apprehensions of H2 workers in just two months in 1956, and it is clear from the interrogation records of those they did catch that many more AWOL guestworkers remained at large. Herbert MacDonald bragged that only 3 percent of West Indians went AWOL, as opposed to 10 percent of Mexican Braceros. Bahamians too, he declared, jumped their contracts with much greater regularity than West Indians (though that may simply have been because they could more easily disappear into Florida's long-standing Bahamian community).[44] Whatever the numbers, guestworkers who ran off might have found better work and wages. Speaking up for oneself or one's fellows meant rapid repatriation and a line on the "U-list." Either way, guestworkers' complaints were rarely heard.

OPERATION WETBACK AND THE BRACERO BOOM

The passage of PL 78 and the McCarran-Walter Act may have silenced guestworkers, but it did not silence critics of guestworker programs. Before the ink was even dry on the McCarran-Walter Act, the Senate Subcommittee on Labor and Labor-Management Relations held yet another round of hearings on the U.S. guestworker programs. For days, speaker after speaker attacked the use of contract labor, alleging that there was no labor shortage that justified it; that contract workers depressed farm labor wages; that guestworkers got preferential treatment; that tax-payers should not have to subsidize the labor costs of a tiny percentage of wealthy farmers; and that family farmers had to compete with large commercial farms hiring Braceros. George Stith, a sharecropper from Arkansas and a member of the National Farm Labor Union, testified that cotton-picking wages began to fall with the arrival of Braceros in Arkansas in 1949. "In many cases," he explained, "local farm workers could not get jobs at all" because Braceros had to be guaranteed four days of work per week. "The Arkansas cotton picker wasn't guaranteed anything," he added, "so he lost his job." Stith's president, H. L. Mitchell, played on Cold War fears of subversives, charging that communist agitators were entering the United States on guestworker contracts. Pro-labor activists from the National Council of Jewish Women to the American Federation of Teachers called for legislation to restrict access to foreign workers and raise standards for domestic workers by establishing a minimum wage in agriculture, federal housing standards, and the extension of collective bargaining rights to farmworkers.[45] In all, the testimony totaled more than two thousand published pages, most of which condemned guestworker programs.

Despite the volume of testimony, lawmakers did not propose terminating the guestworker programs; just the reverse. Although guestworkers raised concerns, the issue of illegal immigration had exploded onto the U.S. political scene, ignited, no doubt, by an INS report that put the number of illegal immigrants in the United States at one million. With titles like "Wetbacks Swarm In," "'Wetback' Roundup," and "Invasion of Wetbacks Lowers Living Standard," the media coverage seemed like a prequel to the Cold War blockbuster, *Invasion of the Body Snatchers*, which would appear on the nation's movie screens a few years later.[46] The more lawmakers worried about "wetbacks" swarming in, the more they re-imagined guestworkers as a solution rather than a problem. Even guestworkers offered in exchange for "wetbacks"—the essence of the Drying Out policy—suddenly seemed like a good idea. Hubert Humphrey noted approvingly that committee member Senator Wayne Morse of Oregon had successfully sponsored a law banning employers from receiving contract laborers if they had been caught using "wetbacks." If growers spurned illegal immigrants, in other words, they would get guestworkers as a reward.[47]

National Farm Labor Union leaders seemed to be caught off guard. To them, there was no real difference between unauthorized immigrant workers and guestworkers; both groups displaced American farmworkers and undermined their organizing campaigns. Freely using nativist rhetoric, they complained that unauthorized immigrants undermined local wages, while guestworkers were guaranteed wages and benefits that local workers didn't get. "The wetbacks are just like poison," Jacinto Cota, Jr., a migratory farmworker and union member from the Imperial Valley testified. "They don't care what the wages are."[48] Still, liberal lawmakers seem to have missed the NLFU's point. Instead of condemning growers' access to an unlimited supply of deportable labor—authorized or unauthorized— the Senate Subcommittee legitimized guestworker programs as a legal alternative to "wetbacks."

The pinnacle of this two-sided policy was "Operation Wetback." The public part of the policy—the Eisenhower administration's brutal removal of unauthorized Mexican residents in the Southwest—is well known. Less well known is the less public policy, which involved the unilateral recruitment of thousands of Mexicans and their metamorphosis into legal, temporary, guestworkers.

Operation Wetback began with another impasse over the renewal of the U.S.-Mexican agreement. This time the key sticking point was U.S. employers' insistence that they should be able to recruit labor at the border, instead of traveling deep into the Mexican interior at official recruitment stations. Once again, negotiations broke off, but this time, Mexican officials banned Mexicans from entering the United States, essentially declaring a state strike against American employers. The Brownsville *Herald* accused Mexico of setting up an "Iron Curtain" along the border. U.S. officials responded by closing its southern border stations. In late January 1954, Mexican men hoping to enter the United States gathered in San Luis, Piedras Negras, Mexicali, and other towns on the Mexican side of the U.S.-Mexican border. Despondent, they waited.[49]

Finally, after months had passed, U.S. officials decided to force the issue a second time by recruiting unilaterally, without having reached a new agreement with Mexico. On January 22, 1954, INS officials opened the barriers at Mexicali, signaling the waiting men to come forward. The crowd surged northward, but this time migrants found their way blocked by Mexican police who positioned themselves between the crowd of men and the border. The police used their fists, clubs, fire hoses, and even guns to prevent their compatriots from seeking work in El Norte. Police in Mexicali shot one man as he scaled the twelve-foot fence that separated the U.S. and Mexican sides of town.[50]

Blocked from crossing at the border stations, prospective Braceros jogged to the edge of town, where border fences abruptly ended. Because they crossed where the border was open, instead of at the official border station, the prospective recruits instantly became "illegal immigrants." Instead of sending them back to Mexico, however, U.S. Border Patrol officials trotted them to the U.S. side of the official crossing and directed them to touch a toe onto the Mexican side, in what Mae Ngai calls "a ritual of sovereignty."[51] When this was done, U.S. Labor Department officials gave the migrants contracts to sign, which completed their transformation from illegal immigrants into guestworkers. The ritual did not always go well. As men stretched their legs back over the border, Mexican officials tried to pull them back into Mexico. U.S. authorities lent their assistance by pulling them toward the United States. One man's picture was taken by a reporter as he hung between nations like a rope in a cross-border game of tug-of-war. Similar scenes were repeated over the next month at multiple points along the U.S.-Mexican border.[52] One critic called it "storm and drag immigration" policy.[53]

The INS may not have intended to act as a tool of U.S. growers; its priority was indisputably to counter the rising number of unauthorized immigrants along the border. But by allowing growers to recruit Mexican Braceros from within the United States, by backing growers' refusal to raise wages, and by taking a cavalier attitude toward enforcing workers' contracts, the INS and the Department of Labor served as the long arm of agricultural capital.

Mexico's leaders responded to U.S. officials' effort to break their boycott by deploying troops to enforce their ban on emigration, but thousands of Mexicans were willing to accept the terms offered by U.S. growers, even if their government was not. Growers joined in the effort to legalize immigrants without Mexico's consent by bringing their undocumented workers to the border to have them "dried out" too. Over the next five days, 3,500 Mexican workers made the crossing and thousands already in the United States were legalized as Braceros. With the strike broken by Mexico's own citizens, Mexican officials capitulated, signing a new bilateral agreement at the old wage. The plan, according to the grower-friendly *Imperial Valley Press,* was "a riotous success."[54]

Six months after the border war, the Eisenhower administration launched its expulsion campaign in an effort to force southwestern growers to shift from unauthorized immigrants to legal guestworkers. The INS claimed victory—apprehensions fell from 920,000 in 1954 to just 23,000 in 1960—but its "success" was at least partly sleight of hand: hundreds of thousands of unauthorized immigrants had simply been legalized as guestworkers. Although the INS did deport thousands, the Bracero Program increased from 309,000 in 1954 to almost half a million in 1956.[55] "Apparently," Congressman John F. Shelly of California noted caustically, "their reasoning is that if we simply remove all restrictions on border crossings . . . all crossings will be legal and we will, therefore, wipe out the wetback problem."[56] Seen as a piece with the border war a few months earlier, it's clear that the plan was designed in part to convince growers to shift to legal temporary workers by undermining Mexico's bargaining power and thus reducing the cost of hiring Braceros. On their way out of the country, deportees passed billboards that read: "NOTICE! The United States needs Legal Farm Workers! The Mayor of Your Town Can Arrange For Your Contracting. WARNING: The Era of the Wetback and the Wire Cutter Has Ended! From This Day Forward Any Person Found in the United States Illegally Will Be Punished by Imprisonment."[57]

The "Era of the Wetback" had not ended, the NFLU warned, it had simply been disguised as state-authorized migration, or as the executive secretary of the American G.I. Forum put it, the Bracero Program was nothing more than "legalized wetbackism."[58] Those who were jubilant about the INS plan outnumbered critics, however. "Not too many months ago," the editors of the Pasadena *Independent* wrote, "Southern California swarmed with 'wetbacks' or Mexican Nationals who had entered the United States illegally in search of work. But today most 'wetbacks' are gone—replaced by the 'Bracero,' a proud and very necessary part of California's agricultural team."[59] Two thousand pages of criticism notwithstanding, guestworkers were golden.

GUESTWORKERS EMBATTLED

The Bracero Program might have continued its charmed existence as a sort of fairy-tale alternative to illegal immigration but for a man, a machine, a movement, and its music. The man, oddly enough, was President Eisenhower's Secretary of Labor, James Mitchell, who probably did more than any person in government to reform the guestworker programs. A "Democrat for Eisenhower," who was rewarded with a cabinet appointment in 1953, Mitchell was not particularly interested in foreign workers at the start of his term, nor did he initially support federal legislation as a solution to domestic farmworkers' ills. He hoped to use his office to encourage states to pass reform legislation, rather than mandate change at the federal level. To this end, he sponsored bills to create a new Interagency Committee on Migrant Labor that would promote state-level farm labor reform legislation. Even that mild measure was too radical for the Republican-dominated Congress; the bill died in committee four times before Eisenhower created the committee by executive order.[60]

Noting that by 1954 there had already been five hundred government studies of migrant workers at the state and federal levels, Mitchell determined to win real change instead of just more hearings. He got nowhere. The Interagency Committee created model guidelines for housing, transportation, and the regulation of crew leaders, but state lawmakers ignored them. Bills designed to establish a minimum wage for agriculture, end child labor, require the registration of crew leaders, and provide federal assistance for migrant housing and education all died in committee. Mitchell could not even get states to accept federal money to create rest stops with clean toilets and drinking water on the routes migrants traveled.[61] Four times he unsuccessfully supported amendments to extend the minimum wage and maximum hour legislation of the Fair Labor Standards Act to farmworkers, and four times he was opposed not just by growers and the leaders of his party but by fellow cabinet member, Ezra Benson, the Secretary of Agriculture, who called federal intervention "repugnant to agriculture."[62]

Frustrated at every turn by the intransigence of the grower lobby, Mitchell drew the only two weapons he had in his arsenal. He had the authority to set the rules under which the U.S. Employment Service supplied employers with domestic labor, and he was responsible under Public Law 78 to ensure that Mexican contract workers did not "adversely affect" the wages and working conditions of domestic workers. Connecting those two roles, Mitchell created minimum wage, housing, and transportation standards for employers who used the Employment Service, and then announced that employers who failed to meet those standards "would not be certified to receive Mexican Braceros."[63] The Labor Department began enforcing his new rules immediately, closing fifty-eight farm labor camps in 1957 alone, and using a new prevailing wage formula to raise wages. In 1959, Mitchell issued new regulations guaranteeing West Indian contract workers free housing and transportation within the United States and restoring the three-quarter guarantee they had lost in 1947.[64] Mitchell also required employers to pay H2 workers an "adverse effect wage," that is, an hourly wage higher than the prevailing wage, so guestworkers would not depress local wages.[65] And when a worker failed to earn the adverse effect wage, either because he cut or picked too slowly or because the price by the row or the bushel was too low, the employer would have to pay enough "build up pay" to make up the difference between what the guestworker earned by the row and what he should have earned by the hour, just as a restaurant owner has to supplement a server's tips if she fails to earn the minimum wage. Rather than doing this quietly, moreover, Mitchell went to the press, noting in interviews that agricultural employers had rejected even the mildest reforms and could hardly be expected to do otherwise as long as cheap foreign workers were supplied by the federal government.[66]

Predictably, growers responded with outrage.[67] Working through Florida senator Spessard Holland, who was a member of the Senate Agricultural Committee and a key supporter of Florida's sugar industry, agricultural interests counterattacked by trying to amend the Fair Labor Standards Act of 1960 to remove the Secretary of Labor's authority over farm labor questions altogether.[68] The Secretary of Agriculture backed them up. Embarrassed by the open rift within his cabinet, Eisenhower forced Mitchell to back down. Nonetheless, Mitchell's stand helped to galvanize reform forces against the special treatment growers received in Washington.[69]

The second strike against guestworkers came in the form of a cotton-picking machine. Mechanical cotton pickers had been available during World War II, but their use boomed in the years that followed, particularly in Texas, where Braceros were initially banned. The INS's willingness to circumvent the Bracero boycott and Mexico's eventual capitulation on this point probably slowed the adoption of the machines, but the more embattled the Bracero Program became in the 1950s, the more growers made the switch. By 1962, 70 percent of all cotton was harvested by machine, causing employers to reduce their requests for Braceros by over half, to about 200,000. The remaining Braceros were concentrated among a tiny number of large fruit and vegetable farms in California. The result was the collapse of the inter-commodity growers' coalition forged during World War II. Lawmakers from cotton districts still generally supported the contract labor schemes, but they increasingly feared that the ill will generated by the Bracero Program would jeopardize other federal agricultural programs they now deemed more important. By 1962, the American Farm Bureau Federation was the lone lobbying organization still pushing forcefully for the Bracero Program.[70]

The third blow against guestworkers came from a familiar source, H. L. Mitchell's old outfit. In the second half of the 1950s, the NFLU, renamed the National Agricultural Workers Union (NAWU), set out to prove that guestworker programs were no more than "legalized Wetbackism." Union officials used volunteers to document the displacement of domestic workers by Braceros and the use of Braceros as strikebreakers. Professor Galarza conducted 350 interviews with Braceros, which he condensed in a pamphlet titled *Strangers in Our Fields* (the United Auto Workers helped fund its dissemination). In it, Galarza quoted Mexican men who told of being housed in barns just vacated by cows; of windows without screens; of rancid food; of picking without knowing what the rate of pay was; and of threats made against those who complained.[71]

Growers dismissed the union's report, but it was enough to force the California branch of the U.S. Department of Labor to investigate. Over a period of months in 1957, William Renner, a compliance officer for the Department's Bureau of Employment Security, studied the Bracero Program. Renner's report confirmed Galarza's findings plus some. He documented a string of abuses, including "payroll falsifications, hours worked but not reported, unauthorized exchanges of Bracero crews among growers, wages set arbitrarily without determination of the prevailing rates, incomplete accounting to the braceros of wages due, overcharges for meals, exorbitant charges for busing to nearby towns . . . filthy over-

crowded camps, and braceros working after their contracts had expired."
Instead of cracking down on employers, however, Renner's supervisors
warned him to withdraw his report, confiscated his official and personal
papers, and then fired him. James Mitchell either didn't know or didn't
save him.[72]

The NAWU and Renner were powerless to pursue their case against
the Bracero Program, but the farm labor movement was about to get an
application of fertilizer. In 1959, as the NAWU was dying, George Meany,
president of the newly joined AFL-CIO, created the Agricultural Workers
Organizing Committee, headed by a United Auto Workers activist with
no experience organizing farmworkers.[73] For all its weaknesses, AWOC
was able to tap into the growing support for Mexican-American or "Chicano" civil rights that was beginning to swell in the Southwest. Picking
up the anti-Bracero baton from the dying NAWU, AWOC, which later
mutated into the United Farm Workers of America, made a direct comparison between the guestworker phenomenon and apartheid in South
Africa. "We believe," AWOC leaders wrote in a statement to the Good
Neighbor Commission, "that America deserves a more honorable place in
the world community than the Union of South Africa, but at the present
time we and South Africa are the only countries on earth which tolerate large-scale alien contract labor programs." (In fact, European nations
did too but working conditions there were generally much better.) "South
African mine owners import Negroes from segregated kraals, under contract, and return them home to their kraals when their labor is no longer
needed," the document continued. "Southwest farm owners import Mexicans, under contract, and return them to Mexico when their labor is no
longer needed."[74]

AWOC's antipathy toward guestworkers deepened in December 1960
when Imperial Valley lettuce farmers used Braceros to break an AWOC-
led strike. Ties with "civil rights organizations, student groups, and liberal
community organizations" helped transform the event from a failed strike
into a social movement. In 1961, Cesar Chavez, who had walked a picket
line for the first time during the NFLU cotton pickers strike of 1949, "led
a march of unemployed workers into the fields near Oxnard, where Braceros were employed." Between 1960 and 1962, 148 strikes in California
helped to raise wages, build the farmworker movement, and focus its supporters on ending the Bracero Program.[75]

Farmworkers' reinvigorated campaign inspired renewed attention
from the national media and from urban lawmakers, who were less be-
holden to growers' lobbies. This time, instead of publishing hysterical
accounts of a farmworker "invasion," newspapers and magazines wrote
exposés of farmworkers' lives. *The Reporter* and *Commonweal* began
covering the issue as early as 1959. *Christian Century, Crisis, Newsweek,*

Time, and the *New York Times* followed soon after. State reports on farm labor conditions appeared in eight states between 1959 and 1963, and in 1960, the NAACP published *No Harvest for the Reaper: The Story of the Migratory Agricultural Worker in the U.S.* CBS hammered the final nail in the coffin of growers' image the day after Thanksgiving in 1960, when the network aired a special report by veteran reporter Walter Murrow, titled "Harvest of Shame," which took advantage of the national day of gluttony to expose the terrible conditions suffered by the men, women, and children who had harvested the food that was even then sitting uncomfortably in Americans' stomachs. The documentary, which focused on Belle Glade, Florida, swayed public opinion against farm employers as never before.[76]

As the farmworker movement grew, so did the roster of voluntary associations and congressmen who made farmworkers their cause. Once largely indifferent to farmworkers' issues or fearful of alienating rural Democrats, urban Democrats began to pay closer attention. And as the "Great Migration" from the countryside to the city made the nation more urbanized in the postwar period, supporting farm labor reform became far less of a political risk, and, for some, an urgent question of conscience. Democrats from states using guestworkers still voted overwhelmingly in favor of the measures backed by growers' lobbyists, but Democrats from other states and from urban districts increasingly voted for reform, and their numbers were rising.[77] In 1959, the National Advisory Committee on Farm Labor, which had A. Philip Randolph and Eleanor Roosevelt among its members, held hearings to document the decline in agricultural wages in relation to factory wages since World War II. "Citizens for Farm Labor" focused on "countering agribusiness propaganda." The National Council on Agricultural Life and Labor had thirty-five member organizations by 1962.[78]

By 1960 the tide had turned to such an extent that both parties' election year platforms promised action on behalf of farmworkers, although only the Democratic platform condemned the Bracero Program. Representative George McGovern and Senator Eugene McCarthy followed with an anti-bracero bill, which failed to pass, but the debate made it clear that the Bracero Program was at risk.[79] By 1961, 120 farmworker bills were under consideration in twenty-four states, and Congress reenacted the Migrant Health program that had been eliminated in 1947 when guestworker programs went private.[80]

Songs written by the troubadours of the old labor movement and the new counterculture fanned the farmworker movement's fire, and put the opposition to guestworker programs to music. After the 1948 crash of an INS plane, which had been repatriating Braceros to Mexico, Woody Guthrie was struck by the fact that the brief *New York Times* story listed the names of the flight crew and security guard but not the names of the twenty-seven Mexican men and one woman who had perished. Naming the poem "Los Gatos Canyon," after the site of the crash, Guthrie chanted the words, including:

> Who are all these friends, all scattered like dry leaves?
> The radio says, "They are just deportees."

A decade later, as the anti-guestworker movement gained momentum, Marty Hoffman put Guthrie's poem to music. Popularized by Pete Seeger, the song, "Deportees," was recorded in the 1960s by the Kingston Trio, Judy Collins, and even sung on Irish television by the Emeralds.[81] Just a few years later, in 1963, folk singer Phil Ochs, who is famous for his anti–Vietnam War songs, wrote his scathing "Bracero":

> Sleep in shacks that could be cages
> They will take it from your wages
> Bracero

Pro-Bracero lawmakers scrambled to protect the program against its growing opposition, but the old notion that Braceros were an alternative to "wetbacks" rang hollow. Illegal immigrants could at least walk away from work they did not like or choose not to cross a picket line. Braceros were legal captives of their employers. Defenders of the programs then tried another tack, arguing, like Senator John Tower of Texas, that "we are denying a number of underprivileged Mexican people work that they need and desire." Opponents parried that argument easily. "We are for assistance to Mexico," the director of the National Catholic Rural Life Conference insisted, "but not at the cost of the poorest people in the U.S."[82] Frustrated by the delay in ending the programs, Representative John Kyl of Iowa noted that "We have made more progress in phasing out prayer in the last three or four years than we have in phasing out the bracero program."[83] The wait would soon be over. In 1963, lawmakers gave growers one more year to wean themselves off Braceros. There would be no future renewals.[84]

Once it became clear that the Bracero Program was on its death bed, some California growers tried to resurrect it by applying for Mexican workers under the H2 rubric. That didn't work, either. Lyndon Johnson's Secretary of Labor, Willard Wirtz, refused to certify western growers' requests for H2 workers, despite enormous pressure to do so. "It became a situation where I could be a hero by doing nothing," Wirtz later recalled, "because if I did nothing they couldn't bring them in." Calling Wirtz "idealistic" and "evangelistic," growers and their allies lobbied harder than ever, hoping to sway Johnson, who had Braceros working on his own farm. Johnson stayed out of it, and Wirtz held his ground. Braceros already in the United States were able to finish out their contracts, but the program was dying.[85]

Not Quite the Final Nail

The same seemed to be true globally. Within ten years of the Bracero Program's fall from grace, European guestworker programs were also brought to an abrupt end. Pressure to expel foreign workers began building in the late 1960s as it became clear that Europe's reconstruction was complete and West Germany's "economic miracle" was no longer so miraculous. Switzerland, Belgium, and the Netherlands all held referenda on expulsion even before the oil crisis of 1973 made the "problem" of foreign workers seem urgent. OPEC's decision to raise oil prices was simply the final nail in guestworker programs' coffin. Germany stopped further recruitment of guestworkers in November 1973. France and Switzerland did the same in 1974.[86] Mine workers in South Africa kept "oscillating," as did Caribbean guestworkers who traveled to and from the United States, but in Europe as on the west coast of the United States, guestworker programs were ending.

Interestingly, European nations ended their guestworker programs but did not expel the guestworkers. Despite rising unemployment in Europe, half of all temporary workers remained in their host countries.[87] Perhaps because forced expulsions had a new and far more insidious connotation after the still recent experience of the Third Reich, or because the more foreigners do a job, the more native-born people tend to disdain it, European governments lacked the will or the inclination to revoke work permits for some 10–12 million foreign workers, many of whom had been in residence for years. Indeed, the number of foreigners rose after the cessation of recruiting, both because unemployed guestworkers were less likely to leave when they had little hope of returning at a later date and because those already admitted were allowed to bring their families.[88] Eventually, the European Union removed the remaining frontiers that blocked the movement of goods, money, services, and people.[89] Guestworker programs seemed to have paved the way for European unity.

In the United States, in contrast, the end of the Bracero Program only led to a hardening of the dividing line between the United States and Mexico. Mexican guestworkers were expected to leave after the termination of the Bracero Program and new omnibus immigration legislation would soon cap the number of Mexicans who could enter the country as permanent immigrants. Neoliberal policies would later lead to the opening of borders to goods, money, and services but not to people.

The comparison to South Africa is also instructive. In the 1970s, South Africa's mining industry bowed to pressure to stabilize its workforce by using migrants in combination with a larger local workforce. The result was a "two-tiered" labor force in which one group lived isolated in company compounds, accepted longer contracts, and could be assigned to more difficult and dangerous mines. Employers must have hoped that this practice would allow them to divide and conquer their workforce. In fact, the presence of a more stable labor force allowed South Africa's miners to organize much more effectively. In the 1970s, South African mines experienced almost continuous outbreaks of violence, rioting, strikes, and slow-downs, despite (or perhaps inspired by) rising wages and improving conditions. By 1979, South Africa had fifty mineworkers' unions, which demanded not just better contracts but limits on the number of guestworkers in the mining industry.[90]

In the United States, in contrast, unions fought to keep guestworkers out. That didn't mean unions didn't care about guestworkers. To the extent that word got out at all about guestworker programs in the 1950s and early 1960s, it was union members and union supporters who did the writing, talking and singing, much of it about how guestworkers were mistreated. But while European unions had struggled to improve guestworkers' condition and smooth their integration into their host societies, and South African miners and guestworkers organized together underground (literally), American union members consistently demanded an end to guestworker programs. The National Agricultural Workers Union and later the United Farm Workers were the key actors in the termination of the Bracero Program. In the 1970s, the fledgling United Farm Workers division in Florida would campaign against the sugar industry's use of H2 workers. American growers' access to guestworkers as strikebreakers and employers' ability to expel guestworkers from the country made unions and guestworkers natural enemies.

Union, journalistic, governmental and musical exposés of the Bracero Program made clear that the program was rife with abuse, despite Mexican workers' model contract, a bilateral agreement, the restoration of federal oversight in 1951, and the Mexican government's effort to protect its citizens abroad. All those protections failed because they weren't meant to succeed. U.S. officials chose not to enforce them with vigilance to tempt growers to choose guestworkers over undocumented immigrants, even if that meant reducing the former to the condition of the latter. The Bracero Program provided a patina of legality to growers' unregulated use of Mexican labor. But if the Bracero Program was a shell game, what can we say about the H-2 Program? Caribbean guestworkers enjoyed a less favorable contract, no bilateral agreement, no federal oversight, and H2 workers' sending governments exerted far less power than Mexico in their negotiations with U.S. growers.

Guestworker programs were a "riotous success," in other words, not because they helped control unauthorized migration or protected domestic workers from competition, but because they created the illusion of state control while giving growers precisely what they wanted. By the end of the 1950s, that patina of legality had worn thin. The National Agricultural Worker Union's campaign against what it called "Legalized Wetbackism" faltered, but a new farmworker-driven, Chicano civil rights movement brought it back to life. Backed at the highest levels by crusading secretaries of labor, and set to music by the folk musicians of the 1950s and '60s, the campaign against guestworkers bore fruit in 1963. By 1965, the Braceros were gone and H2 workers would soon be plucked from vegetable fields and orchards. Only a few thousand guestworkers would remain.

CHAPTER SEVEN

The Worst Job in the World

The Cuban Revolution, the War on Poverty, and the Secret Rebellion in Florida's Cane Fields

ON NEW YEAR'S DAY, 1968, two crews of Caribbean guestworkers refused to cut cane for the row prices offered by the Sugar Cane Growers Cooperative, a 70,000-acre, 7-year-old, 51-member enterprise. "They give us a row of cane to cut," recalled Jamaican Adrian Russell; it was "extra long and bad" and "could not do for that price." The men's demand for more money went up the chain of command until it reached Jim Walls, one of the Co-op's "white bosses," as the all-black cane cutters called them. "Him say 'no'," Jamaican Felix Osbourne later recalled. "If we don't want, we can go home." When Walter Comrie, the cane cutters' liaison officer, agreed with Walls that "the price of the field was in line with prevailing prices," two hundred cane cutters walked off the job.[1]

After the men failed to return to work the following day, Walls and several undercover police gathered in the payroll shack of the Belle Glade camp's courtyard to pay the workers their wages for the previous two weeks and send them home. But strikers, whose numbers had doubled by morning, surrounded the payroll shack, demanding a visit from Jamaica's prime minister and $500 each, the average sum they felt they had been underpaid for cutting quarter-mile-long rows of cane.[2] When the police in the payroll shack called for help, armed deputies who had been waiting at the camp's perimeter stormed the courtyard. "We had reason to believe machetes were hidden in the crowd," Sheriff William Heidtman later told the *Miami Herald*, without mentioning that every worker in the camp would naturally have had a machete. (He later admitted that the men hadn't been brandishing them and that "the camp appeared clean and in good condition.")[3] Within minutes, one hundred heavily armed Palm Beach County deputies and Florida highway patrolmen—rifles pointed, bayonets fixed—were arrayed in a line facing a row of mostly Jamaican guestworkers, who were armed with nothing but Coca Cola bottles and rocks.

The New Year's Day Strike stands out only because it received media attention in two *Miami Herald* articles (that misidentified the strikers as Haitians and Puerto Ricans). The strike was also the first to expose the H2

Program to the new Florida branch of Legal Services, which would spend the next forty years suing the sugarcane industry on farmworkers' behalf.[4] Although the New Year's Day strike was for many years the only cane cutters' strike to generate press coverage, it was just one of many strikes roiling the nine thousand or so guestworkers who labored in Florida's cane fields in the 1960s. Mass strikes that engaged entire labor camps took place as often as once a year at sugar companies where conditions and wages were poorest, and there were hundreds of brief work stoppages or "field strikes" that involved individual work crews. Why the trouble in Florida's fields?[5]

The answer to this question seems obvious. Who wasn't in a state of rebellion in the 1960s? By the time of the Co-op strike, Harlem and Los Angeles had erupted in riots, hundreds of thousands of civil rights activists had marched on Washington, and massive anti-draft demonstrations had taken place around the nation. And that was just in the United States. In the wake of independence in 1962, Jamaica was wracked by strike waves involving dock workers, retail workers, farmworkers on sugar estates, sanitation workers, bus drivers, even Jamaica's two daily newspapers.[6] A rebellion among poor, black, Caribbean workers in the American South seems like little more than a product of the general upset of the 1960s.

Still, that explanation is not sufficient because the H2 Program had been designed to prevent just this sort of turmoil. Growers handpicked guestworkers for passivity, repatriated those who protested too much, and re-invited or "predesignated" men who worked well and without complaint. Beyond that, Jamaican men earned three times more in the United States than most could at home, and they struggled—sometimes for years—to get a "farmworker ticket." Knowing that there were thousands of unemployed men back home who would gladly take their spot, few cane cutters tempted fate by complaining, let alone striking. For fifteen years, this system had kept a lid on militancy in the fields. And then, starting in 1963, Florida's cane fields boiled over. Strike followed strike. Deportation followed deportation. Cane cutters suddenly seemed willing to risk their only real hope of a livelihood to protest their condition. What had changed?

The answer, oddly, is the confluence of two seemingly unrelated events: the Cuban Revolution and Lyndon B. Johnson's War on Poverty. Like the collision of two weather systems, these transformations—a revolution and a reform program—brought unintended but devastating changes to working conditions in Florida's fields. What had been a hard but coveted opportunity for poor black men from the Caribbean became, as Johnson's Secretary of Labor Willard Wirtz put it only somewhat hyperbolically, "the worst job in the world."[7]

AMERICA'S SUGAR KINGDOM

Florida's transformation began with a revolution that was many years in the making. Cuba had been the heart of the American sugar industry since the dawn of the twentieth century. Americans had produced sugar beets and cane on the U.S. mainland and in its new island territories—Hawaii, the Philippines, and Puerto Rico—the latter two acquired as a result of U.S. victory in the Spanish-American War. But all this sugar production paled next to Cuba's mammoth industry, which Americans helped develop into the biggest in the world. American-owned mills, built in Cuba after the 1898 war, produced sugar on a massive scale, drawing workers from the old sugar colonies of the Caribbean, including Jamaica, whose outdated production methods couldn't keep pace.[8]

But Cuba wasn't the only country to take advantage of skyrocketing sugar prices. And as Mauritania, Brazil, Argentina, Australia, and India leaped into production to take advantage of the boom, the market became dangerously volatile. Prices reached their peak in the middle of the 1920s and then began to fall. The stock market crash of 1929 caused hardship among sugar producers in the United States, but in Cuba the result was financial calamity and social upheaval. By the time Franklin Roosevelt moved into the Oval Office in 1932, Cuba's president Gerardo Machado had suspended constitutional protections in response to strikes and student protests. Nine months later, Machado was gone, a socialist academic had replaced him, and Cuban workers were confiscating American-owned sugar plantations and mills.[9]

Americans' dependence on Cuban sugar and Cuba's instability resulted in a strange hybrid of domestic farm policy and foreign policy that would both support and constrain Florida's sugar industry for the next thirty years. U.S. producers of sugar demanded that the federal government respond to the collapse of world sugar prices by hiking tariffs to protect them from Cuban imports. They had considerable backing in the 72nd Congress. The prospect of a tariff probably explains why two sugar companies—Fellsmere and U.S. Sugar—were founded in Florida in 1931, hardly an auspicious year to launch new companies of any kind. But Roosevelt feared full-scale revolution in Cuba as much if not more than he did the collapse of domestic sugar producers. Thus his administration proposed a solution designed to satisfy sugar producers on both sides of the Florida Straits. Instead of trying to raise sugar prices simply by paying U.S. sugar producers to grow less sugar, as the New Deal's Agricultural Adjustment Act (AAA) did in the case of other staple crops, the administration proposed an amendment to the AAA that would divide the

U.S. sugar market equally between domestic and foreign producers, with each group receiving a fixed quota. Domestic producers would divide the domestic quota, foreign producers the foreign quota. U.S. growers would get a subsidy or bonus for every ton of sugar they produced, provided they stayed within their quota and paid a minimum wage set by the U.S. Department of Agriculture, a provision designed to eliminate white child labor from the beet fields of the Midwest. Cuban producers, allotted 64 percent of the foreign quota, were guaranteed access to the U.S. market at a fixed price. The newly independent Philippines followed with 35 percent. The rest of the world, including Jamaica, had to share just 1 percent of the foreign quota.[10]

As Congress debated the legislation that became the Jones-Costigan Act, a coup led by Army Sergeant Fulgencio Batista ousted the rebel-installed professor-president. FDR made his support for the coup known by parking warships off the coast of Cuba. This "cuota y flota" diplomacy became the United States' central way of doing business with Cuba and other Caribbean nations in the decades to come.[11] The Supreme Court soon declared Jones-Costigan unconstitutional (not because of the coup in Cuba), but Congress replaced it in 1937 with the nearly identical Sugar Act, which lasted with minor amendments until 1974.[12]

The Sugar Program made sugar the most regimented of all American crops, which was really saying something in the post–New Deal world. "All of us know," Congressman Harold Cooley (D-NC) remarked, "that this program is saturated with subsidy and control and regimentation and all of these unholy and un-American things that we have been told of from day to day. You fix the amount that a man can grow, the amount that he can market, the amount to be refined, and you pay a tremendous subsidy to the producers . . . Yet, I am for it. [The Agriculture Secretary] is for it. The President is for it."[13] Florida's two sugar companies were not quite sure they were for it. Because the allotment awards were based on production rates in the previous two years, and Florida's industry was then in its infancy, the state got only 6 percent of the domestic quota. U.S. Sugar had begun on a grand scale, so it received a payment of $1,067,665 in the first year after Jones-Costigan's passage, the biggest allotment payment made to a single company. Fellsmere, which had a very bad first year, was devastated by the new law. Still, neither company was allowed to expand, and both bitterly protested rules that reserved quotas for foreign producers while restricting domestic production.[14] In a section of a 1936 pamphlet called "Our men wear shoes," one U.S. Sugar company official complained that: "Diligent search has failed to disclose a single instance, other than the United States where the home producer of a necessity of life is discouraged and restricted for the benefit of alien peoples."[15]

Congress temporarily lifted production quotas during World War II, but Florida's tonnage only rose from 29,000 in 1934 to 175,000 in the 1950s; Cuba measured its production in the millions of tons.[16] For twenty-five years, therefore, the Jones-Costigan Amendment to the AAA kept Florida's sugar industry in a state of arrested development and kept a lid on the boiling cauldron of discontent that was Cuba.

Boom

By the 1950s, however, Cuba was boiling over again. By this time, Cuba's share of the foreign allotment was nearly 99 percent, so there was no way to offer an allotment increase as incentive for good behavior. Having used up all its carrots, Congress tried the stick. In 1956, the year Fidel Castro and his brother Raul returned to Cuba to launch their second attempt at revolution (the first one having ended in jail and exile), Congress cut Cuba's allotment to just 43 percent. Lawmakers' intent was to take the wind out of the revolution's sails by pressuring Cuban elites to oust Fulgencio Batista in favor of a reform-minded leader. What impact that devastating measure had on the success of Fidel's revolutionary mobilization we'll never know, but three bloody years later, Batista packed it in, chose a successor, and left for the Dominican Republic.[17] The Ejército Revolucionario—the Army of the Revolution—soon occupied Havana.

At first it seemed that Congress might embrace post-revolutionary Cuba, and Fidel would simply inherit the U.S. sugar quota. But it soon became clear that Fidel was not the sort of revolutionary you could bring home to mother, at least not at the height of the Cold War. After returning home from a triumphant visit to the United States, during which he met Vice President Nixon and spoke (at length) to an enormous crowd outside Harvard Stadium, Fidel confiscated Cuban estates of over 1,000 acres and barred foreigners from owning Cuban land altogether. In July 1960, Congress struck back by reducing Cuba's quota, but the old "cuota y flota" strategy no longer worked because Communist Cuba had new trading partners in the Soviet Union and its allies. After buying up all the Cuban cigars in Washington, DC, newly elected president John F. Kennedy fired back again with the only thing the United States had left in its holster—an embargo of all trade with Cuba. But when the dust cleared, Fidel was still standing and the United States had lost half its sugar.

In a panic, Congress reassigned Cuba's quota to U.S. producers, lifted the twenty-six-year restriction on domestic sugarcane production (temporarily, lawmakers thought), and gave American growers the green light to plant as much sugar as they could grow.

News of the sugar embargo spread through South Florida like a muck fire. Each new producer angled for a piece of Cuba's suspended production quota. But these weren't homesteaders racing to stake a 160-acre claim in covered wagons. Sugarcane was big business—agribusiness. Sugarcane production required heavy capitalization because, although Florida sugar wasn't refined into table sugar in the state, the cane had to be milled near where it was grown. Once cut, sugarcane loses its sucrose content by the minute, so it has to be milled immediately. Once a cane company expended millions building a modern mill, it needed thousands of tons of sugarcane to feed it.

U.S. Sugar immediately doubled its productive capacity, building a second mill equal to its first. Each mill could process 200,000 tons of sugarcane annually.[18] Vegetable growers and cattle ranchers transformed themselves into sugar planters almost overnight, and either sold their crop to U.S. Sugar or joined together to form their own cooperatives and build their own mills. Fifty-one vegetable farmers and cattle ranchers came together almost immediately to found the Sugar Growers Cooperative. Another fifty formed the Atlantic Sugar Association, which produced 9,500 tons of sugar in 1964 and almost 95,000 in 1984.[19]

Most of the newcomers to the state's sugar region were Cuban exiles who made their way to Florida with whatever liquid capital they had. The most famous were Alfy and Pepe Fanjul, scions of the massive Gómez-Mena sugar empire in Cuba. Even the street on which their Havana office was located was named for their grandfather, Andres Gómez-Mena, who had come to Cuba from Spain in the first half of the nineteenth century and launched Cuba's modern sugar industry. Alfy and Pepe had lived off this inherited fortune, throwing parties for the Duke and Duchess of Windsor, golfing with Leol Guinness, and earning the epithets "parasites and leeches" from their revolutionary detractors.[20]

"On New Year's Eve 1958," Marie Brenner writes, "as Alfy and Pepe Fanjul were watching the fireworks at the Havana Yacht Club, word spread through the party that Batista had fled." Their father was soon arrested and released. He and Pepe fled to New York, leaving twenty-one-year-old Alfy in charge of one of the largest sugar companies in Cuba—ten mills, three alcohol distilleries, 150,000 acres of cane, and thousands of workers. Alfy was alone in the Havana office on the Avenida de Gómez-Mena when soldiers of the Ejército Revolucionario arrived, threw "their machine guns down on the conference table," and announced that the family empire would be theirs. They were right. Alfy's father's mansion became Cuba's national art museum, and Alfy and Pepe's childhood home "in the country-club section of Havana" is one of Fidel Castro's residences. The corporate offices are a mall.[21]

After being threatened and even shot at in the days that followed, Alfy Fanjul left Cuba for good. He joined his brothers and father and thousands of other Cuban landholders in the United States. He and Pepe bought houses in Palm Beach; land from "scores" of cattle, vegetable, and sugar farmers in the Everglades; and a defunct Louisiana sugar mill, which they had dismantled and floated on barges to Florida. Their first crop in 1961–62 "brought in $1 million," but a flood wiped them out the following year. "We lost everything and then some," Alfy recalled.[22] They leased land and started over. By the 1990s, they would be the biggest sugar producers in the United States, with over 190,000 acres in cane, more than the Gómez-Mena family had owned in Cuba. A 1967 photo shows Alfy and his wife Lillian in Palm Beach with King Leopold III of Belgium and his wife. Alfy and Pepe were the princes of Florida sugar.[23]

Cuban exiles alone built eight new sugar mills and hired thousands of skilled Cuban exiles to work in them (Cuban citizens being the one Cuban export the United States didn't embargo). The farms changed hands like stocks and bonds. Fellsmere had gone into foreclosure in 1950 but it came out reorganized in 1959, under the ownership of the South Porto Rico Sugar Company, a multinational based in Puerto Rico and the Dominican Republic that combined German capital, Barbadian technology, Caribbean labor, and New York management. South Porto Rico renamed the farm Okeelanta, and brought in Cubans to run it. It then bought farms called Atlantic and Osceola, the latter being the property the Fanjuls had lost in the 1961 flood. South Porto Rico later sold out to the multinational Gulf & Western, which eventually sold the whole affair back to the Fanjuls.[24]

Not long after the Fanjuls' arrival in Florida, they were followed by diplomat Cold Warrior William Pawley, founder of the legendary World War II Flying Tigers. At various times U.S. ambassador to Cuba, Peru, and Brazil, Pawley was a close confidant of both Batista and the Dominican Republic's dictator, Rafael Trujillo.[25] Besides being a CIA conduit, he was a multimillionaire who owned Cuban mineral rights, sugar plantations, the Havana Bus Company, and Cuba's national airline. Tellingly, when Castro nationalized foreign-owned properties, Pawley's went first. In 1962, Pawley, who already had properties in Miami, joined the exodus to Florida's sugar region, where he bought the Talisman Sugar Corporation in South Bay. With the help of several expatriate Cubans and the financial assistance of Henry Ford II, he produced 325 tons of sugar that year and nearly 95,000 tons two decades later.[26]

The most flamboyant of the new sugar barons was Charles Bluhdorn, the self-made multimillionaire who founded Gulf & Western (G&W), which by then owned Paramount Pictures, Jensen Swimwear, the New York

Knicks, the New York Rangers, and the Miss Universe Pageant. G&W joined the sugar frenzy in 1967, buying the South Porto Rico Company. Bluhdorn's $62 million got him three farms in Florida, totaling 90,000 acres or an area the size of Barbados. The deal made G&W the largest landowner in the Dominican Republic and the owner of the biggest sugar mill in the world. A few years earlier, not many Americans could have bought property in the Dominican Republic because of Trujillo's nationalist policies. After the U.S. embargo of Cuba, however, Trujillo played on his importance as a bulwark against communism in the Caribbean to win the bulk of Cuba's forfeited sugar quota (sugar quota diplomacy could apparently work both ways). He and his cronies then monopolized the land and thus the fruits of the quota. By the early 1960s, however, Trujillo had outworn his usefulness to the United States, and was assassinated in 1961 with the blessing, if not the active participation, of the CIA. In 1965, Lyndon Johnson sent in U.S. Marines to install Trujillo's former vice president as his successor, and stabilized the new president's administration with an even bigger share of the foreign quota. The way was then open for U.S. firms to gain Dominican land and a share of its quota. G&W snapped up the South Porto Rico Company. Whether Bluhdorn colluded in the coup or simply benefited from it remains unclear.[27]

Bluhdorn immediately crushed a strike in the Dominican Republic, after which he turned the mill's bachelors' quarters into a hotel, built a golf course, tennis courts, baseball facilities, a private airstrip, and a full-scale replica of a sixteenth-century European village. As one observer put it, some companies built company towns; Gulf & Western turned the Dominican Republic into a "company country." Bluhdorn's tourism gambit lost money, but the cost of hiring Haitian cane cutters in the Dominican Republic and British West Indian cane cutters in the United States was so low and sugar prices in the United States so high that Gulf & Western's gains more than made up for its losses. Bluhdorn's second-in-command once visited the cane cutter's barracks in Florida and declared them "one degree short of Dachau." Within a decade, G&W's Dominican holdings alone were worth $300 million.[28]

These were Florida's new sugarlords: big men with big ambitions, powerful political connections, and in several cases, well-founded antipathy toward rebels of any kind. They planted sugar on a massive scale, catapulting Florida into the ranks of the world's largest sugar-producing regions. The total acreage of cane in Florida grew nearly eightfold, from less than 36,000 acres in 1955 to over 276,000 in 1973. In 1953, Florida's two sugar-producing farms had produced 173,000 tons of sugar between them. Thirteen years later, Florida's motley crew of Cuban exiles, counterrevolutionaries, corporate magnates, and born-again ranchers and vegetable growers produced nearly a million tons.[29]

FIGURE 7.1 "Big Sugar." An aerial view of the U.S. Sugar Corporation mill on the south side of Lake Okeechobee, Clewiston, Florida, 1958. (Photo courtesy of State Archives of Florida.)

But there was a catch. While the INS obliged Florida's new industry by granting Cuban millworkers permanent immigrant status in the United States, Cuban exiles did not generally take cane-cutting jobs. As legal permanent residents, they could work anywhere. Why cut cane? To secure harvest labor, the new growers looked to guestworkers from the English-speaking Caribbean, adopting without alteration the labor system pioneered by vegetable and sugar producers during World War II and continued, after 1952, as the H2 Program. The trouble was that the Florida boom coincided with the peak of anti-guestworker sentiment. The Bracero Program was dying and, if the Secretary of Labor had his way, the H2 Program would be next.

AMERICANS WON'T WORK FOR STOOP WAGES

In 1963, the year the Bracero Program was given one more year to live, U.S. officials in the Kennedy administration had tried to improve conditions for cane cutters in Florida by raising the "adverse effect wage" growers were required to pay guestworkers from 95 cents an hour to $1.15. The reform backfired. Had the cane cutters been paid by the hour, the pay hike would have been a boon. But because growers paid cane cutters by the row, it was easy for unscrupulous employers to circumvent the wage hike by dropping their row prices. Under the older rules imposed by Eisenhower's Secretary of Labor James Mitchell, which were still in force, growers were supposed to pay "build-up pay" if men paid by the "cut row" made less than the hourly adverse effect wage. But the cane companies got around that requirement, according to liaison officer

Walter Comrie, by training the "ticket writers" who recorded what the men accomplished each day to fabricate the number of hours the men worked, so that the hours recorded on men's time cards matched the amount of cane they cut. The result was that men appeared to earn more per hour than they actually did.[30] So if the mandated hourly wage was $2, a man cutting cane for eight hours would have been entitled to at least $16 for the day, before deductions. If, over the course of that eight-hour day, however, he harvested one "cut row" of cane priced at $8, he would only have earned $1 an hour. His employer would therefore owe him $8 in build-up pay. To avoid that, according to Comrie, the ticket writers would record that the worker had worked only four hours, so it would appear that he had earned the adverse effect wage of $2 an hour. An "R" marked on the man's timecard would indicate that he had "refused work."[31] Men who questioned the hours on their tickets or complained that they had not refused work were told not to worry; they were paid by the row, not the hour. Guestworkers too, ticket writers who challenged the deception would be put "back on the knife."[32]

"Each time the minimum wage went up, say, twenty percent," Walter Comrie recalled, "the sugar wages would go up only five percent, and they'd cut back on the hours to make sure it looked like they'd make the minimum." All sugar producers shaved hours from workers' time cards to greater and lesser degrees, Comrie reported. In 1964, he noted in his diary that fields at the Sugar Cane Growers Cooperative "were so underpriced that it is shocking." "The majority of workers, most of whom worked from seven a.m. to three p.m. seven days a week, were given 3, 4 & 5 hours a day [on their time cards], and in practically every case their time cards were marked 'R,' meaning they had refused additional hours of work."[33]

The cane companies looked for other ways to cut their costs as well, according to Comrie. U.S. Sugar responded to the wage hike by increasing the amount it deducted from each man's pay for meals. Comrie protested this deduction in a letter to the Chief Liaison Harold Edwards, noting that "the increase of the hourly wage . . . as handed down by the Department of Labour was intended to be borne by the sugar producing employers from their profits." Edwards ignored him.[34] The effects of these practices were felt immediately. "Sugar cane used to be one of our best crops," the chief liaison from the Bahamas recalled. "I can remember when our men at Fellsmere made $16 a day and knocked off at 2 p.m. But when the U.S. Agricultural Department . . . raised the minimum hourly wage for cane harvesting to $1.15, production demands on the men went up far more than wages as cane growers tried to get more work out of the men." Bahamians, who only cut cane at Fellsmere, were withdrawn. "It isn't worthwhile working for nothing," the liaison noted.[35]

ANGEL OF MERCY

Caught up in the campaign to end the Bracero Program, Secretary of Labor Willard Wirtz knew little or nothing about what was going on in Florida. The child and grandchild of educators, and a law professor before working on Adlai Stevenson's campaign, Wirtz later became Stevenson's law partner before taking the job of Under Secretary of Labor in the Kennedy administration. He became Secretary of Labor in 1962 when Arthur Goldberg left the post to become associate justice of the Supreme Court. Staying on as Labor Secretary after Kennedy's death, Wirtz, like his new boss President Lyndon Johnson, faced rising prices, rising unemployment, and a slowing economy—a combination of bad news dubbed "stagflation." As a general in Johnson's War on Poverty, Wirtz's mission was to tackle unemployment with a vengeance. He devised programs to train and employ the hardcore unemployed: youths, dropouts, older workers, denizens of the inner city. Ending the importation of guestworkers was one battle in that war.

For Wirtz, it made little sense to import Mexican and Caribbean farmworkers when American farmworkers were unemployed for two-thirds of the year. Growers could not demonstrate the existence of labor shortages, he believed, until they had offered decent conditions and attractive wages. "The false notion that Americans won't do stoop labor was carefully nurtured," Wirtz noted, "from the truer fact that they won't work for stoop wages." Until employers lost access to foreign workers, he reasoned, they would had no incentive to improve the conditions they offered.[36] "He has an evangelical complex about this thing," Florida Senator Spessard Holland complained. "He thinks himself a kind of angel of mercy, a reformer of sorts."[37]

Having hammered nails into the Bracero Program's coffin by refusing to certify western growers' application for Mexican labor through the H2 Program, Wirtz issued new H2 regulations designed to make the program so costly that only growers truly desperate for labor would even consider using it. Eisenhower's Secretary of Labor James Mitchell had already required growers to pay for workers' housing and in-country transportation. In 1964, Wirtz required them to pay workers' transportation costs to and from Kingston, if they finished the season, and he limited H2 workers' contracts to a maximum of 120 days (their contracts had been renewable up to three years), which added to those transportation costs.[38] The new rules also required prospective H2 employers to convince Labor Department officials that they had made a "reasonable" effort to recruit native workers. Whatever guestworkers got, moreover, domestic workers employed by the same companies had to get too.[39]

Certain that there were large numbers of underemployed farmworkers in the United States, Wirtz then denied fruit and vegetable growers' requests for H2 Workers in Florida and the Midwest, and persuaded Connecticut tobacco growers to switch to Puerto Ricans.[40] The results were striking. By late 1965, Bahamian H2 workers, who had been concentrated in fruits and vegetables, dwindled from a high of five thousand to just ten. Within a year, the number of employers importing guestworkers fell from 350 to 37. In four years, the number of Caribbean men imported annually would drop from over 22,000 to 9,000.[41]

Wirtz's reforms resulted in a counterattack in the press and the Senate, calls for Wirtz's job if not his head, and a campaign to remove the labor shortage certification process from the Department of Labor altogether. Legislators from rural states called Wirtz's position "unfortunate and illogical" and predicted agricultural "crises" if H2 workers weren't made available.[42] Florida's senators and congressmen spent hours trying to convince Wirtz not to fire offshore workers, according to Sheffield T. Abood, chair of St. Lucie, Florida's Area Development Council, who insisted that trying to use "local domestic help" was like "trying to convert Castro to democracy." Boynton Beach tomato grower, cattle rancher, and bank executive, Leonard White, was one of the only growers to support Wirtz publicly. "Sure, I could exploit these people," White told a reporter, ". . . but that's not my way. I've found it takes a satisfied person to produce well." White, Kramer noted, wasn't feeling "the bite of the current reported labor shortage" because his 500–600 workers were African Americans, Puerto Ricans, or "Texas Mexicans," not offshore workers. Wirtz "didn't have much choice but to get tough," White insisted. "[A] lot of these farmers exaggerate their labor shortages . . . It makes it harder to tell truth from fiction." Generally, though, growers "howled to high heaven," Wirtz recalled. Eighty pages of the congressional record were devoted to Florida congressmen's complaints, but Wirtz refused to relent.[43] "[T]here has been no significant labor shortages and no significant crop losses due to lack of labor," he boasted in a letter to President Johnson, insisting that newspaper stories featuring photos of rotted fruit had been staged for effect. Employers, he insisted, could do without guestworkers.[44]

Wirtz had killed the H2 Program in most crops, but he wasn't so sure he could do the same for sugar, which was cut exclusively by guestworkers. In April 1965, he traveled to Florida to see for himself how things were. First, he visited the citrus region to see the effects of his ban on the black, white, and Tejano farmworkers who now had more access to work. "I want to find out how we can make things better," he said, striding up to a worker with his hand out in front of him. Citrus growers seized the opportunity to try to convince Wirtz to rescind his ban on H2 workers in their industry, but got nowhere. At a press conference with Florida's governor, Wirtz was "sulky," according to reporter Peter Kramer; with employers he was "reserved." With domestic citrus workers in Winter Garden, however, he was "folksy, friendly, direct, and warm as he shook hands with workers and asked them questions." It was clear which side Wirtz was on.[45]

Arriving in Belle Glade, however, Wirtz was less sure what the sides were. He met with sugar industry officials, and had a long conversation with Harold Edwards, the H2 Program's charming Chief Liaison. Edwards assured him that the H2 Program suffered none of the abuses that had brought down the Bracero Program and that locals would never cut cane. Watching men work, Wirtz was inclined to believe him. "Sugarcane is the worst job in the world," Wirtz told me. "It is the awfulest job . . . They go in there with machetes. It will have been burned over perhaps. It will be full of snakes."[46]

Nonetheless, as a veteran of the battle to defeat the Bracero Program, Wirtz had developed a deep and abiding skepticism of agricultural employers. He wasn't prepared to leave Belle Glade without talking directly to some of the H2 workers. To his surprise, none would meet with him. "[T]hey won't come," he remembered being told, despite the Chief Liaison's assurances that they were well-treated and content. Undaunted, Wirtz waited for nightfall, and arranged an outside meeting in the dark. That night, he stood under a porch light, facing a mass of black men. They could see Wirtz but he couldn't see them, which is how they wanted it. The men's blackened and sticky work clothes smelled of sweat and burnt sugarcane. "I would hear voices—they would ask questions," Wirtz recalled, but "they weren't going to be identified."[47]

Wirtz remembers little beyond those disembodied voices, but his records reveal that he left Florida profoundly ambivalent about the H2 Program. Returning to Washington to make his decision, he found himself beset not just by growers but by the U.S. State Department and by Jamaican officials, who warned of calamitous social and foreign policy consequences if Jamaican guestworkers lost their jobs in the United States. Jamaica was playing its Cuba card, warning U.S. diplomats that Jamaica's friendly orientation "toward the United States and the West," depended on the H2 Program's survival.[48] The Cuban revolution had created Florida's sugar industry; now the threat of its spread would save its guestworker program.

Independence

On August 3, 1962, thousands of Jamaicans cheered Princess Margaret, Queen Elizabeth's sister, as she arrived in Kingston to mark Jamaican independence from England. Three days later, Jamaicans celebrated the birth of their nation, though England had left them with few resources besides pride and people. There was little industry, no social security system, no unemployment insurance, not even a public school system beyond the first few grades of elementary school. The sugar industry was moribund, and agriculture—the nation's biggest employer—still relied primarily on small, peasant farms. Jamaicans were proud of their new university and the island's infant bauxite industry, but both made little difference to the average citizen. The unemployment rate was 25 or 50 percent of the workforce—depending on whether you counted farmers selling home-grown mangos in front of their shacks and women peddling patties from road-side stands as unemployed. There's no doubt that Jamaica needed the jobs created by the guestworker program and the dollars guestworkers sent home.[49]

Britain's parliament celebrated Jamaican independence by passing the restrictionist Commonwealth Immigrant Act, which shut England's doors to immigrants from former colonies in the Caribbean and South Asia, except for the immediate relatives of those who had already made it under the wire. Migrants from former white colonies, like Ireland, were not restricted by the Act, but Jamaica lost a key outlet for its population and a key source of foreign currency. Jamaican officials presumed (reasonably) that the United States would take up the slack, since independent nations in the Western Hemisphere were not subject to U.S. immigration quotas. But, although Jamaica was no longer a colony, U.S. officials delayed lifting its 100-person quota, fearing a flood of poor, black migrants to the United States. Three years after independence, Jamaican leaders' hopes were buoyed by news of the 1965 Hart-Cellars immigration reform bill, which promised to remove the United States' old discriminatory quota system and create equal quotas for all countries. But although Hart-Cellars passed, raising Jamaica's annual immigration quota from 105 to 20,000, Congress delayed its implementation for three years, even as Jamaica's urban poor rioted over unemployment.[50]

Even if Hart-Cellars had been implemented immediately, it wouldn't have been much help to Jamaican farmworkers hoping to emigrate to the United States. Unless they could gain entry as a spouse or child of someone already lawfully admitted for permanent residency, farmworkers remained ineligible for permanent admission. Hart-Cellars allotted 10 percent of the total quota of immigrants to "skilled and unskilled labor," but specifically excluded those performing work "of a temporary or seasonal nature" from permanent status.[51] Poor, rural Jamaicans were stuck with the guestworker program, which Wirtz now threatened.

With avenues for emigration cut off and remittance checks barely flowing, Jamaican society was, in the words of American diplomats in Kingston, "explosive." Jamaicans *with* jobs were demanding better pay and benefits. In the early 1960s, there was a postal strike, a hospital strike, a port workers' strike, and a retail workers' strike. Jamaicans without jobs were rioting. Unemployed people vented their anger first at the Chinese in West Kingston and then against Jamaican leaders more generally. Riots in 1965 were followed by another round of strikes that shut down Jamaica's postal service, customs service, railroad system, water commission, public works department, prisons, food stores, sugar estates, ports, sanitation department, two daily newspapers, and the bus service. The following year, the government declared a state of emergency in Kingston after renewed riots during which protesters chanted, "We want work, we want work, we want work." Robert McGregor, the American General Consul in Kingston, noted in his dispatch to the U.S. State Department that the local papers neglected to mention that the rioters were also chanting, "or we going kill . . . or we going kill." McGregor called Jamaica the "Drunken Helot of West Indian labor-management relations."[52]

Throughout all this, Jamaica's first black prime minister, Alexander Bustamente, lay blind and dying, but still refusing to resign his office. Under intense pressure at home, Jamaica's Acting Prime Minister Donald Sangster unleashed a torrent of warnings in angry conversations with McGregor. Unless Jamaica's farmworker program was retained, Sangster insisted, its infinitesimal share of the U.S. sugar quota enlarged, and its immigration quota expanded, potentially "explosive" problems could "seriously jeopardize U.S. interest[s]."[53]

The State Department was not prepared to take the chance. Sangster may have been exaggerating the risk, but what were a few thousand farmworker jobs against the prospect of the domino effect knocking Jamaica into Fidel Castro's orbit? John R. Kanline, the U.S. State Department's Chief of Jamaican Affairs, explained the department's position: "We at the State Department are sympathetic with the Labor Department's attempts to secure jobs for Americans . . . And the Labor Department apparently has been more successful in finding Americans to do the work than once was thought possible." "It's just that when these efforts affect other countries, the State Department's role is to receive and deal with the complaints of other countries. Therefore we have been working with the Labor Department and others on this matter to see if a drastic reduction in the West Indian farm labor program can possibly be avoided." When the Labor Department was "being too tough on the program," Kanline explained, the Jamaican ambassador would call the State Department, and the State Department would call the Department of Labor to set up a meeting with the ambassador, Wirtz, and perhaps the chief liaison officer. "In general," Kanline noted, Jamaica's Prime Minister's plea "seems to have been that when his people are unemployed they get mad and he doesn't want his government to get unseated."[54]

The State Department thus warned Wirtz not to "get tough" on the H2 Program for fear that if he eliminated Jamaica's source of jobs and remittances in the United States, Jamaica's Labour Party would fall, and the socialist PNP would come to power. "It would be in our nation's interest," Kanline concluded, "that Jamaica remain friendly, quiet and stable in an otherwise restive area that includes Cuba, Haiti and the Dominican Republic."[55]

In the end, the only domino that fell was Wirtz's plan to terminate the H2 Program. Convinced that no Americans would take cane-cutting jobs and that Jamaicans had to have them, Wirtz recertified the need for foreign workers in the sugar and apple industries (the latter only because its harvest complemented the former, which helped sugar growers offset the cost of importing the workers from Kingston). Wirtz also allowed the burgeoning sugar industry to hire all the West Indian workers freed up by the decertification of foreign workers in vegetables, tobacco, and orchards. "All in all," Kanline noted, "the situation has worked out well. At one time the Jamaican leaders were afraid that the program would be cut off completely and abruptly. However, their fears never materialized."[56]

By 1968, all nine thousand of the remaining H2 workers were dedicated to the sugar industry, an increase of five thousand over the sugar industry's pre-embargo years. Eventually, the workforce increased to fifteen thousand—more than triple its pre-boom size—but the sugar industry increased its acreage nearly eightfold. Men wielding machetes had to make up the difference.

NEAR-COMBAT CONDITIONS

The result of the post-embargo sugar boom and Wirtz's reforms was what assembly line workers called a "speed up" and textile workers a "stretch out." The National Committee for Manpower Policy called it "near-combat conditions."[57] The minimum wage went up, but so did the amount of work cane cutters had to do to earn that wage. Neither the U.S. Department of Agriculture nor the Labor Department seemed to have taken into account the fact that cane cutters were paid by the task, not by the hour. Had officials attached the new hourly rate of pay to a minimum production standard—say, a ton of sugarcane or so many feet of cane—the wage hike might have been enforceable, but they didn't and it wasn't. Instead, half-mile-long rows became increasingly common, and men could work all day and never "burst through" the end of a double row over seven football fields in length.[58] "We working by the task and it was very cheap," recalled Clifford Platt.[59] "It was unbelievable," Renford Brown remembered ruefully, shaking his head. "It was a rough, rough place."[60]

No working conditions were comparable to this except coal mining, the National Committee for Manpower Policy noted, and in that job, wages were much higher.[61]

A few small companies dealt with the demands of the harvest by using high wages as an incentive for good work. Jim Beardsley of Beardsley Farm had especially good relations with his workers, according to Comrie, "because he priced the fields based on the speed of the slowest man." But, Comrie noted, Beardsley only hired about thirty men. Large companies and cooperatives hired the vast majority of the workers and they priced their fields based on the speed of good cutters or even the best cutters, so that only the fastest workers could hope to make more than the minimum wage specified in their contracts, and then only by working dangerously fast.[62]

The best cutters were rewarded with jobs as "pushers," which meant instead of cutting, they would walk behind the cane cutters, barking at them to cut faster, neater, and lower to the ground where the sucrose was most concentrated. "Hey," James Matthews recalled the pushers yelling, "cut down them stubble and keep it down!" "Them check you out," if you didn't cut "low, low, low," added another man who only cut cane for one season in the 1960s. Matthews also recalled pushers "checking men out" for cutting the cane too high or too slowly. They'd say: "go to the house. Back a the house." If a worker was "checked out" three times, the employer could "cashier him," sending him home at his own expense.[63]

"[I]n Florida it was really rough, really rough," Noel Porter recalled, "but you know you really fight it out."[64] Driven by fear of repatriation and the need to work long and hard in order to earn the sort of money they had come for, the cane cutters ran to their rows in the morning, stood to eat when the lunch truck arrived, rarely stopped to rest, and fortified themselves with a homemade concoction of Guinness Stout, eggnog, sugar, raw eggs, and carrot juice they called "Petrol."[65] "[T]he cutting of the sugar cane was very tough," Clifford Platt recalled. "It was very hard work. Dirty work. And black because the cane was burned . . . you have to make love with those canes because you have to bring them up on yourself . . . You have to mingle with the cane. It was very hard."[66]

As a means of raising productivity without raising labor costs, the sugar industry's boom-time stretch-out was enormously effective. According to a U.S. Department of Agriculture study, it took 2.4 labor hours to cut a ton of sugarcane in Florida in 1963. A decade later, it took only 1.6 hours, a productivity increase of more than 30 percent.[67]

The result of the accelerated pace was a horrific injury rate, despite the fact that the men wore knee, shin, and foot guards that made them look like partly dressed medieval knights. About 10 percent of the five thousand men employed by the Florida Sugar Producers Association (one of

FIGURE 7.2 Sugarcane as far as the eye can see, Clewiston, Florida. (Photo courtesy of State Archives of Florida.)

the two recruiting organizations) were injured during the 1965–66 season. Dr. James Gray of Belle Glade and his three associates treated about seventy-five offshore workers a day for lacerations, cornea abrasions, severed fingers, cut legs, hernias, and back injuries. About 2 percent, Walter Comrie noted, "would sustain a serious injury, involving permanent partial disability." Roy Johnson, a father of eleven, spent fourteen seasons in

FIGURE 7.3 Noel and Valerie Porter, 2006. Noel had been traveling to the U.S. as a guestworker since he was in his twenties. In 2006, now a father of eight and grandfather of four, he was still traveling to the U.S. to pick apples. (Photo by Renny Hahamovitch.)

Florida, before severing his thumb with a machete in 1984. After that, he says, "They don't send me any more requests." He thinks he was never called back not because of his injury but because he talked to an attorney to file a worker's compensation claim. "When you show them you are not a fool, and like to be treated like somebody, they push you out," he told a reporter.[68]

"Ronald" described the injuries that season. "The first guy that really get injuries, he get cut on his right thumb." He spent about three weeks in the bunks, then "went back out and . . . got cut again." A "second guy," whose "back been pulled," spent over a month in the camp. Then two more men got cut, "just like that, until my time comes around, my lucky time." It was a rainy day, he explained, and the cane had grown sideways, attaching itself to the ground at the joints along the stalks. "You have to chop the cane to get yourself a space to stand on the earth." Not realizing that the cane had grown attached to the ground, Ronald lifted it up. "It pull me back down . . . I lost control and then I got hurt." He spent over three weeks in his bunk, during which he was charged for his board. A few days after his injury, another man got cut. "Just today,"

FIGURE 7.4 Collecting cut sugarcane, Pahokee, Florida, 1987. (Photo courtesy of State Archives of Florida.)

the last day of the season, he told a reporter, "another guy got cut." By the mid-1980s, an injury rate of one-third was accepted as a normal cost of doing business.[69]

FIGHTING IT OUT

The workers responded to these combat-like working conditions with guerilla-style labor negotiations that stopped and started and only escalated into full-scale conventional strikes when all else failed. Bryan Green, who worked five seasons for U.S. Sugar beginning in 1966, recalled, "Sometimes we would rebel before we start. Sometimes we leave it and walk back to the camps. Sometimes we leave it and they check you out. You have to walk back to the camp." "If everybody stop," he noted, "they'd go to the office and negotiate a price and tell us and we'd start to work. We did that a lot of time."[70]

Men from the small islands like St. Vincent and St. Lucia had a reputation for even greater militancy than Jamaicans, which was not surprising since recruiters could hardly have avoided experienced cane cutters and union members in those islands, nor in Antigua, where prospective U.S.

FIGURE 7.5 Jamaican H-2A cane cutter, Belle Glade, Florida, 1991.

guestworkers were required by their government to be union members. Antiguans had such a reputation for assertiveness that growers banned them from the Florida sugar industry altogether in the 1960s. U.S. Sugar's head of personnel told the *St. Petersburg Times* that "The Trinidadian was a mistake for the program. He was not in the least docile, was quite capable of speaking up for himself, and did so vigorously."[71]

The increase in militancy in the early 1960s was marked. The strike wave seems to have begun after the imposition of the 1963 pay raise, when row prices fell instead of rising as the men must have expected they would. In November 1964, a crew of men at the Co-op "refused to work for an entire day," according to a liaison officer, after which fifteen workers were sent home "for agitating and inciting others to strike." A month later, 109 men struck the Co-op again when a white foreman said he would shoot a man for shoddy work. Walter Comrie recalls being involved in at least six field strikes per five-month season, and he was just one of four liaison officers in Florida in the 1960s. In 1965, the senior liaison officer noted in his May report that "the liaison officers were called incessantly to settle price queries," and that growers complained that the Caribbean workers were "more demanding and less manageable" in recent years. "It must be recorded," Comrie wrote the same year, "that the workers have complained more within the past two seasons . . . than ever before." Earl Morrison of U.S. Sugar wasn't being hyperbolic when he said he was called out to negotiate "thousands" of small work stoppages in his thirty-five-year career.[72] Ironically, then, sugar companies in Florida created the sort of "explosive" conditions that the State Department had hoped to avoid in Jamaica by convincing Willard Wirtz to continue the H2 Program.

"Our workers have never in the past acted up the way they have recently," James Paulk, the Co-op's section foreman, told an undercover journalist in 1965. "You'd never find a Jamaican who would burn mattresses and break windows because he was discontent. The nigger used to respect you. You were the boss man." "But in the past three to four years," he continued, "there's been an increasing atmosphere of violence. . . . They watch television and those that can read look at the newspaper, and they hear the U.S. nigger has rights and they think they've got rights too. They eat it up like slop. And they figure 'If those American niggers can run the police off the streets, maybe we can too.' They don't know they ain't got rights in this country."[73]

Whether or not the strikers were inspired by the civil rights movements in the United States or the Caribbean (only one of the men I interviewed was aware of the U.S. civil rights movement at the time), the workers' militancy often resulted in small wage increases. Cane company managers had little choice but to negotiate because once the company prepared a field for cutting by setting it on fire—the flames cleared the cane of leaves, snakes, and rats—the field had to be harvested quickly because the cane's sucrose content would begin to fall. But although company officials made small concessions, they would simultaneously root out and repatriate the men who seemed to be behind the agitation. "If we out there," Noel Porter recalled, "and we say, 'boss, it really rough. It wants some more money on it,' the boss, some of them will really check we out and send we to the camp and when evening come we get our ticket, you will see them write 'refused' on it. But we do not refuse the work . . . we just ask a little more money."[74]

In the 1965–1966 season, according to Comrie, 600 of the 5,200 off-shore workers imported by just one of the two recruiting associations were "breached" and repatriated, most as a result of wage disputes.[75] Not all cane cutters who struck or intentionally slowed their cutting were sent home. That would have been too disruptive to the harvest process. Instead, foremen singled out and deported men who were particularly outspoken, whom they called the "village lawyers."[76]

Strike leaders would try to bring out their fellow workers, sometimes using threats or the occasional airborne rock to convince the most reluctant men to join the strike. "You see, with the strike," Noel Porter explained, "we want some more money on the cane, and everybody will come out of the field. The other one can't stay in there . . . because it will still bring more problem. So you know everybody come out and that's how it go." But, he noted, if a strike stretched on, men who wanted to return to work would sometimes inform on the ringleaders.[77]

When deporting ringleaders didn't quell a dispute, company officials could "breach" whole groups of workers and send them home, docking the price of the round-trip airfare from their accumulated savings. As one official of U.S. Sugar explained: "First we talk to the ringleaders. If they don't go back they are breached immediately. Next we talk to the other men. If you can get one to go back to work, the rest will follow like sheep." "When we get the men back on the job," he added, "the village lawyers often try to talk with us again telling us they changed their minds and want to go back to work. But we refuse their request, breach them and send them home." Paulk looked for "the weak spot." "You give the workers the silent treatment," he explained, "because the more you talk to them the worse it gets. Next you try to get them arguing among themselves. Once you start them arguing, you can bust the strike. On the other hand, they're clannish, so if you don't break them up, you won't move them unless you bring in the border patrol or send them home."[78]

Repatriating the "village lawyers" had the effect of preventing separate acts of militancy from coalescing into a single movement. It also had a chilling effect on those who remained. Asked if Jamaican workers ever went on strike, James Matthews, who spent two seasons in Florida's cane fields in the 1960s, loudly declared: "NOOOO, you can't strike. You can't do that . . . because, if you do that, they're going to send home a plane load a-you."[79]

Since men who breached their contracts went home at their own expense, repatriation may have been bothersome to the cane companies, but a strike was not as devastating as it might have been in other crops, because pre-screened replacements could be in Kingston, ready to fly to Miami with twenty-four hours notice. For the cane companies, work stoppages and the occasional mass strike became a cost of doing business, as was a 30 percent injury rate. The key to the system from growers' perspective was to keep labor costs low and workers at work, without the brutal tactics of the sugar industry's early years. As long as the cane returned, or "ratooned" as cane growers put it, the cane companies needed men to ratoon too.[80]

FOR LOVE OR MONEY

Though thousands stopped work at least briefly every year, some men, perhaps most, kept their heads down and stayed out of trouble. As James Matthews put it, "They're cheap, yes, but you can make something."[81] "I like to cut the cane to get the money," twenty-five-year-old Laford Buchett told a reporter. "I invest it in business."[82] Thirty-two-year-old Irving Wright was a mason by trade (not information he would have shared with recruiters), but work in Florida helped out, he said. "I really like coming back up here every year." He and his wife and two children got things "we couldn't afford if I just had my construction job."[83] The wife of a cane cutter proudly explained that her husband brought "clothes and food and shoes for the children because things are more cheaper over there. It's expensive in Jamaica . . . we all enjoy them a lot."[84] "I've heard people say if you want something, you know you have to run for it," said a man from Hanover Parish, who wouldn't give the *St. Petersburg Times* reporter his name. "I love the farm work program. It changed my life. It's rough, but it means a lot." Colin Plummer despaired of earning enough at home: "I plant things, watch them grow." But, he said, "the money beat me."[85]

Men's letters reveal the immediacy of their needs and the practicality of their purpose. "I didn't get the pot," one Jamaican man wrote home, but I bought the stove, the fridge, and I have 20 days to go. . . . I would like you to order me some materials to work on the house. I would like 10 pieces of $2'' \times 4'' \times 16''$. I would like 50 sheets of zinc and I would like 200 blocks." "[T]ell the carpenter to go ahead and work," he added.[86]

Most earnings went to everyday expenses like bills, children's school fees, and groceries. Some added rooms to their houses, or tried to, but it took many years of labor in the United States to build an entire house.[87] In 1986, after cutting cane for five to six months a year for twenty-three years, Arthur Brown was still building a house for his wife and children in Spanish Town. Samuel Brown explained the problem simply: "Them was cheap," he said of his U.S. employers.[88] Even long-time guestworkers did not appear to accumulate land or livestock as a result of their participation in the program. When I ask former cane cutters James Matthews and Oscar Cottrill whether the money they earned in the United States in a season was enough to buy a piece of land, they just laughed.[89]

Those who tried to use their savings to develop a business tended to buy consumer items to sell or appliances like refrigerators that allowed them to become small shopkeepers at home. "It was the hardest work I have ever done in my life," Leroy McKenzie recalled, "But money is more faster in sugar cane. There are things in America most of us would like to achieve." With the money he earned, he bought small consumer items—radios, watches, clothes—and resold them at home for a little more than he had paid for them. "The situation is not nice," he said; "Other men could not stand the work, but I could stand it," he noted proudly. In the end, though, McKenzie couldn't stand it. In 1984, after seven winters in Florida as a cane cutter, he injured his back stepping into a rabbit hole. The injury left him unable to lift his two-year-old daughter without a flash of pain down the back of his left leg. He would have been deported without workers' compensation, he told a reporter, "if he hadn't taken a taxi to a legal aid office himself." He complained that he received no help from his liaison officer, who favored "sending me back home without anything." A lawyer helped him sue the Sugar Cane Growers Cooperative. While waiting to go to court, his family relied on his wife's income, which she earned by selling Ting (Jamaica's grapefruit soda) and Red Stripe (Jamaica's beer) from the cooler he brought back from the United States.[90]

The pressure to perform, to do well, to send back money, to not come back empty-handed, was enormous. The average Jamaican guestworker supported a family of six and many also sent cash to friends and parents. Fully half had children by women who no longer lived with them, and 90 percent of those men reported that they sent remittances to those "baby mothers," even if the bulk of their savings went to their wives. H2 workers, in other words, had communities to support.[91] "I was so glad for that $5.00 even though it is small," a woman wrote back to "Clifford" in the United States from Portland, Jamaica. "I was so broken it has help me a lot. So when you have [something] if is even $1.00 you can send it."[92] "Remember thing is hard out here, so please try and see what you can get out of it," one woman wrote from Guy's Hill, St. Catherine. She cautioned her man not to "work too much" and to "take thing easy," but closed by saying the children were all right *for the time.*[93]

H2 workers' pride rested on their ability to come back with something. "Here I send you this smalls to help with the light bill," one man wrote to his mother; "Please don't laugh at it." "I don't [want to] come home without anything, so I am saving up to finish up, to do some shopping and to pay for my excess weight, when coming home."[94] "Dear Fatty," a Jamaican cane cutter wrote home to a friend, "How keeping?" "I write you and send you $26 . . . You wouldn't know what I'm going through. We get a cane row for $30. It takes 2 days to cut it. That works out to be some one dollar and some cents an hour. I spoke to the timekeeper . . . and he's ready to eat me up. He says we just have to work fast enough and then we'll make even more than the hourly wages they promised us." "Imagine!" he remarked, "To leave Jamaica, so many hundreds of miles, to come to America and work for one dollar and some cents an hour! Please, don't tell Claudette what I've written," he added in closing. "I don't want her to worry, or think I'm coming home without anything."[95]

Perhaps because men had so little control over what they earned and whether they were called back to work in the United States, few farmworkers seem to have shared the details of their experiences with friends and family. In 2006, when the men in front of the Brandon Hill Dead House set aside their dominoes to talk to me, it became clear that they had never before talked to each other about their experiences, although the tiny community of Brandon Hill had depended heavily on the Farmworker Programme for decades. Three of the men present had cut cane in Florida in the 1960s and they were unanimous about the cheapness of their "bossmen." Yet they were shocked to discover that their neighbor, Wayne Clark, a much younger man who was still "traveling" to the United States, was still experiencing the same treatment they felt they had suffered forty years earlier. As they compared their experiences for the first time, they became more excited and their patois got faster and thicker until I was completely unable to follow the conversation.[96]

Even when men did come home with stories of how "rough" Florida was, few Jamaicans wanted to believe them. "Lots of West Indians always love to come to America," explained "Ronald" because "them don't know the real America . . . they don't care or believe or think about the roughness of the work."[97] "I really give thanks to coming on the contract," one man explained, "but before I travel I really never have the experience about cutting sugarcane in Florida . . . The bossman, the white folks, have you [on] a tight rope for cutting sugarcane."[98] "Anthony" told filmmaker Stephanie Black that "Sometime I . . . explain to my family . . . and tell them the situation up here and they don't believe me." He had to show them his pay stub to prove he had not made much money. "They can't believe how long [I was] up here and did not take home even $1,500 in our pocket, and things for our kids." "Maybe they . . . think that we go to bar and drink our money . . . but it's not true. I really try to keep my money close to my family."[99]

Any little bit earned was enough to convince men to return, even men who were injured or felt they had been underpaid. Carlton Morris, a mason and yam farmer, who had cut sugarcane in Florida for five years and picked apples in Canada and northern U.S. states for four, explained that with the money he earned, he had bought a freezer and materials for a cement block house he was building. At the same time, though, he insisted that he had been underpaid: "If I had a $20 row to cut and I worked eight hours, then they would mark down that I only worked five," Morris said. According to pay stubs from December 1984, which he showed reporter Tim O'Meilia, Morris had only worked sixty-three hours over a two-week period. But he worked much more, he insisted, at least seven hours a day, on most days, and sometimes seven days a week. Morris had also been injured three times, once as a new recruit in 1979 when he cut his knee; again three years later when he injured his eye; and in 1985, when he slipped on a pile of cut cane, damaging a nerve in his neck. He had not been able to return to the United States since. Without his offshore income, he was unable to finish his house and send his two oldest children, aged three and five, to preschool. Despite his complaints about the program, he would have returned to the United States if he were able to do so. "If the company would take me, I would keep going," he said unequivocally.[100] Bryan Green participated in countless work stoppages in his five seasons with U.S. Sugar from 1966 to 1971, but still thought that "[i]t was pretty decent back then."[101] Josh Stone, who cut cane at Okeelanta, got repatriated for striking, returned two years later under a different name, and then was never called back. Asked why he had gone to the United States in the first place, he looked incredulous, then answered, "Well, me get a card and pass and go through."[102] Not going was simply out of the question. Disappointment and desire were opposite sides of the same coin.

Though the H2 Program was a source of pride, it was also a source of frustration and embarrassment because a man could never predict whether he'd be called back. Not getting a card or getting one and then not getting called back was a source of deep shame. "I tried to get a card but I don't get no card to reach," one man told Stephanie Black. Asked why, he said, "I don't know . . . I begged the card. I'd like to get a card. I begged it and I don't get any." Another Jamaican told her that he had worked as a cane cutter for sixteen seasons (twelve of them with Gulf & Western) when he heard he wouldn't be going back to Florida. "They doesn't need me anymore." Of the four men I interviewed in 2006 on the porch of the Dead House in Brandon Hill, two had not worked in the United States in over forty years but were still embarrassed that they had never been asked back to work. After boldly lecturing the young men around him about the importance of hard work, James Matthews lowered his voice to a whisper when noting that he had not been invited back after two years cutting cane in Florida. "It never work out," his neighbor Oscar Cottrill added, by way of explanation.[103] When men did tell their friends about their experiences, no one seemed prepared to listen. "When you come home . . . [and] tell your friends everything about the program . . . they don't believe that," a man told Stephanie Black.[104]

Earning good money and getting called back were especially important but items purchased were also taken as proof of a man's masculinity. "Work is slow in Jamaica," Arthur Brown told a reporter in 1986. "For my wife and kids I try to be a man, so I put my shoulder to the wheel and do this. The dollars are quite good."[105] A successful guestworker displayed his achievement through conspicuous purchases: the pretty dresses brought back for daughters and friends, boom boxes "the larger and louder the better," and in the eighties, motorcycles, which, according to Jarrett Brown, "often ended up either out of gas, in disrepair or in deadly accidents."[106]

To earn the money on which their families depended and to bring back goods unattainable in Jamaica, H2 workers endured long separations, often as much as six months in duration if they tacked the apple harvest onto their months cutting sugarcane. Men missed half their families' lives in order to support them. "I work there [in Florida], Samuel Brown explained, "and it grow them up."[107] "You're away from your family," one man said, standing in front of his Jamaican house. "It's so hard, you feel so depressed . . . you'd like to see them, cause to be away from your family seven months—eight months, it's a hard one—nobody can know how you feel, unless them have the same feeling as the thing that you're doing."[108] During their long absences, without telephones or email to connect them, men and women corresponded about their fears about money and children and farms left untended.[109] "Hello," one woman wrote to a cane cutter working in Florida. "Good day to you. Hope you are fine. Everyone out here is fine. The children are going to school. They will be getting a holiday next week for Christmas—so we all go to the farm and look about the farm—cleaning the yam and the dashine [also a root crop] . . . and sell what we can sell. Next week, school will open so I won't be able to do the amount of work I used to do. So I just stay around the house and look after the chicken and pigs." "Hello, Vin," Patricia Johnson wrote her partner from Guys Hill, St. Mary, "My mother helped me on the farm when you are away; And sometimes she sleep with me." "Whenever I miss you and my mind run on you," she wrote on another occasion, "I just take up the picture and look at it . . . it reminds me of you."[110]

Living for months at a time in Florida, men obsessed about their homes and families. "How is the kids?" Erroll wrote home. "How is the pigs and the cows? Did you get the money from Mr. White?" "Hello Baby, How you doing?" another man asked; "I was so glad to hear from you and so sad to know that you did not get the money in time for Xmas. I would like to know how did you make it through the Xmas without the money." "I did not work six days in January," he continued; "[I]t was raining and cold, so I do not have any money now but in my next letter I will send you some as quick as possible." One man raced home with the help of his liaison officer to attend the birth of child, but found his wife stony and silent, furious at his long absence during her pregnancy.[111] "I reach safe an begin to work but my pay I'm getting is small," a man named Anthony wrote home to his mother. "I am trying to see what i can make out of the crop. Try an see if you can save something out of what I am sending to you for it tuf with me over here Please kiss my kids them for me. Noting more to say."[112]

Some men brought back more than money. They came home with gonorrhea, herpes, and in the 1980s, HIV-AIDS, likely contracted as a result of the widespread availability of prostitutes in farmworkers' camps. "Sometimes ladies come around and yell Pussy for sale, Pussy for sale," Rueben recalled.[113] "We had trouble, from time to time," chief Liaison Harold Edwards agreed, "with American foremen trying to introduce whores into the men's housing camps." "The women who service the offshores . . . come right out to the housing camps," Earl Morrison confirmed. "It's gotten so bad . . . that we're having quite a lot of trouble with venereal disease," added Paulk.[114]

Others didn't come home at all. In the years 1959, 1960, and 1962, a total of 447 men on contract changed their status by marrying American women.[115] One of them was Jarrett Brown's father, who departed for the United States as a farmworker in 1975, leaving his common-law wife with three-year-old twins and Jarrett, who was then a newborn baby. Brown neither returned nor sent money. Several years later, Jarrett's mother traveled to Florida, having heard from an aunt that Brown was living in Fort Lauderdale. When she found him, they rekindled their relationship long enough for her to become pregnant with a fourth child, after which he abandoned her again. Despondent, she ended up in a Florida psychiatric facility. After her fourth child was born a U.S. citizen, she returned to Jamaica to raise her children alone on her mountain top farm, where she remains.[116]

Despite the separation, the injuries, the labor conflicts, and repatriations, the system kept functioning because there were always men willing to take each striker's place. "You leave Jamaica and go to Florida," Noel Porter explained, because "You are looking for something to help ourselves. Ourselves and our family." The cane companies understood that, he explained. They knew the men need the work, wanted it, had to have it, so they treated the cane cutters "anyway they feel like and they give you any price they feel like."[117]

A Case without Clients

Why workers toughed it out at some times and rebelled at others is un-clear, but on New Year's Day 1968, two hundred workers decided not to back down, even if that meant facing off against heavily armed riot police. Standing in the square that day, Walter Comrie watched with concern. Fearing that a sudden move on anyone's part would result in a massa-cre, he stepped in front of the line of workers, presuming that the police wouldn't shoot a white man. Stirred by Comrie's action, one of the strik-ers put his lips to Comrie's ear and whispered, "Please, Mr. Comrie, I just want my money." Comie asked if he meant the pay due since his last check or the extra $500 the strikers claimed they were owed. When the man replied, "just my pay, sir," Comrie took him by the elbow and led him to the window of the payroll shack. Company officials quickly issued the man's pay, which seemed to break the impasse. Other men began to line up behind him to get their pay and go home too. Those who stayed resigned themselves to the row prices they had been offered.[118]

The New Year's Day strike was thus broken, but the events of the day weren't quite over. Four buses pulled into the camp to pick up the depart-ing men. All the men boarded at gunpoint, though not all were strikers. Some had been sick in the infirmary for days; others came from neighbor-ing camps and then decided to take the opportunity to go home. While some men departed voluntarily, field labor boss Jim Walls saw an oppor-tunity to dispense with some of the Co-op's least favorite workers. He handed Sheriff William Heidtman a list of those "we felt were causing the disturbance and the unreasonable ones that you couldn't talk to, or [who] were just unruly."[119] Armed deputies went looking for those men, forcing some from their barracks, others from the mess hall. In the confu-sion, none of the farmworkers noticed that the back of the fourth bus said "Department of Corrections." Eighty men on the second and third buses went to the Miami airport and from there to Kingston. The others went directly to jail.[120]

Irving Frances boarded the fourth bus, thinking he was on his way to the Miami airport, but disembarked at the Palm Beach County jail instead. "All of a sudden I find myself in West Palm Beach coming out of the bus at gunpoint, pointing to a dark room," he recalled in his deposi-tion a few months later.[121] For Frances and the fifty-one other Caribbean cane cutters detained without explanation in the Palm Beach County jail and then moved to the county stockade, the arrival the next day of a small, prematurely balding, Jewish white man with very large glasses and an even larger mouth must have seemed like manna from heaven. Joe Segor represented South Florida Migrant Legal Services (SFMLS), which

—Herald Staff Photo by BATTLE VAUGHAN

Sugar Cane Cutters Marched Into Palm Beach County Jail
. . . on charges of unlawful assembly, inciting to riot

Surveyor Launch | Migrants

Man Ki
Ex-Wife
Then S

By ANNE WILL
Fort Pierce Bureau

FORT PIERCE —
Evans, 56, a former
killed is ex-wife, C
at her beauty par
Tuesday morning a
shot himself to dea
iff's deputies reporte

Evans had been
employe for a nur
years and at one tim
charge of the city ga

He moved away
years ago. Deputies
car had a Washingt
license tag.

The incident
shortly after 9 a.m.
Evans' beauty parlor
in her home at 21(
ware Ave.

Mrs. Gladys Ge
Beau Rivage, Jenser
who was in the beau
said Evans opened
and pointed a gun a
a fe

Mrs. Evans scream
erken said, and Ev
one shot hitting he

FIGURE 7.6 Armed guard watches cane cutters march into the Palm Beach County jail, January 2, 1968. (Battle Vaughan, ©*The Miami Herald*, January 3, 1968, 2A.)

in 1968 meant he was a legal aid attorney on a mission. Privately funded legal aid offices had existed in many cities—mostly northern ones—since the nineteenth century, but they were unheard of in the rural South where the force of law had strikingly different meanings depending on whether one was black or white. A part of the War on Poverty, Legal Services' directive was to make the legal system accessible to even the poorest Americans and to fight poverty systemically. To do so, it chose its cases carefully in order to make the law equitable, win new regulations, and ensure the enforcement of existing ones. Our "mantra was Don't put Band-Aids on cancer," Segor recalled; we just "didn't realize how difficult cancer was at the time."[122]

In 1965, the first Rural Legal Services Office opened in California. A year later, Howard Dixon, Miami's leading civil rights attorney, and Segor, a Miami resident and a recent graduate of the University of Miami's law school, applied for an Office of Employment Opportunity grant to create a multi-county, multi-office legal services organization that would serve farmworkers where corporate farming was most concentrated. Segor and his second in command, Kent Spriggs, knew little about agriculture. Born in the shadow of Yankee Stadium and raised in Queens, New York, before coming to Miami at the age of fifteen, Segor "was one of those city people" who "thought string beans grew in the store or somehow magically appeared." Spriggs grew up in a Washington, DC, apartment building, where his discovery that the black building superintendent's son couldn't play with him on the playground transformed him as a child into an advocate for civil rights. After graduating from NYU's law school, Sprigg's first job was with the New York civil rights firm Rabinowitz and Boudin, where, ironically, he had helped Fidel Castro defend Cuba's right to nationalize U.S.-owned mills and plantations. Little did he know that he would later try cases against the new Florida companies created to replace the ones Castro had nationalized. Anxious to engage southern racists directly, Spriggs answered the SFMLS's want ad.[123]

Segor and Spriggs were excited about fighting for farmworkers, but they spent much of their first year fighting for their jobs. The Miami Bar Association supported the SFMLS's effort, which included hiring organizers to help farmworkers advocate for themselves, but bar associations and lawmakers in rural counties immediately went on the offensive, waging a bitter, yearlong battle to kill or at least hobble the new office. To keep the SFMLS alive, Segor had to agree to drop Florida Congressman Sam Gibbon's district from the office's area of coverage and let local bar associations choose nearly half the members of its board.[124]

After spending several months in boardroom battles, Segor and his idealistic staff of nineteen attorneys were raring for a fight. "We were going to save the world," Segor recalled thirty years later. "That was a little naive, but we thought we could do it."[125] Segor, Spriggs, and their staff of recent graduates did what they were most prepared to do: they wrote a paper. In this case, it was a damning hundred-page study of farmworker health and welfare, which they called "Seasons in the Sun." They learned a lot about Florida agriculture in the process but almost nothing about the sugar industry because they couldn't gain access to the wire-enclosed sugar farms. They were about to get a crash course.[126]

The phone call that would change everything came on the second day of the New Year's strike. It was staff attorney David Bradley who happened to be at the Kennedy Labor Camp when the police roundups of strikers began. Bradley babbled breathlessly about strikers, Jamaicans, and guns. Segor didn't quite catch it all but it was enough to send him and Spriggs racing for the Miami airport. They drove around until they found the warehouse where Caribbean H2 workers waited for their late-night flights and paid their excess baggage fees before departing for home (the facility's owner, William Meranda, made so much money shipping guest workers and their excess baggage that he eventually bought a controlling share of the Florida Marlins).[127]

The attorneys demanded to see the cane cutters, asserting that they had the authority to represent them, "which wasn't entirely true," Spriggs recalled, laughing. Finally, Segor recounted, some of the men were allowed to come outside. Meranda's men told us to come back the next day. Knowing that the men would be gone by then, Segor and Spriggs refused to leave, though Meranda's employees got more menacing by the minute. Finally, some of the men were allowed to come outside, perhaps because they promised to get rid of the attorneys. "You have rights," the attorneys assured them; "We can represent you." The men declined, saying "they wanted to go back." "So, we didn't have clients there," Segor recalled with regret.[128]

Somewhat at a loss, Segor and Spriggs tried the Miami offices of the Associated Press in hopes of finding out what had happened at the Co-op. They learned that fifty-two cane cutters had been taken to the Palm Beach County jail. Assuming that public defenders had been appointed to represent them, Segor and other staff attorneys drove up to Palm Beach the next day just "to help the lawyers." But when they got to the jail they discovered that no public defenders had seen the men, and the cane cutters had not been charged with a crime. With the help of William (Boon) Darden, Florida's first African American police lieutenant and then the SFMLS's chief investigator, the attorneys bluffed their way in "by just brazenly saying we were their lawyers." With Darden present, Segor recalled, the deputy in charge let them in "without checking with the sheriff, who could have easily thrown us out."[129]

Inside they found the cane cutters "really indignant," and "obviously upset at being in jail." "We told them that they had rights in the United States and that we would represent them," Segor recalled, and "We asked them if they wanted legal redress and they did." So Segor and Spriggs "sat down and interviewed them all. We had intake sheets and we simply signed them up." Soon public defenders arrived, as did liaisons from WICLO promising other attorneys.[130] The farmworkers had gone from no lawyers to three sets of lawyers.

Later that day, the fifty-two defendants were marched in leg irons into the county courtroom and arraigned before a judge and a phalanx of attorneys on charges of inciting riot and unlawful assembly. The judge set bail at $11,500 each, more than any of the cane cutters could hope to earn in a decade.[131] The cane cutters were then returned to the stockade for two more days, while prosecutors talked to the sheriff and sat down to watch the film sheriff's deputies had shot during the arrests. They did not share the film with defense attorneys. The film apparently revealed that, despite the Sheriff's statements to the press, workers had not shouted threats, made angry gestures, waved machetes, or barricaded company officials in the payroll shack, at least not after the deputy started filming. There was no evidence of riot, so it was rather difficult for the prosecutor to charge anyone with inciting one, and clearly tenants could not be charged with unlawful assembly in their own place of residence. In a meeting with the prosecutor, the public defender—whose own job had only existed since 1964—pointed out that ten of the defendants had come to Camp Kennedy to see what the excitement was about, and had boarded the first bus voluntarily upon learning that there was an opportunity to go home. The prosecutors declined to prosecute.[132]

The prosecutor had no case but Sheriff Heidtman had a problem on his hands, or, to be precise, fifty-two problems, all of whom now had lawyers. With Legal Services lawyers planning to sue for false arrest, Heidtman decided to resort to the same solution sugar companies had been using for years: deportation. On January 5th, he appeared at the stockade to make the cane cutters an offer, without all the fuss and bother of attorneys and courtrooms: the charges would be dropped, he told them, if they left for Kingston immediately and never came back. Every one of the defendants took the deal. Heidtmen neglected to mention that, as they flew home that very day, the cost of their airfare was being deducted from the savings they had sitting in a Kingston bank.[133]

Joe Segor and Kent Spriggs's discovery that their clients were no longer in the country did not deter them from pursuing the case. "[W]e had signed them up," as Segor put it, and that was that. The fact that the guest-workers had been deported, he reasoned, only made them less vulnerable to further intimidation.[134] Spriggs drew up the complaint against the sheriff and the managers of the Co-op, enlisting Tony Amsterdam, now one of the nation's top death penalty lawyers, to read his draft.

Spriggs then left to become director of Rural Legal Services in Mississippi, and never found out what "the disposition was" in *Clement Cole et al. v. Sheriff William D. Heidtman of Palm Beach County et al.* But Segor sure did. He soon discovered just how risky and expensive it would be to take on the sugar industry and fight for deportable clients whose former employers had some of the most powerful friends in Washington. First, however, Segor had to find his clients. He had their names, parishes, and home villages, but rural Jamaicans don't exactly have street addresses. Few would have had electricity or running water, let alone telephones.[135] Many villages don't appear on maps and some are so hilly and the houses so hidden by lush growth that you can stand right in them and not know that a hundred people live within earshot of you. Fortunately, one of SFMLS's investigators was a well-connected Jamaican named Cyril Armstrong who seemed to know everyone from parish priests to the Prime Minister. Armstrong didn't find all the plaintiffs, Segor recalled, but he located several men willing to come to the capitol to be deposed. During a drought and power shortage crisis that paralyzed Kingston, the plaintiffs waited their turn in a courtroom darkened by rolling blackouts. Armstrong served as translator because Segor and his team of attorneys couldn't understand their clients' patois or, on occasion, their English, though, Segor noted with a laugh, "neither could the other side."[136]

Not all of Segor's clients were anxious to return to the United States for trial. "I am not coming back over there" for "love nor money," H. Cross wrote to Segor. "When I come this time I may not live to come back." "I was born in Jamaica," he continued, "and I never go to jail and I come to America and I never do henny thing and I find my self in Jail."[137] Wilford Reid, who was in the hospital fifteen days before ending up in the Palm Beach Stockade, was too sick or too afraid to come back. His wife would not let him return. "I never know that Slave did not Abbolish," he wrote Segor. "I never know that When You go to America to Work and you are Sick they Send you to Jail and also treat you like a Swine and Leave My Wife and Children to Perish."[138]

Segor was confident he could win the case, even without all his clients participating and without the film, which he eventually heard about but couldn't get his hands on. Still, *Cole v. Heidtman* never went to trial. Instead, South Florida Migrant Legal Services found itself on trial for having had the impudence to fling a stone at Florida's goliath. Nobody walked up to him and said, "drop this case," Segor explained, but the pressure to do so was intense. While up in Washington to testify before Walter Mondale's Senate Subcommittee hearings on Migrant and Seasonal Farmworker Powerlessness, Segor and Spriggs were at first warned off gently by Congressman Paul Rogers of West Palm Beach, who was famous for defending state prerogatives against federal intrusions. "Can't you take it easy?" Rogers asked them in a Washington elevator. "Rogers was a decent guy," Segor recalled, "He realized that these people needed lawyers and were booted out." But "at the same time, his money and his constituency were the growers."[139]

After Spriggs left, Segor passed the case to another attorney who "worked too little and smoked too much pot."[140] As long as the case sat in a drawer, there wasn't too much trouble, but when, out of frustration, Segor subcontracted the case to a local appellate lawyer, who began taking more depositions, asking questions about the missing film, and writing to workers about coming to the United States for trial, Rural Legal Services' enemies turned up the heat. Just as Peter Nimkoff, the private litigator, needed a new infusion of cash to bring the plaintiffs back to the United States for trial, the SFMLS's budget ran out, which gave the sugar industry's allies an opportunity to shut down the case for good. Both federal and state legislators "were all over us," recalled former Legal Services attorney (now judge) Alan Kuker. So were the General Accounting Office and the FBI. The GAO team, which arrived to investigate the SFMLS's annual expenditures of $325,000, had recently returned from investigating the $5.2 billion C-5 transport plane's cost overrun.[141]

The SFMLS appealed to the Office Economic Opportunity for more funding, but the OEO had its own feet to the fire. In 1968, the Nixon administration had proposed abolishing the agency altogether and had settled on lukewarm support. The last thing the OEO wanted was to drag out the SFMLS's nagging controversy in Florida. The OEO ultimately refinanced the SFMLS but demanded Joe Segor as a sacrifice. When the budget negotiations ended, South Florida Migrant Legal Services had a new budget, albeit a much smaller one; its name had been changed to Florida Rural Services, reflecting its expanded territory; its staff had been reduced from nineteen attorneys to eight; there would be no more organizing; and Segor had been forced to step down as director. *Cole v. Heidtman* was doomed. The SFMLS's parent office in Atlanta refused to pay the cost of bringing the plaintiffs to the United States for trial, and after delays and missed motions, the case languished and was finally dismissed in 1972.[142] "[T]he men were screwed," Segor recalled thirty years later. "I still get angry about that whenever I think about it."[143]

For the plaintiffs in Jamaica who were deprived of their income and barred from returning to the United States as H2 workers, the case's dissolution was mystifying. One wrote to Segor to ask whether "you Hall are [waiting until] the world come to an end Befor you Hall deside the case one way are a nother." "If wee Hall was white man," he added tellingly, "some thing would [be] dun about that case from sixty eight and till now."[144] Another plaintiff wrote, "I have been waiting for years since I was lock up in the Palm Beach County jail without a cause," he wrote, "and I haven't heard anything about the next Move."[145] There would be no next move.

Constrained by federal agricultural policy for three decades, Florida's sugar industry boomed in the aftermath of the U.S. embargo of Cuba. But it expanded without a comparable expansion in its guestworker labor force. The result was a brutal stretch-out and, workers alleged, wage fraud. Cane cutters struck back with the sort of tactics that might have served them well on sugar estates, banana plantations, oil fields, and docks around the Caribbean: they complained; they organized; they stopped work while they negotiated; they went on strike. A full two years before California farmworkers launched the famous 1965 campaign against Delano grape growers that made Cesar Chavez the leader of California's farmworker and Chicano movements, Caribbean farmworkers were already striking for higher wages. But the Caribbean movement didn't give rise to a Cesar Chavez, become a national cause célèbre, or even result in tangible change. Few Americans even learned of the cane cutters' protests because Florida's new sugar lords had transplanted Cuba's industry with a twist. They had mixed one of the world's oldest industries with its most modern system of labor supply. If there was a Cesar Chavez among the British West Indians in Florida, he was deported.

CHAPTER EIGHT

Takin' It to the Courts

Legal Services, the UFW, and the Battle for the Worst Jobs in the World

MANUEL CHAVEZ was bored. The cousin of UFW leader and civil rights icon, Cesar Chavez, he had been sent to Florida in the summer of 1971 to coordinate Florida's part in the national boycott of non-union grapes. Formed in 1966 after the dissolution of the Bracero Program, the UFW had blossomed by the early 1970s into a powerful social movement. By then the UFW's boycott was beginning to produce collective bargaining agreements with major California grape growers, and contracts in other crops followed.[1] At meetings in farmworker towns across the Sunshine State, Manuel and other UFW organizers serviced their one Florida contract and dutifully showed slides and films about the California campaign, but they were missing out on all the real action. The real fight was in California's fields.

Then on January 22, 1972, while driving Florida's State Road 27, Manuel happened upon a picket line outside the Talisman Sugar Company. The picketers were two hundred and thirty or so Cuban workers who had struck William Pawley's Talisman Sugar Company when Pawley refused to discuss their grievances. Itching for a fight, Manuel Chavez stopped to talk. When the picketers told them that Pawley was using some of his eight hundred Caribbean guestworkers as strikebreakers, Chavez was hooked. UFW organizers had grown up in the campaign to kill the Bracero Program in the West. Now they had discovered Caribbean Braceros employed in the East! Without holding a meeting or consulting his famous cousin, Manuel offered his services on the spot. Boasting to the press that the UFW would organize every worker at Talisman Farms, he committed the UFW and its allies in Florida Rural Legal Services to a course that would pit guestworkers against domestic workers. The battle for the world's worst jobs had begun.

The UFW enlisted the help of "Florida Rural," which by 1970 had four thousand cases and well over seven thousand clients. Florida Rural Legal Services was working to transform every aspect of farmworkers' lives.[2] Its lawyers sued to gain access to labor camps, to integrate those camps, to get workers transported in buses rather than flatbed trucks, to get any Florida county to set up a Food Stamp program, to get farmworkers paid what they were owed, and to enforce local sanitation and housing ordinances. And although Florida Rural took all sorts of cases—including straight forward divorce and landlord-tenant cases—a great deal of their time would be spent suing on behalf of Caribbean guestworkers who alleged exploitation by sugarcane companies and to prove that domestic workers had been unfairly deprived of those same miserable jobs.

Florida Rural won time and again. "We don't lose," attorney Greg Schell told me matter-of-factly, and he was almost right; Florida Rural rarely lost, but they didn't exactly win either.[3] While attorneys and union organizers battled over who would have "the worst jobs in the world," the nation's fruit, tobacco, and vegetable fields would fill up with farmworkers who lacked the legal right to work in the United States at all and who (after 1982) would not even be entitled to Legal Services representation. Within a decade, the Mexicans, Haitians, and Central Americans who represented a small portion of Florida's workforce in the 1970s would become the vast majority of the seasonal workforce. Mexicans would come to dominate the farm labor force nationwide. Indeed, the more Legal Services attorneys won new regulations and, most importantly, enforcement of those regulations, the more growers seemed to seed their fields with a new crop of deportable workers who found it difficult and dangerous to insist on the legal protections to which they were entitled.

Farmworkers' Old Deal

The 1970s should have been a golden age for farmworkers. The termination of the Bracero Program removed some 200,000 competitors for work from California's and Texas's farm labor markets, and the United Farm Workers of America began to win its battles. California lawmakers passed a bold new Agricultural Labor Relations Act that granted California farmworkers the right of collective bargaining and other protections. Outside California, farmworkers' fortunes seemed to be looking up as well. In Ohio, the Farm Labor Organizing Committee (FLOC), led by Baldemar Velasquez, won over thirty agreements with tomato growers. In 1966, the AFL-CIO and the Southern Student Organizing Committee sent ten college students to Belle Glade in a drive to organize migrants between Florida and Michigan. The campaign culminated the following year in the creation of a United Packinghouse Workers Local, led by twenty-two-year-old Thomas Albert Martin, Jr., of Fayetteville, Arkansas, a "self-styled Ozark hillbilly."[4] Thirty celery workers in Belle Glade soon struck when their employer refused to increase their pay from $1.15 to $1.35 an hour. They later hiked their demand to $1.60 an hour. One hundred and fifty union members then walked off work at a nearby farm when a foreman struck Martin on the nose (the judge let the foreman go but charged Martin with illegal picketing). Insisting that workers were earning $16–$25 a day, growers blamed the unrest on "do-gooders" from churches, civil rights organizations, communists, and the government. Workers said the real figure was more like $6–$10. Despite Martin's arrest, the movement kept building. Organizing spread to Pahokee, Delray Beach, Dade County, and up the Gulf Coast. Eight farmworker support groups in Florida joined together into a Coordinating Committee of Farm Workers, led by Father Martin Walsh of the Catholic Diocese of Miami.

By the 1970s, the Packinghouse Union seems to have vanished but new farmworker organizations had taken its place. Lead by Newlon Lloyd, a former H2 worker from the Bahamas who had jumped his contract and won naturalization fifteen years later, the Florida Farm Workers Organization claimed seven thousand mostly African American citrus workers. Another organization was formed by former SFMLS organizer, Rudy (Rudolfo) Juarez. A former farmworker who had arrived from Texas in the 1950s with his parents and nine siblings, Juarez had worked his way up to crew leader by the late sixties. He then quit and began working for Legal Services because he was disturbed by the many ways his fellow crew leaders exploited their own people. In 1970, when the SFMLS was forced to change its name to Florida Rural Legal Services, increase its territory, and demote Joe Segor, it was also barred from hiring organizers like Juarez. Segor helped Juarez get an OEO grant to form Organize Migrants in Community Action (OMICA), which worked among South Florida's growing population of Mexican Americans from Texas.[5] Both organizations were more advocacy groups than unions. Still, both made a splash. In 1971, Lloyd's outfit marched on the Lakeland city hall, then went to Tallahassee, the state capital.[6]

All this activism and the UFW's nationwide boycott seemed to bear fruit. Most farmworkers still lacked the right of collective bargaining, but in other ways federal farm labor law finally seemed to be catching up to the protections other workers enjoyed. By the early seventies a national registration law required crew leaders to be licensed; farmworkers were finally entitled to a federally mandated minimum wage (albeit a lower one than the national minimum wage); and by 1976, all farmworkers were covered by the Social Security Act.[7]

And yet the new day never quite dawned because agricultural employers organized a powerful counteroffensive. Arizona passed a law banning collective bargaining in agriculture. Florida lawmakers proposed a similar bill. Nationwide, growers dug in their heels. Midwestern tomato growers discovered that they could escape the contracts they had signed with FLOC by switching to different crops. By 1972, FLOC had abandoned all its collective bargaining agreements, admitting they had done little to address members' wages, underemployment, or housing conditions. In Belle Glade, farm-worker advocates soon learned the price of supporting organizing efforts. The Palm Beach Housing Authority forced the Florida Christian Migrant Ministry, whose six hundred volunteers and seven full-time staff members had been running childcare centers, counseling services, youth programs, leadership development programs, and Sunday schools in Belle Glade's farm labor camps for nineteen years, to vacate all the facilities it owned. The Housing Authority gave no reason but "[f]rom the beginnings of the labor unrest in Belle Glade last year," a Migrant Ministry official noted, "charges and accusations have been made against the Florida Christian Migrant Ministry and the National Council of Churches by local leaders and growers."[8] In Florida, growers evaded new housing codes by bulldozing or selling their housing, forcing farmworkers to fend for themselves in motels and mobile home parks that charged cruise ship prices for steerage accommodations. Private labor camps were exempted from local housing ordinances by Florida law. Growers evaded labor law by subcontracting the hiring process to labor contractors whose mobility made them harder to regulate (some crew leaders dutifully made social security deductions from workers' wages and then pocketed the money). Despite the legal gains, by the end of the decade, the southern hub of the East Coast migrant stream was so destitute and desperate that the State Department sent diplomats-in-training to Belle Glade to get a sense of what the developing world was like. For most farmworkers the golden age might as well have been the Stone Age.[9]

As had long been the case, the biggest problem for migrant and seasonal workers in Florida was a lack of work and adequate housing. Harvest work had long been an intermittent profession, but as Florida's sugar industry expanded, it spread into crop areas that had once been the province of domestic workers, particularly African Americans, who still made up half of Florida's 169,000 seasonal farmworkers but 75 percent of its migrants. Even green beans, the crop famously picked by "Tea Cake" and "Janie" in Zora Neal Hurston's *Their Eyes Were Watching God,* were largely supplanted by cane. The exclusion of H2 workers from the vegetable fields and citrus groves in 1965 had opened up thousands of jobs to domestic workers, but the grower-owned housing vacated by Bahamian and West Indian guestworkers was barracks, not housing appropriate for families. Elsewhere, labor camps built by local housing authorities with federal aid offered tin shelters with no screens or glass in their windows, and no indoor plumbing. Privately owned labor camps were even worse. Families paid $10–$15 a week for the privilege of squeezing into a tiny shack. Ten rows of shacks might share one privy. Some farmworkers simply slept in tents or in cars. With work hard to come by and decent housing rare, farmworkers were forced to keep moving. The more they moved, however, the less eligible they were for unemployment insurance and food stamps, both newly available to farmworkers. Florida required proof of three years' continuous residency for benefits.[10]

The African Americans and white workers who had long worked Florida's fields and packinghouses found that they increasingly competed for work and for this abysmal housing with Puerto Ricans, Tejanos, and newcomers from Mexico. Puerto Ricans had been coming to Florida from the Northeast since the 1940s. The Tejanos also began coming to Florida seasonally in the 1940s, when the Bracero Program pushed them out of Texas, but their numbers had increased noticeably in the early sixties as Texas growers prepared for the termination of the Bracero Program by mechanizing the cotton harvest. After the program ended in 1964, Mexicans without authorization, many of them probably former Braceros, followed the Tejanos to Florida. By the 1970s, the Krome Avenue Farm Housing Center in Dade City, Florida, was known as "Mexico City." [11]

FEDERAL PEOPLE

In the winter of 1969–70, conditions in South Florida went from terrible to abysmal. At the height of the harvest season, temperatures suddenly plummeted, ruining crops across the state. In the cane fields, guestworkers were guaranteed work or wages for three-quarters of their contracted period, but in other crop regions the freeze meant immediate unemployment for thousands of domestic farm laborers. Unable to pay rent, many families found themselves evicted from private labor camps. Even where crops survived the freeze, wages fell dramatically; the price per bucket of tomatoes dropped from 30 cents to 12 cents. Just as warm weather returned and work picked up, the skies opened up and torrential rain flooded 70 percent of the crops in seven counties. Farmers got flood loss compensation; farmworkers got nothing. Florida's Secretary for Community Affairs noted the devastation to crops and the local deer population.[12]

Rudy Juarez organized some seven thousand unemployed farmworkers to demand disaster relief, leading caravans of farmworkers to local welfare offices. They got nowhere.[13] The staff at the Collier County welfare office told Juarez the workers did not meet Florida's three-year residency requirement for aid. Migrant farmworkers were "federal people," they said, not the county's responsibility.[14] Juarez then directed OMICA members to the U.S. Employment Service (USES) office where they applied for nonagricultural work, but the staff there refused to consider African Americans and Mexican Americans for jobs other than farmwork or domestic service. Less onerous and better paying jobs were reserved for white people. This segmentation of the labor market into farm and nonfarm work, nonwhite and white work was triply damaging because it shut farmworkers out of more lucrative job markets; lowered farm wages by flooding the agricultural labor market; and lowered prevailing wage calculation that the Labor Department used to set guestworkers' wages.

While Juarez led caravans of farmworkers from office to office, migrants from Texas and Mexico kept arriving in the state. Hearing that there were jobs in citrus, Juarez tried directing new arrivals there, only to discover that Peter Brennan, Richard Nixon's Secretary of Labor, had certified citrus growers' emergency request for 1,800 Caribbean guestworkers, the first H2 workers in citrus since Willard Wirtz's cutbacks of 1965. OMICA members picketed the U.S. Department of Labor's Miami office.[15]

Not even Senator Walter Mondale, chair of the Senate's Subcommittee on Migratory Labor's hearings on Migrant and Seasonal Farmworker Powerlessness, could convince local authorities to do something about farmworkers' desperate straits. When Mondale arrived in Florida to see conditions for himself, Claude Kirk, the first Republican governor in Florida since Reconstruction, told him to leave the state. Mondale did, but not before inviting Rudy Juarez and Joe Segor to Washington to testify before his subcommittee. When Mexican Americans arrived in the groves, Juarez told the assembled audience, they couldn't find housing and could rarely find work. Some returned to Texas, but many lacked the funds to get there. The arrival of migrants from Mexico only made matters worse, he noted, adding that he had personally reported "eight hundred illegals from Mexico" to the INS.[16] Limiting growers' supply of farm labor seemed like farmworkers' only hope.

When organizing locally and testifying before the Senate availed nothing, Florida Rural Legal Services tried the courts, suing the Department of Labor to open its nonfarm job listings to unemployed farmworkers. The case landed in the court of Charles Richey, the U.S. district court judge who would do more than any other to expose the treatment of farmworkers in the coming years. Richey's opinion, issued a year later, found that the Labor Department had indeed discriminated against farmworkers "on the basis of race, sex, age, and national origin," and had also erred by directing farmworkers to employers who violated labor laws, social benefit programs, and local housing and sanitation laws. The Labor Department, he noted, "was unresponsive to farm workers' complaints."[17] Juarez was vindicated, but nothing changed quickly. It took Richey another year to get the U.S. Department of Labor and Migrant Legal Action, a Legal Services-funded support group, to agree to form a committee to oversee the Labor Department's progress in addressing the issue. A year and a half after that, the committee was still haggling over who the committee's chairman would be.[18]

In the meantime, another freeze hit South Florida, this one followed not by a deluge but by a devastating drought. The four-month harvest season was reduced to a few weeks of sporadic work. Having learned the hard way that local officials were unresponsive, Juarez went straight to the top. On March 12, 1971, he led three hundred migrant families to President Richard Nixon's retreat in Biscayne Bay, Florida, where they demanded relief aid, food stamps, and unemployment compensation. Although Nixon was vacationing in the Bahamas, the migrants were forced off the president's lawn by the Secret Service. Instead of leaving, however, the crowd camped on the public beach behind the house. The protest inspired the newly elected Democratic governor, Rubin Askew, to ask the president to declare Dade County in a state of emergency.[19] Aid totaling $5 million was soon flowing into local coffers for food stamps and emergency work relief. For the first time in U.S. history, Joe Segor recalled, federal aid had been granted to farmworkers, not just farmers. Apparently, farmworkers were indeed federal people.

Do-Gooders

The TV people had returned to Florida the previous spring while Rudy Juarez was scrambling to find work for OMICA's members. NBC producer Martin Carr had come to Pahokee to film a documentary to mark the tenth anniversary of Edward R. Murrow's "Harvest of Shame." Carr devoted much of his film to Coca Cola's subsidiary, Minute Maid, whose workers were housed in old guestworker barracks lacking inside plumbing and running water. Carr was getting his information from Philip Moore, a coordinator for Ralph Nader's Campaign for Corporate Responsibility who had gone undercover as a migrant orange picker. "Migrant," which aired in November 1971 in Chet Huntley's "White Paper" series and won Huntley a Peabody Award, made it quite clear that little had changed for Florida farmworkers in the decade since Murrow's famous exposé. Contrasting the storied mansions of nearby Palm Beach with Pahokee's rows of tiny crowded, windowless wooden farmworker huts, the film seemed to suggest that the only thing that had changed in ten years was the advent of signs that said "no Mexicans allowed." The growers Carr interviewed did themselves no favors. A. Duda, the biggest celery producer in the nation (he grossed $20 million in 1970), looked right at the camera and declared without irony that he had lost more money the previous year than all farmworkers had earned combined.[20]

A week after "Migrant" aired on NBC, Senator Mondale and his Senate subcommittee faced Coca Cola CEO Paul Austin who had been called to testify. Coca Cola's Foods Division had been scrambling to improve conditions for Minute Maid's citrus workers in anticipation of "Migrant's" airing, but there was only so much the company could change in a few months. "Our research," Austin admitted to Mondale's committee, "showed that most individual workers' incomes were at dismally low levels." The company had purchased new buses with toilets, was providing free ice for drinking water, and had begun to renovate its barracks, though managers decided that in the long run they would "get out of the housing business." The company hired a firm of architects and chose two sites for model houses they expected workers to buy.[21]

Austin had come to the Senate's subcommittee hearing ready to tout the improvements that Coca Cola had made, but Mondale was ready to push him further. After Austin finished his prepared statement, Mondale pounced, asking Austin whether he thought farmworkers should have the right of collective bargaining. Having just presented himself as a friend of farmworkers, Austin had little choice but to say "yes." George Wedgeworth, the president of the Florida Fruit and Vegetable Association and of the Sugar Cane Growers Cooperative, followed with an equally emphatic "no," accusing NBC and the senate subcommittee of "biased reporting." But Wedgeworth only served as a foil for Austin, whose company appeared enlightened in comparison.

Still, Mondale had more tricks up his sleeve. He had tipped off the United Farm Workers of America (UFW) to have organizers on the ground in Florida, ready to take advantage of Austin's professed commitment to collective bargaining rights. The UFW began organizing Minute Maid's 1,200 workers immediately. Reluctantly, Minute Maid let them do it.[22]

The UFW soon overran every surviving farm labor union in Florida. OMICA had concentrated on Tejano workers; the FFVO, on African American workers. UFW organizers Mack Lyons (who was black), his wife Diane Lyons (who was white), and Manuel Chavez (who was Mexican American) succeeded in bringing Minute Maid's diverse workforce together. Organizing the workers into "ranchos," the UFW helped them articulate and prioritize their grievances, while UFW leaders met with Minute Maid officials. It took four months of negotiations and the threat of a national boycott by Ralph Nader's Citizen's Advocacy organization, but on February 29, 1972, Minute Maid and the UFW signed an unprecedented three-year agreement. The contract banned dangerous pesticides and guaranteed fifty hours of work a week, raised wages 25 percent, and promised pay raises in the coming two years. It required a hiring hall, free food and lodging when workers were bused to different parts of the state, sanitation facilities near the fields, safety equipment, sick leaves, a medical plan, a grievance procedure, even paid vacations. Farmworkers at Minute Maid came out of the negotiations looking like autoworkers.[23]

Inspired by the UFW's success, Florida farmworker and youth organizations began to gear up for a statewide organizing campaign. Groups with names like Cry of the Black Youth, Black Rights Fighters, and Los

Chicanos gathered excitedly to talk union, but UFW leaders in California directed their Florida staff to service the union's new contract and promote the boycott. The union's campaigns in California were the UFW's priority; further organizing in Florida was not on the UFW's agenda.[24]

STAY AWAY FROM SUGAR

That agenda changed when Manuel Chavez discovered the picket line at William Pawley's 38,000-acre farm, 25 miles from South Bay, Florida. The strikers at the entrance to the farm were not cane cutters, who would have been deported for striking, nor mill workers, who were already members of the International Association of Machinists. They were the Cuban field machine operators and haulers whose machines picked up the cut cane and transported it to the mills. During the grinding season, these operators and haulers worked twelve-hour days, seven days a week, without overtime pay. Since most of them lived in Miami, their workday began and ended with a 65-mile drive. Their leader, Nicholas Raymond, who referred to the strikers as *campesinos*, told Chavez that Pawley had promised them a pay increase from $1.80 an hour to $2.20, but raised their pay only to $2.10. When they tried to join the IAM in protest, he refused to recognize them as union members. Two hundred and thirty of the three hundred campesinos walked off the job and, in the weeks that followed, most of the remaining seventy campesinos followed them. Pawley fired them all.[25]

Chavez could hardly have picked a worse cause to champion. In joining forces with the Talisman strikers, the UFW was taking on the founder of the Flying Tigers, the bosom buddy of dictators, the man who had recommended killing Fidel Castro *before* he came to power. Pawley had just fired fellow exiles from Cuba; he certainly wasn't going to sign a labor agreement with shaggy-haired Latino union organizers from California and college student supporters who called themselves names like "Morning Glory." "Had they asked me," Joe Segor later remarked, "I would have told them to stay away from sugar."[26] But Chavez and his staff didn't ask. "The UFW just jumped in," Segor recalled ruefully. Not one to tell organizers what to do, Segor helped bring Tejano families up from Homestead to help picket the farm. Realizing that the picketers had no food, Segor drove back to Miami, cashed in his savings, and fed them.[27]

Three days later, on January 25, 1972, disaster struck. A truck driver who had stopped to take a leaflet before crossing the picket line in the middle of the night accidentally struck and killed one of the four New College students, a young National Merit Scholar named Nan Freeman (aka Morning Glory). Segor was asleep in the Florida Rural Legal Ser-

FIGURE 8.1 Members of the United Farm Workers, Florida Division, on the Talisman strike picket line. (Photo by Joseph Segor.)

vices office in Belle Glade when Freeman's friends pounded frantically on the door, trying to find a phone to call for help (although Legal Services lawyers could no longer represent labor unions, they let Segor, who was assisting the UFW's attorney, sleep on the floor). Pawley's response to the accident was to circulate a rumor that the UFW had killed Freeman and put her body near the gates of his farm to incriminate him (outside investigators hired by Freeman's family later declared the death an accident). The tragedy seemed to turn the tide in the strikers' favor. Horrified by the accident, the truck drivers who supplied Talisman's fuel—all members of the Teamsters Union—began to honor the UFW picket line. Suddenly, it seemed possible that the workers might win.[28]

Pawley was determined to make sure that didn't happen. In early February, a week after Freeman's death, armed guards denied access to the farm to three ministers and Judith Ann Petersen, the UFW's Florida lawyer, who were trying to substantiate reports that the company was illegally using Jamaican cane cutters as strikebreakers. After being told to leave Pawley's property twice, the group drove off the farm, at which time they were arrested for trespassing by one of Sheriff William Heidtman's deputies. No charges were pressed.[29]

Having barred UFW supporters from his farm, Pawley scrambled to turn the tide of public opinion. He invited newsman Bill Moyers and a camera crew to tour his hurriedly spruced up labor camp and interview Jamaican cane cutters, whom Manuel Chavez had called "slaves." Dismissing as an "absolute falsity" the UFW's allegations that working conditions at the camp were poor, he told Moyers, "This is a country club, really." The strikers were "Castroites," he told Moyers. Interviewed in Pawley's presence, Jamaican cane cutters were largely reluctant to speak, though one man acknowledged that he did feel like a prisoner "sometimes." Pawley noted that any cane cutter who became "involved" with the UFW would be "sent back to Jamaica right now."[30]

Although Pawley's bald efforts to manipulate the press probably did him more harm than good, the fight at Talisman consumed the UFW's time and energy. Recognizing perhaps that Manuel Chavez was not a particularly organized organizer (and had gotten the UFW in way over its head), UFW leaders recalled him to the Southwest and replaced him with the brilliant, twenty-six-year-old organizer, Eliseo Medina. The Mexican-born son of a Bracero, Medina had begun working in the fields in Delano after eighth grade. When the Delano grape strike began in 1965, he became an organizer and board member for the UFW, which later sent him to the Midwest to organize the grape boycott there. The UFW's decision to send him to Florida suggests how important beating the sugar industry had become. Medina was immediately occupied by a proposed state law that would have banned collective bargaining in Florida agriculture and by a newly formed growers' organization that was pushing for jail terms for anyone who "forced unionization" on farmworkers.[31]

The UFW continued to commit resources to the strike. Arriving at the end of February to bring attention to the cause, Cesar Chavez spoke first at a memorial service for Nan Freeman, and then addressed a crowd of

five hundred mostly black and Latino workers and their white supporters outside the Belle Glade Civic Center. "We are going to organize the
sugar workers, in time," he promised the assembled crowd. "[T]hey will
be members of the union and benefit from it." But, as Chavez knew, most
of the "sugar workers" were temporary workers from the Caribbean. To
the cries of "Viva Huelga, viva la causa," Chavez said he would seek an
end "one way or another" to their importation. "The low wages paid to
these exploited workers have an effect on not just this industry—but all
farm industries," he said; "they depress the wages of others." Thus Chavez
revealed the contradiction inherent in the union's fight in Florida: To organize the sugar industry, as Chavez promised to do, UFW leaders believed
they had to bar most of its labor from the country. Organizers expressed
sympathy for the Caribbean cane cutters, calling them slaves and victims
of exploitation, but expelling them was the UFW's goal, not organizing
them. The rally ended with a chorus of "We Shall Overcome" in Spanish,
after which Chavez departed for Artesia, New Mexico, where Chicano
city employees were on strike.[32]

The contradiction was clear in the UFW's first Florida court battle.
Still barred from Pawley's farm, UFW attorney Judith Petersen, who was
so poorly paid that she had to sleep on Joe Segor's couch, filed a class
action suit in federal district court on behalf of Jamaican guestworkers,
herself, and the three ministers who had been blocked from interviewing
guestworkers by Pawley's armed guards. The suit alleged that Talisman
and the sheriff had violated the plaintiffs' first amendment rights and, by
preventing the Jamaicans from communicating with outsiders, had also
violated the Thirteenth Amendment, which prohibited involuntary servitude. The judge dismissed the complaint, insisting that only the Jamaicans
could claim that their First Amendment rights had been violated—people
seeking access to them could not sue on their behalf. Yet in rendering his
opinion, the judge noted the conflict between the UFW's professed desire
to help "exploited" guestworkers and their willingness to bar them from
the country. "[I]t rapidly became clear," the judge wrote, "that the plaintiffs' purpose was and is not to help these foreign farm laborers." "If it
was found that Jamaicans were being used in unauthorized positions," he
continued, "the defendant Talisman would lose the right to employ these
workers, and the workers would be immediately deported." This would
benefit the United Farm Workers, he noted correctly, not the Jamaicans.
"[I]f the plaintiffs were truly concerned about the Jamaican farmworkers'
welfare," the judge concluded, "it should not be a cause for their concern
that these workers may be performing tasks easier than cutting sugar cane
with a machete in a burned over field filled with snakes and rats."[33]

Despite the judge's ruling, the UFW pressed on. With Segor's help,
Petersen immediately filed an appeal at the Federal Appeals Court level.

Sheriff Heidtman struck back by pressing the trespassing charges he had held in abeyance.[34] The appeals court agreed with the lower court that Petersen and her colleagues couldn't assert Jamaicans' right to free speech on the Jamaicans' behalf. Nor did uninvited guests have the right to exercise free speech on private property. But, the court asserted, the visitors did have "standing on another ground." By operating a housing camp twenty-five miles from the nearest town with a kitchen, mess hall, chapel, infirmary, laundry, store, a post office and company-run sewage system, Pawley, the judge concluded, had transformed private property into a public place. Pawley's camp may have been a company town, but it was a town nonetheless, and only individual residents of a "town" could bar visitors. Talisman's attorneys countered that the camp couldn't be construed as a town because it housed only single men, but the court rejected that logic.[35] Petersen and Segor had succeeded in winning access for organizers (and lawyers), if not to all labor camps then at least to the biggest and most isolated ones.

The UFW's victory in *Petersen v. Talisman* took over a year, which was too much time to wait for access to cane cutters. In the meantime, Medina took the fight to U.S. Sugar, which did not bar organizers from its property, although company foremen followed them around, stepping close when organizers tried to speak to guestworkers, and summoning cane cutters to anti-union meetings after union members left.[36] In an article called "Solidarity with Sugar," the UFW's newsletter, *Union News*, called on union members at Minute Maid to "get together as many people as we possibly can to go and help the sugar workers attain the same wages and working conditions and other Union benefits as we now enjoy." "In the sugar cane fields that many of us left behind because of the low wages and horrible working conditions," the article noted, "our sisters and brothers need our help and support very badly. While we, at Minute Maid, are enjoying the benefits of our Union contract, farm workers in the cane fields are still living and working under near slave conditions." "It is very difficult for them to help themselves," the article noted, adding, "They need our help desperately."[37]

"They" didn't respond with much enthusiasm. The union made some headway among U.S. Sugar's African American drivers and mechanics—the equivalent of Pawley's campesinos—but only one Jamaican dared to come forward.[38] He brought his time slip to show how little he was paid but asked that organizers not use his name. "[W]e are treated just like in the days of slavery gone," he told Medina bitterly; "Next time I'm going to burn the fucking camp down." Guestworkers' unwillingness to come forward cemented the UFW's position. H2 workers made up 60 percent of U.S. Sugar's 3,600-person peak season workforce. If they couldn't be organized, they would have to be sent home for good.[39]

It didn't take long for the action to shift from organization to litigation. The UFW's campaign to undo the H2 Program began by having UFW members apply for jobs at Talisman, a decidedly odd tactic in the midst of a strike. The forty applicants were met by armed guards wielding shotguns and pistols.[40] But when Pawley refused to hire union members, as expected, the UFW was ready with a federal lawsuit against the Department of Labor, which had certified Pawley's request for labor.[41] While UFW members picketed the Labor Department office in Miami for a second time, the union filed a class action suit in U.S. district court requesting an injunction against the importation of foreign workers, insisting that it had identified hundreds of workers in California, Arizona, Texas, and elsewhere who were ready and willing to cut cane.

The U.S. District Court Judge in Miami rebuffed the UFW's suit, saying that the union's arguments "completely ignored the established history of [the] growers' inability to recruit and retain sufficient domestic laborers throughout the harvest season." Pawley declared victory, but was nonetheless incensed at the suggestion that a judge might have told him whom he had to hire. In a huff, he canceled his request for foreign workers for the following year and mechanized his entire harvest operation, which he could do because his farm was farthest from the soft muck soil around Lake Okeechobee and thus more amenable to mechanization. In October 1972, the UFW went back to court to make its case again, but the argument was declared moot. There would be no guestworkers at Talisman that fall or ever again.[42]

Meanwhile, the campesinos were still on strike. To put that conflict to rest as well, Pawley convinced the owner of the oil company that supplied his farm to threaten drivers who refused to cross the picket line with dismissal. Facing the loss of their jobs, the drivers capitulated and the strike fizzled. In the end, the UFW lost both the strike and H2 workers' jobs at Talisman farm. The lesson the union took from the whole affair was that guestworkers had to be banished from the industry as a whole.

The UFW forged ahead with its campaign to demonstrate that domestic workers were widely available for work as cane cutters. Knowing that in mid-June 1972, U.S. Sugar had requested nearly 10,000 foreign workers for the 1972–73 sugar harvest, activists spent the summer trying to convince UFW members and supporters around the country to apply for cane-cutting jobs. Medina's hope was that, once on the job, UFW members would force U.S. Sugar to the bargaining table. "We of course want contracts," Medina wrote to the UFW office in McAllen, Texas, "and if we can hit them with a quick, effective strike, they cannot bring in anymore Jamaicans, so they'll have to deal with us to get the cane cut. . . . If you can get 500 people . . . great! But naturally the more the better because we would be able to hit more companies and really shut them down. I don't think they would fight too long because you just can't get local scabs for cane-cutting."[43] This was a campaign fought not in the fields but in federal courtrooms.

Visas and Toothbrushes

The district court judge dismissed the UFW's first complaint against the Department of Labor, but the committee set up by Judge Richey to investigate Department of Labor enforcement eventually bolstered the UFW's claims. According to Ronald Goldfarb—the Justice Department prosecutor Richey appointed as special master—sugarcane and apple companies strategically avoided hiring local labor, just as the UFW alleged. They posted their openings as required, but had no intention of hiring anyone but Caribbean H-2 workers. "Departmental regulations required employers to seek American laborers through the State Employment Service network thirty days in advance of the work date," Goldfarb wrote, but by that time employers' labor recruitment associations had already gone through the trouble and expense of recruiting and screening Caribbean workers. "The owner of a big, East Coast apple orchard . . . waits until the last minute and then goes to the local Employment Service office . . . knowing that they [domestic farmworkers] will not be available there at that late date." "State and local officials go through a frantic, expensive search for domestic farm workers," but by this time, Goldfarb wrote, most migrants were either employed or unreachable. To no one's surprise, "once this fruitless charade" was completed, growers would be able "to find a band of, say, Jamaican workers who happen to be at the airport with their visas and toothbrushes and ready to work." Since cane company managers could predict with great certainty when and in what numbers they would need labor, this process had become completely routine.[44]

Despite Goldfarb's findings, the UFW lost its appeal. Undeterred, the UFW fired back with a volley of signed statements from two thousand farmworkers around the country, who informed the Department of Labor that they wanted jobs in Florida's cane fields.[45] The affidavits suggested just how little Florida's cane companies wanted to hire domestic workers. One 1973 affidavit sent by a Major Johnson of Bristol, Virginia, told how, with a friend, he had answered a USES advertisement for a truck driving job at the Sugar Cane Cooperative. Having been promised $200 a week and bus fare to Belle Glade and back if they were not satisfied with the job, they had arrived as instructed at the Trailways depot, but no one was there to meet them. Eventually, someone from the Co-op picked them up and took them to a filthy dormitory. "The walls and floors were black with dirt. Trash was spread all over the floors and on the outside of the buildings. Flies, rats, and roaches were present." The two men were later informed that they would be clearing rocks, planting sugar cane, or cutting sugar cane." They protested that they had been promised truck driving jobs. The following morning, they talked to Jamaicans who described the difficulty and danger of the work they did, and told them that no one made $200 a week. When the two men went to the office and said they wanted their bus fare home, they were told they'd only get it if they finished the season. Eventually someone drove them to the bus station, but they had to buy their own tickets home.[46] Chastened by affidavits such as these, the Labor Department demanded that the sugar industry clarify the guidelines under which it recruited and hired domestic workers.

The result was what Florida Rural Legal Services lawyers still refer to as "the Sikes letter," a simultaneously revealing and misleading statement of industry practice written by Fred Sikes, then Vice President of U.S. Sugar. Sikes wrote to the U.S. Department of Labor on October 17, 1972 on behalf of the Florida Sugar Producers Association, the recruitment agency through which U.S. Sugar imported labor for itself and a few other cane companies.[47] Explaining the terms under which the Sugar Producers Association recruited and hired domestic workers, he said, domestic workers didn't get free airfare but they did get $50 to cover their round-trip bus tickets and meals en route. (The funds were deducted from workers' pay but were reimbursed if they worked at least half the season.) All cane cutters got at least $2.20 an hour, he wrote, but were paid on a task basis. It all seemed straightforward enough.

Sikes's next statements revealed what U.S. Sugar was *not* prepared to do to attract domestic labor. U.S. Sugar offered "barracks-type housing" "for singles," Sikes noted, and would not provide family housing. It never had, he insisted (failing to mention that U.S. Sugar had once showcased its model family cottages). If families found bunk beds in barracks inappropriate, the letter implied, they were free to look for work elsewhere. More importantly, Sikes noted that domestic cane cutters had to meet a minimum production standard. They didn't have to cut as fast as West Indian H2 workers, who "had an average productivity rate of 1 1/2 tons of cane per hour," he wrote, but they had to be able to cut at least one ton of sugarcane an hour for eight hours a day and they had to sustain that rate by their tenth day on the job. That may have sounded reasonable to Labor Department officials and perhaps even to unknowing applicants, but one ton of 12- to 15-foot-high sugarcane as thick as bamboo was still a whole lot of sugarcane. In fact, in 1972, most Caribbean cane cutters were not cutting a ton and a half per hour, according to Walter Comrie, who had seen all the wage and hour records of the men hired by the Florida Sugar Producers since 1962. It took a "good productive man" "an eight hour day" to cut and pile an average of "eight tons of burned cane," Comrie wrote;

only 40 percent of Caribbean contract workers were currently meeting that standard. The "Sikes letter," in other words, inflated what Caribbean men could do, then made that inflated standard the minimum standard. If domestic workers couldn't meet that fast and furious pace by their tenth day on the job, they'd be fired.[48]

Sikes's intention was undoubtedly meant to set a production standard so high that no American would apply for a job as a cane cutter. If some unwittingly did, they'd either be amazingly good at it or easily eliminated. It was a strategy the cane companies would come to regret, for by attaching a tonnage amount to the minimum wage, Sikes inadvertently gave attorneys the ability to calculate precisely what cane cutters should have been earning. Row prices went up and down and varied widely, according to the thickness of the cane, how tangled it grew, whether it was upright or horizontal, or, as far as workers knew, whether Mars and Jupiter were in alignment. But after Sikes's letter, if the contractual minimum wage was, say, $2.79 an hour, and each man was required to harvest at least one ton an hour, then men should have been paid at least $2.79 for every ton of cane they cut. If you knew how much cane a company had harvested, you could easily calculate how much money the average guestworker should have earned. In the late eighties, when farmworker lawyers got their hands on Sikes's letter, they would do just that, and discover that none of the major cane companies budgeted nearly enough money to pay what workers' contracts were owed.[49]

In 1972, however, none of this was yet evident, except to Walter Comrie, who wasn't prepared to publicize what he knew. What mattered was whether the cane companies were refusing to hire domestic workers and whether domestic workers really wanted guestworkers' jobs. Competing claims flew back and forth. The cane companies insisted that they had offered $50 round-trip fares to all the people on the UFW's list, but not one arrived. The UFW said there were 500–1,000 workers in South Texas who would cut cane. U.S. Sugar shot back that it had received applications from eighty Americans, but only twenty-six arrived for the physical and, of the twenty-one who passed, only seven showed up for work.[50] The UFW insisted that the workers who applied got the run-around. "At US Sugar," organizers noted, "more than sixty Am[erican] workers who had traveled 80 miles to look for a job, spent the whole day at the personnel office and still did not get jobs." The workers were made to fill out four-page application forms and wait for hours while standing in the sun. They then underwent extensive interviews with company officials. Some were told their hands were "too soft." One young woman, who was accustomed to carrying 90-pound bags of oranges, was told she was "too slight." All were told there was no family housing. At the end of the day, the applicants were informed they would have to return two days later for physical examinations. No housing was provided in the meantime. Most gave up. Those who did come back and passed the physical were told to report to work five days later. All were fired on their third day for failing to make the quota, although they all said they had improved each day.[51] Growers countered that they couldn't "rely on the sporadic appearances of American workers."[52]

As UFW members and supporters around the country answered Medina's call for applicants for cane-cutting jobs, the UFW discovered that the Labor Department was only requiring the cane companies to advertise in Florida, and only in the summer when few migrants were still there. UFW organizers in Texas tried to get the Texas USES to announce the Florida openings on the radio, but the USES director said he had no knowledge of cane-cutting jobs in Florida. The UFW also learned that, although guestworkers were supposed to be more expensive than domestic workers, the cane companies did not have to make social security and unemployment insurance payments for them.[53]

By the summer of 1972, the UFW had succeeded in winning a second union contract in citrus but the campaign to supply the sugar industry with domestic labor was looking rather ragged and Medina's correspondence was sounding increasingly desperate. On July 31, he wrote to Lupe Gamboa in the San Joaquin Valley, asking him to help organize "Union members and other supporters to sign up to cut cane in Florida." He knew Gamboa's hands were full but noted, "We just barely have our foot in the door with our two citrus contracts, so we really need this momentum in our organizing drive." The UFW even resorted to distributing fliers on college campuses that read: "Wanted: Cane Cutters. See the beautiful Florida Everglades. Help prevent the illegal importation of Jamaican sugar cane cutters by registering as a willing and able farm worker." "By signing as a farm worker you will, if contacted and hired by a sugar company, hold a job for a returning Florida worker. . . . Once a supply of domestic labor is established the sugar companies will be unable to get their automatic certification of foreign labor."[54]

By mid-September, it was clear that the UFW had not convinced the Labor Department to deny growers' requests for Caribbean guestworkers. Medina wrote an organizer named Tony, "we just found out that Sec. Of Labor Hodgson has certified the importation of 9,000+ Jamaicans for this harvest season. So we are going to start picketing the Labor Dept and a little later will picket the farm labor offices. American Jobs for American Workers." He asked Tony to make good on his promise to send 500 to 1,000 union members out here to cut cane.[55] They didn't come. In fact, Joe Segor later admitted, the UFW couldn't cajole its members into cutting cane, not with the wages paid, the danger of the work, the housing offered, and the knowledge that they were not wanted.

Still, the Florida organizers fought on, galled by the presence of guestworkers amid a sea of unemployed and underemployed workers. When in the spring of 1973 the Health Department closed dozens of South Florida labor camps after a typhoid epidemic swept through the domestic farmworker population, the UFW redoubled its efforts to secure cane-cutting jobs for domestic farmworkers, if only to find beds for them to sleep in.[56]

SUPPRESSING SUGARMAN

The following winter, the Labor Department Wage and Hour Division sent a team of inspectors to Florida to make sure that U.S. Sugar and the other sugar companies were making good on the promises Sikes had made in his letter. Led by the aptly named Solomon Sugarman, the survey team examined payroll records, conducted time studies, interviewed cutters, leadmen, ticket writers, cut foremen, and "high company officials."[57]

While Sugarman and his team were investigating Atlantic Sugar in the winter of 1973–74, an entire camp of about 850 workers brought the company "to a standstill" for two days. If the workers were trying to send Sugarman a message, he didn't receive it. Sugarman never learned of the strike or of the repatriation of fifty-nine strikers, which followed it.[58]

Nonetheless, Sugarman issued a damning report on Florida's sugar industry, concluding that timekeepers at U.S. Sugar, Sugar Cane Growers, and Atlantic Sugar had short-changed workers to the tune of one and a half hours per day, or 20 percent of the workers' pay. At Atlantic, all but one worker earned less than the required minimum wage, according to the report. Cutters at U.S. Sugar and the Co-op, Sugarman told reporter Marie Brenner, "were often counted as having started work 30 minutes later than their actual arrival time in the fields," and the sugar companies counted quitting time as the last hour a worker was in the fields. Thus if "let's go time" was at 3:35 p.m., quitting time would be rounded *down* to 3 p.m. At one farm, Sugarman told reporter Marie Brenner, he found ticket writers asleep in the bus. "They knew the bosses would change the tickets anyway," he explained. Only workers at Gulf & Western were paid "in excess of the required minimum wage," according to the report, a finding Walter Comrie attributed to a tip from Chief Liaison Harold Edward that investigators were on their way. "I see where Gulf & Western did a good job of deceiving the Wage & Hour investigators," Comrie noted in his journal.[59]

The report's release should have been a disaster for the industry, which was predicting a record gross of $200 million.[60] With the Carter administration talking about allowing the Sugar Act to lapse after forty-some years of price guarantees, industry officials were anxious to defend their reputation. Determined to keep Sugarman's damning report from surfacing, they called on all their friends and allies. The next thing Sugarman knew, the Labor Department had buried the report and he had been transferred.[61] Then, in the spring of 1974, in a pageant of political theater, the Labor Department held joint hearings with the Department of Agriculture in South Florida. Sitting in the audience were UFW members and Walter Comrie, who wasn't surprised to hear employers deny the charges of wage fraud "to a man." Comrie was furious, however, that "their denial was strongly supported by none other than our own chief liaison officer Mr. Harold F. Edwards," who "stated categorically that he had no knowledge of any wrong doing on the part of employers," and "that liaison officers had received no complaints from workers." Liaison officers had, in fact, received thousands of complaints over the years and, for over a decade, Comrie had been sending Edwards letter after letter alleging exactly the sort of timecard tampering that Sugarman described. The charges were "absolutely true," Comrie wrote in his personal notes. "Make no mistake about it, every employer of West Indian sugarcane cutters in Florida is guilty of underpaying and cheating the workers."[62] Afraid for his own job, Comrie did not insist on testifying.

Jamaica's government was also silent. By the seventies, Jamaica's Prime Minister was Michael Manley, the charismatic son of Norman Manley, founder of the democratic socialist People's National Party. Manley had assumed the leadership of the PNP in 1969, just months before his father's death. Running on the slogan "better must come," the younger Manley electrified supporters, sweeping into power in 1972. Better would come, Manley promised, by nationalizing foreign-owned bauxite mines and failing Jamaican sugar companies. But Manley's government inherited one of the largest foreign debts per capita in the world, most of it owed to the United States, and in the first few years of his administration, the oil embargo sent gasoline prices skyrocketing, forcing Jamaica to borrow even more. With the PNP in power in Jamaica, Florida sugar producers might have anticipated much closer scrutiny of the H2 Program, but Manley was in no better position to challenge the administration of the farmworker program than his predecessors had been. The United States and the IMF responded to Jamaica's debt crisis by lending the new nation more money, but they demanded austerity measures in return, including the devaluation of Jamaica's currency, which caused rampant inflation. As corporate leaders sold off their Jamaican properties and fled the island, fearing socialist economic policies, Jamaica's official unemployment rate shot up from an already dismal 24 percent in 1974 to 31 percent in 1980; the cost of living increased 320 percent; and the value of the Jamaican dollar versus the U.S dollar plummeted from 88 cents to $1.76.[63]

The economic crisis only cemented the H2 Program's significance as a source of revenue and political patronage in Jamaica. The H2 Program is "an aid program," insisted JAG Smith, Jamaica's Minister of Labour under the Labour Party, "the only aid program in the world that does not cost the United States one cent because we earn every cent and every dollar we get from the growers." The ruling PNP was just as inclined to defend the program. The Jamaican government held the farmworkers' mandatory savings without interest, collecting the money in U.S. dollars and exchanging the money into Jamaican dollars at unfavorable exchange rates before paying out workers' funds (it's not clear who or what agency pocketed the interest). The men would have done better exchanging the money themselves on the street, remarked *Palm Beach Post* reporter Beth McLeod.[64]

Jamaicans sought H2 jobs more desperately than ever. In 1978, during riots in two Kingston slums over sharply rising prices and unemployment, "members of one political party were killing those of the other to get a 'ticket,'" reporter Steve Petrow wrote.[65] "[T]he farmworker who has many legitimate sad and sometimes bitter complaints about their experience is the same person who will be at the head of the queue to go next year and the year after," Michael Manley affirmed. The farmworker program "represents an opportunity to earn some money by contrast with a situation, in particular in the rural village, where there is heavy rural unemployment, and often just a blank wall of poverty to face." "I don't call it an economic opportunity," Manley continued perceptively; "it's much simpler than that; it's just an opportunity to earn some money in the course of a year and send some of that money home to families."[66] Although his party had criticized the Labour Party's use of the Farmworker Programme as a source of patronage, Manley admitted that under his government the distribution of farmworker tickets remained a patronage system. "[L]ocal members of parliament within a region find it convenient to recommend different people from year to year," he admitted, "all as a rather superficial way of . . . scoring some political points."[67]

Jamaicans' dependence on the program and the remittances they returned undercut any inclination Manley might have felt to push for reform. "[S]o long as there is massive unemployment in one part of the world," Manley later admitted, "until we begin to develop an international sense of shared responsibility, you are always going to get an undermining of equitable results by the disproportions of bargaining power that are created in these situations." The sending governments could just "walk away from it," Manley noted; but "so far all Jamaican governments, looking at the level of poverty . . . have felt that on balance it was in the interests of people to take advantage of this program, but have frankly faced the bargaining in it in a completely unequal situation."[68]

In early 1974, two tragic accidents seemed to underline Manley's point. In the first accident, a G&W truck overturned, injuring thirty-six guest-workers. The cane cutters had been standing in the back carrying their razor-sharp cane knives, though two weeks earlier, the U.S. Labor Department had ordered cane companies to use trucks with fixed seating. Jamaica's government said nothing. Three weeks after that accident, another G&W truck rolled over, this time injuring all eighty-six passengers, one fatally. The Department of Labor fined G&W a total of $1,800. Unable to remain silent a second time, Jamaica's ambassador paid a visit to the sugar region, where he was asked by a reporter about the problem of growers' lack of compliance with the Labor Department's regulations regarding trucks. If a man came to him with a choice between not working or standing upright in the back of a growers' truck, "and asked my personal opinion of what he should do," he replied, "I think I would have to tell him: Risk the truck."[69]

Two years after the truck accidents, Manley's government showed just how dependent it was on Florida sugar growers' good will by awarding Fred Sikes the honorary title of Commander of the Order of Distinction for his "skillful negotiating on behalf of the growers and for the cooperation he has given us."[70] To the leaders of Jamaica's ruling democratic socialist People's National Party, the "U.S. farmworker programme" was well worth the risk, despite its evident flaws.

With Harold Edwards, the chief advocate for Caribbean farmworkers, denying any company malfeasance, and the largest of the sending governments silent, the Florida hearings seemed to vindicate the growers, who dismissed Sugarman's findings as unsubstantiated exaggerations. "As a result," Comrie wrote privately, "the charges were dropped."[71]

Sugarman's report might have been added to the heap of unheeded farmworker investigations if Legal Services attorneys had not sued the Secretary of Labor to expose it on behalf of working cane cutters, whom the suit named Doe I, II, and III, for fear that they would be deported if exposed.[72] The farmworkers' attorneys intentionally wrangled their way back into Judge Richey's court, with the express purpose of telling him about the censored report. Richey ordered the Labor Department to publish it, which it did as inconspicuously as possible, tacking it on two years later to an unrelated Congressional subcommittee hearing report. Before Sugarman's report was made public, however, the U.S. Department of Agriculture discredited it by convincing an administrative law judge to question the investigators' sample size. The case against the cane companies seemed to evaporate once more.

Slaves for Rent

By that time, the UFW's effort to expose the industry's use of guestworkers had simply vanished, a victim of the union's bitter battles in California. On May 20, 1973, Cesar Chavez insisted in a letter to a supporter in Florida that "The Union is not pulling out of Florida. We have left many offices open there. However," he admitted, "we have had to move many people from Florida to the grape boycott. Our friends in Florida, like you," he concluded, "will need to continue to further our goals and reassure the people that we will return with full force again soon."[73] The union did leave offices open in Florida but that was about it. It left the battle for the worst jobs in the world to farmworkers' lawyers and their advocates in Washington.

In 1977, one such advocate, Jimmy Carter's Secretary of Labor, Ray Marshall, tried to revive the case against the sugar companies without much success. Instead of waiting to be sued, Marshall's Labor Department sued the Sugar Cane Growers Co-op, alleging that it, in Comrie's words, "cheated, robbed, defrauded . . . cane cutters by underpricing cane rows and adjusting the number of hours worked to make it appear as if workers earned the guaranteed minimum hourly wage or more." New hearings were held in West Palm Beach and, this time, dozens of cane cutters stepped forward, in daylight, to testify. According to Comrie, however, before they could give their testimony, company officials and the chief liaison took them aside to warn them of the price of disloyalty. They were informed, "*with our approval,*" Comrie wrote angrily, "that any workers who dared testify against the employer will . . . never again be considered for employment with this Programme." "Realizing this," Comrie noted, "many workers who were slated to give testimony for the U.S. Department of Labor, changed their testimony and denied having knowledge of unfair labour practices on the part of the employer." The workers' suborned testimony "greatly weakened the Labor Department's case." A sympathetic cabinet rank official willing to listen was no match for the fear of deportation.[74]

That last act of intimidation effectively cut off employed cane cutters from legal advocates for nearly a decade. And, with H2 workers isolated from Legal Services lawyers, memory of workers' militancy faded. Caribbean H2 workers became known, not for their standoff against the police in 1968 or for the strikes that had come before and after it, but as captives of the cane companies, as international strikebreakers, as "slaves for rent," as one UFW organizer put it.[75] "You could always recognize the Jamaicans," Rural Legal Services attorney Greg Schell told me years later; "they were the ones who looked terrified."[76]

In fact, the cane cutters were still not terrified into complacency. In 1976 and 1982, there were at least three more hushed up mass repatriations, with 2,400 men repatriated in the latter year alone.[77] No litigation followed these strikes. Cane cutters sought out attorneys when they were injured and about to be sent home but generally steered clear of lawyers while still on the job, having gained so little and risked so much by speaking up in the past.

Secretary of Labor Ray Marshall's attempt to dislodge guestworkers from the sugar industry also went nowhere, but he did make one reform that would eventually have a significant impact. Recognizing that previous Secretaries of Labor had erred in raising guestworkers' wages without preventing the cane companies from increasing the amount of work the men had to do to earn it, Marshall began to require that cane companies state a production standard in the clearance orders they submitted to the Department of Labor. When going through the motions of advertising for domestic workers before they were granted guestworkers, in other words, growers had to state not just the wage they would pay but how much cane workers were expected to cut for that wage (just as Sikes had done in his letter). That way, theoretically at least, the cane companies wouldn't be able to increase the task each man had to accomplish every time the federal government raised the adverse effect wage. In the late 1980s, Sikes's letter and these post-Marshall clearance orders would form the basis for the biggest back wages lawsuit in agricultural history. In the meantime, though, growers and farmworker lawyers continued to battle over whether the cane companies were making an adequate effort to hire domestic workers.

BETTER OFF IN THE GREENVILLE JAIL

Guestworkers were only one of many concerns that occupied Florida Rural Legal Services. In 1975–1976 alone, Florida Rural had nearly 5,800 new cases, only 2,300 of them involving farmworker issues. In addition to the usual run-of-the-mill divorce cases and tenant-landlord disputes, they were still suing labor camp owners over segregation policies, the state for failing to give farmworkers access to food stamps, and growers for gross misrepresentations of wages and conditions.[78] Still, Florida Rural stepped into the breach created by the UFW's departure, taking up the battle to prove that domestic workers would willingly take guestworkers' cane-cutting jobs if conditions were improved.

Fresh out of Harvard Law School in 1980, Greg Schell arrived at Florida Rural and picked up his first clients: 2,000 Haitian refugees who were hired as cane cutters at U.S. Sugar. Soon after they started work, they had gone on strike because they found conditions intolerable. The Haitians decided the jobs "sucked," as Schell put it in his inimitable style. "They [could] get plenty of Haitians to cut cane if they pay more and not push people to go so fast," insisted a Haitian who cut cane briefly for the Co-op. "They want me to cut so fast I stop. I don't want to hurt myself." Schell sprang into action, realizing that if he could prevent U.S. Sugar from getting H2 workers to replace the strikers, the Haitians' protest might finally force a change. Because the Department of Labor was not supposed to certify a labor shortage if the shortage was caused by a strike, Schell took steps to ensure the Labor Department knew a strike was in progress: he sent the strikers marching down U.S. Highway 27 with signs that read "on strike," Schell telegraphed the agency to make doubly sure there was no misunderstanding. It didn't matter. The Labor Department approved the H2 workers anyway. Schell sued.[79]

Later Schell represented a group of sixty-seven African American ex-convicts who had been sent to Florida's cane fields by Mississippi's State Employment Service. After three weeks in the fields, the ex-cons decided they had been better off in the Greenville jail. One told a congressional sub-committee that his hands had gotten so sore and swollen that he "couldn't hold the cane knife." Under pressure from Legal Services to open the jobs to permanent residents, the U.S. Employment Service then tried sending the cane companies Marielitos (Cuban refugees, including Cuban ex-cons and released psychiatric patients, deported to the United States by Fidel Castro). That experiment ended when a Cuban nearly beheaded a Jamaican, and was then stoned by Jamaicans. The suits came fast and furious. In 1989, a judge consolidated twenty-three cases against Okeelanta alone, all alleging that the company favored H2 workers over domestic employees.[80]

In 1983, Schell left Florida to head the Maryland Legal Service office but kept up his campaign against the H2 Program. He filed 150 administrative complaints and a dozen federal lawsuits against H2 employers in Maryland, with most of the action directed against Hepburn Orchards and the nearby German-owned Fairview Orchards Associates, the state's largest fruit grower. According to Schell's complaint against Hepburn, the orchard owner sought to eliminate American workers who applied for apple-picking jobs by requiring that domestic workers pass a grueling set of physical tests with a 45-pound, 25-foot ladder. Caribbean workers, who didn't have to pass the test, always got the jobs. "The big picture," said Schell, "is that the foreign workers program is ideal for growers. You get your labor at the time you specify for how long you specify. The workers cannot strike. If they cause any trouble, you can deport them without a hearing, and then they are blacklisted and not allowed to return to the United States to work. That motivates a work force. It makes a work force nice and docile—and you don't have to deal with things called labor management problems."[81]

Schell and other Legal Services attorneys won that case and many others. In *Caugills v. Hepburn Orchards*, the Federal District Court in Baltimore awarded U.S. workers back pay, having concluded that they had been fired after only three days on the job and unlawfully replaced by H2 workers. *Clarke v. Gardenhour Orchards* found that free housing went to H2 workers but was denied to U.S. farmworkers. Without housing, Florida workers were forced to quit. Some suits were settled out of court, but Legal Services won time and time again. Courts ruled that American apple pickers had been passed over or fired in favor of Caribbean pickers.[82] In 1982, a federal district court in West Virginia found that the Department of Labor wrongfully allowed West Virginia apple growers to offset a wage increase by increasing productivity demands. A Texas court found "massive violations" of regulations by employers of H2 melon pickers. Whether Legal Services' original mandate from the federal government included suing the federal government is not clear, but Schell made a habit of it.[83]

Though Schell and his colleagues won repeatedly, they did not succeed in unseating Caribbean H2 workers from their cane-cutting and apple-picking jobs, though they probably succeeded in restraining the expansion of the program. They did manage to get African American and Haitian workers jobs "around the fringes" of the sugar industry: African American men were hired as truck drivers; Haitian men cut the green seed cane (which paid better than the regular harvest but didn't last as long); Haitian women were hired to drop the short lengths of cut seed cane into furrows.[84] Yet while Legal Services lawyers were expending an enormous amount of time and energy fighting for fifteen thousand H2 jobs, domestic workers were losing hundreds of thousands of jobs outside the cane fields and apple orchards.

SEA CHANGE

While the legal battle raged over whether foreign or domestic workers would get to numb their hands with machetes, the nation's fields were filling with workers who had neither citizenship nor guestworker contracts. No longer called "wetbacks," unauthorized workers were "illegal aliens" in the language of the day or, more politely, "undocumented workers." They were a diverse group. Among them were tens of thousands of Haitians who had been denied asylum but stayed anyway, smaller numbers of Central Americans, and many, many Mexicans.

Like Cubans, Haitians had come to Florida by boats and rafts to escape poverty and oppression, but unlike Cubans, they had the misfortune of having fled an allied rather than an enemy dictatorship. While Cubans won asylum, Green Cards, inside jobs at sugar mills, and places for their kids in Belle Glade's private schools, Haitians who made the mistake of showing up for their immigration hearings were imprisoned and deported back to Haiti. Haitians quickly learned that a berth in the massive farm labor camp just down Krome Avenue was preferable to a cell in the Krome Detention Center (both named for William Krome, the chief engineer of Flagler's Overseas Railway). In 1981, the Reagan administration brokered a small expansion of the H2 Program to slow the out-migration of Haitian "boat people," but a few hundred H2 visas did little to stop Haitians' desperate exodus. Eventually, the Clinton administration would send an invasion force to Haiti in hope of stabilizing the United States' poorest neighbor and keeping Haitians at home. Denied asylum for the most part, thousands of Haitians joined the farmworker migrant stream.

In the early 1980s, Guatemalans and El Salvadorans also came to the United States, fleeing their countries' civil wars. Also usually denied asylum because they too had fled allied dictatorships, some traveled via an underground railroad of safe houses to sanctuary in Canada. A few thousand stayed in the United States and ended up in Florida's fields as well.

By the 1980s, however, Mexicans had become the single largest group of seasonal farmworkers in the United States. The change in Florida was particularly dramatic. In 1970, when the UFW won the Minute Maid contract and when Martin Carr produced the documentary "Migrant," Mexicans comprised only 6.4 percent of the seasonal farm labor force in Florida (and that number probably included many Tejanos, since census takers often failed to distinguish between Mexicans and Mexican Americans). African Americans were the majority at 56 percent, followed by white Americans at 33 percent. Just fifteen years later, the proportions were reversed. Mexicans represented 64 percent of the workforce, and the percentage of African Americans had plummeted to just 14 percent and whites to just 6 percent.[85] By the early eighties, lettuce, strawberry, tomato, and landscape plant producers in Florida all employed Latino crews almost exclusively.[86]

What precipitated this transformation is not clear. Part of the explanation is undoubtedly younger African Americans' decision to spurn fieldwork. The Great Migration from the rural South to the urban North and West was even bigger in the 1970s than it had been during World War II.[87] But the fact of out-migration doesn't explain its cause. Certainly many black people willingly departed the fields—inspired by the Civil Rights movement. The 1964 Civil Rights Act's ban on discrimination in employment and education was slow to take effect in Florida, but its promise probably raised many African Americans' expectations nonetheless. At the very least, black schools no longer closed during Florida's long harvest season, which removed black children from the fields, but even African Americans beyond school age were demanding more of life than farmwork could offer them. Celery king, A. Duda, noted the change in 1970, waxing nostalgic (on camera) about the days when "our darkies" "would come to you to work" for whatever you were paying. In bygone years, he recalled, you could tell them, "here's the situation, here's what we're doing; here's what we're paying," and they would work. But "the same people today," he complained, "the young people, they'll laugh at you."[88] Duda insisted that African Americans preferred food stamps and the dole to hard work.[89] It's more likely that, given any alternative, African Americans would have rejected the migrant farmworkers' life, which paid an average of $802 a year (the average manufacturing job paid over $5,000).[90] Notably, young African Americans still came out to Duda's farm to shuck and pack corn or cut celery—both relatively well paid jobs—but they may well have disdained the wages he and other growers usually offered for fieldwork and Duda's nostalgia for the good 'ole days.[91]

There may have been some truth to Duda's presumption that workers chose the dole to farmwork for, after years of living rough as migrant workers, black, white, Tejano, and Puerto Rican farmworkers may well have preferred the benefits of the Great Society to the hard knock society of the migrant stream, but it probably wasn't the "dole" that kept them out of the fields. Only by "settling out" could farmworkers gain access to new benefits like Head Start, low-income housing, and even the ballot box. Some got assistance from Rudy Juarez, Joe Segor, and the other founders of El Centro Campesino, a Dade County farmworker housing development that helped migrant families buy their own homes. If OMICA's efforts to secure unemployment benefits and emergency aid for farmworkers back in the early 1970s had demonstrated anything, it was that the Great Society, like the New Deal, came to those who stayed still.

Although some domestic workers probably abandoned farmwork for better paying work, older farmworkers were increasingly propelled to "retire" by employers' decision to hire unauthorized immigrants. In fact, the more Legal Services attorneys sued to enforce the new conventions of farm labor law, the more growers seemed to seek workers less likely to take recourse to lawyers. Because of their immigration status, or lack of it, the ACLU noted that many unauthorized workers were unable to protect themselves from exploitation, and were forced to live under "appalling living and working conditions."[92] Labor laws were in force whether the workers were authorized or not, but unauthorized workers who were vulnerable to deportation were more likely to respond to poor conditions by quitting or simply by staying silent. Growers were likely attracted to

Mexican crews recruited seasonally from across the U.S. border not just because they lacked legal status but because they were far more likely to be young and male than were domestic farmworkers.[93] The operative issue was not that the average man could carry more weight than the average woman, though that may have been a factor; men gave more bang for the buck because they could be housed in barracks, often the same barracks built for H2 workers back before Willard Wirtz banned them from citrus orchards and vegetable fields. Men traveling without women and children also prompted less attention from journalists, TV crews, and reformers. By the 1980s, citrus crews were all male; crews in tomatoes and horticultural crops were close behind.[94]

Mexican migrants' youth may have been most important of all. As Gary Geffert, attorney from West Virginia's Rural Legal Services office, put it in 1986, U.S. farm owners prefer foreign workers because "they . . . never get older." If workers began to slow down with age, they were simply replaced with new, eager manpower from Mexico.[95] As in the case of Caribbean H2 workers, foreign workers' youth, sex, and vulnerability to deportation made them more attractive than the older, native born men and women who had come to Florida to stay.

Undocumented workers brought employers an added advantage: the Reagan administration barred Legal Services lawyers from representing them. In 1974, Congress had protected Legal Services from its opponents by removing it from OEO jurisdiction (and therefore from executive branch oversight), reauthorizing it as a separate entity known as the Legal Services Corporation. By the 1980s, however, Legal Services was under attack again. "Of all the social programs growing out of the Great Society," *Time* magazine wrote in 1983, "there is none that Ronald Reagan dislikes more than the Legal Services Corporation."[96] Although Reagan tried to eliminate Legal Services' budget altogether, Congress saved it, though not without major budget reductions and the appointment of Legal Services' enemies to its board. The new board prohibited Legal Services from filing class action suits, representing unauthorized immigrants, and suing for welfare benefits.[97] To continue to represent farmworkers, Legal Services lawyers had to spin off privately funded branches not subject to the Reagan administration's rules.

It's hard to see any results of the work UFW organizers did in Florida in the 1970s, which should have been a Golden Age for farmworkers. Even the UFW contract at Minute Maid was eventually lost when Coca Cola sold its Florida groves in 1997. If conditions for farmworkers improved at all in the 1970s, litigation not organization was likely responsible. Legal Services lawyers exposed abuses, forced the Department of Labor to enforce the law, won a few sugar industry jobs for local workers, and claimed damages from the most recalcitrant employers. But the obsession with H2 workers ultimately proved a distraction. The 15,000 jobs held by H2 workers at the start of the decade were still held by H2 workers by its end, even as hundreds of thousands of workers from south of the border came north, effectively erasing the gains that Legal Services had made in court.

CHAPTER NINE

"For All Those Bending Years"

IRCA, the Dog War, and the Campaign for Legal Status

A PALPABLE SENSE of crisis about immigration permeated American society in the 1980s. In his 1979 presidential campaign, Ronald Reagan made immigration a campaign issue, calling for special measures that would give him the power to shut down roads, airports, harbors, and even cities to head off approaching illegal immigrants. The threat of "aliens" seemed an enduring feature of his campaign, which conjured up images of shadowy subversives skulking in, over, and under the border. Pushing Reagan to make immigration a key part of his campaign was a cleverly named anti-immigration organization called FAIR, or Federation for American Immigration Reform, which released one-sided polling data suggesting that 90 percent of Americans wanted an all-out war on unauthorized immigrants.[1] The sense of crisis only grew when Reagan's election was followed by an economic slump and then the unexpected arrival of hundreds of thousands of Haitian "boat people" and Cuban "Marielitos."[2] The *New York Times* reported "a rising, ugly nativist sentiment."[3] It was a decade fraught with xenophobic anxiety; so fraught, in fact, that in 1989 an infant FOX Network launched a drama series called *Alien Nation*, which featured the travails of the "Newcomers"—aliens from the planet Tencto—as they sought to integrate into Los Angeles society. In the real alien nation, the unauthorized population topped 5 million, and INS agents raided farms in rural communities across the nation, arresting thousands, and frightening terrified migrants into signing English-only voluntary deportation forms.

For Jamaican guestworkers, however, the eighties were years of hope and expectation. It seemed that their years of hard work in the United States would finally be rewarded, either with permanent residency status or a big cash settlement. "Working on the farm was cheap and the hours were curtailed and we did have to keep quiet because we had no legal rights," wrote a Jamaican farmworker to his lawyer in the late 1980s; "I need to be compensated for all those bending years."[4] After forty years, it finally seemed as though Caribbean guestworkers would receive some compensation for all those bending years. The decade brought guestworkers immigration reform legislation known as the Immigration Reform and

Control Act (IRCA—pronounced er-ka), which promised permanent legal status for all "alien farmworkers." It also brought a huge $51 million courtroom victory and unprecedented attention in newsprint, books, and on film. Yet the 1980s ended up being a decade of devastating disappointment. Cane cutters—and only cane cutters—were excluded from the congressional "amnesty" for immigrants; court appeals denied them the back wages awards they had won; and machines replaced them in the cane fields. For Jamaican guestworkers, the eighties left the sort of bitter aftertaste that lasts a lifetime.

Simpson-Mazzoli

Though Ronald Reagan's campaign probably set off the furor over immigration, Reagan wasn't the force behind the immigration reform bills that followed his election. In fact, once in office, Reagan basically ducked the immigration issue, no doubt recognizing the growing split within the Republican Party between employers' desire for continued access to immigrant workers and social conservatives' growing animus toward "illegal" immigrants. Beyond speaking publicly in favor of a 50,000-person guestworker program outside the H2 system, Reagan did little to propel change. Still, the goal of immigration reform was kept in play by the media, the public, and by Senator Alan Simpson (R-WY) and Representative Romano L. Mazzoli (D-KY), the chairmen, respectively, of the Senate and House Immigration Committees. For five years, it was hard to open a newspaper or turn on a radio without hearing the hyphenated words "Simpson-Mazzoli."

The poles of the debate had changed a great deal from the early 1950s, though guestworkers were still in the thick of things. In the 1950s, conservative politicians from both parties had advocated open border policies and fought to reduce border patrol appropriations. Only the most liberal Democrats went on about the "invasion of wetbacks." In the 1980s, the two major parties were much more clearly divided on the immigration issue. Republicans still generally opposed reforms that would restrain employers in any way, but they were feeling increasing pressure to bar the nation's borders to both legal and illegal immigration. Democrats were far more likely to support amnesty for unauthorized immigrants. The parties were also increasingly divided on the issue of guestworker programs. In the 1950s, both Republicans and Democrats had held up guestworker programs as the only legitimate alternative to unregulated immigration. In the eighties, Republicans tended to advocated bigger and less regulated guestworker programs, but many Democrats had become convinced that guestworkers were as abused and exploited as undocumented workers.

The intense fight over guestworkers would hold up immigration reform for half a decade.

In its first iteration, the Simpson-Mazzoli reform bill called for amnesty for unauthorized immigrants already in the country; measures to stop future flows of unauthorized immigration, including a national identification card system that would allow employers to identify who could legally work; and a crackdown on employers who continued to hire unauthorized immigrants.[5]

A wide range of advocacy groups attacked the 1981 bill. Latino and civil rights advocates praised its amnesty provision but opposed employer sanctions, fearing that employers would refuse to hire anyone who looked or sounded Mexican. The Chamber of Commerce opposed criminal sanctions for employers who hired unauthorized immigrants. Agricultural employers argued that farmworkers wouldn't qualify for legalization under Simpson-Mazzoli's legalization provisions because they wouldn't be able to produce the paperwork necessary to show that they had lived and worked in the country since 1982, as the bill required. At the same time, they worried that if farmworkers did qualify for permanent residency, they wouldn't remain farmworkers. Either way, they argued, growers stood to lose their labor source. The price of growers' support was therefore a bigger and less-regulated guestworker program that would guarantee them continued access to immigrant labor. Guestworkers were the only legal workers who would remain in agriculture, they implied, because they were not permitted to work anywhere else. Growers' hopes were buoyed, no doubt, by Reagan's apparent support for a new guestworker program and Senator Samuel Ichiye Hayakawa's (R-CA) proposal to admit one million Mexican nationals on five-year visas.[6]

The Democrats who were the main supporters of the amnesty provision were just as adamantly opposed to the idea of creating a new guestworker program. Increasingly aware of the cascade of litigation filed by H2 workers' lawyers, they saw guestworkers as superexploitable workers whose presence depressed domestic farmworkers' wages. Only immigrants with permanent legal status, they argued, could hope to protect U.S. labor standards. As Charles Schumer (D-NY) put it, legalization was "the only way to assure foreign agricultural workers that they will be able to have the freedom of movement and bargaining power that is enjoyed by every other worker in every other industry in this nation."[7] Democratic lawmakers countered every proposal for a new and less regulated guestworker program with information about past cases of exploitation. When Representative Leon Panetta (D-CA) broke the mold by offering an amendment that would have given growers access to an apparently unlimited number of guestworkers with only seventy-two hours' notice, Representative George Miller (D-CA), chairman of the House Subcommittee on Wages, held hearings on the H2 Program, after which he released a blistering attack on the Labor Department's failure to enforce the very regulations growers thought were oppressive. His report charged Labor Department officials with failing to protect the rights of U.S. workers displaced by guestworkers and accused them of accepting, without verification, whatever the sugar industry told them. Ralph Alewine, the Labor Department official responsible for the H2 Program's oversight, called it the "Miller light-on-facts report."[8] With opposition from all sides, Simpon-Mazzoli died.

The second iteration of the bill offered a little bit more to each camp. To suit opponents of guestworker programs, it dropped the idea of a new, less-regulated program in favor of streamlining and expanding the existing program (though it wasn't exactly clear what streamlining the H2 Program would mean). It dropped the national ID card proposal, which had upset civil libertarians, and courted employers by qualifying employer sanctions with "an affirmative defense" clause. In other words, employers would not be held accountable for hiring unauthorized immigrants if they believed the workers' papers were in order (employers would be required to ask prospective employees for documents, but would not themselves determine whether workers' papers were valid). Versions of this bill passed both houses but died in the conference committee over questions of cost.[9]

By the time the third and final Simpson-Mazzoli bill made it to the House and Senate floors in 1985, new proposals for bigger and better guestworker schemes had garnered strong support among Republicans. Senator Pete Wilson (R-CA) proposed a plan that would have allowed 200,000–300,000 workers to enter the country for periods of up to nine months, during which time they would be confined to particular locales. After their nine months were up, they would be forced to return home to collect the 20 percent of their pay that would have been withheld. Senator Edward Kennedy likened Wilson's plan to the pass laws of South Africa, not realizing perhaps that Wilson's plan was pretty much how the H2 Program already worked.[10] The Senate defeated the measure but then turned around and voted to establish a guestworker program for perishable crops that would admit as many as 350,000 workers a year. Ultimately, both houses of Congress settled on the idea of expanding and streamlining the H2 Program, and dividing it into separate agricultural and nonagricultural components (H-2A and H-2B). Lawmakers did "streamline" H-2B, stripping the newly separated nonagricultural program of the protections and benefits—free travel, free housing, the three-quarter guarantee, and the adverse effect wage—that agricultural workers had long enjoyed. H-2A employers simply got more of what they already had. Even as lawmakers debated Simpson-Mazzoli, the Labor Department was already extending the H2-A Program to all crops and all states.[11]

Growers still resisted Simpson-Mazzoli, insisting on a guestworker program that would give them the benefit of the doubt when they said they needed foreign labor. And as long as growers opposed the bill, their largely Republican allies in Washington promised to vote it down. Growers' "greed knows no bounds," Simpson complained. "I don't [know] what the hell to do with them. I don't know how I can accommodate them. I'll never be right for them; they're the toughest guys to deal with."[12]

Just as it seemed growers were going to scuttle Simpson-Mazzoli a third time, Representative Charles Schumer (D-NY) crafted a compromise. Since growers' allies said they opposed the bill's legalization provision for fear that farmworkers would not qualify for legalization, Schumer and co-sponsors Panetta and Howard Berman (D-CA) offered a special legalization deal for farmworkers to ensure that most would qualify. Other applicants for legalization would have to prove they had been working in the United States since 1982, but under the Special Agricultural Workers or "SAWs" Program, "alien farmworkers" only needed to prove that they had worked ninety days in the year between May 1, 1985 and May 1, 1986. Even with all their coming and going and wages received in cash, most farmworkers would be able to meet that minimal standard. To address growers' fears that, once legalized, farmworkers would abandon the fields altogether, Schumer's amendment allowed for the importation of "replenishment agricultural workers" or "RAWs" at a later time. When even that failed to sway enough growers, the Democrats sweetened the deal by taking the remaining teeth out of the employer sanction policy. The hiring of illegal immigrants would be a civil offense, not a criminal one, and participation in the verification system would be optional (employers could opt not to call an 800-number to verify whether a prospective employee's social security number was valid). Employers had little to fear from "employer sanctions."[13]

All these compromises were too much for Mazzoli, who thought the compromise ceded too much to growers. He called the special legalization program for farmworkers "unparalleled, unprecedented and . . . unacceptable." But Berman warned that there was "no other way" to get the bill passed. "[D]on't try to undo one part of the equation or the whole thing will come tumbling down." With the Schumer amendment attached, IRCA became law on October 19, 1986.[14]

In the aftermath of IRCA's passage, nearly three million unauthorized immigrants raced to file applications for permanent legal status, 1.2 million of them farmworkers. Growers' supporters in Congress celebrated the expansion of the H2 Program. "Potentially, it could become millions of guestworkers," Representative Rick Boucher (R-VA) told the

Sun-Sentinel gleefully. Others predicted more modest growth, but the program was already expanding beyond apples and sugar. Mexican H2 workers were picking oranges in Arizona; soon they would be harvesting tobacco in Virginia, digging irrigation ditches in Idaho, and grooming horses in California.[15] The Caribbean guestworker program quickly became a mostly Mexican program.

Though the expansion of the H2 Program was already under way, the implementation of the SAW's legalization program was delayed by the sugar industry, which challenged the legalization program's applicability to H2 workers. H2 workers came to the United States *with* authorization, so they didn't need "amnesty" per se, but many had been coming to the United States six months out of the year for as much as twenty years, and it seemed peevish to deny them permanent status when men and women who lived in the United States without authorization—including AWOL guestworkers—were going to be legalized. In fact, according to Representative Rodino (D-NJ), the lawmakers who crafted the SAWs compromise fully intended guestworkers to be included, which is why IRCA provided for the legalization of "alien farmworkers," not illegal alien farmworkers. Schumer, Berman, and Panetta had included H2 workers in the SAWs program to placate guestworker opponents like Berman, who "strenuously and irrevocably opposed any massive guestworker program." To win over guestworkers' opponents, in other words, Schumer and the others had arranged for all "alien farmworkers" to become permanent residents so that they would all have the power to defend themselves. Instead of just transforming illegal immigrants into guestworkers as in the days of "drying out the wetbacks," "non-immigrant" guestworkers would be transformed into immigrants.[16]

But while Schumer and friends may have meant to include guestworkers in the amnesty provision, they inadvertently left a loophole in the language of the law. The SAWs program provided for the legalization of "alien farmworkers" involved in "the performance of field work related to planting, cultural practices, cultivating, growing and harvesting of fruits and vegetables of every kind and other perishable commodities *as defined in regulations by the Secretary of Agriculture.*"[17] That definition may have seemed broad enough to include any hired farmworker, but it left the definitions of the words "fruit," "vegetables," and "perishable" to the grower-friendly Department of Agriculture, where the sugar industry had a ringer.

The task fell to Allison T. French, the USDA's recently appointed "temporary acting special assistant for labor affairs" in the Office of Economics. "Al" French wasn't just any federal functionary; he was a consummate sugar industry insider on "special assignment to the USDA."[18] The son of Al French, Sr., the labor manager at Seabrook Farms who had helped engineer New Jersey's use of Bahamian guestworkers during World War II, French, Jr., got his first job with the Management Research Institute, a farm-management consulting business run by Rafael Fanjul, Pepe and Alfy's uncle.[19] He later became the Florida Farm Bureau's director of labor relations and public affairs, which meant, in effect, that he was Florida farm employers' chief lobbyist. Kenny Snodgrass of the United Farm Workers noted that French "fought for the Farm Bureau for years in the legislature. He has opposed collective bargaining for farm workers. He has followed us, taken pictures of us at meetings . . . Time and time again he has been the growers' lackey." [20]

Lackey or not, French would write the language that would determine who would be legalized and who wouldn't. A month after IRCA's passage, as farmworkers and their lawyers awaited French's vocabulary lesson, all hell broke loose in Florida.

THE DOG WAR

When the call came in to Legal Services this time, it was Saturday, November 22, 1986. "Something bad is going down at Okeelanta," reporter Margo Harakas told Greg Schell. "Something crazy."[21] Harakas was co-writing a five-part investigative report on guestworkers in the sugar industry, so when the police tuner began crackling with chatter about Okeelanta, she was paying attention.[22] What was going down at Okeelanta, Schell soon discovered, was a police roundup of striking H2 workers. Within minutes, Florida Rural Legal Services attorneys were racing to the airport, just as their predecessors had in 1968. Arriving at the international terminal, they had little difficulty spotting the H-2A workers among the Jamaicans returning home in their Sunday best and the tourists heading to beach resorts in shorts and Hawaiian shirts: the 350 deportees—all black men from Jamaica, St. Vincent, St. Lucia, Grenada, and Dominica—were lean and muscular; some still wore work clothes covered in black, sticky cane soot; a few wore the slippers and boxer shorts they had on when they were forced at gunpoint onto company buses; some were barefoot; all clutched boarding passes that said "Farmworker" where other travelers' names were printed.[23] The attorneys later located two more cane cutters in the Palm Beach County hospital where they were being treated for bites inflicted by police dogs.

The callousness and violence of the lightning roundup made this repatriation news, as did its proximity to IRCA. The dogs gave the strike its name. IRCA made it possible for attorneys to convince ten cane cutters to stay, apply for legalization under the SAWs Program, and sue.[24]

According to the men who stayed behind, the "Dog War" had begun not long after 6:30 a.m., the day before. On November 21, 1986, each cane cutter had lined up in front of a "cut row" of cane. Spiking his time card onto the top of a piece of cane at the start of his double row, each of the men had begun cutting and topping the cane, stacking the cane and "trash" in two neat rows. As usual, they did so without knowing what they were being paid. "[W]hile we were at work," Dominican McKerril Louis later recalled, "some guys asked the ticket writer the price of the cane." "The ticket writer, knowing the price was so low, did not want to say. So everybody stopped working. That's when it started."[25]

The field supervisor, also a Caribbean guestworker, eventually arrived and announced that the cut row price for the field was $53. Veteran workers murmured to the others that $53 was about half what they had been paid to cut the same field the year before. "We all decided that the price he was giving us was too low," recalled Alfred Campbell, who was in his fourth year as a Florida cane cutter. "We asked for more money, but he refused and said that he would have to speak to the white man."[26]

It's not at all clear why prices would have been half what they were the year before. Sugar prices had tumbled in 1974 when Congress allowed the Sugar Act to lapse as part of the Carter administration's effort to deregulate the U.S. economy. But lawmakers had come to the rescue with massive loans and guaranteed prices. In 1981, that combination of loans and price guarantees formed the basis for a new Sugar Program, crafted by the Reagan administration. Oddly, it worked (and continues to work) just like the old Subtreasury System, proposed but not achieved by Populist farmers in the late nineteenth century. Under the program, the federal government annually loaned sugar producers hundreds of billions of dollars, and set a guaranteed price for sugar (at about twice the world price). Come harvest, if the market price of sugar exceeded the guaranteed price, the industry would sell its sugar and pay back the loans. If the market price fell below the guaranteed price, the federal government would keep the sugar in lieu of repayment. Either way, the cane companies were guaranteed at least twice the price at which sugar sold on the open market (although very little sugar sold on an open market, since most countries subsidized their production). With the Sugar Program firmly in place, a forty plus percent pay cut for cane cutters seems inexplicable.

Alfy and Pepe Fanjul, whose farm the workers struck, didn't seem to be hurting for cash either. In 1983, not long after the new Sugar Program was put in place, the Fanjuls had bought all of Gulf &Western's sugar holdings in the United States and the Dominican Republic, making their company, which they called Flo-Sun, the biggest sugar producer in the United States, bigger even than "Big Sugar."[27]

Ultimately, the strikers didn't worry about why wages were so low; they were just certain that they were. They stopped work at Okeelanta, one of the Fanjuls' properties, hoping, no doubt, for a quick resolution to the conflict. They were in for a surprise. "The white man" did not come out to the fields, and the field supervisor refused to let the strikers ride the bus back to their barracks. A hundred men were forced to walk the eight miles back to Labor Camp #2, part of the sordid housing complex the workers unaffectionately called "Vietnam."[28]

Not all the cane cutters were so quick to put down their machetes, at least according to their later statements. Newman Peters, who was accused by the company of instigating the strike, said he was working in another field when he saw workers walk off the job. The St. Vincent Islander and seven-year veteran of Florida's cane fields insisted that he had only stopped working because "a buddy of mine told me to." "I was worried," he claimed, "that if I did not stop working, I might have trouble later. So I stopped."[29] Horace Clark, who was a first-time cane cutter, said he "had no desire to leave the field" and that he had kept working even after strikers threw rocks at his crew. But when his "pusher," the guestworker assigned to harry the others, stopped working too, Clark followed suit.[30] Realizing, perhaps, that the strikers were calling other men out of the fields as they trekked back to the barracks, Okeelanta's managers eventually sent buses to pick the strikers up.[31]

That night, all was quiet in Vietnam. At breakfast before dawn the men debated what to do. Most men wanted to return to work, but some forty cane cutters preferred to wait to hear "from the bigger officials about the row price."[32] They soon discovered that the choice had been taken out of their hands. Horace Clark, who chose work, headed for the bus that normally took men to the fields in the morning, but when he tried to board, he found the doors closed and the driver missing.[33] The strike had turned into a lockout. Workers sent emissaries to Camp 1 to spread the news.

At about 7:00 a.m., one of the liaison officers arrived to tell the workers that they ought to give up their demand for more money and return to work, which is what some had already tried unsuccessfully to do. Strike leaders insisted that they would not go back to work at row prices that were almost half what they had been the year before. After an hour and a half of fruitless arguing, the liaison left, saying he would speak to the company and try to obtain a raise. He didn't return.[34]

A few minutes later, guestworker Stafford Baptiste watched from his top floor window as a long line of police cars drove up the road toward the camp and then alternated turning left and right, until police cars surrounded the camp's perimeter. "The officers began to gather around our Camp so that we could not leave the Camp to go to Camp One, and no one from Camp One could come to our Camp," recalled Horace Clark.

Newman Peters counted about fifteen police cars. They "were carrying guns, shot guns . . . They had dogs . . . It looked like the army. It looked like South Africa, not the United States." Clarke noticed eight or ten Okeelanta buses bringing up the rear. Then a helicopter landed and policemen and dogs got out.[35]

Although cane cutters moved to board the buses voluntarily, the police began to clear the barracks with their guns drawn. "[T]he police burst into our Camp with dogs," recalled Lansbert Ormsby; they ordered everyone to "Get in the bus; get in the bus." Ormsby tried to grab his suitcase, he said, but fell and was trampled by several fleeing men. Getting up, he tried to explain to the police that he did not want to leave and was willing to work under the terms offered by Okeelanta but "they just told us to shut up and get on the bus."[36] Seeing men run in panic, Stafford Baptiste tried to collect the clothes he had washed and hung on the clothesline the day before, but as he started downstairs a police dog came toward him. Its handler told him to "Get the fuck out of here." When a co-worker bent to pick up his work boots, the dog rushed him. Baptiste fled, leaving behind everything he had.[37] Alfred Campbell and several other men tried barricading themselves into the barracks but were forced onto a bus. Campbell was wearing nothing but his underwear, a vest, and slippers.[38] Newman Peters ran to his barrack and was standing in the doorway when the policemen came in after him. According to his affidavit, he ran, pushing lockers over to keep the dogs off him. Before he reached his bunk, a dog reached him, biting him in three places. Photographs of his stomach taken at the hospital showed teeth marks. He was arrested, charged with battery on a police officer (because one of the lockers he pushed hit an arresting officer), resisting arrest with violence, and inciting to riot. McKerril Louis, who was also bitten by a police dog, was charged with resisting arrest and inciting to riot.[39]

As in 1968, some of the men herded into buses were not strikers at all. Kipling Williams, who had only come over to Camp 1 out of curiosity, ended up on a bus "half naked and wearing his slippers." He asked for permission to get his belongings but was refused.[40] Jamaican Harret Reid was napping in his bunk when a co-worker woke him up and told him something was happening at Camp 2. They walked across the field that separated the two camps to see what was happening and saw sheriff's officers and a group of workers yelling. Reid decided to go back to his camp. As he turned back, an Okeelanta bus drove straight into the field with a jeep full of policemen behind it. The officers jumped out and ordered Reid to board the bus. He tried to explain that he had nothing to do with the strike, he recalled, but a policeman said "he didn't care, and he put his gun across my stomach."[41]

As in 1968, the Palm Beach sheriff's story differed markedly from workers' account of events. Joe Bradshaw, the sheriff's spokesman, said the sheriff's department only came onto the farm when strikers trapped superintendent John Wilkie in his office, attempted to burn a cane field, and threatened fellow cane cutters willing to accept Okeelanta's row prices with rocks and knives. Deputies sent the dog after Newman Peters, Bradshaw told the *Palm Beach Post*, because Peters was moving toward a locker where cane knives were stored. "He pushed lockers into several officers and he struck me," Lieutenant Chuck Lowell told the press.[42]

Whether all or none of this was true, Peters' arrest report makes clear that the police had been organized as a strikebreaking force. It refers to the combined force of law enforcement officers as an "Emergency Field Force Team," which was dispatched in "REFERENCE TO LABOR TROUBLE." "UPON ARRIVAL," he continued, "WE SECURED THE PERIMETER, AT WHICH TIME WE WERE ADVISED BY OUR COMMANDERS TO ASSIST THEM IN TAKING OUT A SUBJECT WEARING A RED TYPE KNIT SWEAT SHIRT, LATE KNOWN TO ME AS NEWTON [*sic*] PETERS. MR. PETERS, WHO WAS AN INSTIGATOR IN THIS INCIDENT, RAN INTO THE LOWER PART OF THE FIRST BARRACKS TRYING TO HIDE FROM THE SHERIFF'S OFFICE AS WE WERE TRYING TO APPREHEND HIM."[43] There was no mention of a burned cane field or of cane cutters trapping Wilkie in the payroll office.

Speaking to reporters in the coming days and weeks, workers argued that the real cause of the strike was the time-shaving practices they had been complaining about for more than twenty years. "[T]here was no riot whatsoever," McKerrill Louis, a father of three and a nine-year veteran of Florida's cane fields, told the *Herald*. "We are on a piece rate. The hour business is just a frame-up, something to show our home government that we are being treated fairly—just to fool people." The *Herald* called Ralph Alewine, the Department of Labor official who oversaw the H2-A Program, for his comment. Alewine promised to investigate but "doubted the claims of under-reported hours." "Okeelanta," according to Alewine, "was the shining example of good time-keeping practices."[44]

That shining example sent several hundred men home, some in their underwear. Police loaded seven buses with men, some by force, and some by telling them they were going back to work. All seven buses headed to the Miami airport. "None of us had a chance to get our belongings," recalled Everard Jarvis of St. Vincent, who had been working in Florida for the first time. "We were driven to Miami and had to go home wearing whatever clothes we had on on Saturday. None of us had a change of clothes," he continued, "and we all had to go home as if we were runaways. On the airplane, all the other passengers were staring at us because we were so dirty. I had to sit on the airplane between two clean passengers . . . I was so ashamed."[45] Sent home without even enough for bus fare, Julius Butcher of St. Lucia had to walk halfway to his house, which was fourteen miles from the airport.[46]

In the days and weeks after the strike, growers, U.S. Department of Labor officials, and Jamaican authorities closed ranks. The Fanjuls refused to comment, but the Florida Cane Sugar League made its views known the afternoon of the strike by announcing that it had elected Pepe Fanjul as its president. Walter Kates, the manager of the Florida Fruit and Vegetable Association's labor division—the grower organization that had recruited the workers and subcontracted them to Okeelanta—insisted that the strike at Okeelanta was an isolated incident. "The industry has been highly regulated for many years by the U.S. Department of Labor," Kates said. "They come down every year and they do payroll audits, interviews with the workers and there has never been a problem in the past."[47] After the ten workers filed a complaint with the Department of Labor, alleging time card tampering, the president of the Sugar Cane Growers Cooperative in Belle Glade told reporters: "It's all just a rehash." "All this has been settled before." "You hear a lot about them not being very educated but if you make one little mistake in his paycheck, he's a CPA," said Bill Miller, U.S. Sugar's agricultural relations manager. JAG Smith, Jamaica's Minister of Labour, declined to talk to reporters about allegations of timekeeping manipulation, saying he "wouldn't dignify that with a response."[48]

These denials failed to stem the flood of negative reporting that followed the Dog War. On November 27, the *Palm Beach Post*'s news editor wrote that sugarcane cutters "may or may not have posed a threat to the safety of superintendent John Wilkie, depending upon whose version of events is accurate." But deportees received no hearings, and were entitled to none, though even illegal immigrants get a hearing. Ironically, the editor noted, those accused of breaking the law [Newman and Louis] stayed, while those facing no charges were deported. "All the laws, federal and state, that have been enacted to protect migrants are of no use to the H-2 worker because he dares not object to mistreatment." The editorial noted that the immigration reform bill, passed the month before, had expanded the program. It should have been abolished, the editor concluded. The *Miami Herald*'s staff editorial didn't go quite so far; still it reasoned that, "If foreign workers are to continue coming to Florida, their rights—including the right to protest employment conditions without the threat of an immediate deportation—must be fully protected."[49]

When Dessert Is Not Food

The Dog War resulted in the very public expulsion of 342 men and a long series of exposés of the H2 Program. It also resulted in ten men deciding to stick around, sue, and test the IRCA's legalization provision. Thus in late 1986, ten men, two of them with dog bites, stayed in the United States and waited anxiously for Al French's ruling on the definition of the words "fruits," "vegetables," and "perishable." One can only imagine their reaction when it came five months later, in May 1987. According to French, who cited the science of botany, sugar was the *only* crop in the country that wasn't a fruit, a vegetable, or perishable. Fruits, according to the published definition, were "the human edible parts of plants which consist of the mature ovaries and fused other parts or structures which develop from flowers or inflorescence." "Vegetables" were the "human edible leaves, stems, roots, or tubers of herbaceous plants." As a grass, sugarcane was neither. And because it had a predictable harvest season, it wasn't perishable.[50] Sugarcane cutters would not get legal status.

In a letter to the Secretary of Agriculture, nine legislators protested that the exclusion of sugarcane cutters from the amnesty program was a "particularly egregious" evasion of congressional intent.[51] It didn't matter. In the days and weeks that followed, the INS began issuing temporary Green Cards to harvesters of Christmas trees, hops, herbs, pecans, tobacco, cut flowers, even clarinet reeds, "human edible" and "perishable" or not. Cane cutters, and only cane cutters, were cut from IRCA's legalization provision. "It was one of the most outrageous things they ever did," former Legal Services attorney Ed Tuddenham said.[52] It was particularly ironic that French deemed sugarcane not perishable, since over the previous forty years its perishability had been used repeatedly as a justification for guestworkers. As late as 1983, when the Department of Labor threatened to deny sugar growers access to foreign workers until growers agreed to pay cutters the full "adverse effect wage," sugarcane growers sought injunctive relief, arguing that "If U.S. Sugar . . . continues to be denied the needed sugar cane cutters, virtually the entire sugar crop will rot in the fields, causing losses of several hundred million dollars."[53] Cane cutters' attorneys challenged the decision in early 1988, filing a lawsuit against the Secretary of Agriculture on behalf of five undocumented Haitian cane cutters, who had gotten their cane-cutting jobs as a result of earlier lawsuits but were denied legalization because of French's rule. (FAIR and other anti-immigration organizations joined the suit against the Department of Agriculture, not because they thought it was unfair to exclude cane cutters, but because they thought the USDA's definition was too broad and would let too many foreign farmworkers gain permanent residency.)[54]

In April 1988, cane cutters won a halfway victory. Judge Thomas Hogan upheld the USDA's definition of perishable commodities but found its exclusion of sugar arbitrary and capricious. He demanded justification "forthwith."[55] While waiting for the USDA's new explanation, the judge required the government to delay deportation proceedings in sugarcane cases, issue cane cutters work authorization forms, and reopen any applications that had already been closed based on the USDA's rule.[56] Some two thousand cane cutters hurriedly applied for permanent status. "To their credit," Greg Schell remarked, the Florida Fruit and Vegetable Association helped workers fill out the paperwork. "We offered to do it," Schell noted, "but they didn't want us anywhere near them."[57]

Publicly, sugar industry officials insisted that it was maintaining a neutral position on the legalization question, but privately, most of the sugar companies fought the legalization program tooth and nail, no doubt fearing that cane cutters with legal status wouldn't cut cane. U.S. Sugar hired "a big law firm" to keep the cane cutters from being legalized, according to Greg Schell. They didn't want to leave it up to the USDA's "usual half-assed job" so they spent "buckets of money."[58]

H2 workers didn't have buckets of money, but they did have the Farmworker Justice Fund (FJF), a national legal advocacy and lobby group, in their corner. The FJF brought in their own big gun: Steve Routh, an attorney from the very big and very reputable Washington, DC, firm Hogan & Hartson (Chief Justice John G. Roberts' firm). Hogan & Hartson was big enough to have a pro bono department, and in 1988, Routh rotated into it. Supplied with clippings on the Dog War and earlier exposés of the industry's labor relations by the Farmworker Justice Fund, Routh decided to take the case. Together, he and FJF attorney Kristine Poplawski tried every angle they could think of to influence the federal judge who would be interpreting the USDA's next effort at semantics. They pointed out that the cane companies themselves called sugarcane perishable, but dropped that line of reasoning because the perishability issue seemed like a nonstarter. They tried to get discovery from the USDA to prove collusion between French and the sugarcane companies, but challenges to government rules fell under the restrictive Administrative Procedures Act, which sets strict limits on what plaintiffs can demand. Unable to find a smoking gun that proved the cane companies were pulling French's strings, Routh and Poplawski filed an "intervenors' reply brief" to make clear that the authors of the SAWs program fully intended to include H2 workers in the legalization program.

On August 19, 1988, the USDA released its new definition, which still excluded sugarcane cutters and only sugarcane cutters from the SAWs program. In this iteration, French continued to rely on a botanical definition of fruits but adopted what the USDA called a "new horticultural definition of vegetables." Although sugarcane might appear to be a vegetable, the new language explained, it was not, because vegetables were eaten "chiefly as the principal part of a meal, rather than as dessert." Because sugarcane was used in dessert, it could not be a vegetable. The new USDA definition was just five lines long, but it came with nine pages of text, which explained, among other things, why rhubarb is a vegetable, despite the fact that it, like sugarcane, is most often eaten for dessert; why cassava, artichokes, and onions are vegetables but parsley is not; and why the fact that sugarcane can be chewed does not make it edible. U.S. Sugar filed comments with the USDA supporting the new definition, and on March 1, 1989, Judge Hogan upheld it. The USDA's definition "didn't even pass the laugh test," Schell remarked, "but it held up in court."[59]

The battle for legalization was over. When H2 workers proudly displayed the temporary Green Cards they had been issued as they returned to the United States for the apple harvest, border officials confiscated them. Cane cutters already in the United States hung on to the cards and used them illegally to get social security numbers and drivers' license numbers. But by remaining in the United States without authorization, they cut themselves off from family members in the Caribbean. With invalid Green Cards, they could never reenter the country if they went home.[60] Some cane cutters, like James Robinson whom I interviewed in Waterbury, Connecticut in 1999, succeeded in bringing family members to the United States to join them, but they lived in fear of exposure. After about an hour of pleasant conversation, Robinson suddenly became reticent and then started to cry as I interviewed him. Struggling to recall what I had said to make him so frightened, I realized that I had made the mistake of casually asking how many children he had and how old they were. I was making chit chat; he was frantically thinking about having to move, hide his children, and start all over. He cried for twenty minutes before I thought to hand over the cassette tape I had been making of the interview.

Former H2 workers who remained in the Caribbean and some who stayed without authorization in the United States sent the Farmworker Justice Fund heartbreaking letters. "Sir, Madam," one man wrote, "I would be very greatful if the government could help us with the green Card so that I could get something better to help myself and my families. I am working over there [in the U.S.] cutting cane and Picking apple more than seventeen seasons, Mon. [A]ll my Strength my working is over there."[61]

BYGRAVE

The two thousand or so men who stayed in the United States were cut off from their families and forced to live in fear of apprehension and deportation, but their presence in the United States made them accessible to Legal Services attorneys, who were beginning to piece together how the cane companies' pay system worked and how to get compensation for cane cutters' "bending years."[62]

In the years after the Dog War, there were countless and seemingly endless lawsuits against Florida's cane companies and the Department of

Labor. And despite Greg Schell's boast that Florida Rural Legal Services never lost, Legal Services gained little ground against the cane companies. A month after the strike, the ten "angry Jamaican sugar cane cutters" who stayed behind when their co-workers left the country filed complaints with the U.S. Department of Labor's Wage and Hour Division in Fort Myers, seeking pay they claimed they were owed and the return of their belongings.[63] FRLS attorneys also filed a civil suit against Okeelanta (*Malcolm v. Okeelanta*), which sought reimbursement for all the property lost by cane cutters when they were deported during the Dog War. Legal Services eventually won a settlement from Okeelanta, but it took nine years.[64] The ten cane cutters who stayed behind became the lead plaintiffs in *Moodie v. Okeelanta*, which focused on time card tampering, and asserted that farm workers were entitled to go to court to enforce their rights under the Wagner National Labor Relations Act. The judge ruled in 1989 that the Wagner Act only protected Americans.[65] Three years after the Dog War, the USDL announced that four sugarcane growers had underpaid Caribbean cutters by more than $1 million in the previous year's sugar harvest. "The investigators looked at one year and found $1 million," FRLS director Rob Williams noted, but "what about all the other years?"[66]

What attorneys really needed was for the ticket writers—the men trained to fill out the time cards—to admit that they had been instructed to falsify men's hours. Some would say so off the record, but only one would do so in court. The rest were either still working for the cane companies or hoping to be called back.

Greg Schell kept digging. He was joined by Jim Green, an ACLU lawyer in West Palm Beach, Yale Law graduate Sarah Cleveland (now an Obama appointee in the U.S. State Department), and Edward Tuddenham, who, like Schell, came from Harvard Law School. Graduating magna cum laude, Tuddenham had driven straight to Hereford, Texas, where he and a couple of friends opened Texas Rural Legal Aid in 1978. Local growers called them "the Harvard idiots." They arrived in Texas just as the Carter administration started allowing the H2 Program to expand beyond apples, sugarcane, and West Indians. Tuddenham found himself representing Mexican H2 workers in Texas and consulting on H2 cases as far away as Virginia. Local cotton farmers fired his clients and sued Texas Rural Legal Aid for "conspiracy to extort minimum wage."[67] In private practice in Austin, Texas, by the late eighties, Tuddenham decided to take on the Florida sugarcane case.

By then, there were boxes and boxes of documents—depositions, payroll records, coded computer printouts of all kinds, correspondence. Going painstakingly through the whole mess, Tuddenham dug out the 1972 Sikes letter in which Fred Sikes, U.S. Sugar's vice president, flatly stated, "We will require all cutters to produce approximately one ton of cane per hour." "It was the 'Eureka! moment," Tuddenham recalled years later.[68] If the cane cutters' contracts guaranteed them a set wage by the hour—the adverse effect wage was $5.30 an hour by the mid-eighties—and if workers were required to cut at least a ton of cane by the hour, then a ton of cane was worth at least $5.30. All Tuddenham needed to know to figure out the difference between what cane cutters were paid and what they should have been paid was the total number of tons harvested each year. The piles of paper also produced clearance orders going back as far as the 1970s. The forms, which Secretary of Labor Ray Marshall had introduced, set the terms of the jobs cane companies offered and contained the one ton an hour statement. Workers never saw these clearance orders nor did their liaison officers, but at least sixty days before workers were needed for a particular season, copies were sent to U.S. Employment Services offices around the country. Only when USES offices failed to secure domestic workers—which they invariably did—were employers allowed to import the H2 workers, who had already been recruited and screened and were standing by for word to proceed to Kingston's airport. Since the cane companies paid by the task not the hour, those clearance orders set out the production standard, the task a man had to complete to earn the $5.30 an hour his contract promised. A ton equaled an hour equaled $5.30. Tuddenham had himself a lawsuit.

The hitch was that Tuddenham couldn't get cane company officials to admit in depositions that eight tons of cane per eight-hour day represented a production standard, and the Department of Labor wouldn't confirm it either. Neither the workers nor the liaisons had ever seen a clearance order. Former Labor Secretary Marshall was ready to testify that the statement in the clearance orders represented a production standard, but he was no longer secretary (though he signed on as an unpaid expert witness). According to current Labor Department officials and company lawyers, the eight-ton statement was just a guideline, not a minimum requirement.[69]

To determine how much workers had been shorted, moreover, Tuddenham still needed to know how many tons of cane had been harvested, and it wasn't at all clear how to figure that out. Cane company officials continued to insist that they didn't employ a tonnage system. The answer finally came from an unexpected source. In 1988, Tuddenham got a phone call from Edward Fountain, a former supervisor at U.S. Sugar, who had kept meticulous records and had taken them with him when he left the company. The cane companies did indeed operate on the basis of a tonnage system, Fountain confirmed, and they budgeted far less per ton—on average $1.60 less—than the workers' contracts required. "In one year, my crew was shorted 11,000 tons," Fountain told him. "It makes me mad—$50,000 would have made such a difference in their lives." Tuddenham couldn't have been more surprised. "He was an Anglo from Belle Glade sticking his neck out for a black Jamaican," Tuddenham told reporter Marie Brenner. "Never in your wildest dreams would you have imagined that."[70]

With Fountain's information, Tuddenham, Schell, and Green were nearly ready to go to court, but they needed named plaintiffs. They found them among the cane cutters who had stayed in the United States after IRCA. Bernard Bygrave became the guestworker whose name would be most associated with the case, but there was one named plaintiff for each of the six companies named in the suit: U.S. Sugar, the Sugar Cane Growers Cooperative, Shawnee Farms, and the three companies owned or controlled by the Fanjuls—Okeelanta, Osceola, and Atlantic. Shawnee, which was defunct by the time the case was filed, was dropped early on. Since, by 1989, Legal Services had been banned from participating in class action suits, Tuddenham and Green—both private attorneys—filed the case on behalf of the 20,000 plaintiffs. Tuddenham brought in David Gorman, a local contracts expert, who had no background in legal aid work, but who could reframe the complaint in a way that the Palm Beach circuit court judge would accept.[71] Together they asked for $100 million in back wages.[72]

Because Florida has a two-year statute of limitations in civil cases, the judge limited the claim to the two seasons before the suit was filed (adding two more years as the case wore on). A class of fifteen thousand cane cutters was certified. Tuddenham, Gorman, and Green demanded more records from the cane companies. Eventually, there would be ninety crates in the county courthouse.[73]

While the plaintiffs' attorneys shelled out more than $100,000 of their own money for travel, court reporters, filing fees, and other expenses, the defendants hired the two most powerful law firms in Miami, choosing as their lead counsel the millionaire personal injury attorney, Willie Gary, who was black. "There was no way I was going to face down a jury trying to argue against thousands of poor black Jamaicans without a black lawyer," the Fanjul's counsel told Brenner. The son of migrant workers, Gary flew to meetings in "the Wings of Justice," his personal jet which had gold-plated fixtures. His strategy was to suggest that poor black farmworkers had been duped into suing by their white, liberal attorneys. "This is not a case about the workers," he told reporters; "It's a case about creative lawyering."[74]

Despite the cane companies' resources, the stars seemed to line up in the plaintiffs' favor. The year Tuddenham, Green, and Gorman filed the Bygrave case, New Yorker author Alec Wilkinson published Big Sugar: Seasons in the Cane Fields of Florida (Knopf), a best-selling and damning indictment of the sugar industry's labor regime, some of which was serialized in the magazine. The following year, Stephanie Black's brilliant documentary film, *H2 Worker*, which she had to film clandestinely after being banned from cane company property, won prizes at the Cannes and Sundance Film Festivals. Coverage by newspapers was relentless and just as incriminating. Pressured by the media exposés, Secretary of Labor Elizabeth Dole threatened to break tradition by enforcing U.S. labor laws in sugar, and the House Education and Labor Committee was preparing a report accusing growers of using low wages and substandard conditions to scare away domestic workers. The U.S General Accounting Office was investigating allegations that H2 workers had paid a million dollars more for health insurance than it actually cost. And in Jamaica, JAG Smith, the former Minister of Labor, went to prison for embezzling guestworkers' savings.[75]

Just when it seemed as though the news couldn't get any worse for the cane companies, it did. On June 25, 1992, the state court in West Palm Beach stunned attorneys on both sides by granting the plaintiffs summary judgment, which meant the farmworkers won without having to go to trial. Two months later, the court awarded the cane cutters damages of $51 million, plus interest. The judge found that the clearance order's guarantee of $5.30 per hour when combined with the 8-ton statement was "clear and unambiguous" in offering workers a piece rate of $5.30 a ton.[76] Clearly stunned by the outcome, all five companies promised to appeal, though U.S. Sugar, always wary of its reputation, announced that it had agreed to a "labor peace" with Florida Rural Legal Services. As part of that peace accord, U.S. Sugar promised a pay increase, an end to the task rate wage system, and full disclosure to workers regarding wages. Each field would be weighed and the cane cutters' pay based on the portion of the tonnage they had cut, a return, in other words, to the system that had been in place during World War II. Time stamp machines would record workers' hours in the field.[77] Robert E. Muraro, U.S. Sugar's general counsel, told reporters that the labor pact did not alter the company's decision to appeal. "This [pact] is not a concession that we were doing things wrong before," he said.[78]

For a while, the good news for farmworkers kept coming. Three days after the cane cutters won summary judgment, the GAO published the report of its investigation, which condemned the Department of Labor for failing to enforce H-2A regulations.[79] It found that workers were being charged for part of their transportation costs, despite DOL regulations to the contrary; that workers had substandard insurance coverage despite "exorbitant premiums"; and that workers were receiving no interest on the 20 percent of their wages they were forced to contribute to a savings plan. The 2.5 percent of those savings that went to WICLO's liaison officers was "un-monitored," the report also concluded.[80]

You All Have the Handle and the Company Has the Blade

It seemed as though everything had turned around for the cane cutters. They had won their case; they had finally been vindicated by a federal agency; all the complaints they had made over the years were before the public in print and on film. But the sweet taste of victory dissolved into bitter defeat. The cane companies responded to the storm of negative publicity and the damage award by doing what they said couldn't be done: they mechanized their harvest operations completely. As though to mock the men who had faced acres of cane with nothing but machetes, massive cane-cutting machines with air-conditioned cabs began appearing in the fields. "Machines don't sue," sugar company executives told reporters.[81]

Mechanization would probably have come anyway because, while still not perfect, cane-cutting technology had improved significantly since the 1940s. Each machine, though costly, could now do the work of fifty men swinging machetes. Still, cane executives were quick to tell any reporter who would listen that liberal lawyers were to blame.

Inevitable or not, the change was final. By 1992, the Co-op had mechanized. The three Fanjul farms followed in 1993. U.S. Sugar began to switch over to machines in 1994, despite its declaration of labor peace. By the 1997–98 cane-cutting season, the H2 Program in sugar was over.[82]

Mechanization may have eliminated dirty, dangerous, and poorly paid work, but it deprived thousands of Jamaican families of their livelihood. In Jamaica, where the Ministry of Finance was boarded up and the evening news included "a cholera watch," many responded to the news with fury. "They're no good," nine-year cane-cutting veteran Anthony Stewart told a reporter, who asked what he thought of the cane cutters' lawyers. "They interfere with our working now. There's no sense in it." Tony Irons, Jamaica's Minister of Labour, also blamed the farmworkers' lawyers "who pressed the back-wage lawsuits." "This is what unwarranted interferences on the part of our bleeding-heart liberals have brought about," said a columnist in the *Gleaner*.[83] But former cane cutters were more ambivalent. With the H2 Program over in sugar, and the Caribbean program in apples offering only a few weeks of work a year, unemployed cane cutters put all their hope in the *Bygrave* payout. "I Agree Upon All Grounds With All Cases brought Against the sugar companies in the U.S.A. for all unjust deal with we Farmers All," one man wrote from St. Vincent. "Human is Human. All Created Equal. Justice is Justice . . . Set it done with discipline, Right, and Honour." "[N]o Doubt we win the case already don't matter what the companies trying to do," another man wrote from the Jamaican Parish of St. Ann, "For God See and Know how we work, and he isn't sleeping." "I Dream it Several times and See the case come to a final," he added. "What I would want you Mr. Schell and the rest of the Bigger Folks is to Stop the Appeal of the Case, for I feel within myself that you all have the handle and the company has the Blade."[84] Schell couldn't stop the appeal, of course, but he and the other attorneys were optimistic that they'd win it in short order. In an interview with the *National Law Journal*, the farmworkers' lawyers predicted that "the appeals process could take a year or long" and that it might take "some time" before their clients saw any money.[85] That turned out to be quite an understatement.

In 1995, a year after the final company mechanized, the state appeals court reversed the judgment in *Bygrave* and broke the case up into five separate jury trials. Three years later, none of those trials had yet occurred, but U.S. Sugar agreed to settle, negotiating its portion of the damages down to a mere $5.65 million, or an average of $250 per cane cutter plus $1 million in legal fees. It was the last cane company money any of the cane cutters would see.[86]

The Co-op and the Fanjuls strung out the appeals, using the time to curry favor and undermine the evidence that had been used against them. In the years following the cane cutters' initial victory, the Fanjuls contributed millions to political candidates from both parties. Alfy co-chaired Clinton's Florida re-election campaign. Pepe was on Bob Dole's finance committee. Their influence was legend. President Clinton took a call from Alfy Fanjul when he was trying to break up with Monica Lewinsky in March 1997 and she was trying to change his mind on her knees. Lewinsky told the Starr Commission the call was from someone whose name was something like "Fanuli." "The most telling thing about Alfy Fanjul," wrote author and columnist Carl Hiaasen, "is that he can get the president on the phone in the middle of a blow job. That tells you all you need to know about their influence."[87] The Fanjuls' influence convinced Clinton's Department of Labor to add a disclaimer in the Okeelanta, Osceola, and Atlantic clearance orders that said the eight-ton-per-day productivity expectation was "not a minimum productivity standard as a condition of job retention."[88]

In 1999, a decade after the case was first filed, the appeal filed by the Atlantic Sugar Company—another Fanjul firm—finally went to court. Marie Brenner described the scene. Atlantic Sugar was represented by "a platoon" of sharply dressed lawyers from Steel, Hector, and Davis. On the plaintiffs' side sat "the entire staff of the Migrant Rural Legal Aid office of Belle Glade, all six of them. Their wardrobe is McGovern-rally casual short-sleeves and knapsacks." Still, Tuddenham was confident. "The beauty of this case is that it is so simple," he told the court. "It is based on a single piece of paper," by which he meant the clearance order.[89] But it was a piece of paper that few in the industry had seen, let alone the farmworkers or liaisons. Willie Gary paraded witness after witness through the courtroom, all of whom testified that they had never heard of a tonnage pay system or a clearance order. At one point in his closing, Gary held up a sign that read, "THIS IS A FRIVOLOUS LAWSUIT." Gorman and Tuddenham fought back with complicated charts showing tonnage rates and wage levels.[90]

After a month of testimony, the judge sent off the six-member jury with strict instructions to consider one question only: Did the workers' contract require Atlantic to pay cane cutters a minimum task rate of $5.30 per ton. The clearance order did, of course, but the contract did not. The jury very reluctantly concluded that it had not. It had required $5.30 an hour. The jurors believed the men had been cheated but were bound by the judge's instructions to return a verdict for the cane companies. "When the jurors returned to the courtroom," Brenner wrote, "one woman was crying." The jury foreman asked the judge to read a statement:

> Atlantic Sugar consistently misrepresented to the cutters the incentive features of their task system of payment. It was shameful. However, the scope of the verdict form presented to us by the court was limited to a single issue— "Does the contract require Atlantic to pay plaintiffs a minimum task rate of $5.30 per ton of harvest cane."

The statement ended with the sentence: "This case is not frivolous." Jury foreman Roger Gamblin later told Brenner that he thought "the judge had decided the case." Inside the jury room, Gamblin had asked the other jurors, "Did the company cheat the workers?" They had all answered, "Yes."[91]

The remaining cases dragged on with costs mounting on both sides. I wondered why the Fanjuls would drag the appeals out so long after the program's termination. "How much could you possibly get out of them if they settled?" I asked. Schell's guess was $4–5 million. "They had to have spent that much on lawyers," I speculated. Schell said they sent "no less than three lawyers in a limo just to say 'we agree' to a motion." It wasn't about the money, Schell insisted. The defendants' lawyers once told Schell that the Fanjuls would not spend a nickel to settle the case. "We're not going to be wimps like U.S. Sugar," she said.[92] "U.S. Sugar had a different, go-out-and-suck-their-ass approach," the Fanjul's counsel told Brenner.[93]

Meanwhile, former H2 workers waited impatiently for their money. "Okeelanta rob us of our Time and money and may the Judge See that," one wrote in 1998. Presumably, he meant the judge on high because the judge in Florida had been no help. He continued: "my brother I think [cutting] cane is one of the hardes work in life and for Too long they suffer us as hell."[94]

In April 1999, the Okeelanta appeal went to trial. This time, Tuddenham and Gorman called to the stand Michael Cameron, a former guestworker who had trained as a ticket writer but who had refused the job when he discovered that it involved falsifying workers' hours. He had been raised as a Christian, he said. "[H]earing the procedure that you have to go through," he said in his deposition, "I thought it was unfair, and I said no, I'm not going to do this." Gary accused him of telling "whoppers." Ultimately, Cameron's testimony counted for nothing because the judge gave the same instructions to the jury. The cane cutters lost the appeal after just four hours of deliberation.[95]

The Osceola appeal was next. Brenner asked Tuddenham: "Is it possible that you will spend the rest of your life working on this case?" He waited a long time before answering "yes."[96] The appeal went to trial in June 2007 but ended in a shouting match between the lawyers. The judge walked out. Then the named plaintiff went missing, so the state court judge decertified the class. As private lawyers, Gorman and Tuddenham were unable to solicit new clients. Only Legal Services lawyers can go looking for clients without running up against Bar Association rules banning "ambulance chasing." Deciding finally not to spend the rest of their lives and savings pursuing the case, Gorman and Tuddenham withdrew. Gregg Schell took the case over once again. By this time, he ran the Migrant Farmworker Justice Project, which had spun off from Florida Rural Legal Services to escape Reagan Era rules banning legal services from participating in class action suits and representing unauthorized immigrants. Schell went back to Jamaica and Barbados to round up plaintiffs. Fifteen hundred men agreed to be named plaintiffs, among them ticket writers who were now free to testify because they had no hope of working in Florida's cane fields again.[97]

The ticket writers' insistence that they were taught to match the number of hours they recorded to the amount of cane each man cut allowed Schell to switch his argument in the Osceola appeal to a much simpler wage and hour case. No complicated charts were required. The companies were supposed to pay a set amount by the hour and they doctored time cards to avoid doing so. The Fanjuls' attorneys accused Schell of pulling a fast one by switching arguments mid-stream, but their motion to dismiss the case failed. Osceola's lawyers then insisted on deposing all the 1,500 plaintiffs, knowing Schell's office couldn't afford to do so. Most recently, in 2009, the cane company's lawyers invoked Florida Statute 57.011, a Reconstruction Era law that requires nonresidents filing a case in Florida to put up a $100 bond against court costs. A case with 1,500 plaintiffs would cost the nonprofit Migrant Farmworker Justice Project $150,000. Schell decided to go with one plaintiff, reasoning that if he won with that one, he could keep going or hope Osceola would settle. At this writing, twenty years after the original $51 million judgment, the case is still pending.

Legalization—Part II

There was one final coda to the whole IRCA-SAWs-Dog War-Bygrave saga. With the H2 Program in sugar gone, the cane companies no longer had any interest in insuring that former cane cutters' status remained temporary. Lead by the Sugar Cane Growers Cooperative, the cane companies now threw their weight behind a last-ditch effort to win legalization for the men they had helped exclude from IRCA's legalization provision. With the sugar industry's express support, Hogan & Hartson sent an emissary to President Clinton's Secretary of Agriculture Mike Espy, asking him to authorize Green Cards for former cane cutters. Even the Fanjuls wrote a letter supporting the effort.

Espy seemed sympathetic. The first African American Secretary of an agency that had recently been sued for racist practices, he knew that very few black immigrants had benefited from IRCA's amnesty provision, and that those who did were H2 workers who had jumped their contracts and become unauthorized immigrants. Those who continued to work legally as guestworkers year after year were denied the right to stay. Sympathetic or not, Espy said no. At stake, he explained, was the H2 Program itself. The program had vanished from the cane fields, but it was alive and well in crops all across the country. If cane cutters could be retroactively granted permanent legal status, the temporary status occupied by current H2 workers nationwide might be jeopardized. So, despite IRCA's legalization program, the Dog War, cane cutters' ephemeral courtroom victory, and the mechanization of their jobs, H2 workers would come to the United States temporarily or not at all. Once a guestworker, always a guestworker.[98]

The 1980s was a dramatic decade for Jamaican guestworkers. They got Green Cards and then had them taken away because sugar was not "human edible." They were bitten by dogs and deported in their underwear. They won the biggest back wages suit in farmworker history, lost the appeals, and then lost their cane-cutting jobs. Jamaican men continued to come to the United States as apple pickers, but the season lasted weeks, not months. Everything changed but, in the end, everything seemed to stay the same. Corporate influence continued to overwhelm federal oversight. Sending governments still chose jobs over justice. H2 workers who spoke up for themselves still got deported. Exposés, hearings, indictments, and reports made temporary ripples in the nation's consciousness but did not end the H2 Program. The Program grew, expanded into more crops and states, and spun off an even less regulated nonagricultural variant. The program survived not just because growers demanded it, moreover, but because it continued to offer a symbolic alternative to unmanaged migration, because it allowed Americans to believe there is a legal, practical, and ethical way to import the world's poor without having to let them stay, because we cling to the idea that we can have our cake—human edible or not—and eat it too.

CHAPTER TEN

All the World's a Workplace

Guestworkers at the Turn of the Twenty-First Century

THREE THOUSAND FEET above the ocean in the high, cool town of Christiana, Jamaica, I followed a winding, narrow road until it disappeared into a rutted path far too uneven for my rental car. Heading up the steep hill on foot, I was just starting to wonder whether the hotel manager's directions were any good when I was startled by an old man coming over the rise with a machete in his hand (a sight that takes getting used to). Greeting me with a "helloooo, white lady!" (a sound I probably won't ever get used to), he confirmed that I was, indeed, on the right path. Down the other side of the hill, I came to several small, unpainted cinderblock houses, one of which belonged to Sheryl Palmer, a twenty-year-old guestworker just back from a stint in the United States.[1] She was waiting for me on her porch with her two small children, one barely three, the other just one. Her mother, who cared for her children in her absence, was in the kitchen, making the cinnamon candy-topped coconut patties she sold for extra income.

Palmer was a lucky woman. She had just spent eight months in the United States as a hotel maid, the longest an H2 worker can now stay in the United States before having to return home. She made less than a sugarcane cutter might have earned a decade earlier less the cost of her airfare, room, and board. And yet she proudly invited me inside to see the room addition her U.S. wages had helped build. As my eyes adjusted to the dark, I could just make out the cardboard barrel she had used to ship clothes and gifts to her children, "barrel children," a Jamaican friend called them later. Home for only a few months, Palmer was eagerly awaiting her next departure.

As I walked back to my car carrying a gift of coconut patties, Palmer's brother, who had clearly been fetched from some distance, ran, panting, up to me, hoping I could get him a job in the United States. This happened often on my trips to the island. I couldn't get anyone a job, I explained; I was merely a university professor writing a book about the "farmworker programme," an explanation that clearly didn't satisfy him. But even if I had been recruiting workers in Jamaica in 2003, I'd have had few jobs for farmworkers like him. There were forty thousand H-2A workers in the

United States that year, but most were from Mexico. Sugar harvest jobs were gone and the apple harvest, which Jamaican men still monopolized, only offered a few weeks of work. H-2A workers were vastly outnumbered by the 400,000 mostly female H-2Bs like his sister, who were working in hotels, food industries, theme parks, resorts, and restaurants.[2]

Palmer's brother had little hope of getting to the United States as a temporary worker, but Palmer herself was part of a booming international "maid trade," the latest and, in some ways, most troubling phase in the global history of guestworkers. This new phase began in the 1970s, as the oil shocks brought an end to Europe's guestworker programs and set off new ones in the oil-rich nations of the Middle East and Pacific Rim. The first guestworkers in the Middle East were Arab, Egyptian, and Palestinian men—construction workers, mechanics, engineers, doctors, and computer analysts—who moved from poorer parts of the Middle East into the oil-rich Gulf states. They were welcomed at first because they allowed for rapid development at little cost, but Middle Eastern guestworkers tended to bolster pan-Arab, Islamist, and fledgling trade union movements. By the early eighties, rich Gulf states had turned to men from South and Southeast Asia. Some of these new migrants were Muslims like their employers, but they were easier to control because they usually spoke no Arabic, were subject to deportation for misconduct, and lived apart from the general population in segregated labor compounds. White-collar guestworkers like doctors and engineers were less constrained than construction workers, but no migrants had legal or political rights in the Gulf States. According to Fred Halliday, in the early 1980s the Saudi press was "replete with advertisements by contractors publishing the details of migrant laborers who have fled from their place of work."[3]

The number of guestworkers in the Middle East quickly skyrocketed. In 1975, 360,000 South and Southeast Asians worked in the region. By 1983, there were 3.6 million (out of a total workforce of about 7 million), most from the oil-importing nations of the Philippines, India, Pakistan, Bangladesh, and Sri Lanka. By 1985, four Gulf states had majority foreign work forces. The United Arab Emirates workforce was almost 91 percent non-nationals; Kuwait, 80 percent; and Saudi Arabia—the most populous of the Gulf states—71 percent. In the small nation of Qatar, most workers were from Pakistan, India, Indonesia, Nepal, and the Philippines. "Actual Qataris," writes Michael Backman, ". . . are somewhat thin on the ground."[4]

For the first few years, guestworkers in the Middle East were almost all men, and they were strictly prohibited from bringing their families. But as ambitious construction projects grew rare in the 1980s, sending governments struggled to keep the remittance dollars flowing by advertising their women as nannies and maids for wealthy Middle Eastern families.

The marketing paid off: soon no Middle Eastern family of means could do without a foreign maid. During the first Gulf War, 400,000 guestworkers were deported from the Middle East, but the number of women workers remained constant.[5]

As demand for guestworkers reached a plateau in the Gulf states in the 1980s, labor demand intensified in Japan, Korea, Hong Kong, Taiwan, Singapore, Brunei, and Malaysia—the so-called Pacific Tigers. Japan's guestworker program was a government response to simultaneous concerns about illegal immigration and the aging of Japan's workforce, though Japan, fearing diversity, limited the migration to Brazilians of Japanese descent. In Hong Kong, the importation of 250,000 Filipina and later Indonesian "domestic helpers" made it possible for local women to take jobs in electronics, toys, and plastics manufacturing.[6] In Malaysia, the discovery of offshore oil combined with high commodity prices for oil, tin, rubber, and timber to create rapid state-led development, which led Malays to abandon the countryside for industrial work. Foreign contract workers arrived to replace them in the fields.[7] Seventy thousand female guestworkers allowed Malay women to enter the paid workforce or simply live a middle-class lifestyle.[8]

As in the United States, guestworker programs tended to lead to large, unauthorized populations. By the summer of 2002, almost 800,000 foreigners worked with authorization in Malaysia, but about half as many foreigners remained in residence without permission. Nevertheless, guestworker programs maintained the illusion of government control over migration. During the late twentieth-century Asian financial crisis, the Malaysian government responded to growing resentment against guestworkers by launching "Operation Go Away," which threatened foreigners with jail and caning if they remained. This led to the swift departure of 320,000 foreign workers. Yet the pageant of state power was little more than a gesture to anti-immigration forces. A few months later, when the construction industry complained of labor scarcity, guestworkers were invited back. "We are a nation that cannot even construct a building with our own hands anymore," observed Sheryll Stothard, a Malaysian writer and social critic. "We have become a nation of subcontractors depending almost totally on foreign labor, money and expertise."[9]

While male guestworkers worked as farmworkers and physicians and everything in between, encountering many of the opportunities and hazards previous guestworkers had experienced before them, the maid trade introduced new perils. Work abroad allowed women to find paid work and send money home as it did men, but it also led to abuses that male guestworkers—working together and in public places—rarely faced. "The home is the most dangerous place because it is private," the executive secretary of a Malaysian shelter for battered women and children explained. In Hong

Kong, where "domestic helpers" earn about $600 (US) per year and where recruiters pocket all their earnings for their first seven months in a position, one woman suffered months of blows and kicks before her employer abandoned her at a local hospital with two broken ribs. She could have quit but was trying to outlast her payless seven-month period. Hong Kong's Mission for Migrant Workers has helped women who had been raped, starved, and, in one case, made to sleep for months with an employer's five dogs. The majority might be well treated and content with their condition but, if they are not, they have little recourse. Women who quit or are dismissed by their employers have two weeks to leave the country.[10]

Although female guestworkers are often imported for intimate but unskilled work (or at least work that is considered unskilled), they are often highly skilled and well-educated. Many Filipina domestic helpers in Hong Kong, for example, are certified as nurses, midwives, or teachers. Standing in for mothers and wives who once performed the same tasks without pay, they enjoy little status and their immigration status reflects it. Other foreign workers in Hong Kong, like engineers, professors, musicians, and bankers, can convert to permanent status after seven years on temporary visas but, like H2 workers in the United States, domestic helpers' status in Hong Kong is permanently temporary. As Cynthia Ca Abdon-Tellez, the director of Mission to Migrants, put it, "Once a domestic helper, always a domestic helper."[11]

Like earlier guestworkers, women travel under contracts that are supposed to protect them, but enforcement is especially hard when workers are spread among individual households. In 1993, the Philippines' Overseas Workers Welfare Administration had just thirty-one labor attachés, twenty welfare officers, and twenty coordinators to deal with the complaints of 4.2 million migrant workers in 120 countries.[12] Competition among labor-exporting nations for the same jobs still undermines standards. Just as Jamaica tried to boycott Florida in 1945, only to capitulate when Bajans stepped in to take the jobs, Bangladesh and Pakistan tried to ban the out-migration of female servants in 1983 in response to reports of abusive employers, but Indonesian women took up the slack with the encouragement of their government. The Bangladeshi and Pakistani governments were forced to capitulate, and in 1986, both recommended *lowering* the wages of their nationals in the Middle East to keep them competitive.[13]

GLOBAL HORIZONS

Guestworkers' experiences in the United States in the years since IRCA have not fallen to the level of Hong Kong or Qatar, but the tales of criminal exploitation have multiplied with the expansion of the H2 Program to more industries, crops, states, and sending countries. For guestworkers in agriculture, all the old regulations still apply but many employers still seem to disregard them with impunity. The biggest and most worrisome post-IRCA innovation has been the proliferation of for-profit recruitment agencies that offer to cut the bureaucratic red tape involved in locating foreign workers, submitting clearance orders, screening workers, applying for their visas, and handling transportation. There have always been grower-organized recruitment agencies, some of which have charged workers for the services recruiters provided to growers. But the post-IRCA agencies seem determined to squeeze far more profit from the work of connecting growers and prospective H2 workers. They have illegally charged workers for their travel and housing, deducted state income taxes in states that don't have any, and, most importantly, charged workers exorbitant fees just to get temporary jobs. Allegations of bribery in the distribution of recruitment tickets have long swirled around the H2 and Mexican Bracero Programs, but nothing like this.[14]

One such company, Million Express Manpower, came to Muangmol Asanok's Thai village in 2005, offering three years worth of work in the United States at $8 an hour. The twenty-eight-year-old jumped at the opportunity, but Million Express demanded an $11,000 fee, a colossal sum to Asanok and his family. To pay it, Asanok mortgaged his farm, took out a bank loan, got another loan from a loan shark, and a fourth from his mother. The recruiter then took Asanok and about thirty other Thai men to Johnston County, North Carolina, collecting their passports and return plane tickets so they couldn't leave. After a couple of days in a motel, they ended up housed in a small storage building behind his residence, where they slept on blankets laid out on the cement floor. Because Million Express collected its fee whether the men worked or not, the recruiter had little incentive to make sure they got full-time work and pay (although by H-2A rules he should have paid them for three-quarters of their time in the United States). Instead, they worked sporadically—without getting paid at all. To keep them from leaving or complaining, the men later reported, the recruiter brandished a gun and left relatives to guard them.[15] It would seem that things couldn't get worse, but they did. As H-2A workers, Asanok and his compatriots were supposed to work only in agriculture, yet when farmwork ran out in mid-October, they were taken to post-Katrina New Orleans, where they lived in the flood-damaged hotel they were tearing down, again without pay. After a few weeks, they managed to buy a cell phone and call the Thai Embassy and a refugee advocacy group called Boat People SOS. The latter group rescued them. The Thai Embassy never called back.[16]

One would hope that such an egregious case of abuse would be anomalous, but it is not. In fact, when *New York Times* reporter Steve Greenhouse called me for comments on Asanok's case, I thought he was talking about a nearly identical case in Washington State. In that case, which also involved Thai workers but a different recruitment company (Global Horizons), the recruiter convinced an apple grower to dismiss workers he already had in favor of Thai guestworkers who, like Asanok, had paid thousands of dollars for the dubious privilege of picking crops in the United States.

H-2A workers weren't the only ones at risk. For H-2B workers—cooks, crab-pickers, construction workers, landscape workers, waitresses, and maids—the potential for disaster is even greater because fewer regulations apply to them. In the aftermath of Hurricane Katrina, Signal International, a marine construction company near New Orleans, took advantage of the Labor Department's willingness to admit guestworkers for cleanup work. Signal imported 550 Indian workers for shipbuilding work. Forty-three-year-old Rajan Pazhambalakode had been living apart from his family for years as a guestworker in the Persian Gulf when he saw Signal's ad for welders and pipe-fitters. Promised Green Cards for himself and his family, he sold his home and paid $20,000 for the chance to be reunited with them "in America." On arrival he discovered that he and the other workers were expected to live twenty-four to a room, a privilege for which he says he paid $1,050 a month. He alleges that he was not permitted to leave the labor camp and was threatened with deportation if he complained. Worse, there would be no Green Card, just a temporary H-2B visa. Calling themselves the Indian Workers' Congress, Pazhambalakode and his countrymen went on strike, throwing their helmets over a fence to attract attention. With the help of a local civil rights organization they charged their employer with human trafficking.[17]

Unfortunately, these weren't the only companies to take advantage of the post-Katrina chaos to switch to guestworkers. Decatur Hotels, a New Orleans firm, asked the Department of Labor for permission to hire up to 290 guestworkers, claiming that hurricane evacuees had not applied for the jobs they offered, despite massive unemployment among those who remained in the city. According to the Southern Poverty Law Center, recruiters found willing workers in Peru, Bolivia, and the Dominican Republic. "Each recruit paid between $3,500 and $5,000 to come to the United States for hotel jobs—maintenance, housekeeping, guest services, etc.—that were scheduled to last just nine months." Given the rate of pay offered, it would have taken each worker three to four months working full time "just to recoup the recruiting fees, not counting any interest on loans they may have taken out." When they arrived, however, they found that the hotel didn't have full-time work for them. "Every one of us has to sell things in order to have the money to come here," said Peruvian worker Francisco Sotelo Aparicio. "I sold some of my land, my belongings, and we leave our families to try to come out ahead. . . . We want to keep working legally, but it is very hard to do so when we make such little money and have so much debt. We become desperate."[18]

What's even more striking than these shocking cases is that the regulatory system that H2 employers complain so bitterly about did not function at all. The Labor Department cited one company and fined it repeatedly for failing to pay the minimum wage and overtime wages, but it did not deny the company's requests for more guestworkers. Indeed, the Government Accountability Office reported in 1997 that "the Department of Labor had never failed to approve an application to import H-2A workers because an employer had violated the legal rights of workers." Never. Legal Services lawyers in the Yakima Valley sued Global Horizons (both on behalf of the local workers displaced by the H-2A workers and later on behalf of the Thai workers who had been deported for complaining). But although Legal Services won both times, Global Horizons paid a fine, promised to behave, and is back in business. Cases like these continue to keep public interest lawyers busy. The Southern Poverty Law Center filed four lawsuits on behalf of H-2B workers in the forestry industry alleging wage and hour violations. Twelve lawsuits filed against ten seafood companies in Virginia and North Carolina alleged virtually identical treatment.[19]

These extreme cases might be just that, exceptionally egregious violations of the law, which resulted in litigation. Yet we should probably worry just as much about the cases that don't make it to court. The recent H2 workers whom I interviewed—without in any way seeking out people with grievances—had more mundane but still serious complaints. Peter Beckford, who had been the cook at my first Kingston hotel, called me from Michigan in 2001, where he had taken temporary work at a resort on an H-2B visa. He had hoped to visit me, he said (he had no inkling of the distance between Michigan and Virginia) but was only getting ten to twenty hours of work a week. With those hours, he could barely pay for the room he shared with another guestworker, let alone a bus ticket to Williamsburg. He was very concerned that he would have nothing saved to bring home to his wife and new baby in Kingston.[20] Sandra Brown, who came home from church just as I was interviewing her father in Effort, also gave me an earful. Her father had worked in Florida in the 1960s. Nearly forty years later, she began traveling to the United States as an H-2B worker. She enjoyed several stints at a Myrtle Beach hotel until a new company bought out the hotel in 2001, after which she got a job at a famous Virginia resort. There she worked as a waitress for $2 an hour plus tips but never received the tips. She still had to pay $110 a week for a single room. "What do you get?" she asked rhetorically. "Nothing." "[W]hen you go up there and work, they work everything to go back to them and you don't come home with nothing . . . Everything they say is how it goes. They no negotiate nothing." Asked whether she complained to her liaison officer, she said the only thing he ever told her was that 8 percent of their pay was going to be deducted for their airfare. When I explained that another portion of her wages was going to the liaisons' pay, a revelation her father confirmed, she was incredulous.[21] Wayne Clark, who joined my 2006 group interview at the "Dead House" in Brandon Hill, Jamaica, was still working seasonally in the United States as an apple picker. He was the one who set off the rapid-fire, patois-laden exchange among the much older men I was interviewing when he made it clear that the sort of intimidation they had experienced in the 1960s was still alive and well: "If you were the ring leader they'd get rid of you," he told the group. "If you speak the right and proper thing dem a go point you out and send you home."[22] The only recent guestworker who didn't complain to me about her pay or experience was Sheryl Palmer, the woman who was just back from the United States, but she had no idea what the terms of her contract were and no knowledge of the U.S. minimum wage or any other rights that might have applied to her. I asked her whether the orientation session run by the Jamaican Ministry of Labour before she left informed new workers of their rights in the United States. The only thing they were told, she said, was how not to offend Americans' sensibilities. None of the recent H2 workers I interviewed had ever contacted a lawyer, despite serious contract violations. These stories suggest no obvious way to "weed out the abuse" from the H2 Program, as a recent Oxfam report advocated.

Ultimately, there is no way to know how many weeds there are, because men and women who complain or approach lawyers still face deportation. There is little doubt that deportations have a chilling effect on those who remain. In any case, the long history of the H2 Program suggests that there is little point in debating what percentage of current H-2A and H-2B workers are happy or discontented or where precisely they are on some abstract spectrum between slavery and freedom. For guestworkers here and around the world, slavery and freedom are not at different ends of a spectrum; they are simultaneous conditions. Jamaican cane cutters returned year after year—sometimes for twenty years or more—and would do so again if they could, yet the same people also insist that they were mistreated and underpaid. Around the world, guestworkers are systematically underpaid, overworked, injured, and threatened with deportation, but they willingly return year after year because they must. This is not real freedom, of course, but only those of us with the luxury to choose our livelihood have any hope of that.

Although the number of guestworkers in the United States today is still tiny relative to the size of the labor force as a whole, the number of guestworkers around the world is astounding and growing. In a 2007 article about Filipino guestworkers, *New York Times* reporter Jason De-Parle writes that if you gathered the 200 million labor migrants around the world and all the family members they support into one "migration nation," they would add up to at least a half a billion people, or the third largest nation on the planet. And in the five years prior to his article, the number of guestworkers around the world had doubled.[23]

The remittance income guestworkers generate is equally astounding. The *Asian Migrant Forum* estimated that in 1992 alone remittances to the Philippines totaled US$4.3 billion, a figure far larger than the country's $3 billion foreign debt. And the more the United States, the World Bank, and the International Monetary Fund responded to the Asian and Latin American debt crises by demanding austerity measures, currency devaluation, and the removal of trade barriers, the more important remittances became. "Today, the temporary labor export industry has become permanently temporary," a Filipino senator noted. "Moreover it has grown . . . from being a stop-gap measure to being a vital life-line for the nation . . . [T]he labor export industry is really the biggest economic story for the country."[24] Worldwide, labor migrants sent home an estimated $300 billion in 2006—nearly three times the world's foreign-aid budgets combined.[25]

As efforts to protect labor standards, make immigration temporary, or manage migration, guestworker programs have failed and still fail, whether they are in the United States, the Middle East, South Africa, or the Pacific Rim. Yet as labor supply systems designed to quarantine immigrant workers from natives and keep them a caste apart, they have been very effective. Guestworker programs have succeeded in holding down the cost of sugarcane harvesting in Florida, diamond mining in South Africa, construction work in the Middle East, and child care in Montreal. They have separated the workers of the world from their "barrel children," leaving their care and the other social costs of reproducing labor to the countries least equipped to pay for it. They have transported the world's young and restless to the world's wealthiest countries in a stunning reversal of the idea of foreign aid. They have drawn nations together in a new, government-crafted dependency, in which the world's wealthy nations import foreigners to do their hardest, dirtiest, and often their most intimate work. This, indeed, was their true purpose and their most pernicious legacy.

Conclusion

IN 2003, after Hurricane Isabel tore through Virginia, I escaped to North Carolina where there was power and a free room at a friend's house. The next day, I tagged along with him on a class trip to meet migrant farm-workers in central North Carolina. Departing from Duke University, we headed deep into the countryside, driving an hour and a half on two-lane roads. The landscape we passed through might have been the eastern shore of Maryland, Southside Virginia, or South Florida. The fields looked flat, hot, and hard-packed. The workers also seemed familiar. Almost every-one we met that day was a Latino man. None had legal status.

To a historian who studies the history of farmworkers since the nine-teenth century, the workers' housing seemed like a throwback to the dis-tant past. Although most of the farmworkers we met were living in trail-ers, not shacks, the quality of their housing seemed to have advanced little from the 1930s (or the 1830s, for that matter). Indeed, the housing we saw seemed to have been ravaged by the hurricane, though Isabel had passed gently over the region. We filed into a long, narrow trailer occupied by eight men despite huge, jagged holes in the metal floor and a tiny kitchen whose walls were blackened by cooking grease. We walked through a small house that had recently housed fifteen people, although the win-dows were broken and the floor was rotted out in places. We talked to four men living in a flea-infested trailer without running water.

At our last stop, we met the only family we saw all day: a husband and wife and their four children who had been living and working on the same farm for four years. The father, José Garcia, complained that since 9/11 two years before, Americans frequently yelled epithets at him, apparently mistaking him for an Arab. "What can I blow up on $5 an hour?" he asked with a grim smile. His wife, Carmela, who fed us tamales she had prepared for our visit, told us of a trip home to visit her dying mother three years earlier when she was six months pregnant, and the harrowing return she made through the desert so that at least one child would be an American citizen. Sitting on the ground, we talked for a while through a translator. Just before we left, the professor leading the trip asked whether the Garcias hoped to become citizens of the United States or aspired only to Green Cards, which would permit permanent residency. Looking puzzled for a second or two, José asked the difference. When I explained that only citizens could vote, he shrugged and simply said, "I want an identity."[1]

Today, as in the 1980s and the 1950s, the nation is debating what to do about people like the Garcias, who now number perhaps 12 million. And, as in the 1980s, the leading immigration reform proposals seek a way to give the Garcias and others like them "an identity" by creating a "path to legalization," if not the instant "amnesty" afforded by IRCA in 1986 (pro-legalization lawmakers now avoid the term amnesty like the plague). As in 1986, legalization proposals are usually paired with demands for stepped-up enforcement of immigration laws. In other words, they would simultaneously shut the gates and integrate those already here (though some proponents of legalization suggest new rituals of sovereignty such as a waiting period, fines, or even a return home, as in the old touch-a-toe-over-the-border days). As in the 1980s, however, any sort of reform seems to hinge on employers' demand for a bigger and less regulated guestworker program that would guarantee "future flows" of immigrant workers.[2] Democrats, who tend to support legalization (or did until the recent anti-incumbent backlash), generally oppose a guestworker solution. (Candidate Obama had a guestworker provision in his platform, but President Obama tried to keep an expanded guestworker program off the bargaining table.)[3] Republican lawmakers generally consider a guestworker program an essential component of any immigration reform package. As one columnist put it, "if guest workers are off the menu, don't expect Republicans to sit down at the table."[4]

If the history of guestworkers in the United States demonstrates anything, however, it's that guestworker programs are not an alternative to illegal immigration. Rather, the two systems of recruiting foreign labor have always existed in symbiosis. The wartime guestworker programs led immediately to an increase in unauthorized border crossers and visa overstayers. In the aftermath of World War II, federal officials tried to wean growers off illegal workers by keeping guestworkers' wages low and by allowing abuses of guestworkers to go unpunished. Unhappy Braceros and H2 workers transformed themselves into illegal immigrants by walking away from jobs they didn't like. When Mexican authorities insisted on improved treatment for Braceros and more control over the recruitment process, U.S. officials encouraged the free flow of migrants across the U.S.-Mexican border and then transformed them—fairy godmother-style—into legal, temporary workers. Originally designed to uplift conditions for all farmworkers, in practice, guestworker programs depressed conditions and systematically undermined the union movements that sought to elevate them. Much like the original guestworker programs in Prussia, South Africa, and Australia, they kept foreign workers vulnerable and isolated.

In South Africa, the oscillating system of labor recruitment that supplied labor to gold and diamond mines helped mold the nation's identity in its formative period. Apartheid's pass laws and "locations" grew out of South Africa's late nineteenth-century guestworker programs. Here in the United States, the story is reversed: a system of apartheid—which Americans called Jim Crow—gave way to a guestworker program. During World War II, just as the federal government finally began to prosecute employers who immobilized black workers in the South with guns, whips, and debt peonage laws, it began allowing growers access to black workers from abroad who could be controlled in a completely new way. As in South Africa, H2 workers were isolated in compounds, separated from native-born workers, and cycled in and out of the country. Forced immobility gave way to forced mobility as the threat of deportation became the world's new whip. H2 workers continue to enter the United States without the harrowing and dangerous journeys that unauthorized migrants from Mexico and Central America now make, but the border follows them into the United States and surrounds them, segregating them from other workers, and from the lawyers who have sought to help them.

At its creation, policymakers justified the H2 Program as a response to the "war emergency" that followed Pearl Harbor. Other crises preserved it: the exigencies of the Cold War; the hysteria over illegal immigration in the Reagan Era; even Hurricane Katrina. But these were rationales, not causes. The real explanation for the H2 Program's existence and survival was the influence wielded by a tiny number of agricultural employers in their home states and in Washington. Just as U.S. senators served as pallbearers for a tomato grower-turned-diplomat, the state supported growers' demands for temporary foreign labor long after the Bracero Program was in its grave. It also propped up the sugar industry that employed most H2 workers. By ceding its monopoly over deportation to those growers, the state gave employers of guestworkers more power than modern employers had ever wielded. The result was a labor system in which workers ran to the fields, maintained a punishing pace, injured themselves with regularity, and got sent home if they called any of this into question. Even without the allegations of wage fraud, the whole H2 system would demand major reform.

But can it be reformed? Past programs do suggest some models. For all their problems and the controversy they engendered, the European guestworker programs of the 1950s and '60s were far better than their U.S. counterparts precisely because European states, not employers, generally decided whether guestworkers stayed or left. Clearly, any guestworker program that isn't going to devolve rapidly into a system of oscillating indentured servitude must protect the very basic human right to quit and to speak freely without fear of deportation.

Still, it's hard to imagine a European-style program working in the United States (or the Middle East or the Pacific Rim, for that matter). European guestworker programs didn't start out as humane as they mostly ended up. They improved over time because powerful labor unions fought for guestworkers' rights (even if they did so to protect their own). Here in the United States, unions have enough trouble defending their own members' rights and conditions, let alone temporary foreign workers'. Even in the 1950s, when American unions were at their peak, the most labor leaders were able to do, it seems, was to protect American workers' jobs and standards by fighting for the termination of guestworker programs.

One American farmworker union has tried tackling the problem of competition from guestworkers in a completely new way. In 2004, the Toledo-based Farm Labor Organizing Committee (FLOC) won an historic collective bargaining agreement with the North Carolina Growers Association, now the nation's largest H-2A recruiter and the supplier of some 8,000 guestworkers to cucumber, tobacco, sweet potato, and Christmas tree growers in North Carolina. "This is tremendous," exclaimed Leticia Zavala, organizing director for FLOC. "It's the first contract ever to cover H-2A workers in the United States, and the biggest contract in the history of North Carolina. It was won by farmworkers, the poorest people, not covered under labor relations law."[5] The contract promised to eliminate the blacklist that intimidated workers who spoke up, sometimes just to request a bathroom or water break. Most remarkably, it set up a hiring system that privileged union members, and created a twenty-one-day, three-step grievance procedure so workers could complain without fear of retaliation. A separately negotiated sidebar agreement with Mt. Olive Pickle Company, the second biggest pickle producer in the country, and the buyer of most of the cucumbers raised in the region, promised to raise workers' wages 10 percent over three years. In the months that followed, 60 percent of the state's 10,000 guestworkers joined the union.[6] FLOC, in other words, got growers and a huge processor to agree to a union hiring hall for guestworkers. William Pawley must have been rolling in his grave.

"The guest worker program has been characterized as an abusive slave labor program by opponents," said FLOC's irrepressible president, Baldemar Velasquez, "but if it's unionized and there is an independent third force to file grievances and hold the program accountable, it removes a lot of the criticism. Why not expand it if you have unions holding it accountable?"[7] Why not indeed? Still, it's hard to imagine this H-2A/union hiring hall idea working on a large scale. FLOC's victory didn't come easily, after all; it was the result of a lawsuit and a five-year boycott of Mt. Olive's products.[8] The union is only now taking on a second company, this time R.J. Reynolds, the cigarette maker, which is supplied by tobacco farmers who frequently use H-2A workers. That means, however, that FLOC is taking on an industry with even deeper pockets and better lawyers. FLOC's effort may be the most Quixotic campaign since the UFW and Legal Services took on Florida's sugar industry. To make matters worse, North Carolina's right-to-work laws prohibit the sort of closed-shop contract that would require all H2 workers to join the union as a condition of their hire. FLOC will thus be forced to continually organize a mobile, international workforce, which is spread across the state, nation, and border. Getting to farmworkers still remains a challenge. FLOC's organizers have found themselves arrested and charged with trespassing for trying to enter labor camps, just as UFW sympathizers were in the 1970s. FLOC tried to solve this problem by reaching out to H-2A workers before they left Mexico, but that strategy resulted in tragedy when FLOC staffer Santiago Rafael Cruz was found bound and beaten to death in the union's Monterrey office, presumably by Mexican contractors who didn't want FLOC spreading the word that Mexican workers could get H-2A visas without paying illegal fees and bribes.[9]

If advocacy by organized labor is not a likely solution in the United States (and many other parts of the world), it's even harder to imagine that more government enforcement would solve anything. Time and time again, the federal officials charged with guarding guestworkers' rights have proven themselves ineffective and sporadically attentive at best, craven and corrupt at worst. The prospect of more enforcement is little comfort. Perhaps a more vigilant Secretary of Labor could do more to safeguard guestworkers' rights and protect domestic workers from unfair competition, but vigilant Labor Secretaries are themselves only one election away from unemployment.

Even with a vigilant Labor Department, there would still never be enough inspectors to monitor every field, mine, factory, hotel, or home. How many Americans have ever seen an OSHA inspector or an investigator from the Department of Labor's Wage and Hour Division after all? If American workplaces are safe and fair—and many of them clearly are not—it's because workers have been vigilant in their own and their fellows' defense. We ensure that our paystubs are correct and our workplaces are safe. If we are effective, it's because when we do see problems, we complain, we quit, and (all too rarely) we organize. Citizenship is no guarantee of workplace safety, of course—as recent mine and oil rig disasters have made clear—but freedom from fear of deportation is a basic prerequisite for justice.

The H2 Program lacks that basic prerequisite. Guestworkers' conditions are not poor because guestworkers come from poor countries and complacently accept whatever they get. Indeed, the Jamaican guestworkers featured here have been as militant and as quick to organize and speak up in their own defense as any farmworkers in this country's history. They have complained to liaisons, written to the press, gone on strike, and gone to court. Yet their struggles remained hidden and their efforts ineffective precisely because deportation is a powerful tool of workplace control, as powerful as the labor spies and Pinkertons of old. As long as employers have the right to hire, fire, and deport, immigrant workers will remain a caste apart and Jamaica, Mexico, and labor-sending countries like them will remain labor reserves like the old "locations" of Apartheid South Africa.

If neither government oversight nor union activism is the key to change, what is? Back in the decades after World War II, labor advocates argued that the only way to improve labor standards for farmworkers was to bar immigrant workers, whether guestworkers or "illegal aliens," and there are certainly many people making the same case now. The anti-immigrant invective in the United States is as virulent as it ever was. However problematic the case for deportation and restriction, however, it was easier to make it in the 1950s when immigrant workers represented a small portion of the workforce. Today, when the nation's hired farm labor force is made up almost entirely of immigrants, at least half of whom are working in the United States without authorization, any notion of surviving without immigrant workers is fanciful. Even domestic farmworkers are generally legalized or naturalized immigrants or the American-born children of immigrant farmworkers.[10] Those of us trying mightily to follow our doctors' orders to eat seven servings of fruits and vegetables a day are dependent on immigrant labor, and should recognize that fact.

Further militarization of the border isn't a solution to the presence of people like the Garcias, either. The billions spent on walls, dogs, searchlights, drone planes, and border patrol agents since IRCA have not blocked U.S. land borders; they have simply made unauthorized crossings more dangerous and expensive and unauthorized workers more desperate to avoid a repeat journey. The costs and dangers of that journey have inspired many unauthorized immigrants to remain in the United States and bring their families to join them, rather than continuing to migrate in and out of the country. As Doug Massey puts it, "[d]espite all the public rhetoric about immigration invasions and floods, the rate of illegal immigration into the U.S. has not changed in 20 years. The only thing that has changed has been the rate of outmigration . . . In other words, the principal result of America's unilateral militarization of the border has been to *increase* the rate of undocumented population growth in the U.S."[11] The result has been a much larger population of vulnerable people living in fear of exposure and repatriation or what the CIA would call "a blowback," a completely unintended consequence of a policy decision.

If there is a long-term solution to farmworker poverty, it will involve opening borders to labor migrants, not closing them. As Massey writes, "Today's advanced industrial societies are caught in a massive contradiction." On the one hand, he says, they promote policies that "facilitate the free movement of raw materials, manufactured goods, capital and credit, information, services, and certain kinds of people." On the other, they "insist on the unilateral right to prevent the free flow of labor and erect daunting barriers to the immigration of workers." "Somehow," Massey says strikingly, "today's wealthy nations wish to create a global economy that integrates all factor markets except one—that for labor." "Thus," he continues, "even as the U.S. has forcefully moved toward greater economic integration with Mexico, it has simultaneously insisted on separation." We welcome tourists, diplomats, exchange students, corporate executives, educators from around the world, and people with skills deemed particularly valuable—nurses, doctors, computer programmers—yet we have hardened the border to low-wage laborers—requiring farmworkers, groundskeepers, nannies, maids, and many others to come the United States illegally or temporarily. And yet still they come. Thus the issue, as Massey puts it, is not "*whether* Mexico and the U.S. will integrate" their labor markets; it is *how* that integration will occur.[12]

Some policy makers, searching for a compromise between those who demand and those who oppose guestworker programs, have proposed temporary visas that don't bind guestworkers to employers or particular jobs (the European model). This would represent a significant reform, but only a partial one. It would force employers to compete for labor by improving wages and conditions, just as the UFW tried to do in Florida in the 1970s. But if guestworkers can only ever be guestworkers—if there is no path to legalization—the United States would still be creating a giant class of second-class citizens—really non-citizens—who would be denied the political power necessary to enforce their basic rights. We've been there before. It was called Jim Crow and it kept millions of African Americans outside the bounds of civil society for a century.

A better idea—and the only one that doesn't seem to have been considered in recent immigration reform debates—is the idea of bumping unskilled or low-wage labor way up the list of priorities that has ordered legal, permanent migration to the United States since 1965. If immigrant workers are essential to the nation's economy, as they clearly are, why should farmworkers (and nannies and roofers and crab pickers) be at the very bottom of the immigration preference list? Not everyone who comes to the United States for temporary work wants to stay, of course. It would be arrogant to assume so. But in the nineteenth century, not everyone who was eligible for naturalization stayed either. Only as immigrants would farmworkers have the power to demand fair wages and conditions. Only as immigrants would their children have the opportunity to achieve the sort of success that Leaford Williams's children have achieved. In Saudi Arabia, Japan, and other countries where naturalization is a rare occurrence, such an immigration policy would represent radical change. But here, in the United States, it would simply mean honoring an American tradition of accepting the world's "tired, poor and tempest tossed," without fear of deportation, without chains upon their feet. The United States has not always lived up to that ideal, of course. Multitudes came to the United States in bondage. Millions of others were excluded by racist immigration policies. But one doesn't have to be a rosy-eyed romantic to believe that this ideal, this fundamental American belief in human equality and possibility, is one worth preserving.

Notes

1. Frank Cundall, *Jamaica in 1924, a handbook of information for visitors and intending settlers with some account of the colony's history*, (Kingston: Institute of Jamaica, 1924), 56.

Introduction

1. The story of Leaford Williams and his brother comes from Leaford C. Williams, *Journey into Diplomacy: A Black Man's Shocking Discovery, A Memoir* (Washington, DC: Northeast Publishing House, 1996), 7–14, 52–59, 64–69, and from my interview with Leaford Williams, Washington, DC, November 18, 2002 (hereafter cited as Leaford Williams interview).

2. Fay Clarke Johnson, *Soldiers of the Soil* (New York: Vantage Press, 1995), 20.

3. The author overheard the expression "our Filipina" in a Montreal neighborhood where every other house seemed to have a Filipina maid or nanny.

4. For general surveys of international labor migration that include sections on guestworkers, see Peter Stalker, *The Work of Strangers: A Survey of International Labour Migration* (Geneva: International Labour Office, 1994); Stephen Castles and Mark J. Miller, *The Age of Migration: International Population Movements in the Modern World* (New York: Guilford Books, 1998, 2nd ed.); and Saskia Sassen, *Guests and Aliens* (New York: New Press, 2000).

5. Before the war, Germans had called foreign workers *fremdarbeiter*—'alien workers'—but in the insidious lexicon of the Third Reich, that term had come to connote subhumans. Thus, the invention of the "more hospitable" *gastarbeiter* was an effort to distinguish West Germany's massive foreign worker programs in the 1950s and 1960s from its slave labor program just a few years earlier. Stephen Castles and Godula Kosack, *Immigrant Workers and Class Structure in Western Europe*, 2nd ed. (London: Oxford University Press, 1985), 13.

6. On Canada's temporary labor program, see Ricardo Trumper and Lloyd L. Wong, "Racialization and Genderization: The Canadian State, Immigrants, and Temporary Workers," 153-191, in *International Labour Migrations*, edited by B. Singh Bolaria and Rosemary von Elling Bolaria (Delhi: Oxford University Press, 1997).

7. In the 1970s, for example, Malaysia admitted a few hundred Filipina and Indonesian domestic workers, by 1994 the official count had risen to 70,000. Chin, 93-124; Benjamin V. Cariño, ed. *Filipino Workers on the Move: Trends, Dilemmas and Policy Options* (Philippine Migration Research Network, 1998), 1.

8. University of North Carolina Press, 1997.

9. Thanks to Will Jones for clarifying the relationship between this project and my former one.

10. Mae Ngai, *Impossible Subjects: Illegal Aliens and the Making of Modern America* (Princeton, NJ: Princeton University Press, 2004), 153.

11. *Palm Beach Post*, December 28, 1986.

12. *Sun-Sentinel*, November 30, 1986.

13. Terry L. McCoy and Charles H. Wood, "Caribbean Workers in the Florida Sugar Cane Industry," Paper No. 2 (Gainesville: Center for Latin American Studies, University of Florida, 1982), 56, 64.

14. Ibid., 44.

15. This was Manley's signature campaign slogan in the 1970s.

CHAPTER 1: Guestworkers of the World, Unite!

1. Saskia Sassen, *Guests and Aliens*, 12–13; Castles and Kosack, *Immigrant Workers*, 16–20. See also Richard Plender, *International Migration Law* (Boston: Martinus Nijhoff Publishers, 1987), who argues that the idea that states had the right to prevent foreigners from crossing their borders is a distinctly modern concept.

2. Jan Lucassen, *Migrant Labour in Europe, 1600–1900: The Drift to the North Sea* (London: Croom Helm, 1986); Leslie Page Moch, *Moving Europeans: Migration in Western Europe Since 1650* (Bloomington: Indiana University Press, 1992): 77–78, 121; Thomas Sowell, *Migrations and Cultures: A World View* (New York: Basic Books, 1996), 175.

3. John Torpey, *The Invention of the Passport: Surveillance, Citizenship and the State* (New York: Cambridge University Press, 2000): 1–56; Erika Lee, *At America's Gates: Chinese Immigration during the Exclusion Era, 1882–1943* (Chapel Hill: University of North Carolina Press, 2003).

4. See most recently Moon Ho Jung, *Coolies and Cane: Race, Labor and Sugar in the Age of Emancipation* (Baltimore: Johns Hopkins University Press, 2006); and Scott Reynolds Nelson, "*After Slavery: Forced Drafts of Irish and Chinese Labor in the American Civil War, or the Search for Liquid Labor,*" In Many Middle Passages: Forced Migration and the Making of the Modern World, edited by Emma Christopher, Cassandra Pybus, and Marcus Rediker (Berkeley: University of California Press, 2007), 150–65.

5. On contract labor in the nineteenth century, see Jung, *Coolies and Cane;* Gunther Peck, *Reinventing Free Labor: Padrones and Immigrant Workers in the North American West, 1880–1930* (New York: Cambridge University Press, 2000); and Andrew Gyory, *Closing the Gates: Race, Politics, and the Chinese Exclusion Act* (Chapel Hill: University of North Carolina Press, 1998). On "white slavery," see Peck, "Making Sense of White Slavery and Whiteness," *Labor: Studies in Working-Class History of the Americas* 1:2 (Summer 2004): 41–63.

6. Aristide Zolberg, "The Great Wall Against China: Responses to the First Immigration Crisis, 1885–1925," in *Migration, Migration History, History: Old Paradigms and New Perspectives*, edited by Jan Lucassen and Leo Lucassen (New York: Peter Lang, 1997): 291–315.

7. Plender, *International Migration Law*; Freda Hawkins, *Critical Years in Immigration: Canada and Australia Compared*, 2nd edition (Montreal: McGill-Queen's University Press, 1991); Carl Solber, *Immigration and Nationalism: Argentina and Chile, 1890–1914* (Austin: University of Texas Press, 1970); Roger

Daniels, "The Growth of Restrictive Immigration Policies in the Colonies of Settlement," in *The Cambridge Survey of World Migration*, edited by Robin Cohen (Cambridge: Cambridge University Press, 1995), 39–44.

8. Ulrich Herbert, *A History of Foreign Labor in Germany, 1880–1980: Seasonal Workers/Forced Laborers/Guest Workers* (Ann Arbor: University of Michigan Press, 1990; German language edition published 1986), 18–34.

9. Herbert, *History of Foreign Labor*, 18–34; David Blackbourn, *The Long Nineteenth Century: A History of Germany, 1780–1918* (New York: Oxford University Press, 1998).

10. Castles and Kosack date the expulsion of Poles to 1907, but Ulrich Herbert clearly shows that tens of thousands of Poles were deported in 1885. Herbert, *History of Foreign Labor*, 12–13; Castles and Kosack, *Immigrant Labor*, 19–20.

11. Herbert, *History of Foreign Labor*, 14–19.

12. Emphasis mine. Ibid., 19–20.

13. This is based on an email communication with Tracey Banivanua Mar. Her 2000 (University of Melbourne) dissertation, "Bulimaen and hard work indenture, identity and complexity in colonial North Queensland," was not available through Inter-Library Loan. James Jupp, *Immigration* (New York: Oxford University Press, 1991), 41–51.

14. See for example, David Birmingham, *Empire in Africa: Angola and its Neighbors* (Athens: Ohio University, Center for International Studies 2006), 20.

15. Rick Halpern makes this point in "Solving the 'Labour Problem': Race, Work, and the State in Louisiana and Natal, 1870–1910," *Journal of Southern African Studies* 30, 1 (2004): 19–40.

16. At least a quarter of them were required by policy to be women; and, after their indentures were up, laborers could choose between free passage home or a small land grant in Natal. Nearly all elected to stay. David Welsh, *The Roots of Segregation: Native Policy in Colonial Natal, 1845–1910* (Cape Town: Oxford University Press, 1971): 1–30; Leonard Thompson, *A History of South Africa* (New Haven, CT: Yale University Press, 1990): 64–100; Rob Turrell, "Kimberley's Model Compounds," *Journal of African History* 25 (1984): 59–75.

17. Turrell, "Kimberley's Model Compounds," 59–75.

18. Francis Wilson, *Labour in the South African Gold Mines, 1911–1969* (London: Cambridge University Press, 1972): 1, 3–5, 10–14; Jonathan Crush, Alan Jeeves, and David Yudelman, *South Africa's Labor Empire: A History of Black Migrancy to the Gold Mines* (Boulder: Westview Press, 1991): 1–32.

19. Crush et al., *South Africa's Labor Empire*; Christopher Saunders and Nicholas Southey, *Historical Dictionary of South Africa*, 2nd ed. (Lanham, MD: Scarecrow Press, 2000): 202–3; Wilson, *Labour in the South African Gold Mines*, 2–5.

20. Irving Abella, "Foreword," in *Whence They Came: Deportation from Canada 1900–1935*, edited by Barbara Roberts (Ottawa: University of Ottawa Press, 1988), vii–x.

21. Nigel Harris, *The New Untouchables: Immigration and the New World Worker* (New York: I. B. Tauris Publishers, 1995), 6.

22. Gary S. Cross, *Immigrant Workers in Industrial France: The Making of a New Laboring Class* (Philadelphia: Temple University Press, 1983), 18–44.

23. Ibid., 38–41.

24. Ibid., 45–98.

25. Cindy Hahamovitch, *The Fruits of Their Labor: Atlantic Coast Farmworkers and the Making of Migrant Poverty, 1870–1945* (Chapel Hill: University of North Carolina Press, 1997), 79–97.

26. My italics. Immigration Act of February 5, 1917. U.S. Department of Labor, Bureau of Immigration (Washington, DC: GPO, 1920), 57–58.

27. Camille Guerin-Gonzales, *Mexican Workers and American Dreams: Immigration, Repatriation, and California Farm Labor, 1900–1939* (New Brunswick, NJ: Rutgers University Press), 44, 61–63; Philip L. Martin and David A. Martin, *The Endless Quest: Helping America's Farm Workers* (Boulder, CO: Westview Press, 1994), 17; Bruno Ramirez, *Crossing the 49th Parallel, Migration from Canada to the United States, 1900–1930* (Ithaca, NY: Cornell University Press, 2001), 35–66.

28. John William Weber, "The Shadow of the Revolution: South Texas, the Mexican Revolution, and the Evolution of Modern American Labor Relations, (Ph.D. Dissertation, College of William & Mary, 2008), 182–85.

29. Crush et al., *South Africa's Labor Empire*, 33–54; Herbert, *History of Foreign Labor*, 127.

CHAPTER 2: Everything but a Gun to Their Heads

1. Ulrich Herbert, *A History of Foreign Labor in Germany, 1880–1980: Seasonal Workers/Forced Laborers/Guest Workers* (Ann Arbor: University of Michigan Press, 1990; German language edition published 1986), 128–29, 153; Wayne A. Cornelius, "Japan: The Illusion of Immigration Control," in *Controlling Immigration: A Global Perspective*, edited by Wayne A. Cornelius, Philip L. Martin, and James F. Hollifield (Stanford, CA: Stanford University Press, 1994), 381; Takashi Oka, *Prying Open the Door: Foreign Workers in Japan* (Washington, DC: Carnegie Endowment for International Peace, 1994), 9, 11–12; J .S. Crush, Alan Jeeves, and David Yudelman, *South Africa's Labor Empire: A History of Black Migrancy to the Gold Mines* (Boulder, CO: Westview Press, 1991), 9; Camille Guerin-Gonzales, *Mexican Workers and American Dreams: Immigration, Repatriation, and California Farm Labor, 1900–1939* (New Brunswick, NJ: Rutgers University Press, 1994), 114–16.

2. After 1938, Germany required non-German workers to register with the police, who reserved the right to deport or take into "protective custody" anyone who refused to work, engaged in political activity, or who was deemed "hostile to the state." Following the invasion of Poland, the treatment of foreign workers deteriorated further, but their numbers grew as Germany expanded its labor force by impressing civilians in the countries it occupied. Herbert, *History of Foreign Labor*, 128–29, 153.

3. Albert A. Blum, "The Farmer, the Army, and the Draft," *Agricultural History* 38, no. 1 (January 1964): 40.

4. American Social History Project, *Who Built America?: Working People and the Nation's Economy, Politics, Culture, and Society*, vol. 2 *Since 1877* (New York: Worth Publishers, 2000), 506; James N. Gregory, *The Southern Diaspora: How The Great Migrations of Black and White Southerners Transformed America* (Chapel Hill: University of North Carolina Press, 2005).

5. For one of many examples of an historian who bases evidence of labor scarcity largely on growers' pronouncements, see Erasmo Gamboa, *Mexican Labor and World War II: Braceros in the Pacific Northwest, 1942–1947* (Seattle: University of Washington Press, 2000), 22–23. On the Depression era glut and growers' claims of labor scarcity, see Cindy Hahamovitch, *The Fruits of Their Labor: Atlantic Coast Farmworkers and the Making of Migrant Poverty, 1870–1945* (Chapel Hill: University of North Carolina Press, 1997), 113–37, 151–81.

6. Office of Labor, FSA Correspondence, 1943–44, box 75, file: 4-FLT-R57, RG 224, NARA, contains over fifty telegrams to Secretary of Agriculture Claude R. Wickard from South Florida potato, bean, and tomato growers demanding imported farm labor, particularly Bahamian labor. They are all dated 29 January 1943 because growers sent them immediately after a meeting held in Homestead to discuss ways to stabilize wages.

7. Hahamovitch, *Fruits of Their Labor*, 123.

8. Ibid., 4.

9. Ibid., 138–39.

10. Ibid., 121.

11. Ibid., 125.

12. Ibid., 154.

13. Ibid., 3–4.

14. L. L. Stuckey to Claude R. Wickard, February 10, 1942, correspondence concerning migratory labor camps, 1935–1943, box 7, file Migratory-120-A thru G, RG 96, NARA.

15. Telegram to Secretary of Agriculture, Claude R. Wickard from Mrs. William J. Krome, January 29, 1943, NARA, RG 224, Office of Labor, FSA correspondence, 1943–44, box 75, file 4-FLT-R57. Similar correspondence is in Correspondence, 1935–1943, box 7, file Migratory-120-A thru G, RG 96, NARA.

16. L. L. Stuckey to Claude R. Wickard, February 10, 1942, correspondence concerning migratory labor camps, 1935–1943, box 7, file Migratory-120-A thru G, RG 96, NARA.

17. Mrs. J. W. Wallace, Sr., Florence, S.C., to Claude Wickard, Office of Labor (WFA), 28 January 1943, General Correspondence, 1943, box 20, file: Farm Labor 15 Problems-Situations Developments Jan. thru Mar. 1943, RG 224, NARA.

18. *Miami News*, 20 March 1962, 7A; Henry S. Marks, *Who Was Who in Florida* (Huntsville, AL: Strode Publishers, 1973), 63–64; *News Leader* (Homestead, FL), March 20, 1962, 1.

19. It's not clear whether whites spurned fieldwork or were never considered for it.

20. David Philip McCally, "Cane Cutters in the Everglades" (M.A. Thesis, University of South Florida, 1991), 33–34.

21. Ibid., 33–36.

22. Ibid., 51–54. For other examples of worker abuse and official corruption, see Jerrell H. Shofner, "The Legacy of Racial Slavery: Free Enterprise and Forced Labor in Florida in the 1940s," *Journal of Southern History* 47, no. 3 (August 1981): 416–26.

23. Shofner, "Legacy of Racial Slavery," 416.

24. Having collected multiple, damaging depositions documenting labor abuses at U.S. Sugar, the investigators were called off by George Smathers, the future U.S. Senator from Florida, who was then U.S. Attorney in Miami. Later a tireless supporter of Florida's sugar industry, in 1941, Smathers forced the FBI to drop the case by demanding evidence of enslavement that agents could not possibly have provided. Frustrated by Smathers's partisan effort to scuttle the investigation, Herbert S. Phillips, the U.S. Attorney General for Tampa, took up the case.

25. McCally, "Cane Cutters in the Everglades," 56–63. The court drew the jury from urban Hillsborough County, where Tampa is located, because of oil and gas shortages that would have made it difficult for jurors to come from farther away. However, the defense challenged the jury selection, arguing that urbanites did not represent a jury of the sugar growers' peers. On that basis, the case was quashed.

26. John M. McCullough, Acting Transportation Supervisor, USDA, FSA, West Palm Beach, FL, to Robert VanHyning, Chief, Farm Labor Supply Section, FSA, WA, 16 February 1943, Box 75, File: Office of Labor WFA 4 - FLT - C80 Cooperation, FSA Correspondence, 1943–44, RG 224, NARA.

27. Hahamovitch, *The Fruits of Their Labor*, 172.

28. Gail Marjorie Hollander, "Raising Cane in the Glades: Regional Development and Agroenvironmental Conflict in South Florida," (Ph.D. Dissertation, University of Iowa, 1999), 194.

29. Ibid., 196–97.

30. *Clewiston News* (Florida), February 12, 1943.

31. Italics mine. Hollander, "Raising Cane," 196–97.

32. Michael Craton and Gail Saunders, *Islanders in the Stream: A History of the Bahamian People*, vol. 2, *From the Ending of Slavery to the Twenty-First Century* (Athens: University of Georgia Press, 1998), 218.

33. Ibid., 217–22.

34. Quoted in Raymond A. Mohl, "Immigration through the Port of Miami," in *Forgotten Doors: The Other Ports of Entry to the United States*, edited by M. Mark Stolarik (Philadelphia: Balch Institute Press, 1988), 83.

35. Ibid., 85.

36. Craton and Saunders, *Islanders in the Stream*, 275–76; Mohl, "Immigration through the Port of Miami," 84–85; Colin A. Hughes, *Race and Politics in the Bahamas* (New York: St. Martin's Press, 1981), 1; *International Historical Statistics: The Americas, 1750–2000*, 5th ed. (New York: Palgrave McMillion, 2003), 3.

37. Hahamovitch, *The Fruits of Their Labor*, 163.

38. Ibid., 156.

39. John Steinbeck, *The Grapes of Wrath* (New York: Viking Press, 1939); Linda C. Majka and Theo J. Majka, *Farm Workers, Agribusiness, and the State* (Philadelphia: Temple University Press, 1982), 123.

40. See Correspondence, 85–58A734, Box 2087, File: 66078/477, RG 85, NARA.

41. A self-proclaimed "tramp athlete" in his youth, the bear-like Cannon grew up on a South Carolina farm, played football in college, and worked as an iceman in Melbourne and later as a policeman in Miami, while attending law school. He ran for office in 1935 on a populist platform. *Washington Post*, January 25, 1966, C3; *New York Times*, February 26, 1943, 12; *Miami News*, January 24, 1966, 1A.

42. Immigration Act, Public Law 301-29, *U.S. Statutes at Large* 39 (1917): 878.

43. My emphasis. Misc. correspondence, 85–58A734, Box 2087, File: 66078/477, RG 85, NARA.

44. Raymond H. Beers, Immigration Inspector, to Inspector in Charge, INS, Miami (following his meeting with Chandler), December 9, 1941, NARA, RG 85, 85–58A734, Box 2087, File 56078/477.

45. Growers working to convince federal officials that there was a labor scarcity crisis were in for a fight. Outside of his ill-advised love life, Schofield had a reputation for doing things by the book. He had made a name for himself in the late twenties as Philadelphia's Director of Public Safety, a position he got because of scandals under his predecessor. He enforced prohibition with so much zeal in Philadelphia that he was replaced in 1932 with an openly anti-prohibition appointee. His reputation for upright behavior suffered during the war, however, when he delayed issuing the order to detain Von Hohenlohe, despite the fact that the FBI had tapped her phone and considered her a "dangerous spy." She was eventually detained after President Roosevelt intervened, but when the war ended, she went back to living with Schofield. "Humble Stephanie Ended Up As Weapon for Nazis; Jewish Girl Who Became Hitler's Spy Princess," *The Express*, May 20, 2004; "Philadelphia's Dodge," *Time*, January 11, 1932; Martha Schad, *Hitler's Spy Princess: The Extraordinary Life of Princess Stephanie Von Hohenlohe*, trans. Angus McGeoch (Stroud, Gloucestershire: History Press, 2004).

46. Misc. correspondence, 85–58A734, Box 2087, File: 66078/477, RG 85, NARA.

47. Raymond H. Beers, Immigration Inspector, to Inspector in Charge, INS, Miami (following his meeting with Chandler), 9 December 1941, NARA, RG 85, 85–58A734, Box 2087, File 56078/477.

48. See Report of the Interbureau Planning Committee on Farm Labor, "Review of the Farm Labor Situation in 1941," 31 December 1941, general correspondence, subject employment, file Labor Oct. 4 to – [1941?], RG 16, NARA; Hahamovitch, *The Fruits of Their Labor*, 151–81.

49. Hahamovitch, *The Fruits of Their Labor*, 166–67.

50. Ibid., 169–70.

51. L. L. Chandler to Senators Claude Pepper, Charles O. Andrews, and Representative Pat Cannon, 24 June 1942, 85–58A734, File 56078 /477, Box 2087, RG 85, NARA.

52. Hahamovitch, *Fruits of Their Labor*, 170; Office of Labor, FSA Correspondence, 1943–33, Box 75, File 4-FLT-R57, RG 224, NARA; David Burgess, "The

Joads—Still Out of Luck," *New Republic* 110, 2 (10 January 1944): 46; FEPC, O File 425g, Report 21 July 1943, FDR Library.

53. L. L. Chandler to Senators Claude Pepper, Charles O. Andrews, and Representative Pat Cannon, 24 June 1942, 85–58A734, File 56078 /477, Box 2087, RG, 85, NARA.

54. 85–58A734, Box 2087, File: 66078/477, RG 85, NARA.

55. *Washington Post*, 8 November 1942, B5.

56. Ibid.

57. Emphasis mine. Ibid.

58. Letter from L. L. Chandler, State Archives of Florida, Tallahassee, Florida, Governor's Papers, Spessard Holland, Series 406, Carton 66, cited in McCally, "Cane Cutters in the Everglades,"66.

59. The U.S.-Mexican agreement was signed July 23, 1942. It was authorized initially by administrative fiat and operated for seven months before Congress authorized it. Kitty Calavita, *Inside the State: The Bracero Program, Immigration, and the INS* (New York: Routledge, 1992), 1–2, 18.

60. Schofield to Cannon, 1 July 1942, 85–58A734, File: 66078/477, Box 2087, RG 85, NARA.

61. Telegram from Secretary of State for the Colonies to Barbados . . . , 20 April 1943, PRO, CO 859, 12261/1/43, Conditions of Employment and International Labour Conventions, West Indies; AACC to Secretary of State for the Colonies, March 20, 1943, PRO, CO 318, 448/10, Recruitment of Labour for U.S.; *Daily Gleaner* (Kingston, Jamaica), 1 April 1943.

62. AACC to Secretary of State for the Colonies, 20 March 1943, PRO, CO 318, 448/10, Recruitment of Labour for U.S.

63. Telegram from Secretary of State for the Colonies to Barbados . . . , 20 April 1943, PRO, CO 859, 12261/1/43, Conditions of Employment and International Labour Conventions, West Indies; AACC to Secretary of State for the Colonies, 20 March 1943, PRO, CO 318, 448/10, Recruitment of Labour for U.S.; *Daily Gleaner*, 1 April 1943.

64. David Greenberg, "The Contract, 'The Project,' and Work Experiences," in *Strangers No More: Anthropological Studies of Cat Island, the Bahamas*, edited by Joel S. Savishinsky (Ithaca, NY: Ithaca College, 1978), 173.

65. J. Harris, 21 May 1943 and Colonel Bruton, WFA to Taussig, AACC, undated, PRO, CO 318, 448/11, Recruitment of Labour for U.S.; *Public Opinion*, 17 May 1943, 1.

66. Calavita, *Inside the State*, 19–20; Hahamovitch, *The Fruits of Their Labor*, 168.

67. PRO, CO 859/95/11; Bahamas, No. 52, Message from his Royal Highness the Governor to the Speaker and Members of the Honourable the House of Assembly .(sic), PRO, WO 166/522; Julia Henderson, "Foreign Labour in the United States during the War," *International Labour Review*, 52 (December 1945): 612–14.

68. Cindy Hahamovitch, "Standing Idly By: 'Organized' Farmworkers in South Florida during the Depression and World War II," in *Southern Labor in Transition*, edited by Robert H. Zieger (Knoxville: University of Tennessee Press,

1997), 15–36; Edward, Duke of Windsor, Governor of Bahamas, to Oliver Stanley, Secretary of State for the Colonies, January 30, 1943, PRO, CO 967/126.

69. FSA Correspondence, 1943–33, Box 75, File 4-FLT-R57, RG 224, NARA.

70. FDR Library, FEPC, O File 425g, Report July 21, 1943.

71. *Kingston Daily Freeman* (NY), 22 February 1943, 10. Chandler's testimony was reproduced in rural newspapers around the United States, including the (Salisbury, North Carolina) *Times*, (Amarillo, Texas) *Daily News*, (Sheboygan, Wisconsin) *Press.*

72. Hahamovitch, *The Fruits of Their Labor*, 167.

73. Emphasis mine. Ibid., 173–74.

74. *Jacksonville Journal,* 6 April 1943; Greenberg, "The Contract," 171–72.

75. Greenberg, "The Contract," 176.

76. Ibid., 177–78, 174.

77. Misc. correspondence, 85-58A734, Box 2087, File: 66078/477, RG 85, NARA.

78. *News Leader*, 22 March 1962, 1.

CHAPTER 3: "Stir It Up"

1. Telegram from Secretary of State for the Colonies to Barbados, Windward Islands, Leewards, Trinidad and Jamaica, April 20, 1943, PRO, CO 859, 12261/1/43, Conditions of Employment and International Labour Conventions, West Indies; AACC to Secretary of State for the Colonies, March 20, 1943, PRO, CO 318, 448/10, Recruitment of Labour for U.S.; Hahamovitch, "In America Life Is Given Away": Jamaican Farmworkers and the Making of Agricultural Immigration Policy," in *The Countryside in the Age of the Modern State: Political Histories of Rural America*, edited by Catherine McNicol Stock and Robert D. Johnston (Ithaca, NY: Cornell University Press, 2001),134–60.

2. Glen Richards, "Race, Class, and Labour Politics in Colonial Jamaica," in *Jamaica in Slavery and Freedom: History, Heritage and Culture*, edited by Kathleen E. A. Monteith and Glen Richards (Jamaica: University of the West Indies Press, 2002), 342.

3. Eric Williams, *The Negro in the Caribbean* (Westport, CT: Negro Universities Press, 1942), 49; Frank Fonda Taylor, *To Hell With Paradise: A History of the Jamaican Tourist Industry* (Pittsburgh, PA: University of Pittsburgh Press, 1993), 37–43.

4. David Edwards, *An Economic Study of Small Farming in Jamaica* (Glasgow: The University Press, 1961), 26–34; McCoy and Wood, "Caribbean Workers in the Florida Sugar Cane Industry," 15–18, 31–32, 70, fn. 9.

5. James C. Riley, *Poverty and Life Expectancy: The Jamaica Paradox* (Cambridge, UK: Cambridge University Press, 2005), 48–72.

6. Elizabeth Thomas-Hope, "The Establishment of a Migration Tradition: British West Indian Movements to the Hispanic Caribbean in the Century After Emancipation," in *Caribbean Social Relations*, edited by Colin G. Clarke. Mono-

graph Series, No. 8. Liverpool: Centre for Latin American Studies, 1978, 68. See Lara Putnam, *The Company They Kept: Migrants and the Politics of Gender in Caribbean Costa Rica, 1870–1960* (Chapel Hill: University of North Carolina Press, 2002).

7. The U.S. Literacy Act, several years earlier, probably barred few Jamaican migrants to the American mainland, since only the more affluent travelers could have afforded the trip.

8. Ken Post, *Strike the Iron*, vol. 1 (Atlantic Highlands, NJ: Humanities Press, 1981); Cedric O. J. Matthews, *Labour Policies in the West Indies* (Geneva: International Labour Office, 1952), 52–53, 116; Dawn Marshall, "A History of West Indian Migrations: Overseas Opportunities and 'Safety-Valve' Policies," in *The Caribbean Exodus*, edited by Barry B. Levine (New York: Praeger, 1987), 23–24; *Amsterdam News*, June 5, 1943, p. 13; Paul Blanshard, *Democracy and Empire in the Caribbean* (New York: MacMillan, 1947), 47 and 91; Thomas-Hope, "The Establishment of a Migration Tradition," 68 and 74.

9. On the Depression Era labor rebellions, see Carl Henry Feuer, "Better Must Come: Sugar and Jamaica in the 20th Century," *Social and Economic Studies* 33, 4 (1984); O. Nigel Bolland, *On the March: Labour Rebellions in the British Caribbean, 1934–39* (Kingston, Jamaica: Ian Randle Publishers, 1995); and Ken Post, *Arise Ye Starvelings: The Jamaican Labour Rebellion and its Aftermath* (The Hague: Martinus Nijhoff, 1978); Trevor Munroe, *Politics of Constitutional Decolonisation, Jamaica, 1944–62*, reprint ed. (Mona: Institute of Social and Economic Research, University of the West Indies, 1983), 28. For a discussion of changing British attitudes toward colonialism during and after World War II, see John Darwin, *Britain and Decolonisation: The Retreat from Empire in the Post-War World* (London: MacMillan, 1988), 3–68.

10. Matthews, *Labour Policies in the West Indies*, 52–53.

11. *Public Opinion*, January 24, 1942.

12. *Amsterdam News,* June 5, 1943, p. 13; James W. Vann, Aug. 1942, general correspondence, box 16, file RP-M-85-183, monthly reports, RG 96, NARA; correspondence, 1943-1944, box 75, file 4-FLT-R57, RG 224, NARA.

13. Blanshard, *Democracy and Empire in the Caribbean*, 90–91.

14. Parliamentary debates (Hansard), Great Britain. Parliament. House of Lords, v. 166, p. 475.

15. Darwin, *Britain and Decolonisation*, 3–68; Munroe, *Politics of Constitutional Decolonization*, 25–26; Blanshard, *Democracy and Empire in the Caribbean*, 94–97.

16. Munroe, *Politics of Constitutional Decolonization*, 36, 38; Blanshard, *Democracy and Empire*, 94–97; PRO, CO 859, 46/16, 12251/1, Minutes of Meetings, 1943.

17. Governor of Jamaica to Mr. Beckett, March 26, 1943, PRO, CO, 448/10, Recruitment of Labour for U.S.; Sheryl Andre Reid, *U.S.–Jamaica Relations: The Farm Worker Programme, 1943–1962*, M.A. Thesis, UWI, 1998, 40–44, 178–79, 181, 150–51, 158–59.

18. Newspapers reprinted some of these letters but, unfortunately, only a few of them ended up in Jamaican, U.S., or British archives. Some may be among the papers of United Fruit, but I was unable to locate them. *Daily Gleaner*, April 8 and December 6, 1943; *Public Opinion*, April 15, 1944.

19. *Daily Gleaner*, May 6, 1943.

20. On the abortion issue, see Hahamovitch, *The Fruits of Their Labor*, 179–80. On Jamaican women and the U.S. migration program, see *Public Opinion*, June 5, 1944, p. 1. Reid, *U.S.–Jamaica Relations*, 40–44, 178–79, 181; *Daily Gleaner*, May 18, 1943, 114–18.

21. Reid, *U.S.–Jamaica Relations*, 40–44; *Daily Gleaner*, May 18, 1943.

22. *Daily Gleaner*, April 30 and May 5, 1943; *Public Opinion*, April 1 and 12, 1943.

23. *Hartford Times*, April 26, 1944, 3; Reid, 133–34.

24. Fay Clarke Johnson, *Soldiers of the Soil* (New York: Vantage Press, 1995), 85.

25. Ibid., 25–29.

26. Ibid., 20.

27. *Daily Gleaner*, May 5 and June 5, 1943; *Public Opinion*, September 25, 1943, 1; AACC to Secretary of State for the Colonies, May 22, 1943, PRO, CO 318/448/10.

28. Leaford C. Williams, *Journey Into Diplomacy: A Black Man's Shocking Discovery, A Memoir* (Washington, dc: Northeast Publishing House, 1996), 69–70; Johnson, *Soldiers of the Soil*, 35–36.

29. It is not clear whether recruits were temporarily based at Monkey Jungle, the nature park founded in Miami in 1933, or whether their encampment had been dubbed that name, simply to be offensive. Johnson, *Soldiers of the Soil*, 35.

30. Williams, *Journey Into Diplomacy*, 71–73.

31. PRO, CO 318/448/10.

32. Williams, *Journey Into Diplomacy*, 73

33. Ibid., 74.

34. Ibid., 75.

35. *Daily Gleaner*, June 7, 1943.

36. *Daily Gleaner*, May 26, June 4–7, August 16, 1943.

37. Johnson, *Soldiers of the Soil*, 62.

38. Williams, *Journey Into Diplomacy*, 76–78, 60.

39. Ibid., 77.

40. *Amsterdam News*, August 28, 1943, 4 and September 25, 1943, 4-A; *Daily Gleaner*, September 8, 1943, 1; The *Protestant Voice* story was reprinted in the *Daily Gleaner*, September 22, 1943, 4.

41. Sir A. Richard, Jamaica, to Secretary of State for the Colonies, June 29, 1943, PRO, CO 318, 448/11, Recruitment of Labour for U.S.; *Chicago Bee*, July 11, 1943, 2.

42. *Public Opinion*, September 25, 1943, 1; Sir A. Richard, Jamaica, to Secretary of State for the Colonies, June 29, 1943, PRO, CO 318, 448/11, Recruitment of Labour for U.S.; Anglo-American Caribbean Commission to Secretary of State

for the Colonies, July 7, 1943, PRO, CO 318, 448/11, Recruitment of Labour for U.S.; *Chicago Bee*, July 11, 1943, 2; Report to Mr. Middleton, July 1 1944, PRO, CO 318/460/1.

43. Leaford Williams interview.

44. *Daily Gleaner*, November 5, 1943.

45. Alfred C. Cairns, Emergency Labor Assistant, Richland Center, Wisconsin, Annual Report for April 1, 1944 to October 31, 1944, Agricultural Extension, County Agricultural Agents, Annual Reports, 1915–1952, Richland County 1918, 1934–1950, Series 9/4/3, Box 102, University of Wisconsin–Archives, College of Agriculture.

46. *Daily Gleaner*, August 6 and 28, 1943.

47. *Waterbury Republican*, June 27, 1943, 14.

48. *Daily Gleaner*, August 6 and 28, 1943.

49. *Daily Gleaner*, August 6 and September 8, 1943. For more comprehensive studies of West Indians' encounters with race in the United States, see, among others: Ira De A. Reid, *The Negro Immigrant* (New York: Columbia University Press, 1939); Lennox Raphael, "West Indians and Afro-Americans," *Freedomways* (Summer 1964): 438–45; Roy S. Bryce-Laporte, "Black Immigrants, the Experience of Invisibility and Inequality," *Journal of Black Studies* 3, 1 (1972): 29–56; Philip Kasinitz, *Caribbean New York: Black Immigrants and the Politics of Race* (Ithaca, NY: Cornell University Press, 1992); and Milton Vickerman, *Crosscurrents: West Indian Immigrants and Race* (New York: Oxford University Press, 1999).

50. Transcript of July 2, 1944 editorial in PRO, 318/460/1.

51. Giles R. Wright, comp. *Looking Back: Eleven Life Histories*, New Jersey Ethnic Life Series, no. 10 (Trenton: New Jersey Historical Commission, Department of State, 1986), 18–19.

52. Ibid., 19.

53. Johnson, *Soldiers of the Soil*, 63–64.

54. Williams, *Journey Into Diplomacy*, 89–90, 93–94.

55. Ibid., 77.

56. *Amsterdam News*, 22 May 1944 (clipping in NARA, RG 224, Box 25, File: Publications 1-1 Negro Press); *Norfolk Journal and Guide*, 17 July 1943.

CHAPTER 4: John Bull Meets Jim Crow

1. *Public Opinion*, June 20, 1944, 1.

2. *Amsterdam News*, November 6, 1943, p. 7-B.

3. Morrison interviewed by the author, 20 April 2000 (hereafter cited as Morrison interview).

4. Morrison interview.

5. Ibid.

6. Bahamians did continue to take cane harvesting work at Fellsmere, the only other sugarcane company in Florida in the 1940s. What Fellsmere offered that U.S. Sugar didn't is unclear. WN RC, RG 224 Office of Labor General Correspondence, 1945, Box 78, 2/45 Redland FLSC.

7. *Public Opinion*, May 17, 1943, 1.

8. J. Harris, May 21, 1943 and Colonel Bruton, WFA to Taussig, AACC, undated, PRO, CO 318, 448/11, Recruitment of Labour for U.S.

9. *Daily Gleaner*, May 17 and 19, 1943.

10. *Daily Gleaner*, September 22, 1943, p. 4.

11. George W. Hill, Special Assistant to the Department Administrator, War Food Administration to Dr. Conrad Taeuber, Acting Chief Div. of Farm Pop and Rural Welfare, Bureau of Agricultural Economics, 11 May 1943 and George W. Hill, WFA to Taylor, 17 May 1943, RG 224, Office of Labor (WFA), General Correspondence, 1943, Box 15, File: Farm Labor 3–4 Jamaican, NARA; Hill to Mason Barr, Director, Management Division, FSA, ibid., Box 10, Army 6 File: Soldiers for Farm Work, 6–12–43.

12. *Daily Gleaner*, September 21, 1943, p.1.

13. The contract stated "if the employer or the Government's agent determine that the worker is unwilling to work in accordance with the terms of the agreement or determine that the worker has committed an act of misconduct or indiscipline . . . the employer shall be entitled immediately to cause the worker to be repatriated at the worker's expense." *Daily Gleaner*, September 21 and 29, 1943; Dohoney, "The Wages of Cane," 111–12.

14. Emphasis mine. Reprinted in the *Daily Gleaner*, October 4, 1943; PRO, CO 318, 448/11, Recruitment of Labour for U.S.

15. See *Panama City* (Florida) *News Herald*, 28 August 1945; *Stuart News*, September 6, 1945; and *Palm Beach Post*, August 29, 1945, p. 2.

16. *Amsterdam News*, November 6, 1943, p. 7-B; *Pittsburgh Courier*, October 30, 1943.

17. Fay Clarke Johnson, *Soldiers of the Soil* (New York: Vantage Press, 1995), 38.

18. Interview with Leaford C. Williams by the author, Washington, DC, November 18, 2002.

19. Leaford Williams, *Journey Into Diplomacy: A Black Man's Shocking Discovery, A Memoir* (Washington, DC: Northeast Publishing House, 1996), 97.

20. Ibid., 99.

21. Ibid., 97.

22. According to historian Sheryl Reid, "The passes were used to distinguish these 'British subjects' from the general 'colored' population and hence protect the Jamaicans (at least legally) from racist whites who were now obligated to treat the Jamaicans with courtesy." Sheryl Andre Reid, *U.S.–Jamaica Relations: The Farm Work Programme, 1943–1962*, M.A. Thesis, UWI, 1998, 197; *Daily Gleaner*, May 26, 1943.

23. *Daily Gleaner*, November 6, 1943, 15; *Palm Beach Post*, October 9 and 15–16, 1943, 12; Herbert G. McDonald (*sic*) to Labour Adviser, Labour Department, Kingston, Jamaica, Office of Censorship, U.S.A, 21 October 1943, PRO, CO 318/460/1.

24. *Pittsburg Courier*, October 26, 1943.

25. This letter still exists only because it was picked up by the "Imperial Censors," Edon, Pelican Lake, Florida, to Dr. F.G. Veitch, J.P., Kingston, July 10, 1943, PRO, CO 318/460/1.

26. Williams, *Journey into Diplomacy*, 99–100.

27. Johnson, *Soldiers of the Soil*, 38–39.

28. Earl Morrison, interviewed by the author, 20 April 2000.

29. Johnson, *Soldiers of the Soil*, 40–41.

30. Nathaniel Allen, Staystonville, Delaware, to Alice Eldemire, Montego Bay, 10 July 1944, PRO, CO 318/460/1.

31. Johnson, *Soldiers of the Soil*, 40.

32. Ibid., 42.

33. *Washington Bee*, July 22, 1944, 2.

34. WNRC RG 224 Office of Labor General Correspondence, 1945, Box 78, File: Camps 11-1 Maryland FLSC 1945, 4 May 1945 Hebron, MD FLSC.

35. For a discussion of conditions for African American migrant farmworkers in the prewar period, see Hahamovitch, *The Fruits of Their Labor: Atlantic Coast Farmworkers and the Making of Migrant Poverty* (Chapel Hill: University of North Carolina Press, 1997), 113–37.

36. For examples of the sort of violence farmworkers faced, see H. L. Mitchell, *Mean Things Happening in This Land: The Life and Times of H. L. Mitchell, Cofounder of the Southern Tenant Farmers Union* (Montclair, NJ: Allanheld, Osmun, & Co., 1979).

37. *Washington Bee*, 22 July 1944, 2.

38. Pahokee Farm Labor Center April 1944 report by George E. Winston, Manager, File: C2-R36 - Florida, Box 51, RG 224, Office of Labor (War Food Administration), General Correspondence, 1943–44, NARA.

39. Remarkably, the War Food Administration was able to keep this incident out of Jamaican and U.S. newspapers. Marvin O. Dickerson and Verdie A. Kile, Farm Labor Supply Assistants, to Mason Barr, Chief, Office of Labor, War Food Administration, 22 November 1943, NARA, RG 224, Box 62, File: 6-R59 Repatriation, January 1944.

40. Peter Kramer, *The Offshores: A Study of Foreign Farm Labor in Florida*. St. Petersburg, FL: Community Action Fund, 1966), 2.

41. General Correspondence, 1943–44, Box 51, RG 224, Office of Labor (WFA), NARA.

42. I have found evidence of only one such hearing and at that meeting, the worker—who alleged that he was struck on the back of his neck with a stalk of cane by a foreman—was not allowed to speak on his own behalf. He tried to leave the camp to escape involuntary deportation and was apprehended by the INS. Indeed, the National Archives file that is supposed to contain the transcripts of the hearings is empty and looks as though it never held anything. December 7, 1956 Apprehension Report, RG 85 (85–59A2038), Box 90, File 56364/42. 95SE (3), Apprehensions, BP–Non-Mexican, Non-Canadian Aliens—SE Region.

43. The recruitment station at Harkers Hall, St. Catherine Parish, was eliminated in 1943 because nearly 50 percent of all applicants had syphilis or gonorrhea. *Daily Gleaner*, August 28, 1944; Reid, *U.S.–Jamaica Relations*, 171–72.

44. *Public Opinion*, August 29, 1944.

45. *Public Opinion*, September 29, 1944, p. 4.

46. In his May 1945 report, Herbert MacDonald estimated that, since the start of program, compulsory deductions had totaled $83,111 for Barbados and $3,459,066

for Jamaicans. Cedric O.J. Matthews, *Labour Policies in the West Indies* (Geneva: International Labour Office, 1952), 118; Chief Liaison's Report for May, 1945, PRO, CO 318/460/2.

47. *Public Opinion*, May 1, 1944, p. 4; July 4, 1944, p. 3; June 19, 1944, p. 1.

48. *Daily Gleaner*, January 12 and 19, 1944, p. 1; April 12, 1944.

49. The remaining five seats went to Independents. *Public Opinion*, December 16 1944; Trevor Munroe, *Politics of Constitutional Decolonisation, Jamaica, 1944–62*, reprint ed. (Mona: Institute of Social and Economic Research, University of the West Indies, 1983), 42; 2 May 1945, PRO, CO 318/460/2.

50. Governor (Sir) Grattan Bushe to the Colonial Office, 29 June and 12 July 1943, PRO, CO 318/448/10, PRO, CO 318, 448/10, Recruitment of Labour for U.S.

51. Ibid.; Letter from L.L.Chandler, Governor's Papers, Spessard Holland, Series 406, Carton 66, State Archives of Florida, Tallahassee, Florida, cited in McNally, 66.

52. Governor (Sir) Grattan Bushe to the Colonial Office, June 29 and July 12, 1943, and decoded telegram from AACC to Secretary of State for the Colonies, 11 March 1944, PRO, CO 318, 448/10, Recruitment of Labour for U.S.; Sir A. Grimble, Windward Islands to Secretary of State for the Colonies, 30 August 1944, PRO, CO 318, 448/11; Telegram from AACC to SSC, 22 March 1945, CO 318, 460/2.

53. The establishment of WICLO saved each sending country from having to negotiate a separate deal and send its own liaisons. K. A. Butler, Acting Director of Labor to Nathan Koenig, Executive Secretary to the Secretary of Agriculture, 24 January 1946, RG 224, General Correspondence 1946, Box 107 POWs, NARA.

54. The Fort Eustis center closed because within a month of its opening, the War Manpower Commission shifted almost two thousand West Indians awaiting repatriation at Fort Eustis into jobs in foundries, airplane and ship engine plants, and other war industries, despite the fact that they had been blacklisted by the WFA and that Public Law 45 restricted temporary foreign workers to agricultural jobs. When word spread that workers facing repatriation in Virginia had been transferred to coveted industrial jobs in New Jersey and Wisconsin, four hundred sugar harvesters in Florida promptly threatened to strike. Their hope was that they too would be transferred to Virginia for repatriation and that, once there, they could sign up for industrial work. Its plan undone, the WFA closed the Fort Eustis center, and opened a new one at Camp Murphy, near West Palm Beach, Florida. Reid, *U.S.–Jamaica Relations*, 3; Report of Herbert MacDonald for December 1944, PRO, CO 318, 460/2.

55. The conflict grew until some 250 men were involved in two hours of stone-throwing (the Jamaicans allegedly shot revolvers) until the police quelled it. Eleven workers (two Barbadians and nine Jamaicans) were tried in court for their part in the disturbance. One was acquitted, nine got three months each, and the other one got six months in a Florida jail. 28 August 1945 clipping in PRO, CO 318/460/2.; *Palm Beach Post*, 29 August 1945.

56. Depositions, 10 September 1945, PRO, CO 318/460/2; Chief Liaison's report for September, 1945, PRO, CO 318, 460/2.

57. Extract of letter from Edon (?) to Hon. And Rev. Dr. P.G. Veitch, J.P., Legislative Council, Kingston, Jamaica, quoted by Imperial Censorship, Jamaica, 10

July 1944 and Chief Liaison's Report for Month Ending 31 May 1945, 2 June 1945, PRO, CO 318/460/1 and 2.

58. Reports by Sadye E. Pryor, home management supervisor, Okeechobee Center, Sept. 1943, and Henry O. Earwood, Okeechobee Camp manager, October 1944, general correspondence, 1943–44, box 51, file C2-R36-Florida, RG 224, NARA.

59. Hahamovitch, *The Fruits of Their Labor*, 175.

60. Italics in the original. Ibid.

61. Sigrid Arne, "West Indian Negroes Shift From Sugar Fields to U.S. Farms," *Waterbury Republican*, 27 June 1943, p. 14.

62. Hahamovitch, *The Fruits of Their Labor*, 176.

63. Ibid.

64. Ibid.

65. Walter S. Comrie, Interviewed by the author, Wellington, Florida, 3 July 2002; Walter S. Comrie, "The West Indian Farm Worker Programme: "Both Sides of the Coin" (unpublished manuscript, 1987) in author's possession, 14–15. Comrie says he wrote it "with a view to promoting and expanding the West Indian Farm Worker Programme." To do that, he argues, the "malignancy" has to be cut out. His knowledge of conditions in the 1940s and 50s is based on discussions with supervisors who had been "in the original lot."

66. Comrie, "The West Indian Farm Worker Programme," 14–15.

67. *Norfolk Journal and Guide*, May 25, 1946.

68. *Palm Beach Post*, August 29, 1945, p. 2.

CHAPTER 5: The Race to the Bottom

1. Leaford C. Williams, *Journey into Diplomacy: A Black Man's Shocking Discovery: A Memoir* (Washington, DC: Northeast Publishing House, 1996), 106–7, 111; Leaford C. Williams, interview by the author, Washington, DC, November 18, 2002.

2. Williams, *Journey into Diplomacy*, 113–15; Williams interview.

3. Williams, *Journey into Diplomacy*, 116; Williams interview.

4. Williams, *Journey into Diplomacy*, 119–20.

5. The major exporters of labor were Ireland, Italy, Portugal, Spain, Finland, Greece, Turkey, Yugoslavia, Algeria, Sudan, Morocco. In 1973, the 6.7 million guestworkers in Europe sent home remittances totaling $6 billion. Stephen Castles and Mark J. Miller, *The Age of Migration: International Population Movements in the Modern World*, 1st ed., 1993, reprint ed, 1998 (London: MacMillan Press), 68–71; John Bendix, "On the Rights of Foreign Workers in West Germany," in *Turkish Workers in Europe: An Interdisciplinary Study*, edited by Ilhan Başgöz and Norman Furniss (Bloomington: Indiana University Turkish Studies, 1985), 28; Philip L. Martin, *Guestworker Programs: Lessons from Europe*, U.S. Department of Labor, Bureau of International Labor Affairs, Monograph No. 5 (Washington, DC: GPO, 1980): 1, 7–10; Peter Stalker, *The Work of Strangers: A Survey of International Labour Migration* (Geneva: International Labour Office, 1994), 16–17.

6. Castles and Kosack contains a detailed discuss of trade unions' various responses to guestworkers in France, Germany, England, and Switzerland. See Stephen Castles and Godula Kosack, *Immigrant Workers and Class Structure in Western Europe*, 2nd ed. (London: Oxford University Press, 1985): 116–79.

7. Cindy Hahamovitch, "Creating Perfect Immigrants: Guestworkers of the World in Historical Perspective," *Labour History* 44, 1 (2003): 84–85.

8. Nigel Harris, *The New Untouchables: Immigration and the New World Worker* (New York: I. B. Tauris, 1995): 9–10; Castles and Miller, *The Age of Migration*, 71.

9. On the comparison to South African migration programs, see Hahamovitch, "Creating Perfect Immigrants," 69–94.

10. Edward A. O'Neal, President, AFBF, to Harry S. Truman, 2 October 1945, File: Public Relations 1 Commendations–Endorsement of the Program 1945, RG 224 Office of Labor General Correspondence, 1945, WNRC, NARA.

11. Frank Seymour, Lakeland, FL, Growers Administration Committee, to Clinton P. Anderson, Secretary of Agriculture, 9 October 1945, File: Public Relations 1 Commendations –Endorsement of the Program 1945, RG 224 Office of Labor General Correspondence, 1945, NARA.

12. *Glades County Democrat*, December 26, 1947.

13. Bureau of Agricultural Economics, U.S. Department of Agriculture, "Farm Manpower Situation and Outlook," *BAE Report*, 30 October 1951.

14. The number of farms declined 56 percent from 1935 to 1970, but their output kept increasing. Farm output increased 25 percent in the 1940s, and 20 percent in the 1950s. Willard W. Cochrane, *The Development of American Agriculture: A Historical Analysis* (Minneapolis: University of Minnesota Press, 1979), 126–40, 148.

15. By 1950, only 14 percent of the approximately 5.5 million Americans who did waged farm work labored more than six months on any one farm. "The Farm Manpower Situation and Outlook," Statement by Louis J. Ducoff, USDA, Bureau of Agricultural Economics, at the 29th Annual Agricultural Outlook Conference in Washington, DC, October 30, 1951, *Workers Defense League Papers*, Box 154, Folder 9.; Robert D. Tomasek, "The Migrant Problem and Pressure Group Politics," *Journal of Politics* 23 (1961): 298.

16. Cochrane, *Development of American Agriculture*, 126–32; Kennett Love, "Migrant Labor in the East: 60,000 Jam Farm Camps," *New York Times*, August 29, 1960.

17. "The Farm Manpower Situation and Outlook," Statement by Louis J. Ducoff, USDA, Bureau of Agricultural Economics, 29th Annual Agricultural Outlook Conference in Washington, DC, 30 October 1951, *Workers Defense League Papers*, Box 154, Folder 9; Tomasek, "The Migrant Problem and Pressure Group Politics," 298.

18. Love, "Migrant Labor in the East."

19. William H. Metzler, *Migratory Farm Workers in the Atlantic Coast Stream: A Study in the Belle Glade area of Florida* (Washington, DC: U.S. Department of Agriculture, Circular No. 966, January 1955).

20. Love, "Migrant Labor in the East."

21. G. Thomas-Lycklama à Nijeholt, *On the Road for Work: Migratory Workers on the East Coast of the United States* (Boston: Martinus Nijhoff, 1980), 17–18; Paul Jacobs, "The Forgotten People, "*The Reporter*, January 22, 1959, 13.

22. These agencies rarely arrived at the same results or defined their terms in similar ways. In 1946, for example, the Bureau of Agricultural Economics put the number of hired farm "hands" at 2,503,000, of whom 550,000 worked on three or more farms a year and over 56,000 were guestworkers. What percentage of those seasonal farmworkers migrated long distances for work was not clear. Other agencies contributed to the swirl of statistics. The Employment Service, which was a branch of the Labor Department, estimated the East Coast migrant population at 10,000 in 1943, 14,000 in 1944, 20,000 in 1945, 25,000 in 1946, and 58,000 in 1949, but since it only counted migrants looking for work through the Employment Service, it is not clear whether the change in numbers reflected an increased supply of labor or the increased use of the Employment Service's offices. The Interstate Commerce Commission counted 123,303 migratory farmworkers in 1945, though it is not clear how it arrived at such a precise figure. Nevertheless, all these agencies recorded an upward trend in the number of seasonal farmworkers. *Farm Labor*, Washington, DC, 13 November 1946, p. 1; Metzler, *Migratory Farm Workers*, 5; *Farm Labor*, Washington, DC, November 13, 1946, 1; Federal Interagency Committee on Migrant Labor, *Migrant Labor . . . a human problem: Report and Recommendations of the Federal Interagency Committee on Migrant Labor*, U.S. Department of Labor, Retraining and Reemployment Administration, 1947, 17 (hereafter called *Migrant Labor . . . a human problem*); Anne B.W. Effland, "The Emergence of Federal Assistance Programs for Migrants and Seasonal Farmworkers in Post–World War II America," Ph.D. Dissertation, Iowa State, 1991, 12–14.

23. *Migrant Labor . . . a Human Problem*, v.

24. Ibid.

25. F. A. Curry, Personnel Manager at the Birds Eye Division of General Foods in Mt. Morris, New York, to Senator Herbert Lehman, 26 November 1952, File C7-6-11, Dec. 1952, Immigration, Legislative Files, Papers of Herbert H. Lehman, Herbert H. Lehman Suite and Library, Columbia University. Thanks to Mae Ngai for sharing this letter with me.

26. Thomas J. Flavin, Asst. to the Sec. to H.G. Winsor, Dir, WMC, NW District, Seattle, 10 October 1942, Box 7, File: Migratory-120-A Thru G, Records of the Farmers Home Administration (Farm Security Administration), RG 96, Records of the Resettlement Administration, 13, General Correspondence, 1935–42, NARA; Howard A. Preston, Chief of Operations, NE Division to Director of Labor—Monthly Report, 9 March 1945, File: Reports 1 Narrative 1945, Box 93, RG 224 Office of Labor General Correspondence, 1945, NARA.

27. Tomasek, "The Migrant Problem and Pressure Group Politics," 308–9; Kitty Calavita, *Inside the State: The Bracero Program, Illegal Immigrants and the INS* (New York: Routledge, 1992), 22–23; See also Allen J. Matusow, *Farm Policies and Politics in the Truman Years* (Cambridge, MA: Harvard University Press, 1967).

28. Tomasek, "The Migrant Problem and Pressure Group Politics," 301–2; Kramer, *The Offshores*, 18; Ellis W. Hawley, "The Politics of the Labor Issue, 1950–1965," *Agricultural History* 40, 3 (1960): 162–63.

29. In 1937, the STFU merged with the newly created United Cannery and Allied Packing and Agricultural Workers Association (UCAPAWA) under the rubric of the Congress of Industrial Organizations (CIO). Two years later, the STFU abandoned the alliance when UCAPAWA refused to support a protest of evicted sharecroppers in Missouri. For the next few years, the STFU and UCAPAWA competed bitterly for members, but in 1941, UCAPAWA withdrew from organizing migrant farmworkers, focusing instead on packinghouse workers because, unlike field workers, they enjoyed the right of collective bargaining. The STFU changed its name to the National Farm Labor Union during World War II. At 20,000 members in 1946, the NFLU was the most significant union of *field* laborers on the mainland U.S. The NFLU later changed its name to the National Agricultural Workers Union.

30. Hahamovitch, *The Fruits of Their Labor*, 182–99.

31. *Farm Labor News*, January 1946, 1, 1, p. 1.

32. *Farm Labor News*, February 1946, vol. 1, no. 2, p. 4.

33. *Report of the Executive Council,* National Farm Labor Union, December 12, 1947, Little Rock, Arkansas, *Workers Defense League Papers*, Box 166, Folder 5, p. 6.

34. *Farm Labor News*, December 1947, vol. 1, no. 12, p. 1.

35. At hearings in February, the House Committee on Agriculture had listened sympathetically as grower representatives testified to their dire need for foreign workers but pressed them on the costs of the program. "The Federal Government will put out over $5,500,000 for transportation this year for labor," Congressman John Flannigan noted, interrupting U.S. Sugar's vice president, Josiah Ferris, Jr., who was testifying to his firm's need for West Indian labor. "[D]o you think it is right," Flannigan asked, "for the Federal Government to pay the transportation bill for the benefit of your company?" Ferris admitted that it wasn't, and the fiscally conservative lawmakers of the 80th Congress agreed, voting soon after to cancel the Labor Importation Program. Farm Labor Supply Program, Hearings before the Committee on Agriculture, House of Representatives, 80th Congress, 1st Session, on H.R. 1388 to provide for the continuance of the farm labor supply program up to and including June 30, 1947 (Washington, DC: GPO, 1947), 82–83.

36. Kramer, *The Offshores*, 3.

37. Earl Morrison, Interview by the author, April 20, 2000.

38. *U.S. Statutes at Large*, vol. 39, Part I (Washington, DC: GPO, 1917), 878.

39. Kramer, *The Offshores*, 1–3; Morrison interview, West Palm Beach, April 20, 2000; Immigration Act of 1917, *U.S. Statutes at Large*, vol. 39, part I (Washington, DC: GPO, 1917), 877.

40. *Union Labor News*, 15 August 1947, p. 3; *Report of the Executive Council*, National Farm Labor Union, 12 December 1947, Little Rock, Arkansas, *Workers Defense League Papers*, Box 166, Folder 5; K.A. Butler, Assistant Director of Labor to Chief of Operations, South East Division, 30 August 1945, File: Welfare 2 Recreation and Child Care, Box 95, WNRC, RG 224 Office of Labor General Correspondence, 1945, NARA; Kramer, *The Offshores*, 51.

41. Richard Steven Street, "Poverty in the Valley of Plenty: The National Farm Labor Union, DiGorgio Farms, and Suppression of Documentary Photography in

Florida, 1947–66," *Labor History* 48, 1 (February 2007), 1; Richard B. Craig, *The Bracero Program: Interest Groups and Foreign Policy* (Austin: University of Texas Press), 147–48.

42. Majka and Majka, *Farm Workers, Agribusiness, and the State*, 147–49; Tomasek, "The Migrant Problem and Pressure Group Politics," 298; J. Craig Jenkins, "The Transformation of a Constituency into a Social Movement Revisited: Farmworker Organizing in California," in *Waves of Protest: Social Movements Since the Sixties*, edited by Jo Freeman and Victoria Johnson (New York: Rowman & Littlefield, 1999), 282; Annual Report of the Executive Board of the National Farm Labor Union, 1948, Folder 24, Box 156, and *Report of the Executive Council*, National Farm Labor Union, 12 December 1947, Little Rock, Arkansas, Folder 5, Box 166 *Workers Defense League Papers*, Walter P. Reuther Library, Wayne State University, Detroit, MI; Tomasek, 303–305.

43. Richard Steven Street tells this fascinating story in "Poverty in the Valley of Plenty," 25–48.

44. On the question of why packinghouse workers had collective bargaining rights when fieldworkers didn't, see Hahamovitch, *The Fruits of Their Labor*, 138–39, 146–48.

45. *Union Labor News*, West Palm Beach, Florida, 10 January 1947, vol. xxi, no. 5, p. 1; 11 April 1947, v. xxi, no. 18, p. 1; 16 May 1947, v. xxi, no. 22, p. 1.

46. Majka and Majka, *Farmworkers, Agribusiness and the State*, 147–49; Ernesto Galarza, *Spiders in the House and Workers in the Field* (Notre Dame: University of Notre Dame Press, 1970), 77.

47. Report on the Function of the BWI CLO, 13 April 1951, CO 1042/189, PRO, Kew Garden, England; Kramer, *The Offshores*, 21–22.

48. It's not clear whether the interest went into government coffers or particular officials' pockets. George E. Winton, November 1947, File: Camps 12-1 Florida, Clewiston, Narrative Report, Box 110, WNRC, RG 224, General Correspondence, 1947, NARA.

49. The name stuck long after MacDonald had left the program (none of the Jamaicans I've interviewed knew why they called the hated deduction by that name).

50. See, for example, statement of Harold D. Cooley, Chairman, Hearings before the Committee on Agriculture, House of Representatives, 82nd Congress, 1st Session (Washington, DC: GPO, 1951), 107.

51. The U-list was maintained for the industry by the Florida Fruit and Vegetable Growers Association. In later years, it would become an online database with codes indicating various workers' failures, such as DDC (disciplinary discharge); NPR (non-productive reason); REF (refusal). "Sugar Cane: The Importation of Temporary Foreign Work," in ACLU/AFSC Report, "The Hands That Feed Us," unpublished report (c. 1987). Report of the Conference of BWI Labour Officers, Kingston, Jamaica, 11–13 December 1950, Appendix II, PRO, CO, 1042/189; Kramer, *The Offshores*, 35, Minutes of the meeting of the Regional Labor Board, 1960, in author's possession.

52. At congressional hearings in 1975 Chief Liaison Officer Harold Edwards testified that "men who are cane cutters in the islands usually do not attempt to

become contract farm workers, so that the majority of the canecutters starts this occupation for the first time after arrival in Florida." Among the applicants, one Florida Fruit and Vegetable Recruiter "automatically rejected were: tradesmen (because of the high cost of workmen's compensation incurred in the event of injury cutting cane), masons (too 'muscle-bound'), and fishermen (chronic backaches)." Dayan Barnett was rejected because he had previously applied to take a trip to the United States. Jo Marie Dohoney, "The Wages of Cane: A Study of Temporary Labor Importation in the U.S. and the Case of West Indian Cane Workers in Florida (M.A. Thesis, Michigan State University), 87; McCoy and Wood, "Caribbean Workers in the Florida Sugar Cane Industry," 21 and 70, fn. 8.

53. David Edwards, *An Economic Study of Small Farming in Jamaica* (Glasgow: University Press, 1961), 26–34; McCoy and Wood, "Caribbean Workers in the Florida Sugar Cane Industry," 15–18, 31–32, 70, fn. 9.

54. Tables 1.6, 6.4, 3.5, 3.6, and 9.8 in Oliver James Claudius Francis, *The People of Modern Jamaica*, (Department of Statistics, Jamaica, 1963), 1–13, 6–9, 3–5, 3–14, 9–22.

55. Kramer, *The Offshores*, 35.

56. Recruitment Video–Rockie Point, Kingston, Jamaica, 1 hour and 46 minutes, *Bygrave v. Atlantic Sugar Corp.*, in author's possession; Dohoney, "The Wages of Cane," 82, fn 7.

57. According to the 1960 census, 6,000 Jamaican men were in the United States working as farmworkers on temporary contracts in 1960. In 1960, there were 258,941 men between the ages of 15 and 34 in Jamaica, many of whom were too young to have participated in the program. Conservatively deducting 20,000 to account for teenagers too young to participate, there would have been a pool of roughly 240,000 men of recruitment age in Jamaica, half of whom would have been agricultural workers. Tables 1.7 and 2.24 in Francis, *The People of Modern Jamaica*, 1–23, 2–36; Kramer, *The Offshores*, 12.

58. Undated correspondence, Stephanie Black files, in author's possession.

59. The East Coast Migrant Conference of 1954 estimated the number of migrant farmworkers in the state at 60,000, of whom 50,000 were registered with the U.S. Employment Service. Of those, there were approximately 6,000 Puerto Ricans, 2,700 whites, 4,000 Bahamians, 6,000 British West Indians, and 41,000 African Americans, most of whom traveled in family groups. Cited in *Migrant Farm Labor in Florida*, State of Florida, Legislative Council and Legislative Reference Bureau, January 1963, 5.

60. Williams, *Journey into Diplomacy*, 85–86.

61. Kramer, *The Offshores*, 28–29.

62. David Gordon, Richard Edwards, and Michael Reich, *Segmented Work, Divided Workers* (New York: Cambridge University Press, 1982).

63. Craig, *The Bracero Program*, 58.

64. I've only seen one reference to Mexican workers in the East before 1950. *Migrant Farm Labor in Florida*, State of Florida, Legislative Council and Legislative Reference Bureau, January 1963, p. 6.

65. The president of the United Brewery Workers complained that foreign contract workers were being deployed to undermine the nineteen union locals the

CIO had established among citrus workers. "Reports are pouring into the state headquarters in Florida from all over the citrus belt," he noted, "of our people working from two to four days per week, while Bahamians are working six and seven days per week." When 5,000 out of an estimated 125,000 citrus workers joined the Brewery Workers, he reported, growers successfully appealed to have Bahamians supplement the West Indians in the orchards. Like the NFLU before them, the Brewery Workers gave up, and no union attempted to organize citrus workers again until the 1960s. Feller claimed to have blocked a proposed 250 percent increase in the number of foreign farmworkers imported into Florida the previous winter. Statement of Karl Feller (President of the International Union of United Brewery, Flour, Cereal, Soft Drink, and Distillery Workers of America–CIO) before the Senate Subcommittee on Labor and Management Relations, 27 February 1952," Folder 2, Box 156, *Workers Defense League Papers; Palm Beach Post*, 17 October 1950, in Folder 7, Box 154, *Workers Defense League Papers*.

66. A.G.H. Gardner-Brown, Colonial Secretary's Office, Bahamas, to F .C. Catchpole, Comptroller, Development & Welfare in the West Indies, Barbados, February 1953, PRO, CO 1042/204.

67. Reports of the BWI CLO in the U.S., PRO, CO 1031/614/240/83/01.

68. "Connecticut Area-Report for April 1952," 2 May 1952, PRO, CO 1031/614.

69. Kramer, *The Offshores*, 7–8.

70. Randall resigned from the Public Service of the Bahamas the same year though it is not clear whether his resignation was related to these events. Herbert Macdonald, chief liaison officer, to chairman, Regional Labour Board, Barbados, BWI, 16 December 1952, PRO, CO 1042/204; Labour Office Report, 1952, PRO, CO 1042/204.

71. 12 September 1951, "Report of British West Indian Workers Picking Cotton In Sugar Land, Texas On An Experimental Basis," W. B. Nelson, Supervisor, BWI Labour, Green Giant Company, Beaver Dam, Wisconsin, PRO, CO 1031/614.

72. Charles A. Browne, "Cotton Harvest: Arkansas," 18 October 1952, PRO, CO 1031/614.

73. David's letter is transcribed in a report written by Herbert G. MacDonald, Chief Liaison Officer, BWICLO, 15 December 1952, CO 1030/614.

74. Kramer, *The Offshores*, 22–23.

75. Ibid., 23.

76. Porter interview.

77. Peter Gordon (name changed on request), interview by the author, April 12, 2000, Chambersburg, PA.

78. Walter S. Comrie, "The Rise, Decline & Fall of the West Indian Farm Worker Programme, 1943–1995," unpublished manuscript (n.d.) in the author's possession.

79. In 1978, Comrie was transferred from U.S. Sugar's territory to the farms supplied with labor by the Florida Fruit and Vegetable Association. Comrie interview, July 3, 2002.

80. Williams interview.

81. Williams interview.

CHAPTER 6: A Riotous Success

1. "Labor Dearth and Cotton Production . . . " *New York Times*, September 27, 1909, p. 6; Anna Rochester, *Why Farmers Are Poor: The Agricultural Crisis in the United States* (Reprint of the ed. published by International Publishers, New York, 1940), 151; Ernesto Galarza, *Merchants of Labor: The Mexican Bracero Story: An Account of the Managed Migration of Mexican Farm Workers in California, 1942–1960* (Charlotte and Santa Barbara: McNally & Loftin, 1964), 49–51. Craig's version of events is slightly different. See Craig, *The Bracero Program*, 69–70; Juan Ramon García, *Operation Wetback: The Mass Deportation of Mexican Undocumented Workers in 1954* (Westport, CT: Greenwood Press, 1980), 75–77.

2. John W. Weber III, "The Shadow of the Revolution: South Texas, the Mexican Revolution, and the Evolution of Modern American Labor Relations." Ph.D. Dissertation, College of William & Mary, 2008; Benjamin Heber Johnson, *Revolution in Texas: How a Forgotten Rebellion and Its Bloody Suppression Turned Mexicans into Americans* (New Haven, CT: Yale University Press, 2003).

3. García, *Operation Wetback*, 5–7.

4. By 1950, over 96,000 out of the approximately 116,000 Braceros in the United States were legalized illegal immigrants, and the majority of Braceros in the United States spent their days on cotton plantations in Texas. Galarza, *Merchants of Labor*, 63; Kitty Calavita, *Inside the State: The Bracero Program, Illegal Immigrants and the INS* (New York: Routledge, 1992), 2.

5. García, *Operation Wetback*, 30–32, 45–46, 70–71, 112–13.

6. On bribery and the Bracero Program, see García, *Operation Wetback*, 36–37. See also *Hayward Daily Review*, May 30, 1956.

7. Truman's appointees, who included the former dean of the University of North Carolina's Law School and the Catholic Archbishop of San Antonio, were clearly meant to represent the public; neither growers nor farmworkers were represented on the commission. García, *Operation Wetback*, 54–55; Effland, "The Emergence of Federal Assistance Programs for Migrants," 18–21.

8. Effland, "The Emergence of Federal Assistance Programs for Migrants," 21–24.

9. García, *Operation Wetback*, 111; "Alien Labor's Rise Arouses Concern," *New York Times*, September 7, 1950.

10. "Brief to the President's Commission on Migratory Labor: West Palm Beach, Florida, October 16–17, 1950," *Workers Defense League Papers*, Box 154, Folder, 7, Walter Reuther Archives, Wayne State University.

11. García, *Operation Wetback*, 112.

12. H. Michael Semler, "Overview: The H-2 Program. Aliens in the Orchard: The Admission of Foreign Contract Laborers for Temporary Work in U.S. Agriculture," *Yale Law & Policy Review* 1, 2 (Spring 1983) 191 (hereafter cited as "Overview").

13. *Migratory Labor in American Agriculture: Report of the President's Commission on Migratory Labor*, 1951, p. 66.

14. Ibid.

15. García, *Operation Wetback*, 120.

16. Hawley, "Politics of the Mexican Labor Issue," 159.

17. *Hearings before the Committee on Agriculture,* House, 82nd Cong., 1s on HR 2955 and HR 3048, March 8,9, 12, and 14, 1951 (Washington, DC: GPO, 1951). Ellender's bill was S. 984.

18. *The West Indies (BWI) Temporary Alien Labor Program, 1943–1977: A Study Prepared for the Subcommittee on Immigration of the Committee of the Judiciary,* U.S. Senate, 95th Congress, 2d session (Washington, DC: GPO, 1978), 14; Craig, *The Bracero Program,* 73–81.

19. *Hearings before the Committee on Agriculture,* House, 82nd Cong., 1s on HR 2955 and HR 3048, March 8, 9, 12, and 14, 1951 (Washington, DC: GPO, 1951), 13, 38, 46, 74.

20. In questioning Assistant Secretary of Labor Robert T. Creasey, for example, Cooley mocked the idea of having to provide medical care to domestic migrant workers' families, obstetricians to deliver "babies born in the camps," "lying-in establishments, and so forth." "No," Creasey answered tersely to all these queries. Suggesting that Yorty's bill would force American families to migrate rather than simply aiding those who did, Cooley ruefully recalled the Farm Security Administration's tenure over the program, when "Pitiful little children were dragged from State to State." Supporters of Yorty's bill, Cooley suggested, favored "a more complete socialization" of agriculture, a point J. C. Baird of the Agricultural Labor Users of the United States echoed, when he testified that "we are confronted on all sides by the evils and abuses of the delegation of legal authority by Congress to the departments, bureaus, and agencies of the Government." *Hearings before the Committee on Agriculture*, House, 82nd Cong., 1s on HR 2955 and HR 3048, March 8, 9, 12, and 14, 1951 (Washington, DC: GPO, 1951), 13, 38, 46, 74.

21. When it was clear that Poage's bill would pass, liberal Democrats tried to amend it to require comparable protections for domestic farmworkers before the Secretary of Labor could certify the need for imported workers, but their amendments failed, and the bill passed overwhelmingly with Republicans voting heavily in favor of it and Democrats split. According to Anne Effland, Democrats and Republicans in the states that used the greatest numbers of contract workers (Arizona, New Mexico, California, Arkansas, Texas, Louisiana, and Florida) voted overwhelmingly in favor of the bill; the most liberal Democrats opposed it, as did the Secretary of Labor. Truman signed it anyway. Effland, "The Emergence of Federal Assistance Programs for Migrants," 35–36; Hawley, "The Politics of the Mexican Labor Issue, 1950–1965," 159; Galarza, *Merchants of Labor,* 64–65.

22. November 26, 1952, F. A. Curry, Personnel Manager at the Birds Eye Division of General Foods in Mt. Morris, New York, to Senator Herbert Lehman, File C7-6-11, Dec. 1952, Immigration, Legislative Files, Papers of Herbert H. Lehman, Herbert H. Lehman Suite and Library, Columbia University. Thanks to Mae Ngai for sending me this letter.

23. *The West Indies (BWI) Temporary Alien Labor Program, 1943–1977: A Study Prepared for the Subcommittee on Immigration of the Committee of the Judiciary,* U.S. Senate, 95th Congress, 2d session (Washington, DC: GPO, 1978), 13.

24. Sir George Seel of Barbados noted that the West Indian delegation had planned to press employers to accept responsibility for a greater share of the program's costs, but given growers' attitudes, they didn't press the point. Seel expressed hoped that, at some point, they would improve their bargaining position. Sir George Seel, BWI Development and Welfare Organization, Barbados, November 17, 1950, PRO, CO 1042/189.

25. Fortunately for Leaford Williams, he got in to the United States before the passage of McCarran-Walter.

26. Title 1 General, Section 101, 15 (H) (ii) read as follows: "an alien having a residence in a foreign country which he has no intention of abandoning . . . who is coming temporarily to the United States to perform other temporary services or labor, if unemployed persons capable of performing such service or labor cannot be found in this country." *U.S. Statutes at Large*, 1952, Vol. 66, 82nd Cong., 163–282.

27. Sec. 203, *U.S. Statutes at Large*, 1952, Vol. 66, 82nd Cong., 163–282.

28. Galarza, *Merchants of Labor*, 62.

29. Article 274 stipulated that employing an illegal worker did not constitute harboring or concealing that person. Galarza, *Merchants of Labor*, 61; Garcia, *Operation Wetback*, 109; Majka and Majka, *Farm Workers, Agribusiness, and the State*, 156.

30. James G. Flanigan, Seabrook Farms, Labor Relations, to James P. McGranery, Attorney General of the U.S., 12/15/1952, NARA, RG 85, 85–59A2038, Box 39, File 59A2038, Subject: Admission of Non-Immigrants for Temporary Labor or Training. Final regulations in *Federal Register*, December 19, 1952.

31. Ibid.

32. The Bahamian statistics are in: Undated Aide-memoire on Recruitment of [Bahamian] Labour for the U.S.A., PRO, WO 166/522.

33. Galarza, *Merchants of Labor*, 94.

34. García, *Operation Wetback*, 209.

35. E. E. Salisbury, District Director, St. Albans, VT, to Argyle R. Mackey, Commissioner, D.C., Re: Public Law 414, 6/30/1952, NARA, RG 85, 85–59A2038, Box 39, File 59A2038, Subject: Admission of Non-Immigrants for Temporary Labor or Training.

36. *New York Times*, January 11, 1953, p. 37.

37. *New York Times*, November 23, 1953, p. 18.

38. In 1954, the INS investigated allegations that a New Hampshire hotel had fired American workers in favor of H2 workers from Canada. Concluding that the hotel's managers were simply ignorant of the law, the INS allowed the hotel to keep its guestworkers. But when the hotel did the same thing again, the U.S. Employment Service withdrew its approval, only to receive a reprimand from the INS, which insisted that the Employment Service lacked the power to revoke a certification once it had been granted. See 14 September 1954 memo in NARA, RG 85, 85–59A2038, Box 39, File 59A2038, Subject: Admission of Non-Immigrants for Temporary Labor or Training.

39. The use of H2 workers in Guam at less than the U.S. minimum wage led to a protracted conflict between the DOD and the Department of Labor over

whether U.S. minimum wage law applied in Guam. David S. North, "Nonimmigrant Workers: Visiting Labor Force Participants," *Monthly Labor Review* 103, 10 (October 1980), 27. Memo from L.W. Williams, Assistant Commissioner of the Examinations Division, INS, 18 February 1957, NARA, RG 85, 85–59A2038, Box 39, File 59A2038, Subject: Admission of Non-Immigrants for Temporary Labor or Training.

40. Kramer, *The Offshores*, 3–9; Memo from L.W. Williams, Assistant Commissioner of the Examinations Division, INS, 18 February 1957, NARA, RG 85, 85–59A2038, Box 39, File 59A2038, Subject: Admission of Non-Immigrants for Temporary Labor or Training. Re: importation of Spanish sheepherders, see NARA, RG 85, 85–59A2038, Box 39, File 59A2038, Subject: Admission of Non-Immigrants for Temporary Labor or Training.

41. *Oakland Tribune*, December 15, 1964.

42. Kramer, *The Offshores*, 39.

43. The INS officer apparently believed Levy's account, and he took the time to let Levy tell his story at length, coaching him to refuse a voluntary departure so that he would be guaranteed an INS hearing, at which he could "tell . . . about the blow [he] got on the head and suffering from it." This is one of the only hearing records I could locate. The file is slim. 7 December 1956 Apprehension Report, RG 85 (85–59A2038), Box 90, File 56364/42. 95SE (3), Apprehensions, BP–Non-Mexican, Non-Canadian Aliens—SE Region.

44. 24 October 1956, Apprehension Reports for Leroy Rolle, Denzel McIntosh, and Alexander Phillip Smith, RG 85 (85–59A2038), Box 90, File 56364/42, 95SE, Apprehensions, BP–Non-Mexican, Non-Canadian Aliens—SE Region.

45. *Migratory Labor*, Hearings before the Subcommittee on Labor and Labor-Management Relations of the Committee on Labor and Public Welfare, U.S. Senate (82nd Congress, 2d session on Migratory Labor, Part I (Washington, DC: GPO, 1952). Stith's testimony is at 226–29.

46. "Wetbacks Swarm In," *Life*, May 21, 1951, 30–37; *Brainerd Daily Dispatch*, September 18, 1951; *Humboldt Standard*, February 11, 1952; "The Wetbacks," *Time*, April 19, 1951, p. 24; and the *New York Times* series by Gladwyn Hill (March 25–29, 1952). Tomasek, "The Migrant Problem and Pressure Group Politics," 311–12.

47. *Migratory Labor*, Hearings before the Subcommittee on Labor and Labor-Management Relations of the Committee on Labor and Public Welfare, U.S. Senate (82nd Congress, 2d session on Migratory Labor, Part I (Washington, DC: GPO, 1952), 3.

48. Ibid., 227 and 231.

49. "'Iron Curtain' Blocks Braceros" (Brownsville, Texas) *Herald*, January 24, 1954, p. 1.

50. Richard B. Craig, *The Bracero Program: Interest Groups and Foreign Policy* (Austin: University of Texas Press, 1971), 112–13; "Mexican Police Battle Braceros to Prevent Crossing of Border," Yuma, Arizona *Sentinel*, January 25, 1954, p.1; "Mexican Troops Patrol Border," Lubbock, Texas *Morning Avalanche*, January 25, 1954, p. 13; "Mexican Police Hose Braceros at Border," Long Beach, California *Independent*, January 28, 1954, p. 6; "Foot Races Mark

Flareups Along the Mexican Border," Albuquerque *Journal*, January 24, 1954, p. 23.

51. Mae Ngai, email communication with the author, April 7, 2006.

52. The *New York Times* presumed it was U.S. officials who brought out tear gas and riot gear to turn back the crowd (February 2, 1954), but according to the Long Beach, California *Independent*, Mexican officials were the ones who used force to turn back their countrymen (February 28, 1954). "Fire hoses quell rush of Mexicans at Border," *New York Times*, January 28, 1954; *New York Times*, February 22, 1954; Fresno *Bee Republican*, February 22, 1954; "Battle of the Wetbacks in Full Swing on Mexican Border," Portsmouth *Herald*, February 23, 1954; "Violent Game of Foot Tag Try to Stop Mexico Border Crossing," Galveston *News*, February 24, 1954; "1158 Braceros Evade Mexico Guards, Sign up For U.S. Jobs," Long Beach, California *Independent*, February 25, 1954; Traverse City, Michigan *Record Eagle*, February 27, 1954.

53. Dick J. Reavis, *Without Documents* (New York: Condor, 1978), 39.

54. HJR 355, 83rd Cong. 2d Sess.; Mae Ngai, *Impossible Subjects: Illegal Aliens and the Making of Modern America* (Princeton, NJ: Princeton University Press, 2004); García, *Operation Wetback*, 83–84, 89.

55. According to INS reports, 540,000 illegal aliens had been apprehended and deported or left voluntarily from California alone. However, according to Juan García, the number of people deported was only 51,784. That means either half a million people left on their own; the INS added a zero; or it converted a huge number of unauthorized immigrants into legal Braceros. García, 199–200; *The Independent*, July 1, 1956, B-6; Galarza, *Merchants of Labor*, 66–71; Craig, *The Bracero Program*, 156–57.

56. García, *Operation Wetback*, 85.

57. Ibid., 184.

58. The G.I. Forum formed to advocate for Chicano civil rights when Latino G.I.s were denied burials in military cemeteries in Texas. Idar, Jr., quoted in García, *Operation Wetback*, 86.

59. García, *Operation Wetback*, 184.

60. Effland, "The Emergence of Federal Assistance Programs for Migrants," 58–68; Henry P. Guzda, "James P. Mitchell: Social Conscience of the Cabinet," *Monthly Labor Review*, August 1991.

61. Effland, "The Emergence of Federal Assistance Programs for Migrants," 61–66.

62. Ibid., 66–67, 75–76, 82; quote is on 76.

63. Ibid., 70–71.

64. *The West Indies (BWI) Temporary Alien Labor Program*, 18; Craig, *The Bracero Program*, 151–53.

65. This calculus was fanciful in sugarcane since there were no domestic workers whose wages could prevail, but the Secretary set the adverse effect wage nonetheless, and sugar growers were supposed to pay it.

66. Paul Jacobs, "An Interview with Secretary Mitchell," *The Reporter*, January 22, 1959, p. 20. Cited in Effland, "The Emergence of Federal Assistance Programs for Migrants," p. 77.

67. Effland, "The Emergence of Federal Assistance Programs for Migrants," 70–76, 144.

68. Ibid., 79.

69. Ibid., 98.

70. Ibid., 99–100, 141–47; and Majka and Majka, *Farm Workers, Agribusiness, and the State*, 165; Craig, *The Bracero Program*,165.

71. Galarza, *Strangers in our Fields*, 251–53. Ernesto Galarza's *Strangers in our Fields* was an eighty-page report to the U.S. section of the Joint U.S.–Mexico Trade Union Committee (University of Michigan, 1956).

72. Galarza, *Merchants of Labor*, 238–42.

73. Majka and Majka, *Farm Workers, Agribusiness, and the State*, 157–58.

74. John Weber, "The Shadow of the Revolution: South Texas, the Mexican Revolution, and the Evolution of Modern American Labor Relations," Ph.D. Dissertation, College of William & Mary, 2008, 377–78. My thanks to John for sharing this quote with me.

75. Majka and Majka, *Farm Workers, Agribusiness, and the State*, 161–62.

76. Effland, "The Emergence of Federal Assistance Programs for Migrants," 106–7.

77. Democrats from states using guestworkers voted 7 to 1 in favor of Holland's amendment, but Democrats from other states voted 40 to 1 against it. Effland, "The Emergence of Federal Assistance Programs for Migrants," 79–80.

78. Effland, "The Emergence of Federal Assistance Programs for Migrants," 86; Craig, *The Bracero Program*, 160.

79. Effland, "The Emergence of Federal Assistance Programs for Migrants," 97; Craig, *The Bracero Program*, 162–63.

80. Effland, "The Emergence of Federal Assistance Programs for Migrants," 137.

81. Since then, "Deportee" has been recorded by some twenty artists, including Dolly Parton, Bruce Springsteen, Nanci Griffith, and Old Crow Medicine Show. See "32 Killed in Los Gatos Airline Disaster Yesterday," *Coaling a Record*, January 29, 1948; "Chartered Immigration Service Plane Crashed," *New York Times*, January 29, 1948.

82. Craig, *The Bracero Program*, 191.

83. Ibid., 195.

84. On the Bracero Program's decline, see Galarza, *Merchants of Labor*; Majka and Majka, *Farm Workers, Agribusiness, and the State*, 1982; and Calavita, *Inside the State*.

85. Interview by the author, May 22, 2001; Craig, *The Bracero Program*, 25.

86. Philip L. Martin and David A. Martin, *The Endless Quest: Helping America's Farm Workers* (Boulder, CO: Westview Press, 1994, 1–2, 10, 17–18.

87. As of 1981, Germany had over 4.5 million resident foreigners (6–7 percent of its population), with Turks, Yugoslavs, and Italians adding up to half the total. Bendix, "On the Rights of Foreign Workers," 25.

88. Martin, *Guestworker Programs*, 11–13, 16–17.

89. The millions of Europeans who had been guestworkers could, by the 1990s, work freely where they willed. Not all guestworkers were treated alike, of course. Turks were last to gain family reunification rights in Germany and the movements of non–EU workers were essentially criminalized. Rogers Brubaker, *Citizenship and Na-*

tionhood in France and Germany (Cambridge, MA: Harvard University Press, 1992); Martin and Martin, *The Endless Quest*; Douglas Massey, Rafael Alarcón, Jorge Durand, and Humberto González, *Return to Aztlan: The Social Process of International Migration From Western Mexico* (Berkeley: University of California Press, 1987).

90. Jonathan Crush, Alan Jeeves, and David Yudelman, *South Africa's Labor Empire: A History of Black Migrancy to the Gold Mines* (Boulder, CO: Westview Press, 1991), 10–31.

CHAPTER 7: The Worst Job in the World

1. Walter S. Comrie, Deposition, *Clement Cole, et al. v. William Heidtman, Sheriff of Palm Beach County, et al.*, in the U.S. District Court in and for the Southern District of Florida, Miami Division, case no. 68-245-Civ-TC (hereafter cited as *Cole v. Heidtman*), 23 July 1969, 25–26.

2. Walter Comrie to Cindy Hahamovitch, July 15, 2008; Depositions of Adrian Russell, Felix Osbourne, Kenneth Williams, Kingston, Jamaica, 7 August 1968; Deposition of James Preston Walls, n.d., *Cole v. Heidtman*; *Miami Herald*, January 3 and 4, 1968.

3. *Miami Herald*, Palm Beach Edition, January 3, 1968, 2A and January 4, 1968, 26A.

4. Ibid. There are too many lawsuits to list.

5. Liaison Walter Comrie, interviewed by the author, Wellington, Florida, July 31, 2002.

6. Robert McGregor, the American General Consul in Kingston, May 7 Dispatch, American Embassy, Kingston to Department of State, 10 October 1965, RG 59, Central Foreign Policy Files 1964–66, Economic Labor and Manpower, Box 1305, File: Lab-Labor and Manpower J.; Foreign Service Despatch, 13 June 1965, NARA, RG 59, CDF 1960–63, Box 2479, 841F.00/3-2860.

7. Interview with the author, May 22, 2001, Washington, DC.

8. Sweeteners from corn syrup would come later. Cesar J. Ayala, *American Sugar Kingdom: The Plantation Economy of the Spanish Caribbean, 1898–1934* (Chapel Hill: University of North Carolina Press, 1999), 203–9.

9. Michael R. Hall, *Sugar and Power in the Dominican Republic: Eisenhower, Kennedy, and the Trujillos* (Westport, CT: Greenwood Press, 2000), 62; Michael Marconi Braga, "To Relieve the Misery: Sugarmill Workers and the 1933 Cuban Revolution," *Workers' Control in Latin America, 1930–1979*, edited by Jonathan Charles Brown (Chapel Hill: University of North Carolina Press, 1997), 38–39; Richard Gott, *Cuba: A New History* (New Haven, CT: Yale University Press, 2005), 129–49.

10. Committee on Agriculture, USDA, *History and Operations of the U.S. Sugar Program* (Washington, DC: GPO, 1962), 2 and 23.

11. Hall, *Sugar and Power in the Dominican Republic*, 68–69, 117.

12. The U.S. Supreme Court declared the Jones-Costigan Act unconstitutional because of the provision that funded the payouts to producers through a tax on processors. The 1937 Sugar Act got around that by taxing processors while paying growers their allotment out of the general treasury. Ahmed Abou-Bakr, "The

United States Sugar Position in the World Sugar Economy," Ph.D. Dissertation, Washington State University, 1976, p. 20–29, 42–44; *History and Operations of the U.S. Sugar Program* (Washington, DC: GPO, 1962), 2 and 23; David E. Price, "The Politics of Sugar," *The Review of Politics* 33, 1 (January 1971), 213; Hall, *Sugar and Power in the Dominican Republic*, 42; Kathleen Mapes, *Sweet Tyranny: Migrant Labor, Industrial Agriculture, and Imperial Politics* (Urbana: University of Illinois Press, 2009), 186–214.

13. Quoted in Hall, *Sugar and Power in the Dominican Republic*, 76.

14. U.S. Sugar and Fellsmere only began planting sugar in 1931. Fellsmere, which started small, got smaller still because of a series of crop failures. Both companies were forced to keep the same acreage until World War II when production quotas were lifted. Gail Marjorie Hollander, "Raising Cane in the Glades: Regional Development and Agroenvironmental Conflict in South Florida" (Ph.D. Dissertation, University of Iowa, 1999), 149–50; J. Carlyle Sitterson, *Sugar Country* (Louisville: University of Kentucky Press, 1953), 376–77.

15. United States Sugar Corporation booklet, "Raising Cane in the Glades," cited in Hollander, "Raising Cane in the Glades," 160–61.

16. Hollander, "Raising Cane in the Glades," 161, 177–78. For a more detailed explanation, see Committee on Agriculture, *History and Operations of the U.S. Sugar Program*, 1962, 23.

17. *History and Operations of the U.S. Sugar Program*, 24; Thomas E. Skidmore and Peter H. Smith, *Modern Latin America Modern Latin America*, 6th ed. (New York: Oxford University Press, 2004), 275–76.

18. George H. Salley, *A History of the Florida Sugar Industry* (Clewiston, FL: Sugar Cane League, 1984), 23–24, 27.

19. The Glades County Sugar Growers Cooperative produced 12,543 tons in 1962 and 48,200 tons just four years later. Salley, *History of the Florida Sugar Industry*, 26.

20. Marie Brenner, "In the Kingdom of Big Sugar," *Vanity Fair* (February 2001), 171–72.

21. Ibid.

22. Ibid., 171–73.

23. Ibid., 114–21, 172.

24. Humberto R. Garcia-Muniz, "*The South Porto Rico Sugar Company: The History of a United States Multinational Corporation in Puerto Rico and the Dominican Republic, 1900—1921*," Ph.D. Dissertation, Columbia University, 1997, abstract; Gordon Patterson, "Raising Cane and Refining Sugar: Florida Crystals and the Fame of Fellsmere," *Florida Historical Quarterly* 75, 4 (Spring 1997), 408–28.

25. Pawley is described in Warren Hinckle and William Turner's *The Fish Is Red* as a CIA conduit and was possibly involved in the run-up to the Bay of Pigs invasion, 33, 44–45, 131, 133, 168, 170–73. Douglas Valentine describes him as a privateer. *The Strength of the Wolf: The Secret History of America's War on Drugs* (New York: Verso, 2004), 78; Don Bohning, *The Castro Obsession: U.S. Covert Operations Against Cuba, 1959–1965* (Washington, DC: Brassey's, 2005), 5.

26. Jim Hougan, *Spooks: The Haunting of America—The Private Use of Secret Agents* (New York: William Morrow, 1978), 340–41; Salley, *History of the Florida Sugar Industry*, 27.

27. 114 *Congressional Record* 6642 (daily edition, 18 July 1968), cited in Kent Spriggs, "Access of Visitors to Labor Camps on Privately Owned Property," *University of Florida Law Review* 21, 295 (1968–1969), 306, n. 60; Garcia-Muniz, "*The South Porto Rico Sugar Company,*" abstract; Paul Monaco, *The Sixties: 1960–1969* (Berkeley: University of California Press), 31; Brenner, "In the Kingdom of Big Sugar," 173; Ruck, *The Tropic of Baseball: Baseball in the Dominican Republic* (Lincoln: University of Nebraska Press), 178–80; Steven M. Davis, *Everglades: the Ecosystem and its Restoration* (Boca Raton, FL: CRC Press, 1994), 101; Alan Riding, *New York Times*, June 24, 1975, 47; Juan de Onis, *New York Times*, February 7, 1977, 2.

28. Garcia-Muniz, "The South Porto Rico Sugar Company," abstract; Monaco, *The Sixties*, 2001: 31; Brenner, "In the Kingdom of Big Sugar," 171–73; Ruck, *The Tropic of Baseball*, 178–180; Davis, *Everglades*, 101; Riding, *New York Times*, June 24, 1975, 47; de Onis, *New York Times*, February 7, 1977, 2.

29. Hollander, *Raising Cane*, 180–86; Abou-Bakr, "The United States Sugar Position in the World Sugar Economy," 46, 99; McCoy and Wood, "Caribbean Workers in the Florida Sugar Cane Industry," 3; Salley, *A History of the Florida Sugar Industry*, Appendix E, 47–78.

30. Comrie's assertions were confirmed a few years later by a Wage and Hour study, whose publication was squelched under pressure from the sugar industry. Its publication was eventually made mandatory by a federal judge. U.S. Department of Labor, 1975: "Wage Survey for 1973–74 South Florida Sugar Harvest," Reprinted as Appendix IV, Department of Labor, Employment Standards Administration (Washington, DC: U.S. GPO, 1974).

31. Interview by author, July 31, 2002, Wellington, Florida; 4 May 1964, Walter Comrie to Harold Edwards, chief liaison. Copy in author's possession.

32. Ticket writers generally refused to expose this system when it still functioned, but now that sugarcane harvesting has been mechanized in Florida, several former ticket writers have verified under oath that they participated in wage fraud. See, for example, Deposition of Leon Luke, who worked as a ticket writer in the 1990s, 12 January 2006, *Alphonso Michaels, et al. v. Osceola Farms Company*, U.S. District Court, Southern District of Florida, West Palm Beach Division, Case No. 05-80825-CI-COHN/SNOW.

33. Comrie interview, July 31, 2002; Walter Comrie to Harold Edwards, chief liaison, 4 May 1964, copy in author's possession; Kramer, *The Offshores*, 41–51; U.S. Department of Labor, "Wage Survey for 1973–74," 97.

34. Fred C. Sikes to Harold F. Edwards, 15 November 1963 and Walter Comrie to Harold Edwards, 20 November 1963, Walter Comrie's files, both in author's possession.

35. Kramer, *The Offshores*, 10, 14.

36. Dohoney, "The Wages of Cane," 81; "Farm Labor: Wirtz Shocked By Camps," *Los Angeles Times*, March 28, 1965, J5.

37. *Miami Herald*, April 3, 1965, 15A.

38. The new regulations are in 29 Fed. Reg. 19, 101, 1964. Wirtz's press release is reprinted in U.S. Department of Labor, Year of Transition: Seasonal Farm Labor 1965, Appendix H at 4, 1965; Kramer, *The Offshores*, 3–4; H. Michael Semler, "Overview: The H-2 Program. Aliens in the Orchard: The Admission

of Foreign Contract Laborers for Temporary Work in U.S. Agriculture," *Yale Law & Policy Review* 1, 2 (Spring 1983): 195; Josh DeWind, Tom Seidl, and Janet Shenk, "Caribbean Migration: Contract Labor in U.S. Agriculture," *NACLA Report on the Americas* 11, 8 (November–December 1977), 26; Dohoney, "The Wages of Cane," 56.

39. The rules also imposed new timing for recruitment. Growers could not request foreign workers until sixty days before they would be needed. Employers had been obtaining certification months in advance, knowing that domestic migrants would not commit that early. The new regulations required that state agencies not process a request more than sixty days nor less than thirty days prior to the date of need, and then review it fifteen days prior to need, so employers couldn't use the certification process to turn away domestic labor. Kramer, *The Offshores*, 3–4; Semler, "Overview," 195; DeWind, Seidl, and Shenk, "Caribbean Migrants," 26. The new regulations are in 29 Fed. Reg. 19, 101, 1964. Wirtz's press release is reprinted in U.S. Department of Labor, *Year of Transition: Seasonal Farm Labor 1965*, Appendix H at 4, 1965; Dohoney, "The Wages of Cane," 56.

40. Wirtz expected President Johnson to call him off, since Johnson had had Braceros on his own farm and needed the support of powerful rural Democrats who supported the program, but Johnson told him he was to do as he saw fit. Willard Wirtz, interview by the author, May 22, 2001, Washington, DC.

41. Kramer, *The Offshores*, 9; DeWind, Seidl, and Shenk, "Caribbean Migrants," 12.

42. Semler, "Overview," 195–97; Senate Committee on Agriculture, Nutrition, and Forestry, Hearings on Importation of Foreign Ag. Labor, 89th Congress, 1st session, January 1965, 15–16.

43. *Fort Pierce News Tribune*, February 23, 1965; "Background Information on Farm Labor," U.S. Department of Labor, 19 March 1965, Willard Wirtz Papers, Case Files, Box 154, John F. Kennedy Library, Boston, MA; Wirtz interview.

44. W. Willard Wirtz, Memorandum to the President, 10 March 1965, White House Central Files, Subject Files, LA5, Box 17, Folder: "Migratory-Seasonal Labor, 22 November 1963–2 June 1965," John F. Kennedy Library, Boston, MA.

45. "Wirtz Florida View Each Other," *St. Petersburg Times*, April 15, 1965, "Wirtz Meets with State Workers, Growers," *St. Petersburg Times*, April 16, 1965.

46. Wirtz interview.

47. Wirtz interview.

48. 13 March 1965, Dispatch A-235 and 5 May 1965, Dispatch A-278, NARA RG 59, Central Foreign Policy Files, 1964–66, POL 2 General Reports and Stats, Box 2372, File: POL 2-3 Politico-Economic JAM.

49. Foreign Service Despatch, 13 June 1961, NARA, RG 59, CDF 1960-63, Box 2479, 841F.00/3-2860.

50. Lydia Lindsey, "A Reexamination of the Significance of the MacCarran-Walters Act on Post–World War II Indian Migration to Britain—An Expository Note," *Journal of Caribbean Studies* 10, 3 (Summer–Fall 1995): 51.

51. *An Act to amend the Immigration and Nationality Act, and for other purposes*, H.R. 2580; Pub.L. 89-236; 79 Stat. 911, 89th Congress; 3 October 1965.

52. Lindsey, "A Reexamination of the Significance of the MacCarran-Walters Act," 195; American Embassy, Kingston to Department of State, October 10,

1965, RG 59, Central Foreign Policy Files 1964–66, Economic Labor and Manpower, Box 1305, File: Lab-Labor and Manpower J.; Foreign Service Despatch, 13 June 1961, NARA, RG 59, CDF 1960–63, Box 2479, 841F.00/3-2860; Despatch A238, American Embassy, Kingston to Department of States, 22 April 1966, RG 59, Central Foreign Policy Files 1964–66, Economic Labor and Manpower, Box 1305; Dispatch A-30, RG 59, Central Foreign Policy Pol. Files, 1967–1969, Politics and Defense, Box 2241, File Political Affairs and Relations, JAM.

53. 13 March 1965, Dispatch A-235 and 5 May 1965, Dispatch A-278, NARA RG 59, Central Foreign Policy Files, 1964–66, POL 2 General Reports and Stats, Box 2372, File: POL 2-3 Politico-Economic JAM.

54. Kramer, *The Offshores*, 81. See also 11 March 1966, RG Central Foreign Policy Files, 1964–66 POL 2 General Reports and States, Box 1305, File LAB-LABOR & MANPOWER; Dispatch A-190, File: POL 2-3 Politico-Economic JAM, Box 2372, RG 59, Central Foreign Policy Files, 1964–66, POL 2 General Reports and Stats.

55. Ibid.

56. 11 March 1966, RG Central Foreign Policy Files, 1964–66 POL 2 General Reports and States, Box 1305, File LAB-LABOR & MANPOWER; Dispatch A-190, File: POL 2-3 Politico-Economic JAM, Box 2372, RG 59, Central Foreign Policy Files, 1964–66, POL 2 General Reports and Stats.

57. 1978 report cited in Lydia Lindsey, "A Reexamination of the Significance of the MacCarran-Walters Act," 48.

58. Dead House interview.

59. Interviewed by Jarrett Brown, June 2004, Effort, Clarendon Parish, Jamaica.

60. Jarrett Brown, interviewed by the author, Effort, Clarendon Parish, Jamaica, January 26, 2003.

61. 1978 report cited in Lindsey, "A Reexamination of the Significance of the MacCarran-Walters Act," 48.

62. Average cutters and slow men could expect to make less than the minimum wage on a regular basis. Kramer, *The Offshores*, 48; Brenner, "In the Kingdom of Big Sugar," 174; Comrie interview, July 3, 2002.

63. Dead House interview.

64. Porter interview.

65. Alec Wilkinson, *Big Sugar: Seasons in the Cane Fields of Florida* (New York: Knopf, 1989), 18.

66. Clifford Platt, interviewed by Jarrett Brown, Effort, Clarendon Parish, Jamaica, June 2004.

67. Though based on the "adverse effect wage" principle, sugarcane-cutting wages should have been higher than wages for domestic citrus harvesters, according to WICLO statistics on workers employed by the Florida Fruit and Vegetable Association. In 1966, the "lowest hourly wage in citrus," which was heavy work but much less dangerous, "was as high as the top hourly wage for cutting sugar cane." USDA, Economic Research Service, *Sugar Policy Options for the United States*, Agricultural Economic Report No. 351, 1977, 33–34, cited in DeWind, Seidl, and Shenk, "Caribbean Migration," 1977: 15; Kramer, *The Offshores*, 45–51.

68. Harakas, "Allegations Plague Foreign Worker Program," *Sun-Sentinel*, November 30, 1986; See also Tim O'Meilia, *Palm Beach Post*, Part 2 of 2, December 29, 1986.

69. "Ronald," interviewed by Stephanie Black, Florida, c. 1986, in author's possession; Kramer, *The Offshores*, 48–49; Beth McLeod, "Cutters Shake Hand that Feeds," *Palm Beach Post*, December 29, 1986.

70. Interviewed by author, Chambersburg, PA, April 12, 2000 [name changed to protect identity].

71. According to Migrant Legal Justice Project attorney, Greg Schell, many Florida growers would have avoided hiring small islanders, if they could have, but they were pressured by the State Department to accept a small number of men from other islands in the British Caribbean that also suffered from high unemployment. Greg Schell, interview by the author, Belle Glade, Florida, July 16, 1994; Dohoney, "Wages of Cane," 113.

72. Morrison interview.

73. Kramer, *The Offshores*, 44–51, 53.

74. Porter interview.

75. Comrie said the companies would not tolerate contradiction and would send home any worker who complained. He attended a number of grievance hearings for individual workers, at which the company would always present evidence that a complaining worker was either a trouble-maker or unproductive (i.e., requiring build-up pay). The best the liaison officer might do was to get the worker transferred to another company. Summary of interview with Walter Comrie, memorandum from Sarah Cleveland to Bruce Goldstein et al., September 19, 1996. Files of Edward Tuddenham in author's possession.

76. Morrison interview.

77. Porter interview.

78. Kramer, *The Offshores*, 39, 51.

79. Dead House interview.

80. Thanks to Alex Lichtenstein for noting that parallel.

81. Dead House interview.

82. *St. Petersburg Times*, November 25, 1979.

83. *St. Petersburg Times*, December 11, 1986, 6A.

84. "Claudette," interview by Stephanie Black, Guystown, Jamaica, c. 1986.

85. Karl Vick, "Bittersweet Harvest," *St. Petersburg Times*, November 21, 1993, A1.

86. Letter transcribed by Stephanie Black, in author's possession, c. 1986.

87. Terry L. McCoy and Charles H. Wood, "Migration, Remittances and Development: A Study of Caribbean Cane Cutters in Florida," *International Migration Review* 19 (1985), 260.

88. McLeod, "Cutters Shake Hand that Feeds," 1A and 4A; Samuel Brown [name changed on request] interviewed by the author and Lindsey Allen, Effort, Clarendon Parish, Jamaica, July 26, 2003.

89. On the question of how remittances were spent, see David Craig Griffith, "The Promise of a Country: the Impact of Seasonal U.S. Migration on the Jamai-

can Peasantry" (University of Florida, Ph.D. Dissertation, 1983). Dead House interview; McCoy and Wood, "Migration, Remittances and Development," 270–71.

90. Tim O'Meilia, "'It was the hardest work I have ever done in my life,'" *Palm Beach Post*, December 28, 1986.

91. David C. Griffith, "Women, Remittances, and Reproduction," *American Ethnologist* 12, 4 (November 1985), 678; McCoy and Wood, "Caribbean Workers in the Florida Sugar Cane Industry."

92. To Clifford, Stephanie Black files, in author's possession, n.d., c. 1987.

93. My emphasis. Letter transcribed by Stephanie Black, in author's possession, n.d., c. 1987.

94. Letter transcribed by Stephanie Black, in author's possession, n.d., [1986].

95. Brenner, "In the Kingdom of Big Sugar," 174.

96. Dead House interview.

97. "Ronald," interviewed by Stephanie Black, no date, copy in possession of the author.

98. "Anthony," interview by Stephanie Black, Guystown, Jamaica, c. 1986.

99. "Anthony," interviewed by Stephanie Black, c. 1986, transcript in author's possession.

100. O'Meilia, "'It was the hardest work I have ever done in my life,'"; Margo Harakas, "Allegations Plague Foreign Worker Program," *Sun-Sentinel*, November 30, 1986.

101. Bryan Green interview.

102. Josh Stone interview.

103. No name, interview by Stephanie Black, Jamaica, c. 1986; "Dudley," interview by Stephanie Black, Jamaica, c. 1986; Dead House interview.

104. "Winston," interview by Stephanie Black, c. late 1980s.

105. McLeod, "Cutters Shake Hand that Feeds," 1A and 4A.

106. Dead House interview; Jarrett Brown interview; according to McCoy and Wood, 60 percent of guestworkers brought back radios, televisions, and tape recorders. McCoy and Wood, "Migration, Remittances and Development," 261.

107. Samuel Brown (name changed at his request) interviewed by Cindy Hahamovitch and Lindsey Allen, Effort, Clarendon Parish, Jamaica, July 26, 2003.

108. "Winston," interviewed by Stephanie Black, Jamaica, c. late 1980s.

109. McCoy and Wood found that wives and children farmed during men's absence in 42 percent of cases, other family members in 37 percent of cases. Friends and paid workers in 14 percent of cases. No one in the remaining cases. McCoy and Wood, "Caribbean Workers in the Florida Sugar Cane Industry," 38.

110. Mrs. Patricia Johnson, Waterford District, Guys Hill PO, St. Mary, Jamaica, transcribed by Stephanie Black, in author's possession, c. 1986.

111. Letters transcribed by Stephanie Black, in author's possession, c. 1986.

112. Anthony to Mrs. Christine Bailey, Stephanie Black files, in author's possession, n.d. [1987].

113. "Reuben," interviewed by Stephanie Black, Haitian Center, Florida, c. 1986, transcript in author's possession.

114. Edwards and Morrison quoted in Kramer, *The Offshores*, 60–61.

115. Reid, "U.S.–Jamaica Relations," 224.

116. Jarrett Brown interview.

117. "Ronald," interviewed by Stephanie Black, no date, copy in possession of the author.

118. George Porter interview.

119. Deposition of Walter Comrie, 23 July 1969, *Cole v. Heidtman*.

120. Depositions of Kenneth Williams and James Preston Walls, 1969, *Cole v. Heidtman*.

121. *Miami Herald*, January 4, 1968; Depositions of Irving Francis and Kenneth Williams, Kingston, Jamaica, 7 August 1968 and Deposition of William B. Darden, 27 February 1970, *Cole v. Heidtman*.

122. Deposition of Irving Francis, *Cole V. Heidtman*.

123. Joseph Segor interview, December 10, 1999.

124. Ibid.; Kent Spriggs, telephone interview by the author, July 16, 2007.

125. Gibbons sat on the congressional committee that had jurisdiction over the OEO. For a discussion of the battle over South Florida Migrant Legal Services (later Florida Rural)'s creation, see Earl Johnson, Jr., *Justice and Reform: The Formative Years of the OEO: Legal Services Program* (New York: Russell Sage, 1974), 93; and Kris Shepard, *Rationing Justice: Poverty Lawyers and Poor People in the Deep South* (Baton Rouge: Louisiana State University Press, 2007), 36.

126. Joseph Segor interview, December 10, 1999.

127. Joseph Segor interview; "Seasons in the Sun: A Preliminary Study of the Seasonal Farmworker in the South Florida Setting," and "Farmworker Legal Problems," Hearings before the Subcommittee on Migratory Labor of the Committee on Labor and Public Welfare, U.S. Senate, 91st Congress, 1st and 2nd Sessions on Farmworker Legal Programs, 7 August 1969, Part 4-A (Washington, DC: U.S. GPO, 1970); 1416–1516 and appendix.

128. Kent Spriggs, telephone interview with the author, July 16, 2007; "The Meranda Company and Holding Center—Miami, Florida," July 9, 1974, in author's possession.

129. Joseph Segor interview; Kent Spriggs interview.

130. Joseph Segor interview.

131. Joseph Segor interview, December 10, 1999.

132. *Miami Herald*, January 4, 1968; Depositions of Irving Francis, Kenneth Williams, and William B. Darden, *Cole v. Heidtman*.

133. This information comes from an investigative report written by Howard A. Glickstein, General Counsel for the U.S. Commission on Civil Rights, which was made later that month. Glickstein talked to the Public Defender, prosecutors, and reviewed the elusive film of the events in the courtyard, but did not share it with Legal Services attorneys. Legal Services knew about the film—Bradley might have seen a deputy filming the day of the arrests—but Segor never knew of Glickstein's report, until I showed it to him in 2007. Glickstein to William L. Taylor, Staff Director, U.S. Commission on Civil Rights, Memorandum, 22 January 1968, Migrant Farmworker Justice Project, Sugar Training, In author's possession.

134. *Miami Herald*, January 4, 1968; Depositions of Irving Francis, Kenneth Williams, and William B. Darden, *Cole v. Heidtman*.

135. Joseph Segor interview, December 10, 1999.

136. Depositions of James Preston Walls, 1969, Kenneth Williams, 7 August 1968, and Felix Osbourne, n.d., *Cole v. Heidtman*; *Miami Herald*, January 3 and 4, 1968.

137. Joseph Segor interviews, December 10, 1999 and August 4, 2007.

138. Segor had left Florida Rural by this time, but these men obviously didn't know that. They were likely replying to appeals that had come much earlier when Segor still hoped to bring the case to trial. H. Cross, Charles Town, St. Ann's Bay PO, to Joseph Segor, South Florida Migrant Legal Services, 4 February 1970, Migrant Farmworker Justice Project Files, *Cole v. Heidtman*—Witness Arrangements, in author's possession.

139. Wilford Reid, 59 Young Street, Spanish Town, Jamaica, 23 March 1970, and 4 February 1970, to Joseph Segor, South Florida Migrant Legal Services, 4 February 1970, Migrant Farmworker Justice Project Files, Cole v. Heidtman-Witness Arrangements, in author's possession.

140. Joe Segor interview, December 10, 1999.

141. Ibid.

142. According to Segor, the GAO came at the behest of Senator Allen Ellender of Louisiana, who was chairman of the Senate Agriculture Committee and the staunchest supporter of the nation's sugar interests. Florida Rural and SFMLS before it received OEO grants totaling $1.3 million between 1967 and 1970. General Accounting Office Audit of the Office of Economic Opportunity Grant to Florida Rural Legal Services, Inc., 18 November 1971, 090745, p. 1, http://archive.gao.gov/f0102/090745.pdf.

143. Segor stayed on for a few more months with the help of private funds that he raised, but in 1969, he set up a separate entity called Migrant Services Corporation, which he ran until 1974, when he was invited to become an appellate lawyer in the firm of Joe Kaplan. Joseph Segor, interview by the author, December 10, 1999 and August 4, 2007, Miami, Florida; Carl W. Turner to Dan Bradley, OEO, Legal Services Division, Atlanta Georgia, 19 August 1970, Migrant Farmworker Justice Project Files, *Cole v. Heidtman*, File: Correspondence, Vol. 3, Misc.

144. Joe Segor, email communication, July 27, 2007.

145. Charles Town, St. Ann's Bay PO, Jamaica, 15 August 1972, to Joseph Segor, South Florida Migrant Legal Services, 4 February 1970, Migrant Farmworker Justice Project Files, *Cole v. Heidtman*—Witness Arrangements, in author's possession.

146. 12 June 1972, Frankfield PO, Migrant Farmworker Justice Project.

Chapter 8: Takin' It to the Courts

1. Joseph A. Califano, Jr., *Inside: A Public and Private Life* (Cambridge, MA: Perseus Book Group, 2004), 211–13.

2. T. Michael Foster, Assistant Director, Florida Migrant Legal Services Program and "Seasons in the Sun: A Preliminary Study of the Seasonal Farmworker

in the South Florida Setting," Hearings before the Subcommittee on Migratory Labor of the Committee on Labor and Public Welfare, U.S. Senate, 91st Congress, 1st and 2nd Sessions on Farmworker Legal Programs, 7 August 1969, Part 4-A (Washington, DC: U.S. GPO, 1970), 1190 and appendix.

3. Greg Schell, interview by the author, July 14, 1994, Belle Glade, Florida; and Greg Schell, phone interview by the author, July 4, 2007.

4. *Miami Herald*, 11 January 1967, 22A. On the SSOC, see Greg L. Michel, *Struggle for a Better South: The Southern Student Organizing Committee, 1964–1969* (New York: Palgrave-MacMillan, 2004), 154–55.

5. Rudolfo (Rudy) Juarez, Hearings before the Subcommittee on Migratory Labor of the Committee on Labor and Public Welfare, U.S. Senate, 91st Congress, 1st and 2nd Sessions, "Who is Responsible," 21 July 1970, Part 8-B (Washington, DC: U.S. GPO, 1970), 5484–5485 (hereafter cited as "Who is Responsible").

6. Patrick Zier, "Farm Worker Progress Report: 'We've Opened Their Eyes to Organization'," Florida Christian Migrant Ministry Papers, Box 6, Folder [?], Walter Reuther Library, Wayne State University, Detroit, Michigan (hereafter cited as Florida Christian Migrant Ministry Papers); (Lakeland, FL) *Ledger View*, June 6, 1971.

7. Rene Perez Rosenbaum, "Unionization of Tomato Field Workers in Northwest Ohio, 1967–1969," *Labor History* 35, 3 (Summer 1994), 330.

8. Florida Christian Migrant Ministry Papers, Box 6, Folder: FCMM, Executive Committee, 1967–68 6–4.

9. Rosenbaum, "Unionization of Tomato Field Workers," 330; Greg Schell, "Farmworker Exceptionalism under the Law: How the Legal System Contributes to Farmworker Poverty and Powerlessness," 139–166, in *The Human Cost of Food: Farmworkers' Lives, Labor, and Advocacy*, edited by Charles D. Thompson, Jr., and Melinda F. Wiggins (Austin: University of Texas Press, 2002), 146–47; Karl Vick, "Bittersweet Harvest," *St. Petersburg Times*, November 21, 1993, A:1; 1965 Senate Subcommittee on Migratory Labor Report, 4–5, quoted in Florida Christian Migrant Ministry Papers, Box 7, Folder 7–8.

10. Florida Christian Migrant Ministry Papers, Box 7, Folder 7–8.

11. Kent Spriggs, "Access of Visitors to Labor Camps on Privately Owned Property," *University of Florida Law Review* 21, 295 (1968–1969): 303, n. 40.

12. "Farmworker Legal Problems," 7 August 1969, Hearings before the Subcommittee on Migratory Labor of the Committee on Labor and Public Welfare, U.S. Senate, 91st Congress, 1st and 2nd Sessions, Part 8-B (Washington, DC: U.S. GPO, 1970), 969 and 1192, 5481; "Declare Disaster in Seven Counties, Kirk Asks U.S.," *Miami Herald*, April 2, 1970.

13. Earl DeHart, "Over 7,000 Migrants Seek Aid," *Miami Herald*, April 1, 1970.

14. "Who is Responsible," 5486–5487; T. Michael Foster, Assistant Director, Florida Migrant Legal Services Program and "Seasons in the Sun: A Preliminary Study of the Seasonal Farmworker in the South Florida Setting," Hearings before the Subcommittee on Migratory Labor of the Committee on Labor and Public Welfare, U.S. Senate, 91st Congress, 1st and 2nd Sessions on Farmworker Legal Programs, 7 August 1969, Part 4-A (Washington, DC: U.S. GPO, 1970), 1201.

15. Brennan was best known for his virulent opposition to affirmative action and his help in instigating the New York City "hard hat riot" during which construction workers pummeled student anti-war demonstrators.

16. Senator Walter Mondale and Rudolfo (Rudy) Juarez, "Who is Responsible," 5486–5487.

17. Ronald Goldfarb, *Migrant Farmworkers: A Caste of Despair* (Ames: University of Iowa, 1981), 67–68.

18. The committee finally settled on a former prosecutor named Ronald Goldfarb, who had worked for the Justice Department's Organized Crime and Racketeering Division. Seven years after that, Goldfarb published *Migrant Farmworkers: A Caste of Despair*, a scathing indictment of the Labor Department's lack of action on behalf of migrant farmworkers. Goldfarb, *Migrant Farmworkers*, 113; *NAACP Western Region v. Brennan et al.*

19. *New York Times*, March 14, 1971.

20. Califano, Jr., *Inside: A Public and Private Life*, 211–13; "NBC White Paper: Migrant," State Archives of Florida.

21. 28 January 1971 talk by W. M. (Bill) Kelly, of the Coca Cola Foods Division re: Coke's Agricultural Labor Project, Florida Christian Migrant Ministry Papers, Box 5, Folder 5-13 (Migrant Labor, Research, Coca Cola, 1971).

22. "Chavez in Tampa to Help Migrants," *Sarasota Herald-Tribune*, September 12, 1971, 7B.

23. The only thing omitted from the contract was a continuation clause which would have ensured that the union contract would be transferred to a new owner if the company were sold. Eventually, Coca Cola sold off Minute Maid, effectively terminating the deal. "A Day Without Sunshine," film by Robert Thurber, 1976.

24. *Playground Daily News*, November 2, 1970, p. 10.

25. Ken Lawrence, "Farmworkers Sign First Florida Contract While Talisman Strike Continues," *Southern Patriot* (published by the Southern Conference Educational Fund), 30, 3 (27 March 1972), 1 and 3.

26. Ibid.

27. Ibid.

28. The Teamsters' decision to honor the picket line is particularly ironic since the UFW and Teamsters were mortal enemies in California. *Florida Times-Union*, January 26, 1972; George H. Salley, *History of the Florida Sugar Industry* (c. 1984), 33.

29. *Judith Ann Petersen, Et al., Plaintiffs-Appellants, v. Talisman Sugar Corporation, et al.*, Defendants-Appellees, No. 72-2057, United States Court of Appeals for the Fifth Circuit, 478 F.2d 73; 1973 U.S. App. LEXIS 10128; 84 L.R.R.M. 2061; 72 Lab. Cas. (CCH), 3 May 1973.

30. "Pawley: Castroites Are Picketing," *Miami Herald*, March 9, 1972.

31. By this time, Segor had created the Migrant Services Organization, a separate legal entity that allowed him to work with the UFW without running afoul of Florida Rurals' constraints. "Jail term asked in union 'pressure,'" *Miami Herald*, January 13, 1972; "Demonstrate against curbs on farmworkers," *The Voice*, May 26, 1972.

32. "Chavez Offers UFW Aid to Sugar Cane Cutters," *Miami Herald*, November 20, 1972, 32-A.

33. U.S. District Court, South District of Florida, *Judith Ann Petersen, et al. vs. Talisman Sugar Corp et al.*, No 72-198-Civ-CF.

34. The local judge dismissed the charges on the grounds that "to prevent their entry might lead to a condition where employees are subjected to a form of involuntary servitude, wherein the masters decide who may communicate with the servants." *State v. Petersen, et al.*, Case No. 72M-8209, Small claims-Magistrate Court, Criminal Division, in and for Palm Beach, Florida.

35. *Petersen v. Talisman*.

36. Eliseo Medina to John Boy, President, U.S. Sugar Corporation, 9 November 1972, Box 25, Folder: Sugar-General Correspondence and Information, UFW Florida Division Papers.

37. *Union News*, October 12, 1972, vol. 2, No. 1. United Farm Workers Florida Division, Box 5, Walter Reuther Library, Wayne State University, Detroit, Michigan.

38. Minutes of meeting on legal pad paper, Box 25, Folder: General Info., Papers of the United Farm Workers Florida Division, Walter Reuther Library, Wayne State University, Detroit, Michigan (hereafter cited as Papers of the United Farm Workers Florida Division).

39. Box 25, Folder: Sugar—General Information 1/73 and Medina to Cesar Chavez, 21 July 1972 Box 16, Folder: U.S. Sugar, Papers of the United Farm Workers Florida Division.

40. Unidentified testimony, Box 25, Folder: Sugar—General Information 1/73, Papers of the United Farm Workers Florida Division.

41. The case was *Kleindist v. Department of Labor*.

42. *Naples Daily News*, November 19, 1972, 9B; "The Florida Rural Legal Services, Inc. & The B.W.I. Farm Worker Program," Comrie's Personal Memoir, 24 January 1979, in the author's possession; Joe Segor interview, August 4, 2007.

43. Eliseo Medina to Antonio Oredain, UFW office in McAllen, 12 October 1972, Folder: Sugar—General Information, Box 25, United Farm Workers Florida Division Papers.

44. Goldfarb, *Migrant Farm Workers*, 136.

45. *Naples Daily News*, November 19, 1972, 9B.

46. Box 25, Folder: Sugar—General Information 1/73, Papers of the United Farm Workers Florida Division.

47. Fred C. Sikes, Vice President, United States Sugar Corporation, to William U. Norwood, Jr., Regional Manpower Administrator, U.S. Department of Labor, 17 October 1972, files of David L. Gorman, Attorney at Law, in author's possession.

48. Walter Comrie, "Underpay Denied by Sugar Firms," 3 May 1974, in author's possession.

49. David Gorman, interview by the author, 17 April 2000, North Palm Beach, Florida.

50. *Naples Daily News*, November 19, 1972, 9B.

51. Unidentified testimony, Folder: Sugar—General Information 1/73, Box 25, United Farm Workers Florida Division Papers.

52. Steven Petrow, "Sugar Cane Slavery," *Southern Exposure* 8, 4 (Winter 1980), 20–21.

53. Jo Marie Dohoney, "The Wages of Cane: A Study of Temporary Labor Importation in the U.S. and the Case of West Indian Cane Workers in Florida" (M.A. Thesis, Michigan State University), 102.

54. Folder: Sugar—General Information, Box 25, United Farm Workers Florida Division Papers.

55. Folder: Sugar—General Information, Box 25, United Farm Workers Florida Division Papers.

56. Segor, August 4, 2007; *News Tribune*, April 3, 1973, 2; *Playground Daily News*, March 9, 1973, 2A; *Naples Daily News*, March 8, 1973, 3A.

57. "Wage Survey for 1973–1974 South Florida Sugar Harvest" was published as part of the Oversight Hearing on Department of Labor Certification of the Use of Offshore Labor, Hearing before the Subcommittee on Agricultural Labor of the Committee on Education and Labor, House of Representatives, 94th Congress, 1st Session, Washington, DC, 20 March 1975 (Washington, DC: GPO, 1975), hereafter cited as "Sugarman Report," 201, 250, 253.

58. DeWind et al., "Caribbean Migration," 16.

59. Comrie alleged that Chief Liaison Harold Edward warned G&W of the impending inspections. Walter Comrie, "Atlantic Sugar Strike . . ." January25–27, 1973, author's possession; Dohoney, "The Wages of Cane," 98–99; Marie Brenner, "In the Kingdom of Big Sugar," *Vanity Fair*, February 2001, 14–15 (online version; http://www.mariebrenner.com/PDF/KingdomOfBigSugar.pdf; accessed 15 July 2009). "Sugarman Report," 201, 250, 253.

60. *Clewiston News*, February 15, 1973.

61. Sugarman later became the DOL's chief of the Wage and Hour Division's Branch of Farm Labor Programs, which oversaw the enforcement of the Migrant and Seasonal Agricultural Worker Protection Act. *Palm Beach Post*, October 19, 1986.

62. Walter Comrie, "Underpay Denied by Sugar Firms," 3 May 1974, in author's possession.

63. Per capita income was $13 a week in U.S. dollars, compared to the average American's $124. Beth McLeod, *Palm Beach Post-Times*, part 1 of 2, 28 December 1986; Laurie Gunst, *Born Fi' Dead* (New York: Macmillan, 1996), xvii–xviii; U.S. Census Bureau, Current Population Survey, United States Department of Labor, Bureau of Labor Statistics, Washington, DC: GPO, 1978; Anthony Payne and Paul Sutton, *Charting Caribbean Development* (Gainesville: University Press of Florida, 2001), 64–87.

64. Beth McLeod, "Jamaican Poverty Helps U.S. Growers Prosper," *Palm Beach Post-Times*, part 1 of 2, 28 December 1986.

65. Steven Petrow, "Sugar Cane Slavery," *Southern Exposure* 8, 4 (Winter 1980), 72–76.

66. Michael Manley, interviewed by Stephanie Black, Kingston, Jamaica, n.d., c. 1986, in author's possession, 2 (hereafter cited as "Manley interview").

67. Ibid., 4.

68. Ibid.

69. The ambassador was Douglas V. Fletcher. "I Would Live Here," *Palm Beach Post*, January 24, 1974, C1.

70. William E. Gibson, "Jamaica Sees U.S. Jobs as Political Plum, *Fort Lauderdale Sun Sentinel*, December 3, 1986.

71. Walter Comrie, "A Strange Union," unpublished memoir, 22 January 1977, in author's possession.

72. The case was handled by Migrant Legal Action in Washington, DC. See *John Doe I, et al., Plaintiffs v. William J. Usery, et al., Defendants*, No. 75-190, U.S. District Court for the District of Columbia, 12 January 1975.

73. Cesar E. Chavez to Awilda Vega, Homestead AFB, 20 May 1973, United Farm Workers Florida Division Papers, Box 25, Folder: Correspondence General 1972–74.

74. His emphasis. Walter Comrie, "A Strange Union," unpublished memoir, 22 January 1977, in author's possession.

75. *Palm Beach Post*, May 23, 1974.

76. Greg Schell, interviewed by the author, July 14, 1994, Belle Glade, Florida.

77. Ibid., 17; Sara Cleveland, interview by the author, November 15, 1999; Tim O'Melia, "The Sugar Harvest," *Palm Beach Post*, November 30, 1986.

78. Report of David J. Lillesand, outgoing executive director of Florida Rural Legal Services, 1 November 1976, Box 6, Folder: Florida Rural Legal Services, United Farm Workers Florida Division Papers; "Federal Slumlord," *New York Times*, April 5, 1975.

79. "Job Rights of Domestic Workers: The Florida Sugar Cane Industry," U.S. House of Representatives, Subcommittee on Labor Standards of the Committee on Education and Labor, July, 1983; Greg Schell, interview by the author, 14 July 1994, Belle Glade, Florida.

80. *Resilien Alfred, et al., v. Okeelanta*, and *Farmworker Rights v. Weatherford*, 84-5119, United States Court of Appeals for the Eleventh Circuit, 767 F.2d 937; 1985 U.S. App. LEXIS 30928, 2 July 1985; Sonia L. Nazario, "Florida in Winter is No Vacation Paradise for a Cane Cutter," *Wall Street Journal*, January 3, 1985, p. 1:4.

81. Sue Anne Pressley, "Dispute Threatens Crop; Md. Grower Barred From Hiring Foreigners," *Washington Post*, October 16, 1986, D1.

82. See *Burnett v. Hepburn Orchards* (Fed. Dist. Court, Baltimore. The West Virginia case is *NAACP, Jefferson County Branch v. Donovan*, 558 F. Supp. 218, No. 82-2315 (D.D.C. Sept. 3, 1982); *St. Petersburg Times*, December 11, 1986; U.S. House of Representatives, Subcommittee on Labor Standards of the Committee on Education and Labor, July 1983.

83. Edward Tuddenham, interview by the author, Austin, Texas, November 15, 1999.

84. Greg Schell, interview by the author, July 14, 1994, Belle Glade, Florida.

85. Leo C. Polopolus and Robert D. Emerson, "IRCA and Agriculture in Florida," *Immigration Reform and U.S. Agriculture*, Publication 3358, edited by Philip L. Martin and Wallace Huffman et al. (Oakland: Regents of the University of California, Division of Agriculture and Natural Resources, 1995), 89.

86. Polopolus and Emerson, "IRCA and Agriculture in Florida," 90.

87. Nearly 11 million Southerners—black and white—left the South during the 1960s and nearly 12 million did so in the 1970s. James N. Gregory, *The Southern Diaspora: How the Great Migration of Black and White Southerners Transformed America* (Chapel Hill: University of North Carolina Press, 2005), 13.

88. "Migrant: NBC White Paper," 1970, Producer Martin Carr, State Archives of Florida, Tallahassee, Florida.

89. "NBC White Paper: Migrant," State Archives of Florida.

90. The figures are from 1965. See Rosenbaum, "Unionization of Tomato Field Workers," 329.

91. Greg Schell, interview by the author, August 14, 1994

92. John Dillin, "Civil rights activists focus on plight of immigrant workers," *Christian Science Monitor*, April 11, 1986, 3.

93. The overall percentage of women only fell from 30 percent to roughly 24 percent between the 1970–71 season and the 1987–88 season but the crops that relied heavily on H2 Workers in the pre-Wirtz period were almost male again by the late eighties. Leo C. Polopolus and Robert D. Emerson, "IRCA and Agriculture in Florida," *Immigration Reform and U.S. Agriculture*, Publication 3358, edited by Philip L. Martin, et al., (University of California, Division of Agriculture and Natural Resources, 1995), 88–90.

94. Polopolus and Emerson, "IRCA and Agriculture in Florida," 90.

95. Dillin, "Civil rights activists focus on plight of immigrant workers," 3.

96. "An Organization at War with Itself," *Time*, October 3, 1983.

97. Francis Regan, Alan Paterson, and Tamara Goriely, *The Transformation of Legal Aid: Comparative and Historical Studies* (Gloucestershire: Clarendon Press, 1999), 26–27; Austin Sarat, Bryant G. Garth, Robert A. Kagan, *Looking Back at Law's Century* (Ithaca and London: Cornell University Press, 2002), 302.

CHAPTER 9: "For All Those Bending Years"

1. Daniel J. Tichenor argues that Reagan cared little about illegal immigration but was egged on by FAIR, which manufactured the sense of crisis. Tichenor, *Dividing Lines: The Politics of Immigration Control in America* (Princeton, NJ: Princeton University Press, 2002), 242–43.

2. Donnel Nunes, "U.S. puts number of illegal aliens under 5 million," *Washington Post*, January 31, 1980, A15.

3. Elizabeth Hull, *Without Justice for All: the Constitutional Rights of Aliens* (Westport, CT: Greenwood Press, 1985), 4.

4. Name withheld, Migrant Farmworker Justice Project Files, Okeelanta.

5. "Hill Chairmen Propose New Immigration Bill," March 18, 1982, *New York Times*, A4.

6. Aristide R. Zohlberg, "Reforming the Back Door: The Immigration Reform and Control Act of 1986 in Historical Perspective," in *Immigration Reconsidered: History, Sociology & Politics*, edited by Virginia Yans-McLaughlin (New York: Oxford, 1990), 322–23; Semler, "Overview," 228, and n. 205.

7. Robert Pear, "Congress; Whither the Immigration Bill?" *New York Times*, July 15, 1986, Section A; Page 20, Column 3.

8. Zohlberg, "Reforming the Back Door," 323–26; Beth McLeod, "Government overseer takes his lumps with a grain of salt," *Palm Beach Post*, (no date). The Miller Report is "Job Rights of Domestic Workers: the Florida Sugar Cane Industry," U.S. House of Representatives, Subcommittee on Labor Standards of the Committee on Education and Labor, July 1983.

9. Zohlberg, "Reforming the Back Door," 323.

10. Ibid., 328.

11. Ibid.

12. Ibid., 327.

13. Declaration of Hon. Howard L. Berman, *NW Forest Workers Association v. Lyng DDC*, 1988, US District Ct., DC (CIV. A. Nos. 87-1487, 87-3303, 29 June 1988; *Washington Post*, June 26, 1986.

14. Mary Thorton, "House Bill Would Add Alien Rights," *Palm Beach Post*, October 19, 1986, A1. Declaration of Hon. Howard L. Berman, *NW Forest Workers Association v. Lyng DDC*, 1988, US District Ct., DC (CIV. A. Nos. 87-1487, 87-3303, June 29, 1988.

15. William E. Gibson, "A Troubled Harvest," Part One of a Five Part Series, *Fort Lauderdale Sun Sentinel*, November 30, 1986, 23A.

16. Steve Routh, interview by the author, 11 July 2007, Washington, DC; 132 Cong. Rec. H9709 (daily ed. Oct. 3, 1986); *Northwest Forest Workers Association et al, Walso Wint, et al, intervenors v. Richard E. Lyng et al, DDC*, 1988, US District Ct., DC (CIV. A. Nos. 87-1487).

17. U.S. Court of Appeals, District of Columbia Circuit, *Walso Wint, et al. Appellants v. Hon. Clayton K. Yeutter, et al.* No. 89-5123, 4 May 1990, 902 F. 2d 76, 284 U.S. App. D.C. III, p. 2; 8 USC § 1160 (h).

18. Ward Sinclair, "USDA Resolves to Exclude Aliens," *Washington Post*, May 28, 1987, p. 4.

19. Brenner, "In the Kingdom of Big Sugar," 176.

20. *Miami Herald*, 1988 (no exact cite). The lackey quote is from Ward Sinclair, "USDA Resolves to Exclude Aliens," *Washington Post*, May 28, 1987, p. 4; see Civil Action No. 87-1487, Mem. Op. (DDC April 25, 1988); *NW Forest Workers Association v. Lyng DDC*, 1988, US District Ct., DC (CIV. A. Nos. 87-1487, 87-3303, 29 June 1988).

21. Brenner, "In the Kingdom of Big Sugar," 175.

22. See, for example, Margo Harakas, "Allegations plague foreign workers program," *Fort Lauderdale Sun Sentinel*, November 30, 1986, and Scott Anderson, "A Troubled Harvest," *Fort Lauderdale Sun Sentinel*, November 30, 1986.

23. Beth McLeod, "Sugarcane cutters gamble on legal battle," *Palm Beach Post*, November 25, 1986; Karl Vick, "Bittersweet Harvest," *St. Petersburg Times*, November 21, 1998, A, 1.

24. McLeod, "Sugarcane cutters gamble on legal battle."

25. *Miami Herald*, November 25, 1986.

26. *Jeptha Malcolm, et al., vs. Okeelanta Corp*, Circuit Court of the 15th Judicial Circuit of Florida, Palm Beach Cty, Civil Action, Case No. CL-91-9901-AN.

This was the suit for the items lost when men were rounded up during the Dog War (hereafter cited as *Malcolm v. Okeelanta*).

27. Brenner, "In the Kingdom of Big Sugar," 119–20; Paul Roberts, "The Sweet Hereafter," *Harper's Magazine* 299, 1794 (November 1999), 54–69.

28. *Malcolm v. Okeelanta.*

29. Affidavit of Newman Peters, *Malcolm v. Okeelanta.*

30. Affidavit of Horace Clark, *Malcolm v. Okeelanta.*

31. *Malcolm v. Okeelanta*; Brenner, "In the Kingdom of Big Sugar," 175–76.

32. Affidavit of Stafford Baptiste, *Malcolm v. Okeelanta.*

33. Ibid.

34. Affidavit of Horace Clark, *Malcolm v. Okeelanta.*

35. Affidavits of Stafford Baptiste and Horace Clark, *Malcolm v. Okeelanta.*

36. Affidavit of Lansbert Ormsby, *Malcolm v. Okeelanta.*

37. Affidavit of Stafford Baptiste, *Malcolm v. Okeelanta.*

38. Affidavit of Alfred Campbell, *Malcolm v. Okeelanta.*

39. Affidavit of Newman Peters, *Malcolm v. Okeelanta.*

40. Affidavit of Kipling Williams, *Malcolm v. Okeelanta.*

41. Affidavit of Harriet Reid, *Malcolm v. Okeelanta.*

42. *Palm Beach Post*, November 23, 1986.

43. *Palm Beach Post*, November 23, 1986; Palm Beach County Sheriff's Office Offense Report, Case No. 86165793, in author's possession.

44. *Miami Herald*, November 23, 1986.

45. Deposition of Everard Jarvis, *Malcolm v. Okeelanta.*

46. Deposition of Julius Butcher, *Malcolm v. Okeelanta.*

47. *Miami Herald*, November 26, 1986.

48. Tim O'Meilia, *Palm Beach Post*, Part 2 of 2, 29 December 1986.

49. *Miami Herald*, November 30, 1986.

50. 52 Fed. Reg., 20,376.

51. Ward Sinclair, "USDA Resolves to Exclude Alien," *Washington Post*, May 28, 1987, 4.

52. Brenner, "In the Kingdom of Big Sugar," 176.

53. Memorandum, Jonathan Abram to Steve Routh and Kevin Lanigan, 3 August 1987, Routh Files, in author's possession.

54. *NW Forest Workers Association v. Lyng DDC*, 1988, US District Ct., DC (CIV. A. Nos. 87-1487, 87-3303, 29 June 1988) (hereafter cited as *NW Forest Workers v. Lyng*).

55. The U.S. government had to accept skeletal SAWS applications from sugarcane workers, waive the $185 application, defer medical exam, and other documentation requirements.

56. See Civil Action No. 87-1487, Mem. Op. (DDC 25 April 1988); *NW Forest Workers v. Lyng.*

57. Greg Schell, telephone communication, July 4, 2007.

58. Mark Calvey, "U.S. Sugar worries dispute may disrupt cane harvest," *Palm Beach Post*, July 29, 1988, B:6 and 11; Mark Calvey, "'Vegetable' root of problem for cane cutters," *Palm Beach Post*, July 12, 1988, B6 and 13.

59. "USDA Applies Linguistic Veg-O-Matic to Would-Be SAW Sugar Cane Workers," *Interpreter Release*, August 22, 1988, 841–842; Mark Calvey, "U.S.

Sugar worries dispute may disrupt cane harvest," *Palm Beach Post*, July 29, 1988, B:6 and 11; *Order, Northwest Forest Association et al. v. Clayton K. Yeutter et al.*, Civil Action No. 87-1487, slip op (DDC, 28 February 1989); Greg Schell, interview by the author, Belle Glade, Florida, July 16, 1994.

60. Greg Schell interview, July 16, 1994.

61. Migrant Farmworker Justice Project Files, Belle Grade, Florida, no date.

62. Brenner, "In the Kingdom of Big Sugar," 176.

63. Tim O'Meilia, *Palm Beach Post*, Part 2 of 2, 29 December 1986.

64. Okeelanta did not admit liability but agreed to pay the workers a total of $355,000 (up to $1000 each plus $20,000 to Florida Rural Legal Services for legal costs). *Palm Beach Post*, September 12, 1995.

65. Rosalind Resnick, "Raising Cane," *National Law Journal*, April 1, 1991, 27.

66. *Palm Beach Post*, January 20, 1989, p. D-1.

67. Brenner, "In the Kingdom of Big Sugar," 116.

68. Sikes letter, in author's possession; Tuddenham quoted in Brenner, "In the Kingdom of Big Sugar," 176.

69. Ibid., 177.

70. Ibid., 176–77.

71. *Bygrave v. Sugar Cane Growers Cooperative of Florida, Inc.*, CL-89-8690 AI.

72. Brenner, "In the Kingdom of Big Sugar," 174.

73. David Gorman, interview by the author, April 17, 2000, North Palm Beach, Florida; Brenner, "In the Kingdom of Big Sugar," 119.

74. Michael Utley, "Lawyer adds spice to sugar's fight," *Palm Beach Post*, July 22, 1998; Brenner, "In the Kingdom of Big Sugar," 178–80.

75. Karl Vick, "Bittersweet Harvest," *St. Petersburg Times*, November 21, 1993.

76. *Bygrave v. Sugar Cane Growers Cooperative*, No. CL-89-8690 (Cir. Ct. Palm Beach Cty, FL).

77. "FJF Reaches Major Accord with U.S. Sugar Corp.," *Farmworker Immigration Policy Report*, vol. 3, no. 1 (Summer 1992), 1 and 4.

78. Rosalind Resnick, "Cane Cutters and Sugar Company Make Peace," *National Law Journal* 15 (28 September 1992), 5.

79. "Foreign Farm Workers in U.S. DOL Action Needed to Protect Florida Sugar Cane Workers," GAO/HRD-92-95.

80. "General Accounting Office Blasts DOL Oversight . . . ." *Farmworker Immigration Policy Report* 3, 1 (Summer 1992), 8.

81. Lisa Shuchman, "Machines Don't Sue," *Palm Beach Post*, n.d.

82. Karl Vick, "Bittersweet Harvest," 21 November 1993, A1.

83. Ibid.

84. "Dillon" to Greg Schell, Tuddenham File, 26 February 1996.

85. Rosalind Resnick, "$50 Million Win for Cane Cutters," *National Law Journal* 14 (13 July 1992), 3 and 43.

86. *National Law Journal*, September 28, 1992, vol. 15, p. 5; "Sugar's payout tastes semisweet," (Fort Lauderdale) *Sun-Sentinel*, July 23, 1996.

87. Brenner, "In the Kingdom of Big Sugar," 116, 119–120.

88. DOL Lets FFVA Reduce Cane Cutters' Protections," *Farmworker Immigration Policy Report* 3, 1 (Summer 1992), 2.

89. Brenner, "In the Kingdom of Big Sugar," 120.

90. Ibid., 179.

91. Ibid., 180; *Palm Beach Post*, October 22, 1999, D: 1–2.

92. Greg Schell, interviewed via email by the author, July 4, 2007.

93. Brenner, "In the Kingdom of Big Sugar," 177.

94. Name withheld, Migrant Farmworker Justice Project Files, File: Okeelanta.

95. Deposition of *Alwyn Smith, Kelroy McDonald, et al., vs. Okeelanta Corporation*, 16 March 1998, Deposition of Michael Cameron, 22 September 1998, West Palm Beach, 15th Judicial Circuit Court, Palm Beach County, Florida, Case No. CL-91-3105 AO; Brenner, "In the Kingdom of Big Sugar," 181.

96. Brenner, "In the Kingdom of Big Sugar," 181.

97. Albert Campbell Deposition, 5 April 2006, Montego Bay, Jamaica, for *Alphonso Mitchell, et al., Plaintiff v Osceola Farms Co., Defendant*, U.S. District Court, for the Southern District of Florida, West Palm Beach Division, Case the Southern District of Florida, West Palm Beach Division, Case No. 05-80825-CIV-COHN/SNOW.

98. Greg Schell, phone interview by the author, July 4, 2007.

CHAPTER 10: All the World's a Workplace

1. Name changed at her request, interview by the author, Christiana, Jamaica, January 29, 2003.

2. *Migration News* 9, 9 (September 2002): http://migration.ucdavis.edu/mn/sep_2002-03.html.

3. Michael Humphrey, "Migrants, Workers and Refugees: The Political Economy of Population Movements in the Middle East," *MERIP* 23, 2 (March/April 1993): 4–9; Fred Halliday, "Labor Migration in the Arab World," *Merip Reports* 14, 4 (May 1984): 6–7.

4. According to Halliday, the oil boom and the turn to foreign workers resulted in "a dangerous neglect of agriculture" and the restriction of industrial development "to a few capital-intensive enterprises." Halliday, "Labor Migration in the Arab World," 3–10. Humphrey, "Migrants, Workers and Refugees," 2–9; Hassan N. Gardezi, "Asian Workers in the Gulf States of the Middle East," in *International Labour Migrations*, edited by B. Singh Bolaria and Rosemary von Elling Bolaria (Delhi: Oxford University Press, 1997): 99–120; J. S. Birks, I. J. Seccombe, and C. A. Sinclair, "Labour Migration in the Arab Gulf States: Patterns, Trends and Prospects," *International Migration* (Geneva, Switzerland) 26, 3 (1998): 267–86; "Capital waves of a human kind wash across Asia's shores," *The Age* (Melbourne, Australia), 26 December 2003, *Business*, p. 15. See also various essays in F. Eelens, T. Schampers, and J. D. Speckmann, eds., *Labour Migration to the Middle East: From Sri Lanka to the Gulf* (New York: Kegan Paul International, 1992).

5. Christine B. N. Chin, *In Service and Servitude: Foreign Female Domestic Workers and the Malaysian "Modernity" Project* (New York: Columbia University Press, 1986), 97–102; Stephen Castles and Mark J. Miller, *The Age of Migra-*

tion: International Population Movements in the Modern World, 2nd ed. (New York: Guilford Books, 1998), 147–48.

6. Cynthia Ca Abdon-Tellez, Director, The Mission for Migrant Workers, interview by the author, June 5, 2009, St. John's Cathedral, Hong Kong; Rhacel Salazar Parrenas, *Servants of Globalization: Women, Migration, and Domestic Work* (Stanford, CA: Stanford University Press, 2001); and Haruo Shimada, *Japan's "Guest Workers": Issues and Public Policies* (Tokyo: University of Tokyo Press, 1994).

7. Chin, *In Service and Servitude*, 45–63.

8. Ibid., 93–124; Benjamin V. Cariño, ed., *Filipino Workers on the Move: Trends, Dilemmas and Policy Options* (Philippine Migration Research Network, 1998), 1.

9. Philip L. Martin and Michael S. Teitelbaum, "The Mirage of Mexican Guest Workers," *Foreign Affairs* 80, 6 (November–December 2001): 117–31; Inter Press Service, 16 August 2002; *Business Times* (Singapore), 3 September 2002; *New York Times*, 20 February 2000, Section 1, p. 10, col. 1; Ahm Zehadul Karim, Moha Asri Abdullah, and Mohd Isa Haji Bakar, *Foreign Workers in Malaysia: Issues and Implications* (Kuala Lumpur: Utusan Publications, 1999), 62.

10. *New York Times*, February 20, 2000, Section 1, p. 10, col. 1; Karim, Abdullah, and Bakar, *Foreign Workers in Malaysia*, 52–55; and Cynthia Ca Abdon-Tellez interview, June 5, 2009.

11. Cynthia Ca Abdon-Tellez interview.

12. Castles and Miller, *The Age of Migration*, 149.

13. Chin, *In Service and Servitude*, 102; Hassan N. Gardezi, "Asian Workers in the Gulf States of the Middle East," in *International Labour Migrations*, edited by B. Singh Bolaria and Rosemary von Elling Bolaria (Delhi: Oxford University Press, 1997), 99–120.

14. See Barry Yeoman's brilliant article on the NC Growers Association: "Silence in the Fields," *Mother Jones*, January/February 2001 (http://barryyeoman. com/articles/silencefields.html, accessed 31 July 2009).

15. Kristin Collins, "Workers: Promise Became a Prison," *News & Observer*, March 10, 2007.

16. Ibid.

17. Sabulal Vijayan and Stephen Boykewich, "American Nightmare: Exploited Indian Workers Demand Justice," *The Indypendent*, June 26, 2008 (http://www. indypendent.org/2008/06/25/american-nightmare/), accessed 24 July 2009.

18. Southern Poverty Law Center Report, "Close to Slavery: Guestworker Programs in the United States," http://www.splcenter.org/legal/guestreport/guest3c. jsp (accessed 31 July 31, 2009).

19. These cases were all settled out of court. Southern Poverty Law Center Report, "Close to Slavery: Guestworker Programs in the United States." http:// www.splcenter.org/legal/guestreport/guest5.jsp" (accessed 31 July 2009) hereafter cited as "Close to Slavery."

20. Peter Beckford (name changed by request), interview by the author, telephone communication, July 15, 2001.

21. Sandra Brown (name changed by request), interview by the author, Effort, Jamaica, January 26, 2003.

22. Dead House interview; Porter interview. Paulk says much the same thing in Kramer, *The Offshores*, 39 and 44–51.

23. Jason DeParle, "A Good Provider Is One Who Leaves," *New York Times*, April 22, 2007, Section 6; Column 1; Magazine; 50.

24. Chin, *In Service and Servitude*, 98–100.

25. Jason DeParle, "A Good Provider Is One Who Leaves," 50.

CONCLUSION

1. Names of the "Garcias" withheld to protect their identity. The friends who put me up were Professor Gunther Peck and writer Faulkner Fox.

2. The term "future flows" was all the rage among policy pundits at an immigration policy conference I attended October 22–23, 2009 at the Woodrow Wilson International Center for Scholars in Washington, DC.

3. Ibid.

4. Ruben Navarrett, Jr., *Washington Post*, July 5, 2009, A15.

5. Reyes Teófilo, "8000 'Guest Workers' Join Farm Union in North Carolina," *Labor Notes*, No. 307, October 2004, http://labornotes.org/node/939 (accessed 28 July 2009).

6. Ibid.; Steven Greenhouse, "North Carolina Growers' Group Signs Union Contract for Mexican Workers," *New York Times*, September 17, 2004.

7. Teófilo, "8000 'Guest Workers' Join Farm Union in North Carolina,".

8. Lecker, "Major Pickle Firm Faces FLOC Boycott in March," *Toledo Blade*, October 11, 1998; Zagier, "Pickle Protest Planned," *Charlotte News and Observer*, October 11, 1998; Carmen, "Organizer of Union for Migrant Workers Takes on Pickle Giant," *Columbus Dispatch*, January 24, 1999; Sengupta, "Farm Union Takes Aim at a Big Pickle Maker," *New York Times*, October 26, 2000.

9. Baldemar Velasquez, "Harvest of Shame," *Huffington Post*, October 25, 2007.

10. According to the National Agricultural Workers Survey, carried out in 2001–2002 by the U.S. Department of Labor's Employment and Training Administration, 78 percent of crop workers nationwide were immigrants; 72 percent were born in Mexico; fifty-three percent lacked legal authorization to work; 21 percent were legal permanent residents; and 25 percent were citizens. Nearly a quarter of the U.S.-born work force self-identified as Mexican or Mexican Americans. National Agricultural Workers Survey, U.S. Department of Labor, Employment and Training Administration, chapter 1, www.doleta.gov/agworker/report9/toc.cfm (accessed 3 July 2009). See also Philip Martin, "Guestworkers: New Solution, New Problem?" Pew Charitable Trust (2002), http://pewhispanic.org/files/reports/7.pdf, 23 (accessed July 1, 2009).

11. On the failure of governments to control immigration, see Wayne A. Cornelius, Philip L. Martin, and James F. Hollifield, *Controlling Immigration: A Global*

Perspective (Stanford, CA: Stanford University Press, 1994); Douglas S. Massey, "International Migration in a Globalizing Economy," *Great Decisions* (2007), 4. See also Massey, *Beyond Smoke and Mirrors: Mexican Immigration in an Era of Economic Integration* (New York: Russell Sage, 2003).

    12. Massey, "International Migration," 4.

Bibliography

MANUSCRIPT COLLECTIONS

Connecticut State Archives, Hartford, Connecticut
  Papers of Governor Robert A. Hurley, 1941–1943
  Papers of Governor Raymond E. Baldwin, 1943–1946
Dwight D. Eisenhower Library, Abilene, Kansas
  U.S. President's Committee on Migratory Labor, Records, 1938–66
State Archives of Florida, Tallahassee, Florida
  Papers of Governor Spessard Holland
Library of Congress
  Papers of the National Association for the Advancement of Colored People,
  Part 13: NAACP and Labor, 1940–1955, Series A, Reel 11 and Part 14: Race
  Relations on the International Arena, 1940–1955
Public Records Office, Kew Gardens, England
  Records of the Secretary of State for the Colonies, Colonial Office Records
John F. Kennedy Library, Boston, Massachusetts
  Willard Wirtz Papers
Franklin Delano Roosevelt Library, Hyde Park, New York
  Fair Employment Practices Commission Records
Walter Reuther Library, Wayne State University, Detroit, Michigan
  Papers of the Workers Defense League
  Papers of the Florida Christian Migrant Ministry
  Papers of the United Farm Workers Florida Division
  Papers of the United Farm Workers Organizing Committee
United States National Archives and Records Administration
  Office of the Secretary of Agriculture, Record Group 16
  U.S. Department of Justice, Record Group 60
  U.S. Department of Labor, Record Group 174
  U.S. Department of State, Record Group 59
  U.S. Farmers Home Administration, Record Group 96
  U.S. Immigration and Naturalization Service, Record Group 85
  U.S. Wage and Hour Division, Record Group 155
  U.S. War Food Administration (Office of Labor), Record Group 224
University of Wisconsin Archives, College of Agriculture, Steenbock Library,
  University of Wisconsin
  Annual Reports of the Richland County Agricultural Agent, 1940s, County
  Agricultural Agents
P. K. Yonge Library, University of Florida, Gainesville, Florida
  Papers of George Armistead Smathers, 1942–1968

INTERVIEWS

Anderson, Winston
Beckford, Sydney
Brown, Denise
Brown, Jarrett
Burgess, David
Ca Abdon-Tellez, Cynthia
Clark, Wayne
Comrie, Walter S.
Cottrill, Oscar
Gorman, David
Grant, Oral
Kuker, Alan
Matthews, James
Morrison, Earl
Porter, Noel
Routh, Steve
Schell, Gregg
Segor, Joseph
Sorn, George
Spriggs, Kent
Stone, Josh
Tuddenham, Edward
Wedgeworth, George
Williams, Leaford
Wirtz, Willard
Zad, Lasing

Interviewees whose names were changed on request
Beckford, Peter
Brown, Samuel
Brown, Sandra
Gordon, Peter
Palmer, Sheryl

NEWSPAPERS AND PERIODICALS

Albuquerque (NM) Journal
Amarillo (TX) Daily News
Amsterdam (NY) News
Baltimore Afro-American
Brainerd Daily Dispatch
Brownsville (TX) Herald

Chicago Bee
Christian Science Monitor
Clewiston News
Express
Farm Labor News
Farmworker Immigration Policy Report
Fort Lauderdale Sun Sentinel
Fresno (CA) Bee Republican
Galveston News
Glades County Democrat
Hartford (CT) Times
Homestead (FL) News Leader
Humboldt Standard
Jacksonville Journal
(Kingston, JA) Daily Gleaner
(Kingston, JA) Public Opinion
Kingston (NY) Daily Freeman
Labor Notes
Lakeland (FL) Ledger View
Life
Long Beach (CA) Independent
Miami Daily News
Miami Herald
Michigan Record Eagle
Migration News
Milwaukee Sentinel
Minneapolis Sunday Tribune
Naples (FL) Daily News
National Law Journal
New Jersey Herald News
New Republic
Norfolk Journal and Guide
Palm Beach Post
Panama City (FL) News Herald
Pittsburg Courier
Portsmouth (NH) Herald
The Reporter
Salisbury (NC) Times
Sheboygan (WI) Press
St. Petersburg Times
Stuart (FL) News
Tampa Daily Times
Texas Morning Avalanche
Union Labor News
Southern Exposure
Time

Union Labor News
Vanity Fair
Wall Street Journal
Washington Bee
Washington Post
Waterbury (CT) Republican
Yuma (AZ) Sentinel

GOVERNMENT PUBLICATIONS

"History and Operations of the U.S. Sugar Program." Committee on Agriculture, USDA. Washington, DC: GPO, 1962, 1–38.
"Immigration Act, Public Law 301–29." *U.S. Statutes at Large* 39 (1917).
"Supplemental Labor Programs." *I & N Reporter* (July 1961): 1–5.
"Temporary Agricultural Labour in the United States West Indies Farm Labour Programme. West Indies Central Labour Organization, 1986.
"The Migration of Workers: Recruitment, Placing and Conditions of Labour." *International Labour Office Studies and Reports* Series O (Migration No. 5), 1–11. Geneva: International Labour Office by P.S. King & Son, Ltd., 1936.
Agricultural Economic Report, No. 110, Washington, DC: U.S. GPO, April 1967.
Anglo-American Caribbean Commission. *The Caribbean islands and the war: A Record of Progress in Facing Stern Realities.* Washington, DC: U.S. GPO, 1943.
Annual Report on the Work of the Labour Department for the Year 1942, Kingston, Jamaica.
Bureau of Agricultural Economics, U.S. Department of Agriculture. "Farm Manpower Situation and Outlook." *BAE Report,* October 30, 1951.
Committee on Agriculture, U.S. Department of Agriculture. *History and Operations of the U.S. Sugar Program.* Washington, DC: GPO, 1962.
Farm Labor, Hearings Before the Committee on Agriculture. House, 82nd Cong., 1st session on HR 2955 and HR 3048, March 8,9,12 and 14, 1951. Washington, DC: GPO, 1951.
Farm Labor Supply Program, Hearings before the Committee on Agriculture, House of Representatives, 80th Congress, 1st Session, on H.R. 1388 to provide for the continuance of the farm labor supply program up to and including June 30, 1947. Washington, DC: GPO, 1947.
Federal Interagency Committee on Migrant Labor. *Migrant Labor . . . a Human Problem.* Washington, DC: U.S. Department of Labor, Retracing and Reemployment Administration, 1947.
Federal Register. Washington, DC: GPO, 1952.
Gabbard, Susan M., Richard Mines, and Anne Steirman. "A Profile of U.S. Farm Workers: Demographics, Household Composition, Income and Use of Services." U.S. Department of Labor, Office of the Assistant Secretary for Policy, 1997.

Great Britain. Public Record Office. *List of Colonial Office Records.* Millwood, NY: Kraus-Thomson Organization, 1976.

Hall, Stuart. "Migration from the English-speaking Caribbean to the United Kingdom, 1950–1980." In *International Migration Today,* vol. 1, *Trends and Prospects,* edited by Reginald T. Appleyard, 264–310. UNESCO, 1988.

Hansard (Parliamentary debates). House of Lords. Parliament. Great Britain.

Hearing Before the Subcommittee on Agricultural Labor of the Committee on Education and Labor, House of Representatives, 94th Congress, 1st session. Washington, DC, March 20, 1975.

Hearings before the Committee on Agriculture, House of Representatives, 80th Congress, 2d session. Washington, DC: GPO, 1948.

Hearings before the Committee on Agriculture, House, 82nd Congress, 1st Session. Washington, DC: GPO, 1951.

Immigration Act of February 5, 1979. U.S. Department of Labor. Bureau of Immigration. Washington, DC: GPO, 1920.

Jamaican Gazette

Jenks, C. Wilfred, International Labour Office, and International Labour Organisation. *The International Labour Code, 1939; a Systematic Arrangement of the Conventions and Recommendations Adopted by the International Labour Conference, 1919–1939.* Montreal, 1941.

Job Rights of Domestic Workers: The Florida Sugar Cane Industry. U.S. House of Representatives, 98th Congress, 1st Session. Washington, DC: GPO, 1983.

Labour Conditions in the West Indies. Report by Major G. St. J. Orde Brown, OBE, Labour Advisor to the Secretary of State for the Colonies, His Majesty's Stationery Office, Cmd., 6070, 1939.

Martin, Philip L. *Guestworker Programs: Lessons from Europe.* U.S. Department of Labor Monograph No. 5, September 1980.

Matthews, Cedric O. J. *Labour Policies in the West Indies.* Geneva: International Labour Office, 1952.

Metzler, William H. *Migratory Farm Workers in the Atlantic Coast Stream: A Study in the Belle Glade area of Florida.* Washington, DC: U.S. Department of Agriculture, Circular No. 966, January 1955.

Metzler, William, Ralph Loomis, and Nelson LeRay. *The Farm Labor Situation in Selected States, 1965–66. Agriculture Economic Report* 110, 1 (1967).

Migrant and Seasonal Farmworker Powerlessness. Hearings before the Subcommittee on Migratory Labor of the Committee on Labor and Public Welfare, U.S. Senate, 91st Congress, 1st and 2nd Sessions. Washington, DC: GPO, 1969.

Migrant Farm Labor in Florida. State of Florida, Legislative Council and Legislative Reference Bureau, January 1963.

Migrant Labor in Florida: A Summary of Recent Studies, State of Florida, Legislative Council and Legislative Reference Bureau, Tallahassee, Florida, 1961.

Migrant Labor...a human problem: Report and Recommendations of the Federal Interagency Committee on Migrant Labor. U.S. Department of Labor, Retraining and Reemployment Administration, 1947.

Migratory Labor in American Agriculture: Report of the President's Commission on Migratory Labor. Washington, DC: GPO, 1951.

Migratory Labor, Hearings before the Subcommittee on Labor and Labor-Management Relations of the Committee on Labor and Public Welfare, U.S. Senate. 82nd Congress, 2d session on Migratory Labor, Part I. Washington, DC: GPO, 1952.

Minutes of Meetings of the Regional Labor Board, multiple years, in author's possession.

National Agricultural Workers Survey, 2001–2002, U.S. Department of Labor's Employment and Training Administration, www.doleta.gov/agworker/report9/toc.cfm (accessed 3 July 2009).

National Planning Agency. *Economic and Social Survey of Jamaica 1989*. Kingston: Planning Institute of Jamaica, 1990.

Office of the Assistant Secretary for Policy, Prepared for the Commission on Immigration Reform, (unpublished) April 1997.

Rasmussen, Wayne D. *A History of the Emergency Farm Labor Supply Program*. Washington, DC: U.S. Department of Agriculture 1951.

Report of the Conference of BWI Labour Officers, Kingston, Jamaica, December 11–13, 1950, PRO, CO, 1042/189.

Report on Farm Labor Importation Urges Greater Protection of U.S. Workers, 23 October 1959, *News from the U.S. Department of Labor.*

Report on Investigation into the Work and Living Conditions of Barbadian Workers on the Farm Labour Programme in the U.S.A. Barbados: Barbados Government, 1965.

Report on the Function of the BWI CLO, April 13, 1951, PRO, CO 1042/189.

Reports of the Chief Liaison Officer (Herbert MacDonald, OBE), PRO, CO 1031/615.

Resources, United States. General Accounting Office, Community, and Economic Development Division. *Sugar program*, 1993.

Runyan, Jack L., United States, and Department of Agriculture. *A Summary of Federal Laws and Regulations Affecting Agricultural Employers, 1992*. Agriculture information bulletin, no. 652. Washington, DC: U.S. Department of Agriculture, Economic Research Service, 1992.

Subcommittee on Labor Standards of the Committee on Education and Labor, U.S. House of Representatives. *Job Rights of Domestic Workers: The Florida Sugar Cane Industry.* Washington, DC: GPO, 1983.

Sugarman, Solomon. *Wage Survey for 1973–74 South Florida Sugar Harvest*. Department of Labor, Employment Standards Administration, Washington, DC: U.S. GPO, 1974.

Summary of Federal Laws and Regulations Affecting Agricultural Employers, 2000. Agricultural Handbook, no. 719; U.S. Department of Agriculture. Washington, DC: U.S. Department of Agriculture, Economic Research Service, 2000.

Trial Transcript of J.A.G. Smith, *The Queen vs. James Smith*, Resident Magistrate's Court for the Parish of Kingston, May 21, 1990–July 2, 1990.

U.S. Agricultural Policy in the Postwar Years, 1945–1963. Washington, DC: Congressional Quarterly Service, 1963, 1–10.

U.S. Congress. House. Committee on the Judiciary. *Guestworker Programs: Hearings Before the Subcommittee on Immigrants and Claims of the Committee on the Judiciary.* 104th Congress, 1st Session, December 7, 1995. Washington, DC: GPO, 1996.

U.S. Congress. Senate. Committee on the Judiciary. Temporary Worker Programs: Background and Issues. Committee Print. 96th Congress, 2nd Session. Washington, DC: GPO, 1980.

U.S. Department of Labor. Bureau of Employment Security, Puerto Rican Farm Workers in Florida. Washington, DC: GPO, 1955.

U.S. Department of State, AACC. *The Caribbean Islands in the War,* 1943.

U.S. President's Commission on Migratory Labor. Stenographic Report of Proceedings, July 13–October 18, 1950. Wisconsin State Historical Society, Microfilm, LaCross, WI: Northern Micrographics, 1977.

U.S. Senate, Committee on the Judiciary. *West Indian Temporary Alien Labor Program, 1943–1977.* Washington, DC: GPO, 1978.

U.S. Statutes at Large. Vol. 39, Part I. Washington, DC: GPO, 1917.

U.S. Statutes at Large. Vol. 66. Washington, DC: GPO, 1952.

Vialet, Joyce C. *The West Indies (BWI) Temporary Alien Labor Program, 1943–1977: A Study Prepared for the Subcommittee on Immigration of the Committee of the Judiciary,* U.S. Senate. Committee Print, ed. 95th Congress, 2nd Session. Washington, DC, 1978.

West Indies (BWI) Temporary Alien Labor Program, 1943–1977: A Study Prepared for the Subcommittee on Immigration of the Committee of the Judiciary, U.S. Senate, 95th Congress, 2d Session. Washington, DC: GPO, 1978.

Theses and Manuscripts

Abou-Bakr, Ahmed. "The United States Sugar Position in the World Sugar Economy." Ph.D. Dissertation, Washington State University, 1976.

Banivanua-Mar, Tracey. "Bulimaen and Hard Work Indenture, Identity and Complexity in Colonial North Queensland." Ph.D. Dissertation, University of Melbourne, 2000.

Dohoney, Jo Marie. "The Wages of Cane: A Study of Temporary Foreign Labor Importation in the U.S.: The Case of West Indian Cane Workers in Florida." M.A. Thesis, Sociology, Michigan State University, 1984.

Effland, Anne B.W. "The Emergence of Federal Assistance Programs for Migrants and Seasonal Farmworkers in Post–World War II America." Ph.D. Dissertation, Iowa State University, 1991.

Gross, Eric Lincoln. "Somebody got drowned, Lord: Florida and the great Okeechobee hurricane disaster of 1928." Ph.D. Dissertation, Florida State University, 1995.

Heitmann, John A. "The Florida Sugar Industry, 1920–1945: Science, Technology and Organization." Unpublished paper delivered at the 1991 meeting of the Organization of American Historians.

Heston, Thomas J. "Sweet Subsidy: The Economic and Diplomatic Effects of the U.S. Sugar Acts—1934–1974." Ph.D. Dissertation, Case Western Reserve University, 1975.

Hollander, Gail Marjorie. "Raising Cane in the Glades: Regional Development and Agroenvironmental Conflict in South Florida." Ph.D. Dissertation, University of Iowa, 1999.

Jaffe, Erwin Alan. "Passage of the McCarran-Walter Act: The Reiteration of American Immigration Policy." Ph.D. Dissertation, Rutgers University, 1961.

McCally, David Philip. "Cane Cutters in the Everglades," M.A. Thesis, University of South Florida, 1991.

Mehra, Rekha. "International Labor Migration and Florida Sugarcane Production: A Political-Economic Analysis." Ph.D. Dissertation, University of Florida, 1985.

Reid, Sheryl Andre. "U.S.–Jamaica Relations: The Farm Worker Programme, 1943–1962." M.A. Thesis, University of West Indies-Mona, Jamaica, 1998.

Weber, John W. III. "The Shadow of the Revolution: South Texas, the Mexican Revolution, and the Evolution of Modern American Labor Relations." Ph.D. Dissertation, College of William & Mary, 2008.

PUBLISHED BOOKS AND ARTICLES

"Special Report: The Farm Worker Controversy." *Caribbean Labour Journal* 1 (September 1991), 25–32. "The Cane Contract: West Indians in Florida." *NACLA Report* (Nov./Dec. 1977), 10–37.

Abella, Irving. "Foreword." In *Whence They Came: Deportation from Canada 1900–1935*, edited by Barbara Roberts, vii–x. Ottawa: University of Ottawa Press, 1988.

Ahmed, Belal, and Sultana Afroz. *The Political Economy of Food and Agriculture in the Caribbean.* Kingston, Jamaica: I. Randle; London: J. Currey, 1996.

Albert, Bill, and Adrian Graves. *The World Sugar Economy in War and Depression, 1914–40.* New York: Routledge, 1998.

American Social History Project. *Who Built America?: Working People and the Nation's Economy, Politics, Culture, and Society.* Vol. 2, Since 1877. New York: Worth Publishers, 2000.

Ayala, César J. *American Sugar Kingdom: The Plantation Economy of the Spanish Caribbean, 1898–1934.* Chapel Hill: University of North Carolina Press, 1999.

Baker, Gordon E. *Rural v. Urban Political Power.* New York: Random House, 1955.

Bakan, Abigail B. *Ideology and Class Conflict in Jamaica: The Politics of Rebellion.* Montréal: McGill-Queen's University Press, 1990.

Baldwin, Sidney. *Poverty and Politics: The Rise and Decline of the Farm Security Administration.* Chapel Hill: University of North Carolina Press, 1968.

Barrow, Christine. *Family in the Caribbean.* Kingston: Ian Randle, 1996.

Beachey, R. W. *The British West Indies Sugar Industry in the Late 19th Century.* Oxford: Blackwell, 1957.

Beckford, George L., and Michael Witter. *Small Garden—Bitter Weed: the Political Economy of Struggle and Change in Jamaica.* Mona, Kingston, Jamaica: Institute of Social and Economic Research, 1991.

Beckles, Hilary. *A History of Barbados: From Amerindian Settlement to Nation-State.* New York: Cambridge University Press, 1989.

Behar, Joseph. "Diplomacy and Essential Workers: Official British Recruitment of Foreign Labor in Italy, 1945–1951." *Journal of Policy History* 15, 3 (2003): 324–44.

Beinart, William. "Transkeian Migrant Workers and Youth Labour on the Natal Sugar Estates 1918–1948." *Journal of African History* 32, 1 (1991): 41–63.

Bendix, John."On the Rights of Foreign Workers in West Germany." In *Turkish Workers in Europe: An Interdisciplinary Study*, edited by Ilhan Başgöz and Norman Furniss. Bloomington: Indiana University Turkish Studies, 1985.

Bernstein, Ann, and Myron Weiner. *Migration and Refugee Policies.* New York, NY: Continuum International Publishing Group, 2002.

Bhabha, Jacqueline, Francesca Klug, Sue Shutter, Women, Immigration, and Nationality Group. *Worlds Apart: Women under Immigration and Nationality Law.* London: Pluto Press, 1985.

Birks, J. S., I. J. Seccombe, and C. A. Sinclair. "Labour Migration in the Arab Gulf States: Patterns, Trends and Prospects." *International Migration* (Geneva, Switzerland) 26, 3 (1998): 267–86.

Birmingham, David. *Empire in Africa: Angola and its Neighbors.* Athens: Ohio University, Center for International Studies, 2006.

Black, Clinton V. *The History of Jamaica.* Longman Caribbean, 1994.

Black, Earl, and Merle Black. *Politics and Society in the South.* Cambridge: Harvard University Press, 1987.

Blackbourn, David. *The Long Nineteenth Century: A History of Germany, 1780–1918.* New York: Oxford University Press, 1998.

Blanshard, Paul. *Democracy and Empire in the Caribbean.* New York: MacMillan, 1947.

Blum, Albert A. "The Farmer, the Army and the Draft." *Agricultural History* 38 (1964): 34–42.

Bohning, Don. *The Castro Obsession: U.S. Covert Operations Against Cuba, 1959–1965.* Washington, DC: Brassey's, 2005.

Bolland, O. Nigel. *On the March: Labour Rebellions in the British Caribbean, 1934–39.* Kingston: Ian Randle, 1995.

———. *The Politics of Labour in the British Caribbean: the Social Origins of Authoritarianism and Democracy in the Labour Movement.* Princeton, NJ: Markus Wiener, 2001.

Bolles, A. Lynn. "'Goin' Abroad': Working Class Jamaican Women and Migration." In *Female Immigrants to the United States: Caribbean, Latin American and African Experiences*, edited by D. Mortimer and R. Bryce-Laporte, 56–85. Occasional Paper, No. 2. Washington, DC: Smithsonian Institution RIIES, 1981.

Bolles, Augusta Lynn. *Sister Jamaica: A Study of Women, Work, and Households in Kingston.* Lanham: University Press of America, 1996.

Borstelmann, Thomas. *The Cold War and the Color Line: American Race Relations in the Global Arena.* Cambridge: Harvard University Press, 2001.

Braga, Michael Marconi. "To Relieve the Misery: Sugarmill Workers and the 1933 Cuban Revolution." In *Workers' Control in Latin America, 1930–1979,* edited by Jonathan Charles Brown, 16–44. Chapel Hill: University of North Carolina Press, 1997.

Brenner, Marie. "In the Kingdom of Big Sugar." *Vanity Fair* (February 2001): 114–21, 171–81.

Brochmann, Grete. "Migrant Labour and Foreign Policy: The Case of Mozambique." *Journal of Peace Research* 22, 4 (December 1985): 335–44.

Brubaker, Rogers. *Citizenship and Nationhood in France and Germany.* Cambridge, MA: Harvard University Press, 1992.

Bryce-Laporte, Roy S. "Black Immigrants, the Experience of Invisibility and Inequality." *Journal of Black Studies* 3, 1 (1972): 29–56.

Bunche, Ralph J. "The Anglo-American Caribbean Commission: An Experiment in Regional Cooperation." American Council Panel No. 7. Ninth Conference of the Institute of Pacific Relations. New York: American Council, 1945.

Burawoy, Michael. "The Functions and Reproduction of Migrant Labor: Comparative Material from Southern Africa and the United States." *American Journal of Sociology* 81, 5 (March 1976): 1050–87. Calavita, Kitty. *Inside the State: The Bracero Program, Illegal Immigrants and the INS.* New York: Routledge, 1992.

Califano, Jr., Joseph A. *Inside: A Public and Private Life.* Cambridge: Perseus Book Group, 2004.Cariño, Benjamin V. ed., *Filipino Workers on the Move: Trends, Dilemmas and Policy Options.* Philippine Migration Research Network, 1998.Carr, Barry. "Identity, Class, and Nation: Black Immigrant Workers, Cuban Communism, and the Sugar Insurgency, 1925–1934." *Hispanic American Historical Review* 78, 1 (February 1998): 83–116.

Castles, Stephen, and Godula Kosack. *Immigrant Workers and Class Structure in Western Europe,* 2nd ed. London: Oxford University Press, 1985.

Castles, Stephen, and Mark J. Miller. *The Age of Migration: International Population Movements in the Modern World.* 2nd ed. New York: Guilford Books, 1998.

Cater, Douglas. *Power in Washington: A Critical Look at Today's Struggle in the Nation's Capital.* New York: Random House, 1964.

Cecil, R .G., and G. E. Ebanks. "The Caribbean Migrants Farm Workers Programme in Ontario: Seasonal Expansion of West Indian Economic Spaces." *International Migration* (Switzerland) 30, 1 (1992): 19–37.

Chambers, Clarke A. *California Farm Organizations: A Historical Study of the Grange, the Farm Bureau, and the Associated Farmers, 1929–1941.* Berkeley: University of California Press, 1952.

Chaney, Elsa M. "The World Economy and Contemporary Migration." *International Migration Review* 13, 1 (Summer 1979): 204–13.

Chin, Christine B. N. *In Service and Servitude: Foreign Female Domestic Workers and the Malaysian "Modernity" Project.* New York: Columbia University Press, 1986.

Chin, Rita. *The Guest Worker Question in Postwar Germany*. 1st ed. New York: Cambridge University Press, 2009.

Chullén, Jorge, and David Lincoln. *Sugar World: Information and Analysis for Sugar Workers, 1977–1997*. ICCSASW-CCSTAM, 1998.

Clarke, Colin G. *Caribbean Social Relations*. Centre for Latin-American Studies, University of Liverpool, 1978.

Cochrane, Willard W. *The Development of American Agriculture: A Historical Analysis*. Minneapolis: University of Minnesota Press, 1979.

Cogan, John. "The Decline in Black Teenage Employment: 1950–1970." Working Paper No. 685, National Bureau of Economic Research, May 1981.

Comaroff, Jean. "Alien-Nation: Zombies, Immigrants, and Millennial Capitalism." *South Atlantic Quarterly* 101, 4 (Fall 2002): 779–805.

Cornelius, Wayne A. "Japan: The Illusion of Immigration Control." In *Controlling Immigration: A Global Perspective*, edited by Wayne A. Cornelius, Philip L. Martin, and James F. Hollifield, 375–410. Stanford, CA: Stanford University Press, 1994.

Craig, Dennis. *Education in the West Indies*. Mona: University of the West Indies, 1996.

Craig, Richard B. *The Bracero Program: Interest Groups and Foreign Policy*. Austin: University of Texas Press, 1971.

Craton, Michael. *Searching for the Invisible Man: Slaves and Plantation Life in Jamaica*. Cambridge: Harvard University Press, 1978.

Craton, Michael, and Gail Saunders. *Islanders in the Stream: A History of the Bahamian People*, vol. 2, *From the Ending of Slavery to the Twenty-first Century*. Athens: University of Georgia Press, 1998.

Cross, Gary S. *Immigrant Workers in Industrial France: The Making of a New Laboring Class*. Philadelphia: Temple University Press, 1983.

Cross, Malcolm, and Gad J. Heuman. *Labour in the Caribbean: From Emancipation to Independence*. Macmillan Caribbean, 1988.

Crush, J. S., Alan Jeeves, and David Yudelman. *South Africa's Labor Empire: A History of Black Migrancy to the Gold Mines*. Boulder, CO: Westview Press, 1991.

Cundall, Frank, *Jamaica in 1924, A Handbook of Information for Visitors and Intending Settlers with Some Account of the Colony's History*. Kingston: Institute of Jamaica, 1924.

Curtin, Philip. "The British Sugar Duties and West Indian Prosperity. *Journal of Economic History* 14, 2 (Spring 1954): 157–64.

Dalton, John E. *Sugar: A Case Study of Government Control*. New York: Macmillan, 1937.

Daniel, Cletus E. "Radicals on the Farm in California." *Agricultural History* 49, 4 (October 1975): 629–46.

Daniel, Pete. "The New Deal, Southern Agriculture, and Economic Change." In *The New Deal and The South*, edited by James C. Cobb and Michael V. Namorato, 37–61. Jackson: University Press of Mississippi, 1984.

———. *Standing at the Crossroads: Southern Life in the Twentieth Century*. New York: Hill & Wang, 1986.

Daniels, Roger. "The Growth of Restrictive Immigration Policies in the Colonies of Settlement." In *The Cambridge Survey of World Migration*, edited by Robin Cohen, 39–44. Cambridge: Cambridge University Press, 1995.

Darwin, John. *Britain and Decolonisation: The Retreat from Empire in the Post–War World.* London: MacMillan, 1988.

Davis, Steven M. *Everglades: the Ecosystem and its Restoration.* Boca Raton, FL: CRC Press, 1994.

De Schmidt, Aurora Camacho, and Frank O'Loughlin. "The 'H-2' Enemy: Institutionalized Injustice in Our Fields." *Civil Rights Quarterly* (Summer 1983): 8–9.

DeLone, Sarah. "Farmers, Growers, and the Department of Labor: The Inequality of Balance in the Temporary Agricultural Worker Program." *Law and Liberation* 3, 1 (Fall 1992): 100–144.

DeWind, John, et al. "The Cane Contract: West Indians in Florida." *NACLA Report on the Americas* 11, 8 (November–December 1977): 12.

DeWind, Josh, Tom Seidl, and Janet Shenk. "Caribbean Migration: Contract Labor in U.S. Agriculture." *NACLA Report on the Americas* 11, 8 (November–December 1977): 4–37.

Dunn, Richard. "'Dreadful Idlers' in the Cane Fields: The Slave Labor Pattern on a Jamaican Sugar Estate, 1762–1831." In *British Capitalism and Caribbean Slavery: The Legacy of Eric Williams*, edited by B. Solow and Stanley Engerman, 163–90. Cambridge: Cambridge University Press, 1987.

———. "The Pursuit of 'Higher Wages' and 'Perfect Personal Freedom'" St. Kitts-Nevis, 1836–1956." In *From Chattel Slaves to Wage Slaves: The Dynamics of Labour Bargaining in the Americas*, edited by Mary Turner, 275–301. Bloomington: Indiana University Press, 1995.

Dye, Alan, and Richard Sicotte. "The U.S. Sugar Program and the Cuban Revolution." *Journal of Economic History* 64 (2004): 673–704.

Eaton, G. E. *Alexander Bustamante and Modern Jamaica.* Kingston: Kingston Publishers, 1975.

Edid, Maralyn. *Farm Labor Organizing: Trends and Prospects.* Ithaca, NY: ILR Press, 1994.

Edie, Carlene J. *Democracy in the Caribbean.* Santa Barbara, CA: Praeger, 1994.

Edwards, David. *Report on An Economic Study of Small Farming in Jamaica.* Institute of Social and Economic Research, University of the West Indies. Glasgow: University Press, 1961.

Eelens, F. T. Schampers, and J. D. Speckmann, eds. *Labour Migration to the Middle East: From Sri Lanka to the Gulf.* New York: Kegan Paul International, 1992.

Eisner, Gisela. *Jamaica, 1830–1930.* Westport, CT: Greenwood Press, 1974.

Engerman, Stanley L. "Contract Labor, Sugar, and Technology in the Nineteenth Century." *Journal of Economic History* 43, 3 (September 1983): 635–59.

Feuer, Carl Henry. "Better Must Come: Sugar and Jamaica in the 20th Century." *Social and Economic Studies* 33, 4 (1984): 1–49.

———. *The Struggle for Workers' Rights at Hampden Sugar Estate.* Kingston: Social Action Centre, 1989.

Foner, Nancy. *Status and Power in Rural Jamaica*. New York: Teachers College Press, Columbia University, 1973.

———, ed. *Islands in the City: West Indian Migration to New York*. Berkeley: University of California Press, 2001.

———, ed. *New Immigrants in New York*. New York: Columbia University Press, 2001.

Foner, Nancy. *In a New Land: A Comparative View of Immigration*. New York: New York University Press, 2005.

Foner, Nancy, and Richard Napoli. "Jamaican and Black-American Migrant Farm Workers: A Comparative Analysis." *Social Problems* 25, 5 (1978): 491–503.

Fouron, Georges E. "The Black Immigrant Dilemma in the United States: The Haitian Experience." *Journal of Caribbean Studies* 3 (1987): 242–65.

Fox, Annette Baker. *Freedom and Welfare in the Caribbean: A Colonial Dilemma*. New York: Harcourt Brace, 1949.

Fragínals, Manuel Moreno. *The Sugarmill: the Socioeconomic Complex of Sugar in Cuba*. New York: Monthly Review Press, 1976.

Francis, O. C. *The People of Modern Jamaica*. Kingston: Department of Statistics, 1963.

Frucht, Richard. "Emigration, Remittances and Social Change: Aspects of the Social Field of Nevis, West Indies." *Anthropologica* 10, 2 (1968): 193–208.

Füllberg-Stolberg, Claus, and E. Peter Jacobs. *Jamaica 1938*. Mona: Social History Project, Department of History, University of the West Indies, 1990.

Gabbard, Susan M., and Richard Mines. "Farm Worker Demographics: Pre–IRCA Field Workers." In *Immigration Reform and U.S. Agriculture*, Publication 3358. Edited by Philip L. Martin et al., 63–71. Davis: University of California, Division of Agriculture and Natural Resources, 1995.

Galarza, Ernesto. *Merchants of Labor: The Mexican Bracero Story: An Account of the Managed Migration of Mexican Farm Workers in California, 1942–1960*. Charlotte and Santa Barbara: McNally & Loftin, 1964.

———. *Spiders in the House and Workers in the Fields*. Notre Dame: University of Notre Dame Press, 1970.

Gamboa, Erasmo. *Mexican Labor and World War II: Braceros in the Pacific Northwest, 1942–1947*. Seattle: University of Washington Press, 2000.

García, Juan Ramon. *Operation Wetback: The Mass Deportation of Mexican Undocumented Workers in 1954*. Westport, CT: Greenwood Press, 1980.

Gardezi, Hassan N. "Asian Workers in the Gulf States of the Middle East." In *International Labour Migrations*, edited by B. Singh Bolaria and Rosemary von Elling Bolaria, 99–120. Delhi: Oxford University Press, 1997.

Gerber, David J. "The U.S. Sugar Quota Program: A Study in the Direct Congressional Control of Imports." *Journal of Law and Economics* 19, 1 (1976): 103–47.

Gilroy, Paul. '*There Ain't No Black in the Union Jack': The Cultural Politics of Race and Nation*. Chicago: University of Chicago Press, 1991.

Gmelch, George. *Double Passage: The Lives of Caribbean Migrants Abroad and Back Home*. Ann Arbor: University of Michigan Press, 1992.

Goldfarb, Ronald L. *Migrant Farmworkers: A Caste of Despair.* Ames: University of Iowa, 1981.

Gordon, David, Richard Edwards, and Michael Reich. *Segmented Work, Divided Workers.* New York: Cambridge University Press, 1982.

Gott, Richard. *Cuba: A New History.* New Haven: Yale University Press, 2005.

Grant, Philip A., Jr. "Southern Congressmen and Agriculture, 1921–1932." *Agricultural History* 53 (1979): 338–51.

Grantham, Dewey W. *The South in Modern America: A Region at Odds.* New York: HarperCollins, 1994.

Gray, Obika. *Radicalism and Social Change in Jamaica, 1960–1972.* Knoxville: University of Tennessee Press, 1991.

Green, William A. *British Slave Emancipation: The Sugar Colonies and the Great Experiment, 1830–1865.* New York: Oxford University Press, 1991.

Greenberg, David. "The Contract, 'The Project,' and Work Experiences." In *Strangers No More: Anthropological Studies of Cat Island, the Bahamas,* edited by Joel S. Savishinsky, 170–207. Ithaca, NY: Ithaca College Press, 1978.

Gregory, James N. *The Southern Diaspora: How the Great Migration of Black and White Southerners Transformed America.* Chapel Hill: University of North Carolina Press, 2005.

Griffing, Michael P. *Impact of the Adverse Effect Wage Rate on the Domestic Farm Labor Market: A Theoretical Discussion.* Legal Action Support Project, Bureau of Social Science Research, 1976.

Griffith, David. "Women, Remittances, and Reproduction." *American Ethnologist,* 12, 4 (November 1985): 676–90.

Griffith, David. "Peasants in Reserve: Temporary West Indian Labor in the U.S. Farm Labor Market." *International Migration Review* 20, 4 (1986): 875–98.

———. "Social Organizational Obstacles to Capital Accumulation Among Returning Migrants: The British West Indies Temporary Alien Labor Program." *Human Organization* 45, 1 (1986): 34–42.

———. *American Guestworkers: Jamaicans and Mexicans in the U. S. Labor Market.* University Park: Pennsylvania State University Press, 2007.

Griffith, David, Ed Kissam, and Jeronimo Campaseco. *Working Poor: Farmworkers in the United States.* Philadelphia: Temple University Press, 1995.

Guerin-Gonzales, Camille. *Mexican Workers and American Dreams: Immigration, Repatriation, and California Farm Labor, 1900–1939.* New Brunswick, NJ: Rutgers University Press, 1994.

Gunst, Laurie. *Born Fi' Dead.* New York: Macmillan, 1996.

Guzda, Henry P. "James P. Mitchell: Social Conscience of the Cabinet." *Monthly Labor Review* (August 1991): 23–29.

Gyory, Andrew. *Closing the Gates: Race, Politics, and the Chinese Exclusion Act.* Chapel Hill: University of North Carolina Press, 1998.

Hahamovitch, Cindy. *The Fruits of Their Labor: Atlantic Coast Farmworkers and the Making of Migrant Poverty, 1875–1945.* Chapel Hill: University of North Carolina Press, 1997.

———. "Standing Idly By: 'Organized' Farmworkers in Florida During the Second World War." In *Organized Labor in the New South*, 2nd ed., edited by Robert Zieger, 15–36. Knoxville: University of Tennessee Press, 1997.

———. "In America Life Is Given Away": Jamaican Farmworkers and the Making of Agricultural Immigration Policy." In *The Countryside in the Age of the Modern State: Political Histories of Rural America*, edited by Catherine Mc-Nicol Stock and Robert D. Johnston, 134–60. Ithaca, NY: Cornell University Press, 2001.

———. "Creating Perfect Immigrants: Guestworkers of the World in Historical Perspective." *Labor History* 44, 1 (January 2003): 69–94.

———. "The Worst Job in the World": Reform, Revolution, and the Secret Rebellion in Florida's Cane Fields." *Journal of Peasant Studies* 4, 35 (October 2008): 770–800.

Hahamovitch, Cindy, and Rick Halpern. "Not a 'Sack of Potatoes': Why Labor Historians Need to Take Agriculture Seriously." *International Labor and Working Class History* 65 (Spring 2004): 3–10.

Hall, Michael R. *Sugar and Power in the Dominican Republic: Eisenhower, Kennedy, and the Trujillos*. Westport, CT: Greenwood Press, 2000.

Halliday, Fred. "Labor Migration in the Arab World." *Merip Reports* 14, no. 4 (May 1984): 3–10.

Halpern, Rick. "Solving the 'Labour Problem': Race, Work, and the State in Louisiana and Natal, 1870–1910." *Journal of Southern African Studies* 30, 1 (2004): 19–40.

Harris, Nigel. *The New Untouchables: Immigration and the New World Worker*. New York: I. B. Tauris Publishers, 1995.

Harrison, Michelle. "Living with the Sugar Legacy: International Policy Change and Local Level Impact in Rural Jamaica." In *Resource Sustainability and Caribbean Development*, edited by Duncan F. M. McGregor, David Barker, and Sally Lloyd Evans, 232–49. Kingston, Jamaica: University of the West Indies Press, 1998.

Hawkins, Freda. *Critical Years in Immigration: Canada and Australia Compared*, 2nd edition. Montreal: McGill-Queen's University Press, 1991.

Hawley, Ellis W. "The Politics of the Mexican Labor Issue, 1950–1965." *Agricultural History* 40, 3 (1966): 157–76.

Heitmann, John A. *The Modernization of the Louisiana Sugar Industry, 1830–1910*. Baton Rouge: Louisiana State University Press, 1987.

———. "The Beginnings of Big Sugar in Florida, 1920–1945." *Florida Historical Quarterly* 77, 1 (Summer 1998): 39–61.

Henderson, Julia. "Foreign Labour in the United States during the War." *International Labour Review* 52 (December 1945): 609–31.

Herbert, Ulrich. *A History of Foreign Labor in Germany, 1880–1980: Seasonal Workers/Forced Laborers/Guest Workers*. Ann Arbor: University of Michigan Press, 1990; German language edition published 1986.

Heston, Thomas J. "Cuba, the United States, and the Sugar Act of 1948: The Failure of Economic Coercion." *Diplomatic History* 6, 1 (1982): 1–22.

Heuman, Gad J. *The Killing Time: The Morant Bay Rebellion in Jamaica.* Knoxville: University of Tennessee Press, 1994.

Hinckle, Warren, and William W. Turner. *The Fish Is Red: The Story of the Secret War Against Castro.* New York: Harper & Row, 1981.

Hoerder, Dirk. "Changing Paradigms in Migration History: From 'To America' to World-Wide Systems." *Canadian Review of American Studies* 24, 2 (1994): 105–26.

Holder, Calvin B. "The Causes and Composition of West Indian Immigration to New York City, 1900–1952." *Afro-Americans in New York Life and History* (January 1987): 7–27.

Hollander, Gail M. *Raising Cane in the 'Glades: The Global Sugar Trade and the Transformation of Florida.* Chicago: University of Chicago Press, 2008.

Hollifield, James F. *Immigrants, Markets, and States: The Political Economy of Postwar Europe.* Cambridge, MA: Harvard University Press, 1992.

Holt, James S. "Labor in Florida Agriculture." In *Migrant Labor in Agriculture: An International Comparison*, edited by Philip Martin, 19–30. Oakland: Agricultural and Natural Resource Publications, University of California, 1984.

Hougan, Jim. *Spooks: The Haunting of America—The Private Use of Secret Agents.* New York: William Morrow, 1978.

Hughes, Colin A. *Race and Politics in the Bahamas.* New York: St. Martin's Press, 1981.

Hull, Elizabeth. *Without Justice for All: The Constitutional Rights of Aliens.* Westport, CT: Greenwood Press, 1985.

Humphrey, Michael. "Migrants, Workers and Refugees: The Political Economy of Population Movements in the Middle East." *MERIP* 23, 2 (March/April 1993): 2–9.

Hurston, Zora Neale. *Their Eyes Were Watching God.* New York: HarperCollins, 2000.

Ilhan, Başgöz, and Norman Furniss, eds. *Turkish Workers in Europe: An Interdisciplinary Study.* Bloomington: Indiana University Turkish Studies, 1985.

International Historical Statistics: The Americas, 1750–2000, 5th ed. New York: Palgrave McMillan, 2003.

James, Winston. *Holding Aloft the Banner of Ethiopia: Caribbean Radicalism in Early Twentieth Century America.* New York: Verso, 1998.

Jenkins, J. Craig. "The Transformation of a Constituency into a Social Movement Revisited: Farmworker Organizing in California." In *Waves of Protest: Social Movements Since the Sixties*, edited by Jo Freeman and Victoria Johnson, 277–302. New York: Rowman & Littlefield, 1999.

Johnson, Anthony S. *J.A.G. Smith.* Kingston Publishers in association with J.I.P.E., Jamaica Institute of Political Education, 1991.

Johnson, Benjamin Heber. *Revolution in Texas: How a Forgotten Rebellion and Its Bloody Suppression Turned Mexicans into Americans.* New Haven, CT: Yale University Press, 2003.

Johnson, David Gale. *The Sugar Program: Large Costs and Small Benefits.* Washington, DC: American Enterprise Institute for Public Policy Research, 1974.

Johnson, Earl, Jr. *Justice and Reform: The Formative Years of the American Legal Service Program.* New York: Russell Sage, 1974.

Johnson, Fay Clarke. *Soldiers of the Soil.* New York: Vantage Press, 1995.

Johnson, Howard. "Bahamian Labor Migration to Florida in the Late Nineteenth and Early Twentieth Centuries." *International Migration Review* 22 (1988): 84–103.

———. *The White Minority in the Caribbean.* Kingston: Ian Randle Publishers, 1998.

Joseph, Gilbert Michael, Catherine LeGrand, and Ricardo Donato Salvatore. *Close Encounters of Empire.* Durham, NC: Duke University Press, 1998.

Jung, Moon Ho. *Coolies and Cane: Race, Labor and Sugar in the Age of Emancipation.* Baltimore: Johns Hopkins University Press, 2006.

Jupp, James. *Immigration.* New York: Oxford University Press, 1991.

Karim, Ahm Zehadul, Moha Asri Abdullah, and Mohd Isa Haji Bakar. *Foreign Workers in Malaysia: Issues and Implications.* Kuala Lumpur: Utusan Publications, 1999.

Kasinitz, Philip. *Caribbean New York: Black Immigrants and the Politics of Race.* Ithaca, NY: Cornell University Press, 1992.

Kaufman, Michael. *Jamaica under Manley: Dilemmas of Socialism and Democracy.* London: Zed Books, 1985.

———. "Democracy and Social Transformation in Jamaica." *Social and Economic Studies* 37, 3 (1988): 45–73.

Kessler, Mark. *Legal Services for the Poor: A Comparative and Contemporary Analysis of Interorganizational Politics.* Westport, CT: Greenwood Press, 1987.

Kirstein, Peter N. "Agribusiness, Labor and the Wetbacks: Truman's Commission on Migratory Labor." *Historian* 40, 4 (1978): 650–67.

Knight, Franklin W. "Who Needs a Guest Worker Program? They Do, We Do." *Caribbean Review* 11, 1 (Winter 1982): 46–47.

———. "Jamaican Migrants and the Cuban Sugar Industry, 1900–1934." In *Between Slavery and Free Labor: The Spanish-speaking Caribbean in the Nineteenth Century*, edited by Manuel Moreno Fraginals, Frank Moya Pons, and Stanley L. Engerman, 94–114. Baltimore: Johns Hopkins University Press, 1985.

Koslofsky, Joanne. "Where Sugar Is King." *NACLA: Report on the Americas* 15, 1 (January–February 1981): 8–23.

Kramer, Peter. *The Offshores: A Study of Foreign Farm Labor in Florida.* St. Petersburg, FL: Community Action Fund, 1966.

Kurlansky, Mark. *A Continent of Islands: Searching for Caribbean Destiny.* New York: Da Capo Press, 1993.

Lake, Marilyn, and Henry Reynolds. *Drawing the Global Colour Line: White Men's Countries and the International Challenge of Racial Equality.* 1st ed. Cambridge: Cambridge University Press, 2008.

Langley, Lester D. *The United States and the Caribbean in the Twentieth Century.* Athens: University of Georgia Press, 1985.

Lee, Erika. *At America's Gates: Chinese Immigration during the Exclusion Era, 1882–1943.* Chapel Hill: University of North Carolina Press, 2003.

Le Franc, Elsie. *Consequences of Structural Adjustment: A Review of the Jamaican Experience*. Kingston, Jamaica: Canoe Press, 1994.

Le Franc, Elsie, and Andrew Downes. "Measuring Human Development in Countries with Invisible Economies: Challenges Posed by the Informal and Remittance Sectors in Jamaica." *Social and Economic Studies* 50, 1 (2001): 169–98.

Legg, L. G. Wickham, and E. T. Williams. *The Dictionary of National Biography, 1941–1950: With an Index Covering the Years 1901–1950*. New York: Oxford University Press, 1959.

Leo-Rhynie, Elsa. *The Jamaican Family*. Kingston: The Grace, Kennedy Foundation, 1993.

Levi, Darrell E. "Fragmented Nationalism: Jamaica Since 1938." *History of European Ideas* 15, 1–3 (1992): 413–17.

Levine, Barry B. *The Caribbean Exodus*. New York: Greenwood, 1987.

Lewis, Gordon K. *The Growth of the Modern West Indies*. Kingston: Ian Randle Publishers, 2004.

Lewis, W. Arthur. *Labour in the West Indies*. 2nd ed. London: New Beacon Ltd., 1977.

Libby, Ronald T. "The United States and Jamaica: Playing the American Card." *Latin American Perspectives* 17, 1 (Winter 1990): 86–109.

Lindsey, Lydia. "A Reexamination of the Significance of the McCarran-Walter Act on Post–World War II Indian Migration to Britain—An Expository Note." *Journal of Caribbean Studies* 10, 3 (Summer–Fall 1995): 182–206.

Liss, Samuel. "The Concept and Determination of Prevailing Wages in Agriculture During World War II." *Agricultural History* 24 (1950): 4–18.

———. "Farm Wage Boards Under the Wages Stabilization Program During World War II." *Agricultural History* 30 (1956): 128–37.

Looney, Ginny. "Biting the Budget at Legal Services." *Southern Changes* 4, 4–5 (1982): 19–22.

Lopez, Paul. *The Braceros: Guest Workers, Settlers, and Family Legacies*. 1st ed. Dubuque, IA: Kendall Hunt Publishing, 2009.

Lowenthal, David. "Black Power in the Caribbean Context, "*Economic Geography* 48 (January 1972): 116–34.

Lowi, Theodore. "How the Farmers Get What They Want." *The Reporter* 21 (May 1967): 34–37.

Lucas, María Elena. *Forged Under the Sun: The Life of María Elena Lucas*. Ann Arbor: University of Michigan Press, 1993.

Lucassen, Jan. *Migrant Labour in Europe, 1600–1900: The Drift to the North Sea*. London: Croom Helm, 1986.

Lungren, Daniel E., and Kevin P. Holsclaw. "An Analysis of the H-2 Program: The Admission of Temporary Foreign Agricultural Workers into the United States." *Yale Law and Policy Review* 1, 2 (Spring 1983): 24–254.

Maingot, Anthony P. *Caribbean Migration as a Structural Reality*. Latin American and Caribbean Center, Florida International University, 1983.

———. *The United States and the Caribbean*. Boulder, CO: Westview, 1994.

Majka, Linda C., and Theo J. Majka. *Farm Workers, Agribusiness, and the State.* Philadelphia: Temple University Press, 1982.

Mapes, Kathleen. *Sweet Tyranny: Migrant Labor, Industrial Agriculture, and Imperial Politics.* Urbana: University of Illinois Press, 2009.

Marks, Arnaud F., and Hebe M. C. Vessuri. *White Collar Migrants in the Americas and the Caribbean.* Leiden: Royal Institute of Linguistics and Anthropology and Department of Caribbean Studies, 1983.

Marks, Henry S. *Who Was Who in Florida.* Huntsville, AL: Strode Publishers, 1973.

Marshall, Dawn. "The History of Caribbean Migrations: The Case of the West Indies." *Caribbean Review* 11, 1 (Winter 1982): 6–9, 52–53.

———. "A History of West Indian Migrations: Overseas Opportunities and 'Safety-Valve' Policies." In *The Caribbean Exodus,* edited by Barry B. Levine, 15–31. New York: Praeger, 1987.

Martin, Philip. "Guestworkers: New Solution, New Problem?" Pew Charitable Trust (2002), http://pewhispanic.org/files/reports/7.pdf", 23 (accessed July 1, 2009).

Martin, Philip, and Richard Mines. "Alien Workers and Agriculture: The Need for Policy Linkage." *Yale Law and Policy Review* 1, 2 (Spring 1983): 255–69.

Martin, Philip L., and David A. Martin. *The Endless Quest: Helping America's Farm Workers.* Boulder, CO: Westview Press, 1994.

Martin, Philip L., and Michael S. Teitelbaum. "The Mirage of Mexican Guest Workers." *Foreign Affairs* 80, 6 (November–December 2001): 117–31.

Martin, Philip L. et al., eds. *Immigration Reform and U.S. Agriculture.* Publication 3358. University of California, Division of Agriculture and Natural Resources, 1995.

Massey, Douglas S. *Beyond Smoke and Mirrors: Mexican Immigration in an Era of Economic Integration.* New York: Russell Sage Foundation Publications, 2003.

Massey, Douglas, Rafael Alarcón, Jorge Durand, and Humberto González. *Return to Aztlan: The Social Process of International Migration From Western Mexico.* Berkeley: University of California Press, 1987.

Matusow, Allen J. *Farm Policies and Politics in the Truman Years.* Cambridge, MA: Harvard University Press, 1967.

McCally, David Philip. *Cane cutters in the Everglades.* Tampa: University of South Florida, 1991.

McConnell, Grant. *The Decline of Agrarian Democracy.* Berkeley: University of California Press, 1953.

McCorkle, James L. Jr. "Agricultural Experiment Stations and Southern Truck Farming." *Agricultural History* 69, 2 (1988): 234–43.

McCoy, Terry L. "A Primer for U.S. on Caribbean Emigration." *Caribbean Review* 8, 1 (January–March 1979): 10–15.

McCoy, Terry L., and Charles H. Wood. "Caribbean Workers in the Florida Sugar Cane Industry." Paper No. 2. Center for Latin American Studies. Gainesville: University of Florida, 1982.

McCoy, Terry L., and Charles H. Wood. "Migration, Remittances and Development: A Study of Caribbean Cane Cutters in Florida." *International Migration Review* 19, 2 (Summer 1985): 251–77.

McCune, Wesley. *Who's Behind Our Farm Policy?* New York: Praeger, 1956.

McGregor, Duncan F., and M. Lloyd-Evans. *Resource Sustainability and Caribbean Development.* Kingston, Jamaica: The Press, University of the West Indies, 1998.

McKean, David. *Peddling Influence: Thomas ("Tommy the Cork") Cocoran and the Birth of Modern Lobbying.* Hanover, NH: Steerforth, 2005.

McKeown, Adam. "Global Migration 1846–1940." *Journal of World History* 15, 2 (June 2004): 155–89.

McKeown, Adam M. *Melancholy Order: Asian Migration and the Globalization of Borders.* 1st ed. New York: Columbia University Press, 2008.

Meeks, Eric V. *Border Citizens: The Making of Indians, Mexicans, and Anglos in Arizona.* Austin: University of Texas Press, 2007.

Michel, Greg L. *Struggle for a Better South: The Southern Student Organizing Committee, 1964–1969.* New York: Palgrave-MacMillan, 2004.

Miller, Mark J. *Foreign Workers in Western Europe.* New York: Praeger, 1981.

Mintz, Sidney Wilfred *Caribbean Transformations.* New York: Columbia University Press, 1989.

Mintz, Sidney Wilfred. *Sweetness and Power.* New York: Penguin Books, 1986.

Mintz, Sidney Wilfred, and Sally Price. *Caribbean Contours.* Baltimore: Johns Hopkins University Press, 1985.

Mintz, Sidney Wilfred, Sally Price, and Woodrow Wilson International Center for Scholars. Latin American Program. *Focus—Caribbean.* Latin American Program, Woodrow Wilson International Center for Scholars, 1985.

Mitchell, H. L. *Mean Things Happening in This Land: The Life and Times of H. L. Mitchell, Cofounder of the Southern Tenant Farmers Union.* Montclair, NJ: Allanheld, Osmun, & Co., 1979.

Moch, Leslie Page. *Moving Europeans: Migration in Western Europe Since 1650.* Bloomington: Indiana University Press, 1992.

Mohl, Raymond A. "Black Immigrants: Bahamians in Early Twentieth-Century Miami." *Florida Historical Quarterly* 65, 3 (January 1987): 271–97.

——. "Immigration through the Port of Miami." In *Forgotten Doors: The Other Ports of Entry to the United States*, edited by M. Mark Stolarik, 81–98. Philadelphia: Balch Institute Press, 1988.

Momsem, Janet Henshall. "Gender Roles in Caribbean Agricultural Labour." In *Labour in the Caribbean From Emancipation to Independence*, edited by Malcolm Cross and Gad Heuman, 141–59. London: MacMillan, 1988.

Monaco, Paul. *The Sixties: 1960–1969.* Berkeley: University of California Press, 2001.

Morin, Alexander. *The Organizability of Farm Labor in the United States.* Cambridge, MA: Harvard University Press, 1952.

Mortimer, Delores M., and Roy S. Bryce-Laporte. *Female Immigrants to the United States.* Washington, DC: Research Institute on Immigration and Ethnic Studies, Smithsonian Institution, 1981.

Munroe, Trevor. *Politics of Constitutional Decolonisation, Jamaica, 1944–62*, reprint ed. Mona: Institute of Social and Economic Research, University of the West Indies, 1983.

Nelson, Lawrence J. "The Art of the Possible: Another Look at the 'Purge' of the AAA Liberals in 1935." *Agricultural History* 57 (1983): 416–35.

Nelson, Scott. "After Slavery: Forced Drafts of Irish and Chinese Labor in the American Civil War, Or the Search for Liquid Labor." In *Many Middle Passages: Forced Migration and the Making of the Modern World*, edited by Emma Christopher, Cassandra Pybus, and Marcus Rediker, 150–65. Berkeley: University of California Press, 2007.

Nettleford, Rex M. *Mirror Mirror: Identity, Race and Protest in Jamaica*. Kingston: William Collins and Sangster, 1970.

———. *Jamaica in Independence: Essays on the Early Years*. Kingston: Heinemann, 1989.

Newton, Velma. *The Silver Men: West Indian Labour Migration to Panama, 1850–1914*. Kingston: Ian Randle, 2004.

Ngai, Mae. *Impossible Subjects: Illegal Aliens and the Making of Modern America*. Princeton, NJ: Princeton University Press, 2004.

North, David S. "Nonimmigrant Workers: Visiting Labor Force Participants." *Monthly Labor Review* 103, 10 (October 1980): 26–30.

Oka, Takashi. *Prying Open the Door: Foreign Workers in Japan*. Washington, DC: Carnegie Endowment for International Peace, 1994.

Orrenius, Pia M., and Madeline Zavodny. "Do Amnesty Programs Reduce Undocumented Immigration? Evidence from IRCA." *Demography* 40, 3 (August 2003): 437–50.

Pactor, Howard S. *Colonial British Caribbean Newspapers: A Bibliography and Directory*. New York: Greenwood Press, 1990.

Paine, Suzanne. *Exporting Workers: The Turkish Case*. University of Cambridge, Department of Applied Economics, Occasional Paper 41. New York and London: Cambridge University Press, 1974.

Palmer, Colin. "Identity, Race, and Black Power in Independent Jamaica." In *The Modern Caribbean*, edited by Franklin W. Knight and Colin A. Palmer, 111–28. Chapel Hill: University of North Carolina Press, 1989.

Palmer, Ransford. "A Decade of West Indian Migration to the United States, 1962–1972: An Economic Analysis." *Social and Economic Studies* 23, 4 (1974): 571–87.

Parrenas, Rhacel Salazar. *Servants of Globalization: Women, Migration, and Domestic Work*. Stanford, CA: Stanford University Press, 2001.

Patterson, Gordon. "Raising Cane and Refining Sugar: Florida Crystals and the Fame of Fellsmere." *Florida Historical Quarterly* 75, 4 (1997): 408–28.

Payne, Anthony. *Politics in Jamaica*. Kingston: Ian Randle, 1994.

Payne, Anthony, and Paul Sutton. *Charting Caribbean Development*. Gainesville: University Press of Florida, 2001.

Peck, Gunther. *Reinventing Free Labor: Padrone and Immigrant Workers in the North American West, 1880–1930*. New York: Cambridge University Press, 2000.

Peck, Gunther. "Making Sense of White Slavery and Whiteness." *Labor: Studies in Working-Class History of the Americas*1, 2 (Summer 2004):41–63.

Petras, Elizabeth McLean. *Jamaican Labor Migration: White Capital and Black Labor, 1850–1930.* Boulder, CO: Westview Press, 1988.

Phaup, Jimmie Darrell. "*The Politics of Poverty*: Controversy in Three South Florida Migrant Programs." Ph.D. Dissertation, University of Arizona, 1975.

Phillips, Peter. "Race, Class, Nationalism: A Perspective on Twentieth Century Social Movements in Jamaica." *Social and Economic Studies* 37, 3 (1988): 97–124.

Plender, Richard. *International Migration Law.* Boston: Martinus Nijhoff Publishers, 1987.

Polopolus, Leo C., and Robert D. Emerson. "IRCA and Agriculture in Florida." *Immigration Reform and U.S. Agriculture*, Publication 3358. Edited by Philip L. Martin, et al. University of California, Division of Agriculture and Natural Resources, 1995, 77–96.

Portes, Alejandro, and Robert L. Bach. *Latin Journey: Cuban and Mexican Immigrants in the United States.* Berkeley: University of California Press, 1985.

Post, Ken. *Arise Ye Starvelings: The Jamaican Labour Rebellion and its Aftermath.* The Hague: Martinus Nijhoff, 1978.

———. *Strike the Iron,* vol. 1. Atlantic Highlands, NJ: Humanities Press, 1981.

Potter, Robert B., Dennis Conway, and Joan Phillips. *The Experience of Return Migration.* Aldershot, UK: Ashgate Publishing, 2005.

Price, David E. "The Politics of Sugar." *Review of Politics* 33, 1 (January 1971): 212–32.

Proudfoot, Malcolm J. *Population Movements in the Caribbean.* New York: Negro Universities Press, 1950, 1970.

Proudfoot, Mary Macdonald. *Britain and the United States in the Caribbean: A Comparative Study in the Methods of Development.* London: Faber & Faber, 1954.

Putnam, Lara. *The Company They Kept: Migrants and the Politics of Gender in Caribbean Costa Rica, 1870–1960.* Chapel Hill: University of North Carolina Press, 2002.

Rabe, Stephen G. *Eisenhower and Latin America: The Foreign Policy of Anticommunism.* Chapel Hill: University of North Carolina Press, 1998.

Ramirez, Bruno. *Crossing the 49th Parallel, Migration from Canada to the United States, 1900–1930.* Ithaca, NY: Cornell University Press, 2001.

Raphael, Lennox. "West Indians and Afro-Americans." *Freedomways* (Summer 1964): 438–45.

Raymond, Nathaniel. "Cane Fires on a British West Indian Island." *Social and Economic Studies* 16 (1967): 280–88.

Reavis, Dick J. *Without Documents.* New York: Condor, 1978.

Regan, Francis, Alan Paterson, and Tamara Goriely. *The Transformation of Legal Aid: Comparative and Historical Studies.* Gloucestershire: Clarendon Press, 1999.

Reid, Ira De A. *The Negro Immigrant.* New York: Columbia University Press, 1939.

Reid, Sheryl Andre. "U.S.–Jamaica Relations: The Farm Work Programme, 1943–1962." M.A. Thesis, UWI, 1998.

Reimers, David M. *Still the Golden Door*. New York: Columbia University Press, 1992.

Richards, Glen. "Race, Class, and Labour Politics in Colonial Jamaica." In *Jamaica in Slavery and Freedom: History, Heritage and Culture*, edited by Kathleen E. A. Monteith and Glen Richards, 340–62. Jamaica: University of the West Indies Press, 2002.

———. "The Pursuit of 'Higher Wages' & 'Perfect Personal Freedom' St. Kitts-Nevis, 1836–1956." In *From Chattel Slaves to Wage Slaves: The Dynamics of Labour Bargaining in the Americas*, edited by Mary Turner, 275–301. Bloomington: Indiana University Press, 1995.

———. "'Driber Tan Mi Side': Creolisation and the Labour Process in St. Kitts-Nevis, 1810–1905." *Questioning Creole: Creolisation Discourses in Caribbean Culture*, edited by Kamau Brathwaite, Verene Shepherd, Glen L. Richards, 202–226. Kingston: Ian Randle Publishers, 2002.

Richardson, Bonham C. *Caribbean Migrants: Environment and Human Survival on St. Kitts and Nevis*. Knoxville: University of Tennessee Press, 1983.

———. *The Caribbean in the Wider World, 1492–1992: A Regional Geography*. New York: Cambridge University Press, 1992.

———. *Economy and environment in the Caribbean*. Gainesville: University Press of Florida, 1997.

Riley, James C. *Poverty and Life Expectancy: The Jamaica Paradox*. Cambridge: Cambridge University Press, 2005.

Roberts, G. W. "Emigration from the Island of Barbados." *Social and Economic Studies* 4, 3 (September 1955): 245–88.

———. *The Population of Jamaica*. London: Conservation Foundation at the University Press, 1957.

———, ed. "Recent Population Movement in Jamaica." Paris: Census Research Programme, University of the West Indies CICRED Series, 1974.

Roberts, G. W., and D. O. Mills. "Study of External Migration Affecting Jamaica, 1953–1955." *Social and Economic Studies* 7, 2 Supplement (June 1958): 10.

Roberts, George W., and Sonja A. Sinclair. *Women in Jamaica: Patterns of Reproduction and Family*. Millwood, NY: KTO Press, 1978.

Roberts, Paul. "The Sweet Hereafter: Our Craving for Sugar Starves the Everglades and Fattens Politicians." *Harper's Magazine* (November 1999): 54, 55–68.

Rochester, Anna. *Why Farmers are Poor: the Agricultural Crisis in the United States*, reprint ed. New York: International Publishers, 1940.

Rodgers, Gerry, Eddy Lee, Lee Swepston, and Jasmien Van Daele. *The International Labour Organization and the Quest for Social Justice, 1919–2009*. Ithaca, NY: Cornell University Press, 2009.

Rosenbaum, Rene Perez. "Unionization of Tomato Field Workers in Northwest Ohio, 1967–1969." *Labor History* 35, 3 (Summer 1994): 329–44.

Rowley, Charles Kershaw. *The Right to Justice: The Political Economy of Legal Services in the United States*. Brookfield, VT: Edward Elgar, 1992.

Rubenstein, Hymie. "Remittances and Rural Underdevelopment in the English-Speaking Caribbean." *Human Organization* 42, 4 (1983): 295–306.

Ruck, Rob. *The Tropic of Baseball: Baseball in the Dominican Republic.* Lincoln: University of Nebraska Press, 1998.

Safa, Helen I., and Brian M. Du Toit. *Migration and Development: Implications for Ethnic Identity and Political Conflict.* The Hague: Mouton, 1975.

Salley, George H. *A History of the Florida Sugar Industry.* Clewiston, FL: Sugar Cane League, 1984.

Saloutos, Theodore. "Agricultural Organizations and Farm Policy in the South after World War II." *Agricultural History* 5, 3 (1979): 377–404.

Sanchez, Guerra-Ramino. *Sugar and Society in the Caribbean.* New Haven, CT: Yale University Press, 1964.

Sarat, Austin, Bryant G. Garth, and Robert A. Kagan. *Looking Back at Law's Century.* Ithaca and London: Cornell University Press, 2002.

Sassen, Saskia. *Guests and Aliens.* New York: New Press, 2000.

Saunders, Christopher, and Nicholas Southey. *Historical Dictionary of South Africa*, 2nd edition. *African Historical Dictionaries*, No. 78. Lanham, MD: Scarecrow Press, 2000.

Saunders, Gail, and Edward Carson. *Guide to the Records of the Bahamas.* Nassau: Government Print Department, Commonwealth of the Bahamas, 1973.

Schad, Martha. *Hitler's Spy Princess: The Extraordinary Life of Stephanie von Hohenlohe.* trans. Angus McGeoch. Stroud, Gloucestershire: History Press, 2004.

Schapsmeier, Edward L., and Frederick H. Schapsmeier. "Farm Policy from FDR to Eisenhower: Southern Democrats and the Politics of Agriculture." *Agricultural History* 53 (January 1979): 352–71.

Schell, Greg. "Farmworker Exceptionalism under the Law: How the Legal System Contributes to Farmworker Poverty and Powerlessness." In *The Human Cost of Food: Farmworkers' Lives, Labor, and Advocacy*, edited by Charles D. Thompson, Jr., and Melinda F. Wiggins, 139–66. Austin: University of Texas Press, 2002.

Schmidt, Louis B. "The Role and Techniques of Agrarian Pressure Groups." *Agricultural History* 30 (April 1956): 49–58.

Scruggs, Otey M. "Evolution of the Mexican Farm Labor Agreement of 1942." *Agricultural History* 34 (July 1960): 140–49.

Semler, H. Michael "The New Immigration Law and Guestworkers (H-2 Program)." *The Progressive* 46 (March 1982): 42–44.

Semler, H. Michael. "Overview: The H-2 Program. Aliens in the Orchard: The Admission of Foreign Contract Laborers for Temporary Work in U.S. Agriculture." *Yale Law & Policy Review* 1, 2 (Spring 1983): 187–239.

Shepard, Kris. *Rationing Justice: Poverty Lawyers and Poor People in the Deep South.* Baton Rouge: Louisiana State University Press, 2007.

Shepherd, Verene. *Working Slavery, Pricing Freedom: Perspectives from the Caribbean, Africa, and the African Diaspora.* New York: Palgrave, 2002.

Shepherd, Verene, Bridget Brereton, and Barbara Bailey, eds. *Engendering History: Caribbean Women in Historical Perspective.* New York: St. Martin's Press, 1995.

Sherlock, Philip Manderson. *The Story of the Jamaican People / Bennett, Hazel.* Kingston, Jamaica: I. Randle Publishers; Princeton, NJ: M. Wiener Publishers, 1998.

Sherrill, Robert G. "The Power Game: George Smathers, the Golden Senator from Florida." *The Nation*, December 7, 1964, 426–37.

Shimada, Haruo. Translated by Roger Northridge. *Japan's 'Guest Workers' issues and public policies.* Tokyo: University of Tokyo Press, 1994.

Shofner, Jerrell H. "The Legacy of Racial Slavery: Free Enterprise and Forced Labor in Florida in the 1940s." *Journal of Southern History* 47, 3 (August 1981): 411–26.

Siebert, Wilbur. "The Early Sugar Industry in Florida." *Florida Historical Quarterly* 35, 4 (1956–57): 312–19.

Singer-Kérel, Jeanne. "Foreign Workers in France, 1891–1936." *Ethnic and Racial Studies* 14, 3 (July 1991): 279–93.

Sitterson, J. Carlyle. "Ante-Bellum Sugar Culture in the South Atlantic States." *Journal of Southern History* 3, 2 (May 1937): 175–87.

———. *Sugar Country.* Louisville: University of Kentucky, 1953.

Skidmore, Thomas E., and Peter H. Smith. *Modern Latin America.* 6th edition. New York: Oxford University Press, 2004.

Smith, T. E. *Commonwealth Migration: Flows and Policies.* London: MacMillan Press, 1981.

Solber, Carl. *Immigration and Nationalism: Argentina and Chile, 1890–1914.* Austin: University of Texas Press, 1970.

Southern Poverty Law Center Report, "Close to Slavery: Guestworker Programs in the United States." http://www.splcenter.org/legal/guestreport/guest3c.jsp" (accessed 31 July 31, 2009).

Sowell, Thomas. *Migration and Cultures: A World View.* New York: Basic Books, 1996.

Spencer, Ian R. G. *British Immigration Policy Since 1939: The Making of Multi-Racial Britain.* New York: Routledge, 1997.

Spriggs, Kent. "Access of Visitors to Labor Camps on Privately Owned Property." *University of Florida Law Review* 21, 295 (1968–1969): 295–323.

Stalker, Peter. *The Work of Strangers: A Survey of International Labour Migration.* Geneva: International Labour Office, 1994.

Stark, H. N. "War Poses Problems for the British West Indies." *Foreign Commerce Weekly* 9, 12 (1942): 8–12.

Steinbeck, John. *The Grapes of Wrath.* New York: Viking Press, 1939.

Sternstein, Jerome L. "Corruption in the Gilded Age Senate: Nelson W. Aldrich and the Sugar Trust." *Capitol Studies* 6, 1 (Spring 1978): 13–37.

Stone, Carl. "Political Aspects of Postwar Agricultural Policies in Jamaica (1945–1970)." *Social and Economic Studies* 23 (December 1974): 145–75.

Stone, Carl. *Class, State, and Democracy in Jamaica*. New York: Praeger, 1986.
———. "Running Out of Options in Jamaica: Seaga and Manley Compared." *Caribbean Review* 15, 3 (Winter 1987): 10–12.
———. *Power and Policy Making in Jamaica*. Kingston: C. Stone, 1987.
Street, Richard Steven. "Poverty in the Valley of Plenty: The National Farm Labor Union, DiGorgio Farms, and Suppression of Documentary Photography in Florida, 1947–66." *Labor History* 48, 1 (February 2007): 25–48.
Sugar World: Information and Analysis for Sugar Workers, 1977–1997. Toronto: ICCSASW-CCSTAM, 1998.
Sutton, Constance R., and O. Nigel Bolland. *Revisiting Caribbean Labour*. Kingston: Ian Randle, 2005.
Sutton, Constance R., and Elsa Chaney. *Caribbean Life in New York City*. Center for Migration Studies of New York, 1987.
Taylor, Frank Fonda. *To Hell with Paradise: A History of the Jamaican Tourist Industry*. Pittsburgh, PA: University of Pittsburgh Press, 1993.
Teitelbaum, Michael S., Myron Weiner, and American Assembly. *Threatened Peoples, Threatened Borders*. New York: W. W. Norton, 1995.
The National Cyclopaedia. Vol. 6. New York: John White and Co., 1946.
The State, Politics and Violence in the Anglophone Caribbean. Centre for Caribbean Studies, University of Warwick, 1985.
Thomas-Hope, Elizabeth. "The Establishment of a Migration Tradition: British West Indian Movements to the Hispanic Caribbean in the Century After Emancipation." In *Caribbean Social Relations*, edited by Colin G. Clarke, 66–81. Monograph Series, No. 8. Liverpool: Centre for Latin American Studies, 1978.
———. "Caribbean Diaspora, the Inheritance of Slavery: Migration from the Commonwealth Caribbean." In *The Caribbean in Europe: Aspects of the West Indian Experience in Britain, France and the Netherlands*, edited by Colin Brock, 15–35. England: Frank Cass & Co., Ltd., 1986.
Thomas-Lycklama à Nijeholt, G. *On the Road for Work: Migratory Workers on the East Coast of the United States*. Boston: Martinus Nijhoff, 1980.
Thomason, Holly J. *An Economic Analysis of the Role of the Sugar Industry in the South Florida Economy*. Gainesville: University of Florida Press, 1979.
Thompson, Leonard. *A History of South Africa*. New Haven, CT: Yale University Press, 1990.
Tichenor, Daniel J. *Dividing Lines: The Politics of Immigration Control in America*. Princeton, NJ: Princeton University Press, 2002.
Tomasek, Robert D. "The Migrant Problem and Pressure Group Politics," *Journal of Politics* 23 (1961): 295–319.
Torpey, John. *The Invention of the Passport: Surveillance, Citizenship and the State*. New York: Cambridge University Press, 2000.
Tucker, Barbara M. "Agricultural Workers in World War II: The Reserve Army of Children, Black Americans, and Jamaicans." *Agricultural History* 68, 1 (Winter 1994): 54–73.

Turner, Mary, ed. *From Chattel Slaves to Wage Slaves: The Dynamics of Labour Bargaining in the Americas*. Kingston: Ian Randle, 1995.

Turrell, Rob. "Kimberley's Model Compounds." *Journal of African History* 25 (1984): 59–75.

Valentine, Douglas. *The Strength of the Wolf: The Secret History of America's War on Drugs*. New York: Verso, 2004.

Vickerman, Milton. *Crosscurrents: West Indian Immigrants and Race*. New York: Oxford University Press, 1999.

Von Escher, Penny M. *Race Against Empire: Black Americans and Anti-colonialism, 1937–1957*. Ithaca, NY: Cornell University Press, 1997.

Wallace, Elisabeth. *The British Caribbean: From the Decline of Colonialism to the End of Federation*. Toronto: University of Toronto Press, 1977.

Walne, Peter, ed. *A Guide to Manuscript Sources for the History of Latin America and the Caribbean in the British Isles*. London, Oxford University Press [for] the Institute of Latin American Studies, University of London, 1973.

Walter, John C. "West Indian Immigrants: Those Arrogant Bastards." *Contributions in Black Studies: A Journal of African and Afro-American Studies* 5 (1981–1982): 17–27.

Walter, Rodney. *The Groundings with My Brothers*. London: Bogle-L'Ouverture, 1969.

Waters, Anita M. *Race, Class and Political Symbols: Rastafari and Reggae in Jamaican Politics*. New Brunswick, NJ: Transaction Books, 1985.

Waters, Mary C. *Black Identities: West Indian Dreams and American Realities*. Cambridge, MA: Harvard University Press, 1999.

Weber, Arnold R. "The Role of the U.S. Department of Labor in Immigration." *International Migration Review* 4, 3 (Summer 1970): 31–46.

Weintraub, Sidney, and Stanley Robert Ross. *"Temporary" Alien Workers in the United States*. Boulder, CO: Westview Press, 1982.

Wells, Miriam J. *Strawberry Fields: Politics, Class, and Work in California Agriculture*. Ithaca, NY: Cornell University Press, 1996.

Welsh, David. *The Roots of Segregation: Native Policy in Colonial Natal, 1845–1910*. Cape Town: Oxford University Press, 1971.

Who Was Who. Vol.6, 1961–1970: A Companion to 'Who's Who' Containing the Biographies of Those Who Died During the Decade 1961–1970. London: A. & C. Black, 1972.

Wilkinson, Alec. *Big Sugar: Seasons in the Cane Fields of Florida*. New York: Alfred A. Knopf, 1989.

Williams, Eric. *The Negro in the Caribbean*. Westport, CT: Negro Universities Press, 1942.

Williams, Leaford C. *Journey into Diplomacy: A Black Man's Shocking Discovery, A Memoir*. Washington, DC: Northeast Publishing House, 1996.

Wilson, Carlton. "'In Their Own Words': West Indian Technicians in Liverpool During World War II." *Journal of Canadian Studies* 8, 1–2 (Winter 1990 and Summer 1991): 71–88.

Wilson, Francis. *Labour in the South African Gold Mines, 1911–1969.* London: Cambridge University Press, 1972.

Woodruff, Nan Elizabeth. "Pick or Fight: The Emergency Farm Labor Program in the Arkansas and Mississippi Deltas During World War II." *Agricultural History* 64, 2 (Spring 1990): 74–121.

Worrell, DeLisle. *Small Island Economies.* New York: Praeger, 1987.

Wright, Giles R., comp. *Looking Back: Eleven Life Histories,* New Jersey Ethnic Life Series, no. 10. New Jersey Historical Commission, Department of State, 1986.

Yeoman, Barry. "Silence in the Fields." *Mother Jones,* January/February 2001.

Young, Lung-chang, Helen Icken Safa, and John M. Raynor. *Different People.* Center for Cross-cultural Education, College of Education, Georgia State University, 1983.

Zolberg, Aristide. "The Great Wall Against China: Responses to the First Immigration Crisis, 1885–1925." In *Migration, Migration History, History: Old Paradigms and New Perspectives,* edited by Jan Lucassen and Leo Lucassen, 291–316. New York: Peter Lang, 1997.

Zolberg, Aristide R. *A Nation by Design: Immigration Policy in the Fashioning of America.* New York: Russell Sage Foundation, 2006.

Index